Visual J++ 1.0 Publi

G000091489

Microsoft® Corp. Visual J++™ Publishers Edit
ROM allows you to create your own Visual J+
commercial version. The Publisher's Edition de
in some ways. These include no database support _____ databases through
Data Access Objects (DAO) and Remote Data Objects (RDO), no JET engine for cre-
ating programs that work with Access and other DAO databases, no Zoomin and
WinDiff Tools, no third-party tools and libraries that integrate with Visual J++™, no
redistribution of Java Virtual Machine and Internet Explorer, no code samples, no
Microsoft technical support, and no free or discounted upgrades to later versions of Visual
J++™ Professional Edition.

Microsoft Corp. Visual J++™ Publishers Edition requires the following to operate:

○ Personal computer with a 486 or higher processor running MS Windows® 95
  or Windows NT® Workstation version 4.0 or later operation systems
○ 8MB of memory (12MB recommended) if running Windows 95; 16MB (20
  recommended) if running Windows NT Workstation

Hard-disk space:

○ Typical installation: 20MB
○ Minimum installation: 14MB
○ CD-ROM installation (tools run from the CD): 14MB
  (Total tools and information on CD: 50MB)
○ A CD-ROM drive
○ VGA or higher resolution monitor (super VGA recommended)
○ Microsoft Mouse or compatible point device

Web Programming with Visual J++™

by Mike Cohn,
Jay Rutten, and
James Jory

sams
net

201 West 103rd Street,
Indianapolis, Indiana 46290

Copyright© 1997 by Sams.net Publishing

FIRST EDITION

International Standard Book Number: 1-57521-174-2

Library of Congress Catalog Card Number: 97-69400

2000   99   98   97   4   3   2   1

Interpretation of the printing code: the rightmost double-digit number is the year of the book's printing; the rightmost single-digit, the number of the book's printing. For example, a printing code of 97-1 shows that the first printing of the book occurred in 1997.

Composed in AGaramond and MCPdigital by Macmillan Computer Publishing

Printed in the United States of America

Publisher and President:	*Richard K. Swadley*
Publishing Manager:	*Greg Wiegand*
Director of Editorial Services:	*Cindy Morrow*
Assistant Marketing Managers:	*Kristina Perry*
	Rachel Wolfe

Acquisitions Editor
Christopher Denny

Development Editor
Richard W. Alvey, Jr.

Software Development Specialist
Brad Myers

Production Editor
Mary Inderstrodt

Copy Editors
Heather Butler
Keith Davenport

Indexer
Cheryl Dietsch

Technical Reviewers
Chris Stone
Matt Stone

Editorial Coordinator
Katie Wise

Technical Edit Coordinator
Lynette Quinn

Resource Coordinator
Deborah Frisby

Editorial Assistants
Carol Ackerman
Andi Richter
Rhonda Tinch-Mize

Cover Designer
Tim Amrhein

Book Designer
Alyssa Yesh

Copy Writer
Peter Fuller

Production Team Supervisors
Brad Chinn
Charlotte Clapp

Production
Rick Bond
Carol Bowers
Jenaffer Brandt
Paula Lowell
Timothy Osborn

Overview

Part VII Appendixes 565

Contents

xi

About the Authors

Mike Cohn is the Director of Information Technology at Access Health, Inc., the leading provider of personal health management services. Before that he was with Andersen Consulting and the Adler Consulting Group in New York. He holds a Masters degree in Computer Science from the University of Idaho and has been programming for 16 years. Mike lives in Cameron Park, California, with his wife Laura and their daughter Savannah. Mike was the lead author of *Database Developer's Guide with Borland C++ 5.0* and *Java Developer's Reference*. When not programming, Mike is usually thinking about programming, reading about programming, or writing about programming.

Jay Rutten is a Software Engineer at Access Health, Inc., where his fire-fighting skills range from database replication to writing C++, Delphi, and Java code. He is involved in designing the company's next generation database and Internet products. Jay lives in Rocklin, California, with his wife Paula and their son Christopher. When not chained to his desk, he can be found on the volleyball court, on his bike, or just spending time with his family.

James Jory is a Lead Programmer/Analyst with the Information Technology Group at Access Health, Inc. He has been programming for seven years and has experience on several platforms ranging from personal computers to mainframes. Before joining Access Health, James was a Systems Engineer at Electronic Data Systems where he specialized in network programming and GUI development and was an intranet Webmaster. He has also been an independent consultant to Dentisoft Inc., a supplier of Windows-based dental office management software.

Tell Us What You Think!

As a reader, you are the most important critic and commentator of our books. We value your opinion and want to know what we're doing right, what we could do better, what areas you'd like to see us publish in, and any other words of wisdom you're willing to pass our way. You can help us make strong books that meet your needs and give you the computer guidance you require.

Do you have access to CompuServe or the World Wide Web? Then check out our CompuServe forum by typing GO SAMS at any prompt. If you prefer the World Wide Web, check out our site at http://www.mcp.com.

> **Note:**
>
> If you have a technical question about this book, call the technical support line at (800) 571-5840, ext. 3668.

As the publishing manager of the group that created this book, I welcome your comments. You can fax, e-mail, or write me directly to let me know what you did or didn't like about this book— as well as what we can do to make our books stronger. Here's the information:

Fax: 317/581-4669

E-mail: programming_mgr@sams.mcp.com

Mail: Greg Wiegand
         Sams Publishing
         201 W. 103rd Street
         Indianapolis, IN 46290

Introduction

By now there is little doubt that the Java language will profoundly impact both how we write programs and the programs we write. Java influences how we write programs because it achieves a new level of power combined with simplicity. Java influences the programs we write because Java is an enabling technology. With Java you can write programs you could not write without it. There are, of course, the simple things that Java enables, such as adding animation to Web pages. However, with Java so much more is possible. With Java you can write a single program that will run on Windows NT, Windows 95, a Macintosh, or UNIX. With Java you can write a distributed program that can access resources on any machine on the Internet. In less than 10 lines of Java code, you can write a program to display an image retrieved from a computer 5,000 miles away. And even better, your 10-line program can be run from almost any computer in use today or in the future.

When a powerful language like Java is combined with a powerful development environment, you have an unbeatable combination. In this book you will learn how Java and Visual J++ work together to be this unbeatable combination. While there are now many Java development environments available, Visual J++ is unique in extending Java with the ability to use ActiveX controls from within Java. This opens an entire world of existing components to your Java programs.

Who Should Buy This Book?

This is an advanced book. We assume that you are already familiar with Java, or at least with object-oriented programming in general. Unlike most other Java books, this one does not include 300 pages teaching you the basics of the language. Starting right with the first chapter we assume you know the basics of Java syntax. Appendix A provides a whirlwind tour of the Java language in case you need a refresher before getting started with Chapter 1.

You should buy this book if you are looking for a book that goes into more detail than do other books. This book does not "scratch the surface" of any topics. If a topic was worth covering, this book covers it in detail. You should also buy this book if you are looking for lots of examples. Almost every concept discussed in this book is accompanied by one or more examples.

This book is not an API reference. Although there should be room on every Java programmer's bookshelf for a good API reference, there should also be room for a book, like this one, that tells how to use the language to solve problems.

You should buy this book if you're a practicing programmer with a job to do or a deadline to meet. If you're a manager trying to understand Java or figure out if it has a place in your organization, this isn't the book for you. This book is intended for programmers who are either starting to use Java on the job or who are learning it in their spare time.

We do encourage you to e-mail us at the following addresses:

mcohn@spider.innercite.com

pjrutten@pacbell.net

jjory@ibm.net

What's in This Book?

Chapter 1, "Web Programming and Visual J++," presents some of the reasons why Web programming with Java, and with Visual J++ in particular, will be an important part of the World Wide Web's future. If you're not fully convinced of the benefits of Java programming this chapter finishes the job. You'll also get an overview of some of the Visual J++ features that make Java development easier. Among these are the Developer Studio, the Applet Wizard, the Dialog, Menu, and Graphic Editors, the Resource Wizard, and the debugger.

Chapter 2, "Creating Your First Applet with Applet Wizard," introduces the Java Applet Wizard. This is the first of a handful of wizards you'll encounter when using Visual J++. In this chapter you'll learn how to use the Applet Wizard to generate an initial applet. By the end of this chapter you'll have created a powerful applet that makes use of multithreading and animation.

Chapter 3, "Using the Developer Studio," describes the Visual J++ integrated development environment. The Developer Studio is a proven productivity aide from its use in Microsoft's Visual C++. In this chapter you'll see how the Developer Studio can speed your Java programming tasks. You'll learn about project workspaces and how to manage multiple projects and configurations within a single workspace. You'll discover the Project Workspace window and its FileView, ClassView, and InfoView windows. Using the ClassView, you'll learn how to let Visual J++ help you create new classes and add methods and variables to existing classes.

Chapter 4, "Applet Programming Fundamentals," covers a lot of ground. You'll see how an applet's init, start, stop, and destroy methods are executed over the life of the applet. Handling events such as keypresses and mouse clicks are an important part of Java programming, so this chapter presents numerous examples of how to handle events. You'll learn about generic event handling with the handleEvent method, as well as how to handle events with mouse- and keyboard-specific methods. This chapter also demonstrates how to customize the behavior of an applet by using applet parameters embedded in the host HTML file. Finally, this chapter also gives a quick preview of loading a graphics resource from a URL and displaying it in an applet.

Chapter 5, "Java's User Interface Components," describes the Component class and all of its subclasses. These include Button, TextField, TextArea, Label, Checkbox, List, Choice, and Scrollbar. This chapter includes examples of how to create and use each of these classes. This chapter also describes the layout classes and shows how they can be used to control the placement of components in the user interface.

Chapter 6, "Working with Frames, Dialogs, and Menus," describes Java's container classes: Container, Panel, Frame, Dialog, and FileDialog. Here you will learn how to create and place panels on other containers in order to group components. You'll also learn how to use the Frame and Dialog classes to create windows that are not part of the browser's window. This chapter also demonstrates how to control the appearance of the mouse pointer. Finally, you will learn about Java's menu classes: MenuBar, Menu, MenuItem, and CheckboxMenuItem.

Chapter 7, "Saving Time with the Resource Wizard," describes the Resource Wizard and how it can free you from some of the difficulties of hand-coding your user interface. You'll learn how to visually design dialogs, frames, and menus, and then convert these designs into Java classes that can be used in your projects.

Chapter 8, "Debugging with the Visual J++ Debugger," explores the usefulness of the integrated debugger. Control of the executing program is handled by the ability to set a breakpoint on any source line of a successfully complied program. Once the breakpoints are set, you can run to the next breakpoint, step through the source line by line, or execute until the current line is reached. Data can be inspected in a number of ways including DataTips, QuickWindow, the Watch window, or the Variable window, which the debugger automatically populates. Additionally, the debugger has support for catching exceptions and specifying the thread to be debugged.

Chapter 9, "Documenting Your Visual J++ Code," describes how to acquire and use the JavaDoc program to automatically create documentation for your Java classes. Here you'll learn how to embed special tags into your code to document the parameters, return values, and exceptions of each method. You'll also see how HTML commands can be embedded directly in your code to control the appearance of the documentation.

Chapter 10, "Working with Java Strings," describes the String and StringBuffer classes, two of the most commonly used classes in Java programming. Included are many examples of using the member methods of the String class, including changing the case of a string, trimming whitespace, and accessing substrings. This chapter also shows how to convert variables of other types into strings and how to search and compare strings. The StringBuffer class is described, and reasons are presented about why it is a more useful class for strings that change size or content.

Chapter 11, "The Java Utility Classes," gives you a thorough overview of the classes in the java.util package. You will learn how to use the BitSet class to store large amounts of Boolean data, how to manipulate dates and times with the Date class, how to generate random numbers, and how to tokenize strings. You'll learn how the Observable class works in conjunction with the Observer interface to allow you to decouple your code. The Hashtable class is described, and you'll see how the Properties class can be used in applications to stream data to and from files. This chapter also teaches you how the Vector class can be used as a resizable array and how the Stack class extends Vector.

Chapter 12, "Moving Up to Multithreading," shows how to take advantage of one of Java's most useful language features—threads. Creating a usable thread is as easy as creating a class that implements the Runnable interface. This interface has a single run method, which is called after the thread is started. Synchronization of multiple threads writing to common variables is covered on a block level or a method level. Additional capabilities that allow threads to be started and stopped are discussed. This chapter describes how to use the ThreadGroup class to group-related threads and assign a priority to the group.

Chapter 13, "Using Java Streams," covers the java.io package in detail. Streams provide an effective abstraction for data flow between two sources, and this package includes classes for streaming between buffers, files, and processes. This chapter also describes the input/output stream filter classes that can be attached to streams to add buffering, formatting, and handlers for streaming primitive data types. The examples in this chapter also establish a foundation that is built upon in Part IV, "Networking with Java."

Chapter 14, "Incorporating Graphics," presents an in-depth look at the Graphics class and how you can use the methods of this class to enhance the appearance of your Java programs. In this chapter you will learn how to draw outlined and filled shapes such as lines, arcs, ovals, rectangles, and polygons. You will also learn about the Image class and how to filter, crop, and modify images prior to display. You will also see how the ImageObserver interface allows you to monitor the progress of an image that is being retrieved.

Chapter 15, "Multimedia Programming with Java," covers two popular topics: animation and sounds. The MediaTracker class is used to load multiple images and then notify the application that it has completed. Once you have multiple images loaded, basic animation can be accomplished by displaying closely related images in quick succession. A couple of additional techniques to improve the appearance of the animation are also discussed. An alternate approach to loading and displaying multiple images is manipulating a single image, displaying only parts of it. Supporting sounds is simple with Java by using the play method of the Applet class.

Chapter 16, "Sprucing Things Up with Colors and Fonts," illustrates how to set colors and fonts. A sample dialog is created that allows you to set the color by either selecting a predefined color or creating a unique color by setting the components of the color. A similar dialog is created for selecting the font.

Chapter 17, "Accessing URLs," focuses on tapping the power of the Uniform Resource Locator (URL) collection of classes to access resources on the Internet. This chapter begins by exploring the syntax of URLs and will show you how to implement your own URL handlers by creating support for the mailto URL. This chapter will also show you how to interact with common gateway interface (CGI) scripts from your applets.

Chapter 18, "Networking with Datagrams and Sockets," gets into the low-level details of network programming with Java. The datagram example implements a live national debt server that broadcasts datagram packets to one or more datagram client applets. A socket example implements a post office protocol (POP) client that can be run as an applet or application to retrieve electronic mail from a POP server on the Internet. By the end of this chapter, you will understand the strengths and weaknesses of the datagram and socket methods of communication and how they can be used in your programs.

Chapter 19, "Client/Server Programming," takes socket programming one step further by describing how robust and efficient server programs can be written in Java. The primary example implements an Internet dictionary that is capable of handling multiple simultaneous requests from client applets and applications over a network. This chapter also discusses Java's contribution to client/server development and the emerging technologies that will make Java an even more serious player in the future.

Chapter 20, "Keeping Out the Riff-Raff: Java Security," lays out the security scheme implemented by the Java development and runtime environments. Without a doubt, the security challenges of Internet development should not be taken lightly and certainly no language or platform is inviolable. However, by the end of this chapter you will have a clear understanding of Java's multilayer security model and see how it provides a nearly impenetrable barrier against both intentional and unintentional security violations.

Chapter 21, "Using ActiveX Controls with Java," covers some of the basics of ActiveX controls, commonly referred to as COM objects in the Java world. First, creation of the Java interface to any ActiveX control is accomplished through the use of the Java Type Library Wizard. Once you have an interface, communication channels are discussed so that the COM object can be controlled by an applet, or the applet can be used as an event handler of the COM object events. To show the versatility of the Java language, a COM object is created using Java and the COM object is then securely packaged in a signed .CAB file.

Chapter 22, "Using the Data Access Objects," introduces you to the Data Access Objects (DAO) and shows how to use them in your Java programs. You'll learn about `Database`, `Recordset`, and `Field` objects and how to combine these objects to perform useful tasks. You'll see examples of using DAO to browse a database, add new records, update existing records, delete records, search for records, and execute SQL.

Chapter 23, "Software Cost Estimator," presents a complete Java applet example that combines much of what you learned in prior chapters. The applet created in this chapter is a software cost estimation calculator based on the Constructive Cost Model. It demonstrates in-depth user interface programming, including the use of an imagemap to control the appearance of the applet.

Chapter 24, "Development Request Online," is a complete applet that shows the use of Database Access Objects to implement a request tracking system. The chapter contains a complete project overview including a class overview and database schema. The key classes are described in detail, including the database access classes, common user interface classes, and the classes used to implement the specific panels used in the applet.

Appendix A, "A Whirlwind Tour of the Java Language," is a quick overview of the Java language. If you are already familiar with Java, this appendix can serve as a handy reference. On the other hand, if you are not familiar with Java but are experienced in another object-oriented language, this appendix might be all you need to read to get started with Java.

Appendix B, "Pointers and Memory Management," offers a reminder of how Java simplifies programming by eliminating pointers and using garbage collection to automatically reclaim unused memory.

P a r t

Using Visual J++

Web Programming
and Visual J++

- Why Web Programming?
- Why Java?
- Why Visual J++?

This chapter addresses the three questions implied by this book's title:

○ Why Web Programming?
○ Why Java?
○ Why Visual J++?

The first question is answered by considering the tremendous growth of all activity that surrounds the Internet and the World Wide Web. The second question is answered by examining the capability of Java to address the shortcomings of existing Web technologies and through the consideration of the general purpose strengths of the language. The question of why you should use Visual J++ is answered with a brief overview of the product's many features.

Why Web Programming?

The tremendous growth in the popularity of the Internet, and of the World Wide Web in particular, has created entire new worlds of programming possibilities. The Internet and corporate intranets have been posed as both the death of client/server programming and as the next logical step in client/server programming. At the center of all of this is the Java language, a language originally designed for use in video-on-demand systems but which found a more natural fit in the World Wide Web.

Of course, as exciting and important as Web programming is, it is not without its problems. In particular, there are two problems that have traditionally plagued World Wide Web development:

○ Currently, Web content is passive and static.
○ Delivery of Web content is dependent on the configuration of each user's Web browser.

Although these problems are related, each warrants independent consideration.

Passive and Static Content

Current Web pages are very good at conveying some types of information but are inadequate for conveying other types. In particular, Web pages excel at conveying passive, static information. This type of information changes infrequently (static) and doesn't change in response to user interactions with it (passive).

For example, there are many Web pages that let you enter a company's name or stock ticker symbol and receive current price quotes. One of the best is the APL Quote Server located at `http://qs.secapl.com/cgi-bin/qs` and shown in Figure 1.1. This page is static because it isn't automatically updated with new quotes while the page is being browsed. It is passive because the user cannot interact with the page, other than to request to see a similar page.

Figure 1.1.
Retrieving passive, static stock prices.

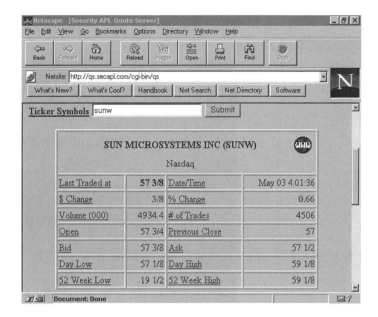

Older Web development technologies excelled at displaying this type of page. Much of human communication is passive, static, or both. A highway billboard is a perfect example of a conventional means of communication that is both passive and static. Television is an example of nonstatic, but passive, communication.

Just as not all billboards will go the way of Burma Shave, not all passive, static Web content needs to become active and dynamic (the opposites of passive and static). However, there is a tremendous demand for technologies that enable the creation of active, dynamic World Wide Web content.

Dependence on Browser Capabilities

In the pre-Java world of the Web, as a developer of Web content and pages, you could not count on your users having a specific browser configuration. You could create a Web page with leading edge graphics, sound, and real-time multimedia. Unfortunately, if any of the visitors to your Web site did not configure a browser add-on to handle the latest whiz-bang features, these users wouldn't get the full impact of your site.

The inability to know what features will be supported by the visitors to your Web site has traditionally led many sites to be developed to a lowest common denominator. These problems are compounded by the differences in a user's browser, his hardware, and his operating system.

Why Java?

Much of the excitement over Java comes from the capability of Java to solve the problems of passive content and browser dependence. Java is a nearly ideal language for programming the World Wide Web. However, applications for Java programs go beyond the Web and reach far into the domain of traditional programming languages.

Active and Dynamic Content

By using Java, you can take your Web pages beyond the world of passive, static content and into a world of active, dynamic content. This is more than just an esthetic difference. It is a difference that affects the types of problems that can be solved on the World Wide Web. Because of this, Java is an *enabling* technology. With Java you are able to solve entire classes of problems that you would not be able to solve without Java.

Take a moment to look back again at Figure 1.1. This static, passive Web page shows the price of a stock at a specific moment in time. There is so much more that could be, *should be*, on this page. This is where Java comes in. With Java, you could create a page that shows a graph of the stock's price over time and have that graph continue to update in real time while you browse the page. Because Java is a full-featured programming language, Web pages like this become much more feasible. Sun Microsystems has created a page that does exactly this. It is located at `http://java.sun.com/java.sun.com/applets/applets/StockDemo/index.html` and is shown in Figure 1.2.

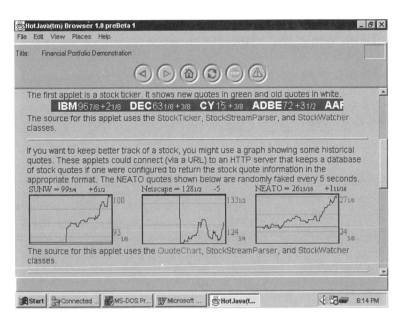

Figure 1.2.

A Java version of a stock price Web page.

On the Java Web page shown in Figure 1.2, there is a line of stock ticker symbols and prices that scrolls across the top of the screen. Below that are graphs for the stock of three different companies. Each of these graphs is updated every five seconds based on the latest trades. (As described in Figure 1.2, this page is just an illustration, and the prices of the NEATO company are randomly generated.)

Browser, Hardware, and Operating System Independence

In addition to being an enabling technology that enables your Web pages to become active and dynamic, Java again serves as an enabling technology by freeing you from concerns about how each user has configured his browser. Java enables you, as a Web developer, to create Web pages that will be delivered consistently to all users with a Java-enabled browser.

Not only does Java free you from concerns about how users have configured their Web browsers, but it also frees you from concerns about which hardware and operating system platform they are using. Because Java source code is interpreted, if a Java interpreter exists for a specific hardware and operating system platform, you can write programs with the knowledge that they will be usable on that platform.

Java Is a General Purpose Language

Of course, the use of Java extends beyond the Web, and there is much to recommend Java as a general purpose development language. The same hardware and operating system independence that Java brings to the Web is a benefit to other programming tasks as well.

Because Java borrows much of its syntax and many of its concepts from C and C++, there is a pre-existing pool of programmers who could quickly learn Java. However, Java goes far beyond being a mere derivative of C++. It adds to C++ in the areas of automatic memory management and language-level support for multithreaded applications. On the other hand, Java remains easier to learn and simpler to use than C++ because of those C++ features that were left out of Java: multiple inheritance, pointers, and the goto statement, among others.

Because implementations of the Java Virtual Machine can be very efficient, it is possible for Java programs to run almost as quickly as C++ programs. This is a key feature in convincing developers that Java is a viable language for non-Internet development. Because of Java's strengths as an Internet language, many of these same strengths apply when Java is used as a language for client/server development. It is very likely that as corporations do more and more Internet development in Java, they will begin to apply these same Java developers to their client/server projects. Java's strengths in terms of network-awareness, security, portability, and performance make it ideally suited for corporate client/server development, as well as Internet development.

> **NOTE:**
>
> In discussing Java programs, it has become standard to refer to Java programs that are embedded in another language as *applets* and to stand-alone programs as *applications*. For example, when using Java to augment a World Wide Web page, the Java code is embedded within HTML code. Therefore, this is referred to as an applet. On the other hand, a Java program that is not embedded within HTML, or any other language, and can stand on its own is referred to as an application.
>
> Of course, there is a subtle implication here that applications are larger (and, therefore, presumably more complex) than applets. However, this is not necessarily true. Applications and applets alike can range from simple one class programs to programs with hundreds of classes. The implication that an applet is somehow less than an application is unfortunately a connotation it is necessary to live with in an otherwise valid distinction.

Key Features of Java

Having seen that Java is equally suited as a language for development both on and off the Internet, it's time to look more closely at the Java language itself. The creators of Java at Sun Microsystems have defined the Java language as "A simple, object-oriented, distributed, interpreted, robust, secure, architecture-neutral, portable, high-performance, multithreaded, and dynamic language." Well, they managed to fit all of the important 1990s buzzwords into one sentence, but we need to look more closely at Java to determine whether they managed to fit all these concepts into one language.

Simple

If you have experience with any object-oriented language, especially C++, you will probably find Java to be easier than your high school prom date. Because Java started out as C++ but has had certain features removed, it is certainly a simpler language than C++. Some of the most difficult aspects of C++ programming are related to memory management and the use of pointers. Many, if not most, C++ programs contain memory leaks that will eventually cause the system to run out of memory.

Java prevents this by not allowing a program to directly manipulate memory addresses through the use of pointers. Additionally, Java performs automatic memory management, sometimes called *garbage collection*. With garbage collection you do not need to remember to free every memory resource you allocate. The system keeps track of allocated resources for you and automatically releases each when you are finished with it.

Object-Oriented

Of course, Java is object-oriented. In fact, in the mid-1990s it's hard to imagine someone developing a new language and declaring it the greatest new thing without it being object-oriented. In its approach to object-orientation Java follows most closely along the lines of languages such as SmallTalk than C++. Except for its primitive data types, everything in Java is an object. In contrast, C++ is much more lax in that you are entirely free to mix and match object-oriented code (classes) and procedural code (functions). In Java, this is not the case. There are no global functions in Java: All functions are invoked through an object.

Java's support for object orientation does not include multiple inheritance. The designers of the language felt that the complexity introduced by multiple inheritance was not justified by its benefits. Multiple inheritance has been replaced in Java with the concept of *interface inheritance*. While a Java class can only be a subclass of one other class, it can implement multiple interfaces.

Java classes are comprised of methods and variables. Class methods are the functions to which an object of the class can respond. Class variables are the data that define the state of an object. In Java, methods and variables can be declared as private, protected, or public. Private methods and variables are not accessible outside of the class. Protected members are accessible to subclasses of the class, but not to other classes. Finally, public methods and variables are accessible to any class.

Distributed

Java facilitates the building of distributed applications by a collection of classes for use in networked applications. By using Java's URL (Uniform Resource Locator) class, an application can easily access a remote server. Classes are also provided for establishing socket-level connections.

Interpreted

Because Java is interpreted, once the Java interpreter has been ported to a specific machine, that machine can instantly run the growing body of Java applications. As the body of existing Java source code increases, this becomes an increasingly important advantage. This means that by porting a single application—the Java virtual machine—all existing Java programs become available for use on that machine.

Also, when using an interpreter, programmers are freed from some of the concerns of intermodule dependencies. You no longer have to maintain a make file that is sometimes as complicated as the hardest part of your program.

Another advantage to using an interpreter is that the time-consuming, edit-compile-link-test cycle is broken. Without the compile and link steps, working in an interpreted environment is a much simpler edit-test cycle. Even with today's quick C++ compilers, it is not uncommon for a complete recompile and relink of a large program to be measured in hours and take the better part of a day. Without having to wait for lengthy compiles and links, Java promotes prototyping and easier debugging.

Robust

The designers of Java anticipated that Java would be used to solve some very complex programming problems. Writing a distributed, multithreaded program that can run on a variety of operating systems with a variety of processors is not a simple task. To do it successfully, you need all the help your programming language can offer you. With this in mind, Java was created as a strongly typed language. Data type issues and problems are resolved at compile-time and implicit casts of a variable from one type to another are not allowed.

Memory management has been simplified in Java in two ways. First, Java does not support direct pointer manipulation or arithmetic. This makes it impossible for a Java program to overwrite memory or corrupt data. Second, Java uses runtime garbage collection instead of explicit freeing of memory. In languages like C++ it is necessary to delete or free memory once a program has finished with it. Java follows the lead of languages such as Lisp and SmallTalk by providing automatic support for freeing memory that has been allocated but is no longer used.

Secure

Closely related to Java's robustness is its focus on security. Because Java does not use pointers to directly reference memory locations, as is prevalent in C and C++, Java has a great deal of control over the code that exists within the Java environment.

It was anticipated that Java applications would run on the Internet and that they could dynamically incorporate or execute code found at remote locations on the Internet. Because of this, the developers of Java have hypothesized the existence of a hostile Java compiler that would generate Java byte codes with the intent of bypassing Java's runtime security. This led to the concept of a byte code verifier. The byte code verifier examines all incoming code to ensure that the code plays by the rules and is safe to execute.

Architecture-Neutral

Back in the dark ages of the early 1980s there was tremendous variety in desktop personal computers. You could buy computers from Apple, Commodore, Radio Shack, Atari, and eventually even from IBM. Because developing software is such a time-consuming task, very little of the software developed for use on one machine was ever ported and then released for use on a different machine.

In many regards this situation has improved with the acceptance of Windows, the Apple Macintosh, and UNIX variations as the only valid personal computer options. However, it is still not easy to write an application that can be used on Windows NT, UNIX, or a Macintosh. And it's getting more complicated with the move of Windows NT to non-Intel CPU architectures.

There are a number of commercially available source code libraries (for example, Zinc, ZApp, and XVT) that attempt to achieve application portability. These libraries attempt this by focusing on either on a lowest common denominator among the operating systems or by creating a common core API (Application Programming Interface).

Java takes a different approach. Because the Java compiler creates byte code instructions that are subsequently interpreted by the Java interpreter, architecture neutrality is achieved in the implementation of the Java interpreter for each new architecture.

Portable

In addition to being architecture-neutral, Java code is also portable. It was an important design goal of Java that it be portable so that as new architectures (either due to hardware, operating system, or both) are developed, the Java environment could be ported to them.

In Java, all primitive types (integers, longs, floats, doubles, and so on) are of defined sizes, regardless of the machine or operating system on which the program is run. This is in direct contrast to languages like C and C++ that leave the sizes of primitive types up to the compiler developer.

Additionally, Java is portable because the compiler itself is written in Java and the runtime environment is written in POSIX-compliant C.

High Performance

For all but the simplest or most infrequently used applications, performance is always a consideration. It is no surprise then to discover that achieving high performance was one of the initial design goals of the Java developers. A Java application will not achieve the performance of a fully compiled language such as C or C++. However, for most applications, including graphics-intensive ones such as are commonly found on the World Wide Web, the performance of Java is more than adequate. For some applications, there may be no discernible difference in performance between C++ and Java.

Many of the early adopters of C++ were concerned about the possibility of performance degradation as they converted their programs from C to C++. However, many C++ early adopters discovered that while in some cases a C program will outperform a C++ program, the additional development time and effort doesn't justify the minimal performance gains. Of course, since we're not all programming in assembly language, there must be some amount of performance we're willing to trade for faster development.

It is very likely that early experiences with Java will follow these same lines. While a Java application may not be able to keep up with a C++ application, it will normally be fast enough, and Java may enable you to do things you couldn't do with C++.

Multithreaded

Writing a computer program that only does a single thing at a time is an artificial constraint that we've lived with in most programming languages. With Java, we no longer have to live with this limitation. Support for multiple, synchronized threads is built directly into the Java language and runtime environment.

Synchronized threads are extremely useful in creating distributed, network-aware applications. Such an application may be communicating with a remote server in one thread while interacting with a user in a different thread.

Dynamic

Because it is interpreted, Java is an extremely dynamic language. At runtime, the Java environment can extend itself by linking in classes that may be located on remote servers on a network (for example, the Internet). This is a tremendous advantage over a language like C++ that links classes prior to runtime.

In C++, every time member variables or functions are added to a class, it is necessary to recompile that class and then all additional code that references that class. Of course, the problem is exacerbated by the fact that you need to remember to recompile the files that reference the changed class. Using make files reduces the problem but for large, complex systems doesn't eliminate it.

Java addresses this problem by deferring it to runtime. At runtime, the Java interpreter performs name resolution while linking in the necessary classes. The Java interpreter is also responsible for determining the placement of objects in memory. These two features of the Java interpreter solve the problem of changing the definition of a class used by other classes. Because name lookup and resolution is performed only the first time a name is encountered, only minimal performance overhead is added.

Why Visual J++?

This section answers the question of why Visual J++ is the best choice for Web programming with Java. The most compelling reason to select Visual J++ as your Java development environment is the strength of the product itself. Visual J++ features a proven IDE (Integrated Development Environment) in its Developer Studio. The Visual J++ Developer Studio is essentially the same IDE as is provided with Microsoft's Visual C++. In addition to providing an established IDE, Visual J++ offers a number of Java-specific features. Included among these are the Java Applet Wizard, the Resource Wizard, and a debugger that lets you debug a Java applet running in a browser.

The Developer Studio

The Developer Studio serves as the focal point for the tools and features of Visual J++. While in the Developer Studio you can edit source code, create new projects, compile projects, start a debugging session, and use visual tools to design dialogs and menus. For example, Figure 1.3 shows the Developer Studio while being used to simultaneously edit a Java source code file, view help information, and design a new dialog.

Figure 1.3.

The Visual J++ Developer Studio.

The Developer Studio features a Project Workspace window that enables you to view your project. From the Project Workspace you can view a project in the old-fashioned, file-oriented view. You can see a list of files included in the project, double-click a file, and then edit that file. Alternatively, you can use what is called the ClassView. The ClassView presents a more natural, and more useful, view of a project's components. Instead of selecting an item to edit from a list of files, you select the class or method within that class you want to edit. A source code editing window is automatically opened and the cursor positioned to the correct place. The ClassView is also shown in Figure 1.3, along the left side of that figure.

The Applet Wizard

The Java Applet Wizard is a very useful little tool that helps you quickly get an applet started and running. The Applet Wizard is a one-way tool that asks you questions on a series of five screens and then generates skeleton Java files and a project. Although the Applet Wizard does not contain any earth-shattering technology, it is a very convenient and time-saving tool. The Applet Wizard can be used to generate significant applets, including applets using animation, event handling, applet parameters, and multiple threads. As an example of the type of questions asked by the Applet Wizard, see Figure 1.4, which shows the first screen of this wizard.

Figure 1.4.

The first screen of the Java
Applet Wizard.

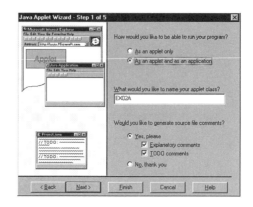

The JView Stand-Alone Interpreter

The JView stand-alone Java interpreter can be used to run any Java application, including those not written with Visual J++. JView includes a very fast implementation of the Java Virtual Machine. Using JView to run Java applications provides a viable alternative to Web-based applets, in many cases. Because the main subject of this book is the creation of Web-based Java applets, JView will be used very infrequently. However, it is still a useful tool in your collection.

Editing Resources

Visual J++ facilitates applet development by providing visual tools for designing dialogs, menus, and images.

The Dialog Editor

The Dialog Editor, which is shown in Figure 1.5, can be used to visually place components such as edit fields, list boxes, radio buttons, and check boxes. As components are placed on the screen, you can set various properties about the components, such as its name and how it will be displayed.

Figure 1.5.
The Visual J++ Dialog
Editor.

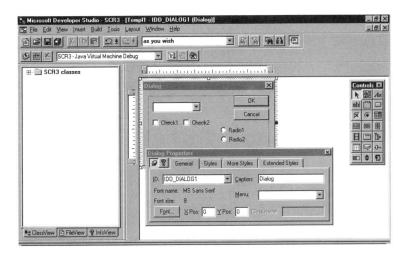

Despite its name, the Dialog Editor is useful for editing more than just dialogs. The Dialog Editor can be used to design the placement of the components on Java dialogs, frames, panels, and applets themselves.

The Menu Editor

The Menu Editor, which is shown in Figure 1.6, enables you to visually design a program's menus. Using the Menu Editor, you can easily create one or more menus for use in your program.

Figure 1.6.
The Visual J++ Menu
Editor.

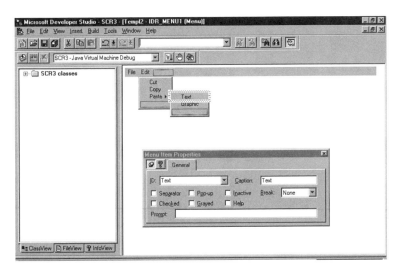

The Graphics Editor

The Graphics Editor, which is shown in Figure 1.7, can be used to create and edit the graphic images you may use in your Java programs. The Graphics Editor is a relatively simple image editing program, similar to numerous other programs, including, of course, the Microsoft Paint program.

Figure 1.7.

The Visual J++ Graphics Editor.

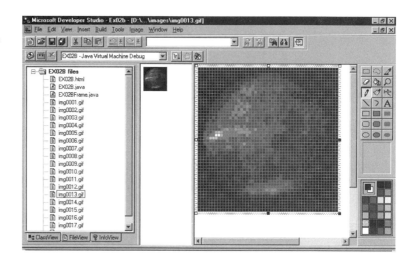

The Resource Wizard

If you are familiar with Microsoft Windows programming, you are used to creating dialog and menu resources in a special resource file that is linked into your final program. In Java, dialogs and menus are, instead, created at runtime by code. The Resource Wizard converts the dialogs and menus stored in Windows-style resource files into Java source code that can be added to your project.

The Debugger

Visual J++ includes a very powerful and easy-to-use debugger. Through the debugger Visual J++ can control an applet running in the Internet Explorer. All the features you'd expect to be present are there. You can step through an applet in a variety of ways to step, set breakpoints, and inspect variables. The Visual J++ Debugger is shown in Figure 1.8.

Figure 1.8.

The Debug and Variable Watch windows of the Visual J++ Debugger.

Summary

This chapter presented some of the reasons why Web programming with Java, and with Visual J++ in particular, will be an important part of the World Wide Web's future. Java takes the Web into a new world of active and dynamic content. You learned the reasons that support the claim that Java is "a simple, object-oriented, distributed, interpreted, robust, secure, architecture-neutral, portable, high-performance, multithreaded, and dynamic language." Finally, you learned about some of the Visual J++ features that make Java development easier. Among these are the Developer Studio, the Applet Wizard, the Dialog, Menu, and Graphic Editors, the Resource Wizard, and the debugger. In the next two chapters you will learn more about the Applet Wizard and the Developer Studio.

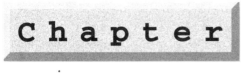

Chapter 2

Creating Your First Applet with Applet Wizard

This chapter introduces you to the Applet Wizard. The Applet Wizard is the first of many wizards that Microsoft has built into Visual J++ to help simplify Java development. In this chapter you learn how to jump start your development effort by using Applet Wizard to create an initial applet for you. You also learn how to add to and customize this applet.

Saying "Hello, World" Visual J++ Style

The Visual J++ Applet Wizard creates a *skeleton applet*. A skeleton applet is aptly named because, although it's fully functional, there is little meat on its bones. Using a skeleton applet created by Applet Wizard, however, can be a great way to get a project started on the right foot. Applets created by Applet Wizard include all the code necessary to run the applet from within an HTML page. Additionally, Applet Wizard includes five pages of customization options that control if and how the skeleton applet makes use of features such as multithreading, animation, event handling, and applet parameters.

Because your first goal is to create a typical Hello World application, you'll instruct Applet Wizard to leave most of the advanced features out the first time through. To create a Hello World applet, you will perform the following steps (each of which is explained in more detail in the sections that follow):

1. Create a new project workspace.
2. Start the Applet Wizard.
3. Set the Applet Wizard options.
4. Generate the skeleton project.
5. Set project settings.
6. Add the Hello World message.
7. Build and execute the applet.

Create a New Project Workspace

Every Visual J++ project you create must reside in what is known as a *project workspace*. A project workspace groups a project's code with its configuration and builds information as a way to help you manage the project. Therefore, the first step in creating a new applet is creating a new project workspace. To do this, select File | New from the menu, and you will be presented with the New file dialog as shown in Figure 2.1. In this dialog select Project Workspace and select the OK button.

Figure 2.1.

Creating a new project
workspace.

Start the Applet Wizard

After following the first step, you will be presented with the New Project Workspace dialog shown
in Figure 2.2. In this dialog you need to select Java Applet Wizard. You can then change the name
of the applet and its location. Once you've done this, select the Create button to start the Applet
Wizard.

Figure 2.2.

Starting the Applet Wizard.

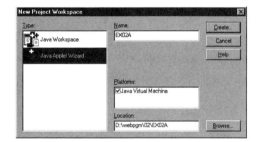

Set the Applet Wizard Options

The Java Applet Wizard itself is a set of five screens that are displayed sequentially and can be used
to determine which features will initially be included in the applet. In the first Applet Wizard
screen, shown in Figure 2.3, you should select the radio button labeled "As an applet and as an
application."

Figure 2.3.

The first screen of options
in the Applet Wizard.

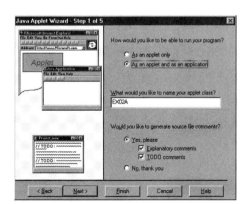

Selecting this option tells the Wizard to include startup code in the applet so that it can also be run as a stand-alone Java application. When ready, select the Next button to move to the next page of the Applet Wizard, as shown in Figure 2.4.

> ## NOTE:
>
> Remember an applet is a Java program run within a browser, and an application is a stand-alone program that is run using the Java interpreter.

Figure 2.4.

The second screen of options in the Applet Wizard.

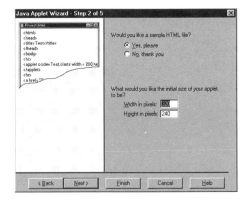

For this sample applet, you can leave the fields on the second page with their default values and move to the third page by selecting the Next button. Because the goal of your first applet is only to display "Hello World," your applet does not need to be multithreaded. This means you can select the "No, thank you" radio button when asked this question on the third page, as shown in Figure 2.5.

Figure 2.5.

The third screen of options in the Applet Wizard.

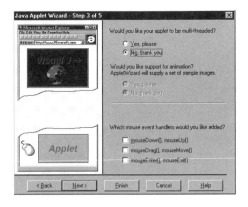

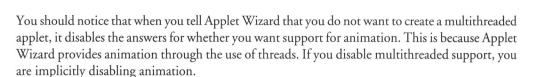

You should notice that when you tell Applet Wizard that you do not want to create a multithreaded applet, it disables the answers for whether you want support for animation. This is because Applet Wizard provides animation through the use of threads. If you disable multithreaded support, you are implicitly disabling animation.

This page of the Applet Wizard also enables you to trap various mouse actions by adding event handlers to your applet. If you want to install handlers for whenever the mouse button is pressed or released, select the `mouseDown()`, `mouseUp()` check box. To install handlers for mouse dragging or movement notification, select the `mouseDrag()`, `mouseMove()` check box. Finally, if the applet needs notification whenever the mouse enters or leaves the area covered by the applet on the screen, select the `mouseEnter()`, `mouseExit()` check box shown in Figure 2.5.

Once you've correctly set the options on this screen, select the Next button to move to the fourth options screen of the Applet Wizard. On this screen, which is shown in Figure 2.6, you can specify any parameters that your applet will read at runtime. Applet parameters are stored in the HTML file in which a Java applet is contained and can be used by an applet similar to how command-line parameters are used by a conventional program. The applet you're starting with doesn't need any applet parameters, so simply press the Next button to move to the fifth screen of the Applet Wizard.

Figure 2.6.

The fourth screen of options in the Applet Wizard.

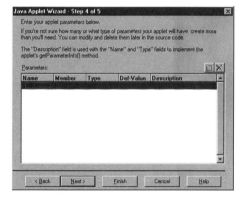

The fifth and final options screen of Applet Wizard is shown in Figure 2.7. In this screen you can enter whatever text you would like the applet to respond with when queried by the `getAppInfo` method. By default, it should show your name and the version of Visual J++ that was used, as shown in Figure 2.7. When you've finished with this screen, press the Finish button to tell the Applet Wizard that you are done setting options.

Figure 2.7.
The fifth screen of options
in the Applet Wizard.

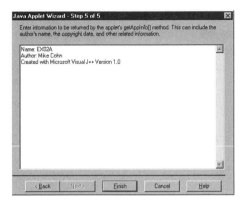

Generate the Skeleton Project

After you select the Finish button, you are presented with the New Project Information dialog, as
shown in Figure 2.8. This dialog gives you a final chance to confirm that you made the correct
selections in the Applet Wizard.

Figure 2.8.
The New Project Informa-
tion dialog allows you to
confirm your Applet
Wizard selections.

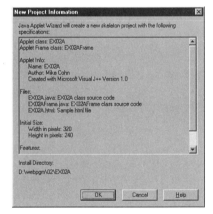

TIP:

You can select the Finish button from any of the options pages of the Java Applet
Wizard. If you wanted to accept the default for all pages after the first, you could have
selected Finish directly from the first page.

Once you've confirmed that you want the Applet Wizard to create the applet, select the OK button. Doing so will create the files necessary for the new applet and the new project workspace. Table 2.1 summarizes the files that are created by the Applet Wizard.

Table 2.1. Files created by the Applet Wizard.

Filename	Purpose
EX02A.java	This file contains the main class for the applet.
EX02AFRAME.java	This file contains a frame class that is used to provide a top-level window for when the program is run as a stand-alone application.
EX02A.html	This is an HTML file in which the applet is embedded.
EX02A.mak	This is the make file that Visual J++ uses to know how to build the applet.
EX02A.ncp	This is the program database that is used by Visual J++. You do not need to directly manipulate this file.
EX02A.mdp	This is the project workspace file. It contains various configuration settings and switches that can be set in the Visual J++ Developer Studio.

Set Project Settings

Now that you've successfully generated the applet, you need to set some Visual J++ options so that you can run the applet and view your masterpiece. To do this, select Settings from the Build menu. This will display the Project Settings dialog, which will be similar to Figure 2.9.

Figure 2.9.

Setting options on the Debug page of the Project Settings dialog.

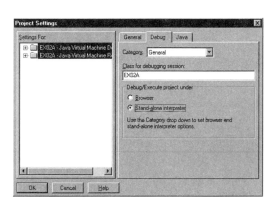

The Project Settings dialog lets you set options for a debug version of your applet as well as for a release version. To simultaneously set options for both versions, ensure that both versions are selected in the tree at the left of this dialog. Select the Debug page and the General category on the page. Indicate that you want to execute the applet under the stand-alone interpreter.

TIP:

As with many Windows controls, you can select multiple items by holding the Ctrl key down while selecting an item with the left mouse button.

Add the Hello World Message

You've now generated the applet source code and have configured Visual J++ to run the applet under the stand-alone interpreter. There's no point in giving the applet a trial run yet, however, because we haven't told the applet to do anything. At this point you need to add the code that will display the Hello World message.

The easiest way to do this is to use the ClassView pane of the Developer Studio. The ClassView can be accessed by selecting the first tab at the bottom of the Project Workspace window. The ClassView will display a tree of the classes in the project. Classes can be expanded to show their members by clicking the plus (+) symbols to the left of each class name.

NOTE:

Use of the Project Workspace window is fully described in Chapter 3, "Using the Developer Studio." The current chapter covers just enough so that you can edit, build, and run your first project. A full explanation of the Developer Studio is deferred until the next chapter.

Your ClassView should show two classes: one representing the applet itself and a second representing the frame that will house the applet when it is run outside a browser. If you fully expand the applet class your ClassView should appear similar to the one shown in Figure 2.10.

Figure 2.10.

The ClassView of the Project Workspace with the applet class fully expanded.

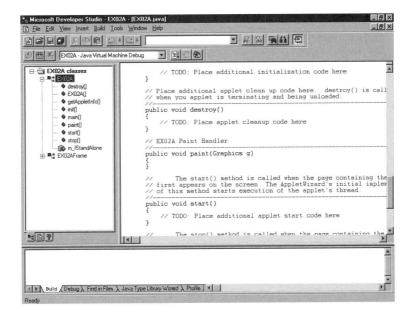

Listed beneath the class are its members. If you double-click a method, the right pane of the Project Workspace will be repositioned to the declaration of that method. Try this on the paint method and modify that method so that it appears as follows:

```
public void paint(Graphics g)
{
    g.drawString("Hello, World", 10, 10);
}
```

This line will draw the string "Hello, World" at position 10, 10 in the window represented by g.

Build and Execute the Applet

At this point, all that's left to do is to build and execute the applet. To do this, select Execute from the Build menu. You will be asked to confirm that you want to build the project. After the project is built, the JVIEW.EXE interpreter will automatically start and will run your application. The results will appear as shown in Figure 2.11.

Figure 2.11.
The Hello World applet,
EX02A, running in the
JView interpreter.

Examining the Source Code

Because the Applet Wizard generates the initial applet source code for you, you may be tempted to ignore the generated code. However, because this code serves as the foundation of your applet, it is well worth examining. In this section, you'll dissect the generated code and see exactly what using the Applet Wizard has saved you.

The Applet Class

The Applet Wizard generated two Java source code files and one HTML file. The first Java file is EX02A.java and is shown in Listing 2.1. This file contains the definition of class EX02A, which extends the Applet class. This class contains definitions for the following methods:

- ○ public static void main(String args[])
- ○ EX02A()
- ○ public String getAppletInfo()
- ○ public void init()
- ○ public void destroy()
- ○ public void paint(Graphics g)
- ○ public void start()
- ○ public void stop()

Listing 2.1. EX02A.java.

```
//************************************************************
// EX02A.java:    Applet
//
//************************************************************
import java.applet.*;
import java.awt.*;
import EX02AFrame;


//============================================================
// Main Class for applet EX02A
```

```
//
//================================================================
public class EX02A extends Applet
{
    // STANDALONE APPLICATION SUPPORT:
    // m_fStandAlone will be set to true if applet is run
    // standalone
    //----------------------------------------------------------
    boolean m_fStandAlone = false;

    // STANDALONE APPLICATION SUPPORT
    // The main() method acts as the applet's entry point when it
    // is run as a standalone application. It is ignored if the
    // applet is run from within an HTML page.
    //----------------------------------------------------------
    public static void main(String args[])
    {
        // Create Toplevel Window to contain applet EX02A
        //------------------------------------------------------
        EX02AFrame frame = new EX02AFrame("EX02A");

        // Must show Frame before we size it so insets() will
        // return valid values
        //------------------------------------------------------
        frame.show();
        frame.hide();
        frame.resize(frame.insets().left+frame.insets().right +320,
                     frame.insets().top+frame.insets().bottom+240);

        // The following code starts the applet running within the
        // frame window. It also calls GetParameters() to retrieve
        // parameter values from the command line, and sets
        // m_fStandAlone to true to prevent init() from trying to
        // get them from the HTML page.
        //------------------------------------------------------
        EX02A applet_EX02A = new EX02A();

        frame.add("Center", applet_EX02A);
        applet_EX02A.m_fStandAlone = true;
        applet_EX02A.init();
        applet_EX02A.start();
        frame.show();
    }

    // EX02A Class Constructor
    //----------------------------------------------------------
    public EX02A()
    {
        // TODO: Add constructor code here
    }

    // APPLET INFO SUPPORT:
    // The getAppletInfo() method returns a string describing the
    // applet's author, copyright date, or miscellaneous
    // information.
    //----------------------------------------------------------
```

continues

Listing 2.1. continued

```java
public String getAppletInfo()
{
    return "Name: EX02A\r\n" +
           "Author: Mike Cohn\r\n" +
           "Created with Microsoft Visual J++ Version 1.0";
}


// The init() method is called by the AWT when an applet is
// first loaded or reloaded. Override this method to perform
// whatever initialization your applet needs, such as
// initializing data structures, loading images or fonts,
// creating frame windows, setting the layout manager, or
// adding UI components.
//--------------------------------------------------------------
public void init()
{
    // If you use a ResourceWizard-generated "control creator"
    // class to arrange controls in your applet, you may want
    // to call its CreateControls() method from within this
    // method. Remove the following call to resize() before
    // adding the call to CreateControls(); CreateControls()
    // does its own resizing.
    //----------------------------------------------------------
    resize(320, 240);

    // TODO: Place additional initialization code here
}

// Place additional applet clean up code here. destroy() is
// called when when your applet is terminating and being
// unloaded.
//--------------------------------------------------------------
public void destroy()
{
    // TODO: Place applet cleanup code here
}

// EX02A Paint Handler
//--------------------------------------------------------------
public void paint(Graphics g)
{
    g.drawString("Hello, World", 10, 10);
}

// The start() method is called when the page containing the
// applet first appears on the screen. The AppletWizard's
// initial implementation of this method starts execution of
// the applet's thread.
//--------------------------------------------------------------
public void start()
{
    // TODO: Place additional applet start code here
}

// The stop() method is called when the page containing the
// applet is no longer on the screen. The AppletWizard's
```

```
        // initial implementation of this method stops execution of
        // the applet's thread.
        //------------------------------------------------------------
        public void stop()
        {
        }

        // TODO: Place additional applet code here

}
```

The class EX02A includes a variable, m_fStandalone, which is used to indicate whether the code is being run from within a browser (as a true applet) or from within a stand-alone interpreter as an application. If m_fStandalone is true, the main method will be invoked. When run in stand-alone mode, the program cannot rely on the browser to provide a window in which it can run. Because of this, the main method creates a frame window in which the program will run. It sizes the window as appropriate and starts the program by calling the applet's init and start methods.

Because no special processing is required when an instance of EX02A is created, an empty constructor is provided. Similarly, the destroy method that is called when the applet is terminated is provided but is empty. The getAppletInfo method simply returns the string message that was entered when Applet Wizard was run.

The init method resizes the window. You'll alter this method when displaying one of Visual J++'s control creator classes. You've already seen the paint method because you added the call to drawString to display "Hello, World." Finally, empty start and stop methods are provided in case you need to supply code for them.

The Frame Class

The second Java file created by the Applet Wizard is EX02AFRAME.java and is shown in Listing 2.2. This class is a very simple descendant of Java's Frame class. This class provides a window in which the program can run when it is run outside of a browser as a stand-alone application.

Listing 2.2. EX02AFRAME.java.

```
//****************************************************************
// EX02AFrame.java:
//
//****************************************************************
import java.awt.*;

//===============================================================
// STAND-ALONE APPLICATION SUPPORT
// This frame class acts as a top-level window in which the applet appears
// when it's run as a stand-alone application.
//===============================================================
```

continues

Listing 2.2. continued

```
class EX02AFrame extends Frame
{
    // EX02AFrame constructor
    //-----------------------------------------------------------
    public EX02AFrame(String str)
    {
        // TODO: Add additional construction code here
        super (str);
    }

    // The handleEvent() method receives all events generated within the
    // frame  window. You can use this method to respond to window events.
    // To respond to events generated by menus, buttons, etc. or other
    // controls in the frame window but not managed by the applet, override
    // the window's action() method.
    //-----------------------------------------------------------
    public boolean handleEvent(Event evt)
    {
        switch (evt.id)
        {
            // Application shutdown (e.g. user chooses Close from the
            // system menu).
            //-----------------------------------------------------------
            case Event.WINDOW_DESTROY:
                // TODO: Place additional clean up code here
                dispose();
                System.exit(0);
                return true;

            default:
                return super.handleEvent(evt);
        }
    }
}
```

Only two methods are needed in the EX02AFrame class: a constructor and handleEvent. The constructor is passed a String that will appear on the title bar of the frame. The handleEvent method catches the WINDOW_DESTROY message that is generated when the user closes the application.

The Host HTML File

Finally, the Applet Wizard also created an HTML file that will host the applet when run under a browser. Listing 2.3 shows the contents of EX02A.html, which is a very simple HTML page that uses the applet tag and specifies the name of the applet and its dimensions.

Listing 2.3. EX02A.html.

```
<html>
<head>
<title>EX02A</title>
```

```
</head>
<body>
<hr>
<applet
    code=EX02A.class
    id=EX02A
    width=320
    height=240 >
</applet>
<hr>
<a href="EX02A.java">The source.</a>
</body>
</html>,
```

Seeing What the Wizard Can Do

Example EX02A is a very stripped-down example of what the Applet Wizard can do. To create this sample applet, you disabled multitasking and animation. What would Applet Wizard have done if you hadn't disabled them? If you had left animation enabled when generating the applet, Applet Wizard would have created an applet that displayed an animated view of the Earth rotating, as shown in Figure 2.12.

Figure 2.12.

An animated applet generated by the Applet Wizard.

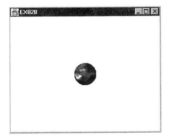

This applet is provided on the CD-ROM as EX02B, but to create it yourself, start Applet Wizard and create a new Project Workspace as before. On the first step of the Applet Wizard, tell the Wizard to create the program as an applet and an application. At this point, select the Finish button instead of using the Next buttons to move through the remaining Applet Wizard steps. If you're satisfied with the defaults (and animation is on by default), there is no need to move through each step.

This will create the program, but before running it, remember to use the Build | Settings menu item to indicate that you want to run the program through the stand-alone interpreter instead of through a browser. Finally, to run your program, select Execute from the Build menu.

Listing 2.4 shows the source code for the applet class of example EX02B. As you can tell from this listing, the Applet Wizard is capable of doing much more work for you than was done in the Hello, World example of EX02A. Taking advantage of this can save you hours at the start of a project.

Listing 2.4. EX02B.java.

```
//**********************************************************************
// EX02B.java:    Applet
//
//**********************************************************************
import java.applet.*;
import java.awt.*;
import EX02BFrame;


//====================================================================
// Main Class for applet EX02B
//
//====================================================================
public class EX02B extends Applet implements Runnable
{
    // THREAD SUPPORT:
    //        m_EX02B    is the Thread object for the applet
    //----------------------------------------------------------------
    Thread     m_EX02B = null;

    // ANIMATION SUPPORT:
    // m_Graphics   used for storing the applet's Graphics context
    // m_Images[]   the array of Image objects for the animation
    // m_nCurrImage the index of the next image to be displayed
    // m_ImgWidth   width of each image
    // m_ImgHeight  height of each image
    // m_fAllLoaded indicates whether all images have been loaded
    // NUM_IMAGES   number of images used in the animation
    //----------------------------------------------------------------
    private Graphics m_Graphics;
    private Image    m_Images[];
    private int      m_nCurrImage;
    private int      m_nImgWidth  = 0;
    private int      m_nImgHeight = 0;
    private boolean  m_fAllLoaded = false;
    private final int NUM_IMAGES = 18;

    // STANDALONE APPLICATION SUPPORT:
    // m_fStandAlone will be set to true if applet is run
    // standalone
    //----------------------------------------------------------------
    boolean m_fStandAlone = false;

    // STANDALONE APPLICATION SUPPORT
    // The main() method acts as the applet's entry point when it
    // is run as a standalone application. It is ignored if the
    // applet is run from within an HTML page.
    //----------------------------------------------------------------
    public static void main(String args[])
    {
        // Create Toplevel Window to contain applet EX02B
        //------------------------------------------------------------
        EX02BFrame frame = new EX02BFrame("EX02B");

        // Must show Frame before we size it so insets() will
        // return valid values
        //------------------------------------------------------------
```

```
        frame.show();
        frame.hide();
        frame.resize(frame.insets().left+frame.insets().right+320,
                    frame.insets().top+frame.insets().bottom+240);

    // The following code starts the applet running within the
    // frame window. It also calls GetParameters() to retrieve
    // parameter values from the command line, and sets
    // m_fStandAlone to true to prevent init() from trying to
    // get them from the HTML page.
    //--------------------------------------------------------------
    EX02B applet_EX02B = new EX02B();

    frame.add("Center", applet_EX02B);
    applet_EX02B.m_fStandAlone = true;
    applet_EX02B.init();
    applet_EX02B.start();
    frame.show();
}

// EX02B Class Constructor
//------------------------------------------------------------------
public EX02B()
{
    // TODO: Add constructor code here
}

// APPLET INFO SUPPORT:
// The getAppletInfo() method returns a string describing the
// applet's author, copyright date, or miscellaneous
// information.
//------------------------------------------------------------------
public String getAppletInfo()
{
    return "Name: EX02B\r\n" +
           "Author: Mike Cohn\r\n" +
           "Created with Microsoft Visual J++ Version 1.0";
}


// The init() method is called by the AWT when an applet is
// first loaded or reloaded. Override this method to perform
// whatever initialization your applet needs, such as
// initializing data structures, loading images or fonts,
// creating frame windows, setting the layout manager, or
// adding UI components.
//------------------------------------------------------------------
public void init()
{
    // If you use a ResourceWizard-generated "control creator"
    // class to arrange controls in your applet, you may want
    // to call its CreateControls() method from within this
    // method. Remove the following call to resize() before
    // adding the call to CreateControls(); CreateControls()
    // does its own resizing.
    //--------------------------------------------------------------
    resize(320, 240);
```

continues

Listing 2.4. continued

```
      // TODO: Place additional initialization code here
   }

   // Place additional applet clean up code here.  destroy() is
   // called when when your applet is terminating and being
   // unloaded.
   //-------------------------------------------------------------
   public void destroy()
   {
      // TODO: Place applet cleanup code here
   }

   // ANIMATION SUPPORT:
   // Draws the next image, if all images are currently loaded
   //-------------------------------------------------------------
   private void displayImage(Graphics g)
   {
      if (!m_fAllLoaded)
         return;

      // Draw Image in center of applet
      //----------------------------------------------------------
      g.drawImage(m_Images[m_nCurrImage],
               (size().width - m_nImgWidth)   / 2,
               (size().height - m_nImgHeight) / 2, null);
   }

   // EX02B Paint Handler
   //-------------------------------------------------------------
   public void paint(Graphics g)
   {
      // ANIMATION SUPPORT:
      // The following code displays a status message until all
      // the images are loaded. Then it calls displayImage to
      // display the current image.
      //----------------------------------------------------------
      if (m_fAllLoaded)
      {
         Rectangle r = g.getClipRect();

         g.clearRect(r.x, r.y, r.width, r.height);
         displayImage(g);
      }
      else
         g.drawString("Loading images...", 10, 20);

      // TODO: Place additional applet Paint code here
   }

   // The start() method is called when the page containing the
   // applet first appears on the screen. The AppletWizard's
   // initial implementation of this method starts execution of
   // the applet's thread.
   //-------------------------------------------------------------
   public void start()
   {
```

```
    if (m_EX02B == null)
    {
        m_EX02B = new Thread(this);
        m_EX02B.start();
    }
    // TODO: Place additional applet start code here
}

// The stop() method is called when the page containing the
// applet is no longer on the screen. The AppletWizard's
// initial implementation of this method stops execution of
// the applet's thread.
//-----------------------------------------------------------
public void stop()
{
    if (m_EX02B != null)
    {
        m_EX02B.stop();
        m_EX02B = null;
    }

    // TODO: Place additional applet stop code here
}

// THREAD SUPPORT
// The run() method is called when the applet's thread is
// started. If your applet performs any ongoing activities
// without waiting for user input, the code for implementing
// that behavior typically goes here. For example, for an
// applet that performs animation, the run() method controls
// the display of images.
//-----------------------------------------------------------
public void run()
{
    m_nCurrImage = 0;

    // If re-entering the page, then the images have already
    // been loaded.
    // m_fAllLoaded == TRUE.
    //-------------------------------------------------------
    if (!m_fAllLoaded)
    {
        repaint();
        m_Graphics = getGraphics();
        m_Images   = new Image[NUM_IMAGES];

        // Load in all the images
        //---------------------------------------------------
        MediaTracker tracker = new MediaTracker(this);
        String strImage;

        // For each image in the animation, this method first
        // constructs a string containing the path to the
        // image file; then it begins loading the image into
        // the m_Images array. Note that the call to getImage
        // will return before the image is completely loaded.
        //---------------------------------------------------
        for (int i = 1; i <= NUM_IMAGES; i++)
```

continues

Listing 2.4. continued

```
    {
        // Build path to next image
        //---------------------------------------------
        strImage = "images/img00" + ((i < 10) ? "0" : "") +
                i + ".gif";
        if (m_fStandAlone)
            m_Images[i-1] =
            Toolkit.getDefaultToolkit().getImage(strImage);
        else
            m_Images[i-1] = getImage(getDocumentBase(),
                    strImage);

        tracker.addImage(m_Images[i-1], 0);
    }

    // Wait until all images are fully loaded
    //-------------------------------------------------------
    try
    {
        tracker.waitForAll();
        m_fAllLoaded = !tracker.isErrorAny();
    }
    catch (InterruptedException e)
    {
        // TODO: Place exception-handling code here in
        // case an InterruptedException is thrown by
        // Thread.sleep(), meaning that another thread
        // has interrupted this one
    }

    if (!m_fAllLoaded)
    {
        stop();
        m_Graphics.drawString("Error loading images!", 10,
                40);
        return;
    }


    // Assuming all images are same width and height.
    //-------------------------------------------------------
    m_nImgWidth  = m_Images[0].getWidth(this);
    m_nImgHeight = m_Images[0].getHeight(this);
}
repaint();

while (true)
{
    try
    {
        // Draw next image in animation
        //-------------------------------------------
        displayImage(m_Graphics);
        m_nCurrImage++;
        if (m_nCurrImage == NUM_IMAGES)
            m_nCurrImage = 0;
```

```
            // TODO:  Add additional thread-specific code here
            Thread.sleep(50);
        }
        catch (InterruptedException e)
        {
            // TODO: Place exception-handling code here in case
            // an InterruptedException is thrown by
            // Thread.sleep(), meaning that another thread has
            // interrupted this one
            stop();
        }
    }
}
// TODO: Place additional applet code here
}
```

Summary

This chapter introduced you to the Java Applet Wizard, the first of a handful of helpful Wizards you'll encounter when using Visual J++. You learned how to use the Applet Wizard to generate source code that would run both as an applet and an application. You studied the generated source code and learned how to use the ClassView to modify the code so that you could say "Hello, World". Finally, you generated a more powerful applet that included support for multithreading and animation. You did all of this work within the Visual J++ Developer Studio, a powerful integrated development environment. In the next chapter you will learn more about the Developer Studio and the time-saving features it provides.

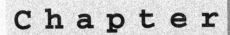

Chapter 3

Using the Developer Studio

In this chapter you learn how to use the Microsoft Developer Studio. The Developer Studio is an integrated development environment that is designed to make a programmer's life easier. It includes tools and features for managing a project's source code and configuration setting and for visually designing its resources, an editor that understands Java and HTML syntax, and even an integrated debugger that can step through code executing in a browser. If you're familiar with Microsoft Visual C++, you've already met the Developer Studio, and you might want to skip ahead to Chapter 4, "Applet Programming Fundamentals."

What Is the Developer Studio?

The Developer Studio is a fully integrated development environment (IDE). From within the Developer Studio you can do anything you could possibly want to while developing a Java program. In the dark ages of programming, a programmer used to rely on a collection of different tools. (The "dark ages of programming" is defined as any period five years prior to the current date.) Each programmer had a separate editor, a compiler, a debugger, and other tools as necessary. With an IDE, not only are these tools collected into one environment but they also are designed to work together in order to improve the productivity of the programmer.

Figure 3.1 shows the Developer Studio while being used to develop example EX02B, which was built in Chapter 2, "Creating Your First Applet with Applet Wizard." In the figure the left portion of the screen displays the ClassView pane of the Project Workspace window. Also displayed are a source code editing window, a graphic image editing window, and an InfoView topic. The rest of this chapter is devoted to covering some of the key concepts in using the Developer Studio.

Figure 3.1.

Creating a new project workspace.

Understanding Workspaces

When programming in Visual J++, all your work is performed in a *workspace*. A Visual J++ workspace is a way of logically associating project source code and configurations for building that source code. For example, a typical workspace will define a *project* that is comprised of one or more Java source files and Debug and Release configuration settings that describe how to build the project.

As you saw in Figure 3.1, the Developer Studio features a Project Workspace window that is located prominently on the left of the Visual J++ desktop. The Project Workspace window is one of the most important in Visual J++ because it enables you to quickly navigate through a workspace's projects, classes, and files. It also provides easy access to online documentation through the InfoView. To consolidate all this information into one place, the Project Workspace window contains three panes of information—ClassView, FileView, and InfoView. Each of these panes is activated by selecting the tab at the bottom of the Project Workspace window.

Working with FileView

The FileView pane of the Project Workspace window enables you to view and work with the files in your projects. It is displayed as a hierarchical list box as shown in Figure 3.2. In this figure you can see that the project EX02B contains an HTML file, a pair of Java files, and then a series of GIF files. To select one of the files for editing, double-click the mouse over the desired filename. In Figure 3.2, the file EX02BFRAME.JAVA was selected in the FileView pane, and a window for editing it was displayed to the right of the Project Workspace.

Figure 3.2.

Using the FileView to edit a Java source file.

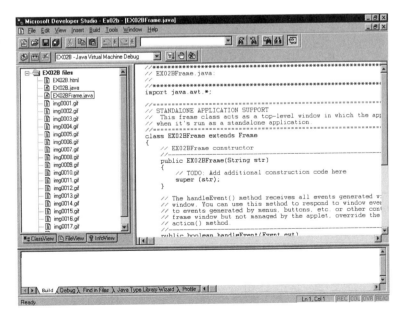

Because a project can contain files other than simple text files, such as source code, the Project Workspace lets you edit and display other file types. Figure 3.3 illustrates this by showing how a graphic image—a filenamed IMG0013.GIF—is displayed. As you can see in Figure 3.3, the image is shown at its actual size and at a magnified size. A palette of graphics editing tools is also provided.

Figure 3.3.

Using the FileView to edit a graphic file.

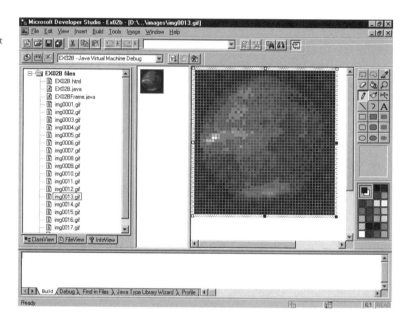

Using Dockable Windows

So far, the Project Workspace window has always been on the left side of the screen. The Project Workspace window, like many windows in Visual J++, is a *dockable* window. A window is dockable if you can move it into a position and have it become anchored in that position. When you do this, the window will usually reshape itself to dimensions appropriate for its new position.

Because the Project Workspace window is a dockable window, you can move it from its default home at the left of the Developer Studio. You can even undock it by moving it to the middle of the Developer Studio desktop where it becomes a free-floating window, as shown in Figure 3.4.

To move a dockable window, position the mouse pointer near the border of the window and hold the left mouse button down. While holding the mouse button down, begin moving the mouse. As you do, an outline of the window will move with you, changing shape as you move the window across the desktop. Once you've found a suitable location, release the mouse button and the window will move. You should experiment with various locations for the dockable windows until you've found an arrangement that suits your working style.

Figure 3.4.

Undocking the FileView by
moving it to the middle of
the Developer Studio
desktop.

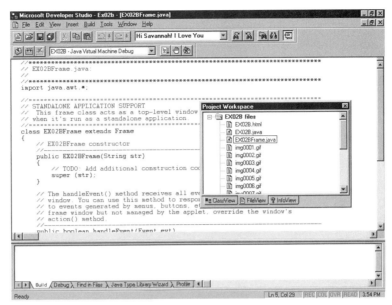

Working with ClassView

The ClassView pane of the Project Workspace window will probably be the one you'll use most frequently. (Looking at a project through its files is a somewhat artificial approach.) More useful is the capability to look at the classes that are used by a project and then to be able to see the methods and variables that are members of the classes. This is precisely what the ClassView enables you to do. The ClassView is shown in Figure 3.5.

Like the FileView, the ClassView can be used to open an edit window by double-clicking an item in the Project Workspace. In Figure 3.5, a double-click on the getAppletInfo method of the EX02B class has opened the edit window to the right of the Project Workspace window. A key difference between the FileView and the ClassView is that the ClassView has opened the Edit window and positioned it at the desired function. In this way, it is possible to use the ClassView to navigate a class without regard to the file in which the class is stored.

Adding Variables, Methods, and Classes

Throughout the Developer Studio of Visual J++, the right mouse button can be used to display a menu of actions relevant to the current context of the program. When working with the ClassView, you can highlight a class name and press the right mouse button. Doing so activates a menu that, among other things, lets the user add variables or methods to the highlighted class.

Figure 3.5.

Using the ClassView to edit the `getAppletInfo` method.

Adding Variables

To add a member variable to a class, select Add Variable from the context menu displayed when the right mouse button is clicked. This will display the dialog shown in Figure 3.6. On this dialog you can set the variable type, name, an initial value, and select the desired access modifiers.

Figure 3.6.

Creating a new `String` variable from the ClassView.

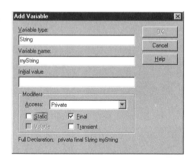

Adding Methods

It is just as easy to add a new method to a class as it is to add a new member variable. Select Add Method from the context menu, and the dialog shown in Figure 3.7 will appear. Here you can specify the return type of the method, its name, and any modifiers. After pressing the OK button, the appropriate source code is added to the class and the editor is positioned at the start of the new

method. In the case of the method being added in Figure 3.7, the following code will be added to the class:

```
private static String myMethod()
{
}
```

Figure 3.7.

Creating a new method
from the ClassView.

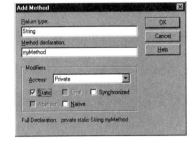

Adding Classes

Finally, it is also possible to create a new class from the ClassView pane of the Project Workspace. From the context menu you can select Create New Class to be presented with the Create New Class dialog as shown in Figure 3.8.

Figure 3.8.

Creating a new class from
the ClassView.

To create the new class, press the OK button. This will create a new class in the ClassView and a new File in the FileView. If you were to move to the new class in the ClassView, you could then continue using the ClassView to add the appropriate methods and variables.

Working with InfoView

The final pane of the Project Workspace is the InfoView. The InfoView is used to view the online books provided with Visual J++. Included with Visual J++ are online books such as a User's Guide, a two-volume API (Application Programming Interface) reference, a Test Drive book introducing Visual J++, and other reference books. The InfoView provides a very powerful viewer for these online books. The InfoView as it appears when viewing the java.awt package is shown in Figure 3.9.

Figure 3.9.

The InfoView while reading about the java.awt package.

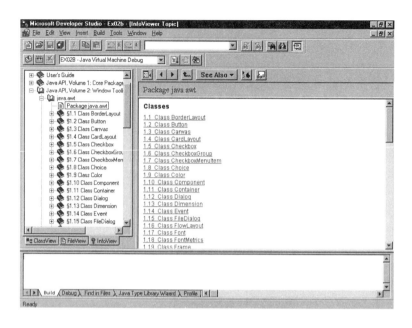

Opening Books

To use the InfoView, highlight the book you are interested in and continue opening chapters in it until you find a page display. In Figure 3.9, the chapter *java.awt* within the book *Java API, Volume 2* has been opened. Within that chapter, a page titled "Package java.awt" has been selected in the InfoView pane and the contents of the page have been displayed in a window to the right of the InfoView.

Searching

If you know what you want to read and where it's located, opening a book and moving to the page can be a very quick way to get to the information you need. However, usually you don't know where to find what you need to know. In these cases, you need to search the online books. You can use the InfoView to search either by topic or for any word in the full text. To search, click the right mouse button while the mouse pointer is over the InfoView or select the search button from the standard toolbar. Doing so will display the Search dialog as shown in Figure 3.10.

If when searching by topic you don't find what you're looking for, you can select the Query page of the Search dialog, as shown in Figure 3.11. Doing so will enable you to enter one or more words to be searched for. You can search the entire set of books or limit the scope of the search to a particular topic or a subset of topics.

Figure 3.10.
The Index page of the
InfoView Search dialog.

Figure 3.11.
The Query page of the
InfoView Search dialog.

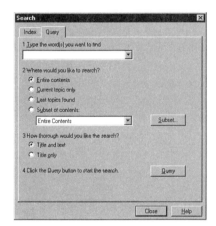

Working with Projects

You've already seen how the Project Workspace window organizes a project's files and classes into an easy-to-navigate structure. However, files and classes are only part of a project. In addition to the files that comprise a project, the Developer Studio also organizes the configuration settings you use when building a project.

Configuring Projects

Each project must be associated with at least one configuration. The configuration indicates how the project will be compiled (optimization, output directories, compiler options, and so on) and how it will be run from the Developer Studio. A project can be run as a stand-alone application or under the control of a browser. If under a browser, the configuration can specify the filename of the browser and any options needed to run it.

A typical Visual J++ project will include two configurations: one for creating a debuggable version and a second for creating a releasable version. If you use the Applet Wizard to create your project, it will create these two configurations for you. Each project will have a default configuration. You can set the default configuration by selecting Set Default Configuration from the Build menu.

You can manage a project's configurations by selecting Configurations from the Build menu. This will activate the Configurations dialog, as shown in Figure 3.12.

Figure 3.12.

The Configurations dialog.

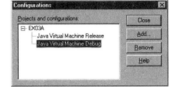

You can add or remove configurations using the Configurations dialog. To add a new configuration, select the Add button. This will display the Add Project Configuration dialog, as shown in Figure 3.13.

Figure 3.13.

The Add Project Configuration dialog.

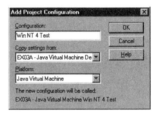

To edit the configuration settings, select Settings from the Build menu. This will display the General page of the Project Settings window as shown in Figure 3.14. In addition to this page, the Project Settings dialog contains pages for setting Debug and Java options. These pages are shown in Figures 3.15 and 3.16.

Figure 3.14.

The General page of the Project Settings dialog.

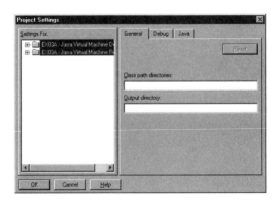

Figure 3.15.

The Debug page of the
Project Settings dialog.

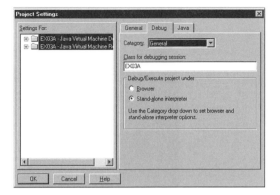

Additionally, the Debug page contains a list box named Category that allows you to set general
debugging options, browser-specific debugging options, and stand-alone interpreter specific debugging options.

Figure 3.16.

The Java page of the Project
Settings dialog.

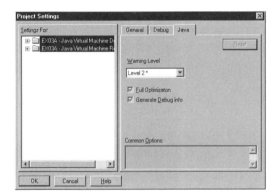

Working with Subprojects

Sometimes you are working on a set of related programs that are built and released together. For
example, you might be developing an applet that will let World Wide Web users order items from
your store. The applet displays a searchable list of available items and lets users examine each item
and select some for purchase. Although all items are displayed, only items that are in stock can be
purchased. You are writing a second applet to manage inventory levels that lets an inventory receiving clerk update the database as new items are received.

Clearly, these two applets have much in common and, if designed correctly, would share some
common classes. The Visual J++ Developer Studio facilitates working on two related projects by
enabling you to include subprojects in the Project Workspace. To create a new subproject, select
Subprojects from the Build menu and select the New button. The Insert Project dialog, as shown
in Figure 3.17, will be displayed.

Figure 3.17.
The Insert Project dialog.

This dialog should look familiar because it is similar to the New Project Workspace dialog you've already used. However, on the Insert Project dialog you can specify whether the new project is a top-level project or is subproject of an existing project in your workspace.

Setting the Default Project

Many Visual J++ operations are performed on the default project. The default project is always based on the default configuration. Earlier in this chapter you learned that you can set the default configuration by selecting Set Default Configuration from the Build menu. The default project is indicated in bold text in the FileView and ClassView panes of the Project Workspace window.

Building a Subproject

There are three ways you can build a subproject. These are as follows:

1. Make the project the default project and select Build from the Build menu.
2. Select Rebuild All from the Build menu.
3. Select Batch Build from the Build menu, and select the projects and configurations you want to build.

Removing a Project

Sometimes a project outlives its usefulness. To remove a project from the Project Workspace, select Configurations from the Build menu, highlight the desired project, and press the Remove button. You will be asked to confirm that you want to remove the project before it is deleted from the Project Workspace.

Summary

This chapter showed you how to use the Developer Studio. You learned about project workspaces, and how to manage multiple projects and configurations within a single workspace. You saw how to use the FileView, ClassView, and InfoView panes of the Project Workspace window to navigate through the files and classes of your projects. Using the ClassView, you learned how to let Visual J++ help you create new classes and add methods and variables to existing classes. Now that you're comfortable with the Developer Studio, you're ready for the next chapter where you'll learn the fundamentals of applet programming.

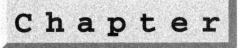

Chapter 4

Applet Programming Fundamentals

In this chapter you learn the fundamentals of Java applet programming. You learn about the four methods that control the life span of an applet. You also learn how to write code to respond to events generated by an applet's graphical user interface. In this chapter you also see how to use applet parameters to control the behavior of a program. Finally, you learn about Uniform Resource Locators (URLs) and how to display simple graphics.

The Applet Class

To create your own applets, you derive a class from Java's Applet class and then add the desired functionality. The Applet class contains methods for actions such as interacting with the browser environment in which it is running, for retrieving images, for playing sound files, and for resizing its host window. In this section you learn about the most frequently used methods in this important class.

The Life and Death of an Applet

On a typical Java-enhanced Web page, Java applets start and stop frequently as the user switches among pages. As pages are loaded into the browser, viewed and then left, applets are started and terminated in response to messages passed to the Applet class. The four most important methods in the life of an applet are init, start, stop, and destroy. They are described in Table 4.1.

Table 4.1. Important methods over the life of an applet.

Method	Purpose
init	Called when the applet is initially loaded.
start	Called each time the user loads the host Web page.
stop	Called each time the user leaves the host Web page.
destroy	Called to release resources allocated by the applet.

The init Method

When an applet is first loaded by either a browser or a stand-alone interpreter such as is provided with Visual J++, the init method is called. This allows the applet to execute any startup code that is necessary. Usually an applet will resize itself at this point. The applet may also acquire and load resources such as images or sound at this point. The init method will be called only once for each time the applet is loaded.

The **destroy** Method

The `destroy` method is called when the browser is closing an applet. Ideally this method should be used to release any resources that have been allocated during the life of the applet; however, because Java performs garbage collection, it is not necessary to release resources.

> ## TIP:
>
> Although you do not need to explicitly release resources, it is generally a good practice to do so. By explicitly releasing a resource, rather than waiting for Java's garbage detection to notice a resource has been released, your program will be able to reuse the resource sooner.

The **start** and **stop** Methods

The `start` method is similar to `init` except that `start` is called each time the Web page in which the applet is embedded is loaded. The most frequent use of the `start` method is to create a new thread. Similarly, the `stop` method is called whenever the browser moves off the Web page that hosts the applet.

The distinction between a method that gets called when an applet is first loaded and when its host page is first loaded might seem like a fine distinction, but understanding this distinction enables you to write more efficient applets. In Netscape Navigator 3 and Microsoft Internet Explorer 3, when a page containing a Java applet is first loaded, the `init` and `start` methods are called. Following a link from the page calls the applet's `stop` method. Backing up to the page calls the applet's `start` method, but not its `init` method.

In Netscape Navigator, reloading a page that contains an applet will stop and then start the applet. Performing the equivalent function in Microsoft Internet Explorer, however, causes the `stop`, `destroy`, `init`, and `start` methods all to be invoked in that order. For convenience, this information is summarized in Table 4.2.

Table 4.2. Applet method calls under Navigator and Internet Explorer.

What	Navigator	Internet Explorer
Page first loaded	init + start	init + start
Forward then backward	stop + start	stop + start
Reload/Refresh	stop + start	stop + destroy + init + start

An Example

The best way to understand how the init, start, stop, and destroy methods interact is to build an applet to demonstrate their use. Listing 4.1 shows a class that does exactly this. The class EX04A includes a private string member named history that is empty initially. As the various methods are called, text is added to this string to indicate the sequence in which the methods were called. Parentheses are placed around the start and stop messages to improve readability.

Listing 4.1. EX04A.java.

```java
import java.applet.*;
import java.awt.*;

public class EX04A extends Applet
{
    private String history = "";

    public EX04A()
    {
    }

    public void init()
    {
        history = history + "init ";
        resize(320, 240);
    }

    public void start()
    {
        history = history + "(start ";
    }

    public void stop()
    {
        history = history + "stop) ";
    }

    public void destroy()
    {
        history = history + "destroy ";
    }

    public void paint(Graphics g)
    {
        g.drawString(history, 10, 10);
    }
}
```

Even though the code in the destroy method of Listing 4.1 will execute, the results of adding this text will not be apparent. Because the history string is displayed only by the paint method and paint is not called after destroy, you will not be able to see the destroy message. You've got two options: Either trust me or run EX04A in the debugger after setting a breakpoint in destroy.

The result of a sample run of EX04A is shown in Figure 4.1. In this case, Netscape Navigator was used to run this applet. After the applet was loaded, the Reload button was pressed repeatedly. This had the effect of stopping and starting the applet each time, as you can see in Figure 4.1. Closing Navigator will stop the applet and then destroy it.

Figure 4.1.

Example of reloading an applet in Netscape Navigator.

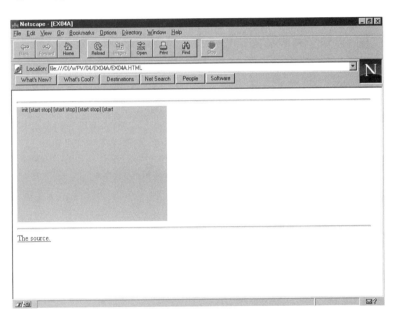

Unlike Navigator, Microsoft Internet Explorer does not simply stop and start an applet when refreshing a page. Figure 4.2 shows Internet Explorer while running EX04A after the Refresh button was pressed repeatedly. As you can see, only init and start have been used. This is because Internet Explorer completely reloads an applet when refreshing it. This causes the history string to be reset each time the applet is reloaded.

Figure 4.2.

Example of reloading an
applet in Microsoft
Intenet Explorer.

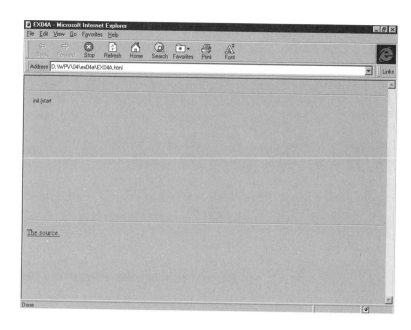

Event Handling

The Java Virtual Machine works by sending messages to Java applets whenever specific events
occur. For example, if the user presses a key, a message named KEY_PRESS is passed to the applet.
If a Java applet wants to respond in a particular way to a message, a *handler* for that message is
written. The complete list of Java messages follows:

Java messages

WINDOW_DESTROY	MOUSE_DRAG
WINDOW_EXPOSE	SCROLL_LINE_UP
WINDOW_ICONIFY	SCROLL_LINE_DOWN
WINDOW_DEICONIFY	SCROLL_PAGE_UP
WINDOW_MOVED	SCROLL_PAGE_UP
KEY_PRESS	SCROLL_ABSOLUTE
KEY_RELEASE	LIST_SELECT
KEY_ACTION	LIST_DESELECT
KEY_ACTION_RELEASE	ACTION_EVENT
MOUSE_DOWN	LOAD_FILE
MOUSE_UP	SAVE_FILE
MOUSE_MOVE	GOT_FOCUS
MOUSE_ENTER	LOST_FOCUS
MOUSE_EXIT	

The Component Class

In Java, events are generated in response to a user's interaction with the graphical user interface (GUI) of a program. As events are generated, they are sent to the component in or over which they occurred. The Component class is an abstract class, so instances of it cannot be created directly. However, it serves as the superclass for almost all parts of a program's user interface. This allows events to be sent to the specific part of the user interface that will be best able to interpret the message.

For example, if the user presses the mouse button down while the mouse pointer is over a button, the MOUSE_DOWN event is sent to the button object. This works because Button is a subclass of Component. If the button object chooses not to handle the event, it can be passed up to the object on which the button is located, usually a Window or Dialog object. That object will then have the option of handling the event, ignoring it, or passing it up to a higher level. Figure 4.3 shows a class hierachy of the subclasses of Component, which is a very active superclass.

Figure 4.3.

The descendants of Component.

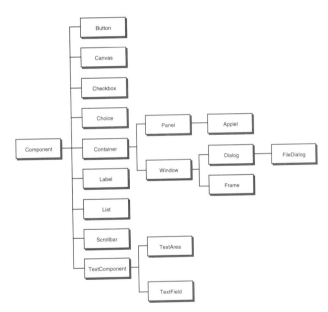

The Event Class

When an event occurs, it is passed to the event handling methods of a component as an instance of the Event class. This class is defined in the java.awt package. At the time the event occurs, an instance of Event is created and member variables are used to store information about the event and the state of the system at the time. For example, if a KEY_PRESS event occurs, it may be useful to know whether the Shift key was being held down at the time. Similarly, when the mouse is clicked, it is usually important to know the x and y coordinates of the mouse pointer when the click occurred. All relevant information about an event is stored in the member variables of the Event class, as shown in Table 4.3.

Table 4.3. The member variables of Event.

Member	Purpose
arg	Contains arbitrary, event-specific data.
clickCount	The number of consecutive mouse clicks. (For example, 2 indicates a double-click.)
evt	The next event.
id	A number representing the type of event.
key	The key that was pressed if this is a keyboard event.
modifiers	Indicates the state of the modifier keys (Shift, Ctrl, and so on).
target	The target component for the event.
when	The time at which the event occurred expressed in seconds since midnight January 1, 1970 (GMT).
x	The x coordinate where the event occurred.
y	The y coordinate where the event occurred.

In addition to the member variables shown in Table 4.3, the Event class includes some public methods you will find useful in handling events. These are shown in Table 4.4. Many of these public variables and methods are described in detail and used in examples in the following sections of this chapter where mouse and keyboard event handling are covered.

Table 4.4. The public, nonconstructor member methods of Event.

Member	Purpose
boolean controlDown	Returns true if the Ctrl key was down.
boolean metaDown	Returns true if the meta key was down.
boolean shiftDown	Returns true if the Shift key was down.
String toString	Returns a formatted string showing information about the event, which can be useful for display while debugging.
void translate	Translates the x and y coordinates of an event relative to a component.

Handling Any Event

Java provides a single method, handleEvent in the java.awt.Component class that can be used to process all events. This method is passed an Event object that contains all of the information necessary to handle the event. As an example, consider the code for EX04B, shown in Listing 4.2.

Listing 4.2. EX04B.java.

```java
import java.applet.*;
import java.awt.*;

public class EX04B extends Applet
{
    private int xPosStart=0, xPosEnd=0;
    private int yPosStart=0, yPosEnd=0;
    private boolean drawing = false;

    public void init()
    {
        resize(320, 240);
    }


    public void paint(Graphics g)
    {
        if (drawing)
            g.drawLine(xPosStart, yPosStart, xPosEnd, yPosEnd);
    }

    public boolean handleEvent(Event event) {
        boolean result;

        switch (event.id) {
        case Event.MOUSE_DOWN:
            drawing = true;
            xPosStart = event.x;
            yPosStart = event.y;
            xPosEnd   = xPosStart;
            yPosEnd   = yPosStart;
            repaint();
            result = true;
            break;
        case Event.MOUSE_UP:
            drawing = false;
            repaint();
            result = true;
            break;
        case Event.MOUSE_DRAG:
            xPosEnd = event.x;
            yPosEnd = event.y;
            repaint();
            result = true;
            break;
        default:
            result = super.handleEvent(event);
            break;
        }
        return result;
    }
}
```

This example includes a handleEvent method that uses a switch statement to act on the MOUSE_DOWN, MOUSE_UP, and MOUSE_DRAG events. This applet implements a very simple drawing program in which a line is drawn from the location where the mouse button is pressed to the mouse pointer's current location while the mouse is being dragged. When the mouse button is released, the drawing stops.

When the MOUSE_DOWN event occurs, a private member variable, drawing, is set to true to indicate that the user wants to draw a line while the mouse button is held down. The current location of the mouse pointer is retrieved from the x and y members of event and stored in private member variables. These will serve as the starting and ending points for the line that the applet will draw.

The MOUSE_DRAG event is caught and also retrieves values from event.x and event.y. This time, however, these values indicate the end of the line being drawn. After being stored, the repaint method is called to tell the applet to redisplay itself. This causes the paint method to be invoked. The paint method of EX04B is written so that it will draw a line between the stored locations if the value of drawing is true. Because drawing was set to true when the mouse button was pushed down, the line will be drawn and updated as long as the mouse button remains depressed. This can be seen in Figure 4.4. When a MOUSE_UP event is caught, it sets drawing to false to indicate that the user is done drawing the line and then repaints the screen.

You may have noticed in Listing 4.2 that handleEvent is a boolean method. In order to indicate that the event has been successfully dealt with, handleEvent must return true. If an event is received that handleEvent would prefer not to deal with, but would rather pass up to its parent, false can be returned.

<u>Figure 4.4.</u>

The results of running EX04B.

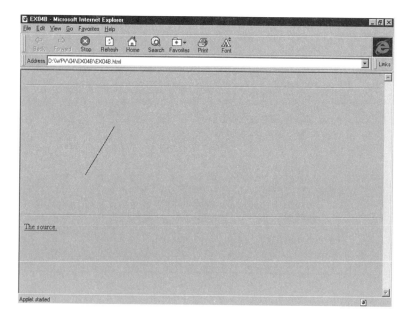

Event Handling for the Mouse

While `handleEvent` provides a very flexible and powerful way of catching and acting on Java events, it is sometimes tedious to have to look inside the supplied `Event` object for the necessary values. Because mouse and keyboard events are so common, Java includes a simple set of methods customized for use with these events. Mouse event handling is made simpler by the methods listed in Table 4.5.

Table 4.5. Methods for handling mouse events directly.

Member	Purpose
mouseDown	Called when the mouse button is pressed.
mouseDrag	Called when the mouse pointer is dragged while the button is held down.
mouseEnter	Called for a component when the mouse pointer is moved over the component.
mouseExit	Called for a component when the mouse pointer moves off the component.
mouseMove	Called when the mouse pointer is moved while the button is not held down.
mouseUp	Called when the mouse button is released.

The signature for each of these methods is the same. For example, the signature for `mouseDrag` is as follows:

```
public boolean mouseDrag(Event evt, int x, int y)
```

In handling a mouse event, the first thing a method usually looks at is the location of the mouse pointer (as given by its x and y coordinates) when the event occurred. Because these values are so frequently used, they are passed directly to the mouse event-handling methods. There is an additional advantage to using the event-specific methods instead of the generic `handleEvent`. By using these functions, you can reduce the clutter that is caused by involving many case statements inside `handleEvent`.

As a simple example of how to use one of the mouse event methods, consider the code for class `EX04C` in Listing 4.3. `EX04C` is similar to `EX04B` in allowing the user to draw a line on the screen. However, `EX04C` differs in a few small ways:

○ `EX04C` uses point `0,0` as the start of each line.

○ A line is always drawn by the `paint` method, even if it is between `0,0` and `0,0`.

○ The line is not cleared when the mouse button is released.

Listing 4.3. EX04C.java.

```java
import java.applet.*;
import java.awt.*;

public class EX04C extends Applet
{
    private int xPos=0, yPos=0;

    public EX04C()
    {
    }

    public void init()
    {
        resize(320, 240);
    }

    public void paint(Graphics g)
    {
        g.drawLine(0, 0, xPos, yPos);
    }

    public boolean mouseDrag(Event evt, int x, int y)
    {
        xPos = x;
        yPos = y;
        repaint();
        return true;
    }
}
```

Because of the simplifications to the applet, EX04C requires only the use of the mouseDrag method. Similar to the MOUSE_DRAG case of handleEvent, mouseDrag stores the location of the mouse pointer and then repaints the applet. Of course, because x and y have been provided as parameters they are used directly instead of evt.x and evt.y.

The simplifications of EX04C are removed in EX04D, which is shown in Listing 4.4. In this case, mouseDown, mouseUp, and mouseDrag are all used. The applet will respond by drawing a line from the location where the mouse button was pushed down, to its current location while the mouse is dragged, and then remove the line once the mouse button is released.

Listing 4.4. EX04D.java.

```java
import java.applet.*;
import java.awt.*;

public class EX04D extends Applet
{
    private int xPosStart=0, xPosEnd=0;
    private int yPosStart=0, yPosEnd=0;
    private boolean drawing = false;
```

```
public EX04D()
{
}

public void init()
{
    resize(320, 240);
}

public void paint(Graphics g)
{
    if (drawing)
        g.drawLine(xPosStart, yPosStart, xPosEnd, yPosEnd);
}

public boolean mouseDown(Event evt, int x, int y)
{
    drawing = true;
    xPosStart = x;
    yPosStart = y;
    xPosEnd    = xPosStart;
    yPosEnd    = yPosStart;
    return true;
}

public boolean mouseUp(Event evt, int x, int y)
{
    drawing = false;
    repaint();
    return true;
}

public boolean mouseDrag(Event evt, int x, int y)
{
    xPosEnd = x;
    yPosEnd = y;
    repaint();

    return true;
}
}
```

Keyboard Event Handling

Directly handling keyboard events is similar to handling mouse events. Two methods, keyDown and keyUp, are provided. These methods are summarized in Table 4.6. The signature for each method is the same and is as follows:

```
public boolean keyDown(Event evt, int key)
```

Table 4.6. Methods for directly handling keyboard events.

Member	Purpose
keyDown	Called when a key is pressed down.
keyUp	Called when a key is released.

In addition to the keys that generate displayable characters, Java supports the usual set of navigational and function keys. The Event class defines values for the following special keys:

Values for Java keys

HOME	RIGHT	F7
END	F1	F8
PGUP	F2	F9
PGDN	F3	F10
UP	F4	F11
DOWN	F5	F12
LEFT	F6	

Each of these values can be accessed through the event class. For example, Event.LEFT represents the left arrow key on the keyboard.

The Shift, Control, and Meta Modifiers

Sometimes a key is augmented by the use of shift, control, or other modifiers. In Java you can distinguish between an unmodified key and one combined with the Shift or Ctrl key.

Earlier in this chapter you learned that the Event class contains a member named modifiers. When an event is generated, modifiers holds the state of the Shift, Ctrl, and meta keys. To discern the state of these keys, you can either look directly at modifiers or you can use the provided utility methods controlDown, shiftDown, and metaDown.

An Example of Keyboard Event Handling

As an example of keyboard event handling, consider class EX04E in Listing 4.5. This example uses the keyDown method to trap for the up, down, left arrow, and the alphabetic (upper- and lower-case) keys.

Listing 4.5. EX04E.java.

```java
import java.applet.*;
import java.awt.*;

public class EX04E extends Applet
{
    int    yRow = 1;

    public void init()
    {
        resize(320, 240);
    }

    public void paint(Graphics g)
    {
    }

    public boolean keyDown(Event event, int key) {
        boolean result = false;

        Graphics g = getGraphics();

        switch(key) {
        case Event.UP:
            g.drawString("the up key", 10, yRow++ * 10);
            result = true;
            break;
        case Event.DOWN:
            g.drawString("the down key", 10, yRow++ * 10);
            result = true;
            break;
        case Event.LEFT:
            StringBuffer str = new StringBuffer("you pressed: ");
            if (event.controlDown())
                str.append("control + ");
            if (event.shiftDown())
                str.append("shift + ");

            str.append("left");

            g.drawString(str.toString(), 10, yRow++ * 10);
            result = true;
            break;
        default:
            if((key >= 65 && key <= 90) ||          // upper case
                  (key >= 97 && key <= 122)) {      // lower case
                Character ch = new Character((char)key);
                g.drawString(ch.toString(), 10, yRow++ * 10);
                result = true;
            }
            break;
        }
        return result;
    }
}
```

In this example, the applet will write a message to the display describing the key that is pressed. Class EX04E starts by defining a member variable, yRow, that will be used to keep track of the number of rows written so that each call to g.drawString can write at a higher y coordinate, so the messages appear to move down the applet's window. This can be seen in Figure 4.5, which was created after several keys had been pressed. Before the applet window will receive the keypress messages, the browser window needs to have focus. Click the mouse while the pointer is over the applet area.

In the keyDown method of EX04E, a switch statement is used to distinguish between the keys. If the up or down arrow is pressed, a simple message is displayed on the screen. However, if the left arrow is pressed, the applet uses the controlDown and shiftDown methods to determine which keys were down when the left arrow key was pressed. A string is created to display the modifier information and then the string is displayed.

In the default case, the value of key is checked. If the key is an upper- or lowercase letter, the key is converted from an integer and displayed.

Figure 4.5.

The results of running EX04E.

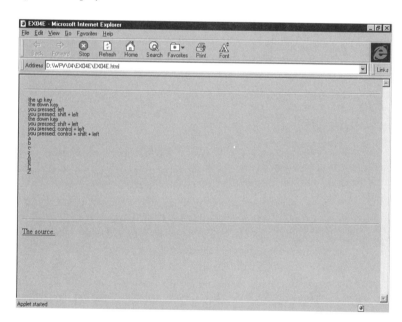

Using Applet Parameters

In the traditional, non-Java programming world, it is common to write a program that uses command-line parameters to modify its behavior. For example, the grep program searches for string patterns in files. To search for java.awt in all files with a Java extension, you would use the following command line:

```
grep java.awt *.java
```

Without command-line parameters, the grep program would be useless because it wouldn't know either the pattern to look for or the files to search. Because Java applets are not run from a command line, as is grep, an applet cannot be passed a parameter in this fashion. However, a Java applet is embedded in a host HTML file, and parameters to the applet can be embedded in the HTML file.

Embedding Parameters in HTML

To embed a parameter in a host HTML document you use the <param name> tag. For each parameter you create with this tag, you specify a name and a value. For example, Listing 4.6 is the host HTML file for EX04F. It describes three parameters: message, xPos, and yPos. The message parameter will be displayed in the browser window by the applet and is set to "Hello, World". The xPos and yPos parameters indicate the coordinates at which the message will be displayed.

Listing 4.6. EX04F.html.

```
<html>
<head>
<title>EX04F</title>
</head>
<body>
<hr>
<applet
    code=EX04F.class
    id=EX04F
    width=320
    height=240 >
    <param name=message value="Hello, World">
    <param name=xPos value=30>
    <param name=yPos value=40>
</applet>
<hr>
<a href="EX04F.java">The source.</a>
</body>
</html>
```

Reading Applet Parameters

An applet can read parameters from its host HTML file by using the getParameter method of the Applet class. The signature of getParameter is as follows:

```
public String getParameter(String name)
```

The getParameter method is passed the name of the parameter to read, and it returns the value of that parameter as a string. Although all parameters are read as string values, they can easily be converted to integers or any other more appropriate data type. This is illustrated in Listing 4.7, which shows the class EX04F. This applet reads the message, xPos, and yPos parameters that were embedded in the HTML file of Listing 4.6. An example of running this applet is shown in Figure 4.6.

Listing 4.7. EX04F.java.

```java
import java.applet.*;
import java.awt.*;

public class EX04F extends Applet
{
    private String message = "";
    private int xPos = 10;
    private int yPos = 10;

    public void init()
    {
        String param;

        param = getParameter("message");
        if (param != null)
            message = param;

        param = getParameter("xPos");
        if (param != null)
            xPos = Integer.parseInt(param);

        param = getParameter("yPos");
        if (param != null)
            yPos = Integer.parseInt(param);

        resize(320, 240);
    }

    public void paint(Graphics g)
    {
        g.drawString(message, xPos, yPos);
    }
}
```

TIP:

You can use the Applet Wizard to simplify the use of parameters. The fourth step of the Applet Wizard lets you enter parameter names, types, and default values. When the wizard generates the applet, it will generate class member variables to hold the parameter values and will place code in the init method to retrieve the values.

Figure 4.6.

EX04F displays a parameter from its host HTML file.

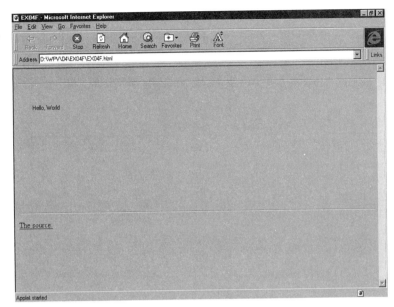

Working with URLs and Graphics

One of the most common things for a Web page to do is display a graphic. Because of this, the Applet class includes a method for retrieving an image from a URL (a Uniform Resource Locator, the way in which files are addressed on the Internet). The signature for getImage is as follows:

```
public Image getImage(URL url)
```

Accessing a URL

Because getImage loads an image from a URL, you must first create an instance of a URL. This can be done by using the following URL constructor:

```
public URL(String spec) throws MalformedURLException
```

This constructor is simply passed to the URL as a string, as in the following example:

```
myURL = new URL("http://mtngoat/java/test.jpg");
```

However, because the constructor can throw a MalformedURLException exception, the constructor must be enclosed in a try...catch block that catches the exception. This could be done as follows:

```
try {
    myURL = new URL("http://mtngoat/java/test.jpg");
}
catch (MalformedURLException e) {
    // handle error
}
```

An Example of Displaying an Image

The getImage method retrieves an image from a URL but does not display it. To display the retrieved image, use the Graphics.drawImage method in the paint method of the applet. This can be seen in EX04G, which is shown in Listing 4.8.

Listing 4.8. EX04G.java.

```java
import java.applet.*;
import java.awt.*;
import java.net.*;


public class EX04G extends Applet
{
    private Image m_image;
    private URL m_URL;
    private String error = "";

    public void init()
    {
        resize(600, 440);

        try {
          m_URL = new
            URL("http://spider.innercite.com/~lcohn/savannah.jpg");
          m_image = getImage(m_URL);
        }
        catch (MalformedURLException e) {
          error = "Image is unavailable.";
        }
    }

    public void paint(Graphics g)
    {
        g.drawString("Here's a cute baby:", 10,10);

        if (error.length() == 0)
            g.drawImage(m_image, 10, 30, this);
        else
            g.drawString(error, 20, 30);
    }
}
```

This example creates a URL object and then uses that object as a parameter to getImage. If an exception occurs, the image is not loaded but an error message is formatted. The paint method displays a string above the image and then displays either the image or the error message. The results of running this applet can be seen in Figure 4.7.

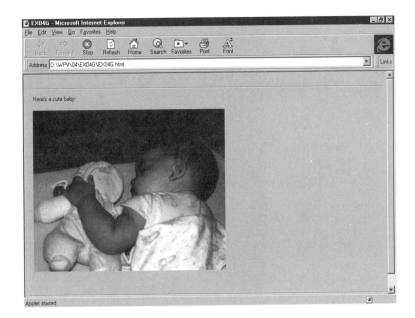

Figure 4.7.
Displaying a graphic
loaded from a URL.

Summary

This chapter covered a lot of ground. You learned how an applet's init, start, stop, and destroy methods are executed over the life of an applet. Because understanding event handling is critical to applet development, this chapter presented numerous examples of how to handle events. You learned about generic event handling with the handleEvent method as well as how to handle events with mouse- and keyboard-specific methods. This chapter also demonstrated how to customize the behavior of an applet by using applet parameters embedded in the host HTML file. Finally, you got a quick introduction into loading a graphics resource from a URL and displaying it in an applet. In the next chapter, you will turn your attention to enhancing applets by using windows and dialogs.

Chapter

5

Java's User Interface Components

Back in the days before the graphical browser, the World Wide Web was dominated by boring, text-only pages, and the only people using the Web were researchers, programmers, and some college students. The graphical browser changed all that by presenting more visually appealing pages. Suddenly, everyone is surfing the Web. Clearly, the change to an appealing, graphical user interface has much to do with the growth in popularity of the Web. The information in this chapter teaches you how to create an appealing user interface for your Java applets. Without an appealing, intuitive, easy-to-use user interface, it is very likely your Java applets will not have the success you desire for them.

Elements of an Applet's Interface

In Java, an applet's user interface is created mostly by combining classes that represent the following elements:

- Buttons
- Text fields
- Text areas
- Labels
- Checkboxes
- Lists
- Choices
- Scrollbars

These visual elements can be combined in any manner to create the user interface your applet needs. For example, Figure 5.1 shows a Web-based applet that enables golfers to enter their scores and submit them to a remote server.

This figure shows all the common elements of a Java user interface. The golfer's name is collected in a text field. The number of holes played (9 or 18) is a Checkbox group. A List is used for the course and a Choice is used for the time of day. The score can be entered directly into a text field or can be increased or decreased by using the adjacent scrollbar. The amenities (Golf Cart and Caddy) are checkboxes. The comment area is a multiline text area. The use of each of these user interface elements is explained in detail in the following sections.

Figure 5.1.

The Golf Scorekeeper applet illustrates most user interface components.

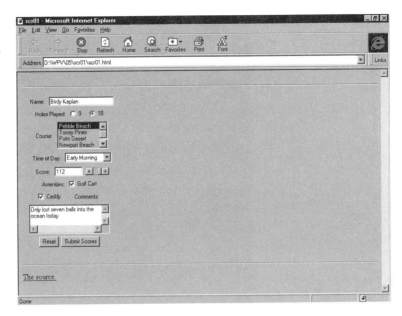

Everything Is a Component

You were introduced to the Component class in Chapter 4, "Applet Programming Fundamentals," because of its importance in passing events from one subclass of Component to another. Component serves as the base class for most of Java's user interface classes.

As the base class for Java's user interface classes, Component does much more than provide a common set of event handlers for each user interface object. Component is a very large class that makes over 70 methods available to its subclasses. The most important or frequently used of these are shown in Table 5.1.

Table 5.1. Some useful public members of Component.

Method	Purpose
action	An event-handling method called when action events occur.
disable	Disables the component.
enable	Enables the component.
getBackground	Returns the background color of the component.
getFont	Returns the font in use on the component.
getFontMetrics	Returns the font metrics (character height, width, and so on) of the component's font.
getForeground	Returns the foreground color of the component.

continues

Table 5.1. continued

Method	Purpose
getGraphics	Gets a reference to the graphics object for the component.
getParent	Gets the component's parent.
gotFocus	An event-handling method called when the component receives the focus.
handleEvent	A generic event-handling method.
hide	Makes the component invisible.
inside	Determines whether a position given by x, y coordinates is inside the component.
isEnabled	Returns true if the component is enabled.
isVisible	Returns true if the component is visible.
lostFocus	An event-handling method called when the component loses the focus.
minimumSize	Returns the minimum size required by the component.
mouseDown	An event-handling method called when the mouse button is pressed down.
mouseDrag	An event-handling method called when the mouse is moved while the button is held down.
mouseEnter	An event-handling method called when the mouse enters the component.
mouseExit	An event-handling method called when the mouse exits the component.
mouseMove	An event-handling method called when the mouse is moved without holding the button down.
mouseUp	An event-handling method called when the mouse button is released.
move	Relocates the component.
nextFocus	Gives focus to the next component.
paint	Paints the component.
preferredSize	Returns the preferred dimensions of the component.
repaint	Causes the component to be repainted.
resize	Changes the dimensions of the component.
setBackground	Sets the background color of the component.
setFont	Sets the font that will be used by the component.
setForeground	Sets the foreground color of the component.
show	Makes the component visible.

Buttons

Buttons are one of the simplest Java user interface classes and are therefore a good starting point. To create a button you can use either of the constructors shown in Table 5.2. Of course, you'll find the constructor that takes a label as a parameter much more useful than the one that does not, unless you want users to have to guess what a button does.

Table 5.2. Button constructors.

Constructor	Purpose
Button()	Creates a button without a label.
Button(String label)	Creates a button with the specified label.

As an example of how to construct and use a button, consider EX05A as shown in Listing 5.1. This is a no-frills example of placing a button on an applet and then displaying a message when the button is pressed. After the button is created the add method is used to add the button to the applet. Because add is defined in java.awt.Container and Applet is a subclass of Container, the button is added to the applet and will be displayed when the applet is run. The results of running this applet can be seen in Figure 5.2.

Listing 5.1. EX05A.java.

```java
import java.applet.*;
import java.awt.*;

public class EX05A extends Applet
{
    Button myButton;

    public void init()
    {
        resize(320, 240);

        myButton = new Button("Push me!");
        add(myButton);
    }

    public boolean action(Event evt, Object obj)
    {
        boolean result=false;

        if("Push me!".equals(obj)) {
            getGraphics().drawString("You pushed it!", 20, 20);
            result = true;
        }
        return result;
    }
}
```

Figure 5.2.

EX05A after the button has
been pushed.

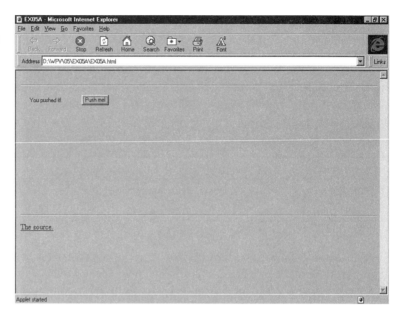

Handling Button Events

In Chapter 4, you learned how to process mouse and keyboard events. Although a button may be
pushed as a result of the user clicking a mouse button, Java provides a different message-handling
method for use when a button has been pushed. In Listing 5.1, you may have noticed the inclusion of the action method, a method that hasn't been mentioned so far. The action method is
used to handle a variety of events such as button presses, checkbox selection, or menu selection.

The action method is passed the event that has occurred and the object to which the event happened. In Listing 5.1 the equals method is used to compare the Object parameter and the button's
label. If equal, the object was the button. In this example a message is displayed.

TIP:

In Listing 5.1, the allocated button was stored in a member variable. However, because
the button can later be referenced by its label (for example, "Push me!") and because Java
supports automatic memory management, this is not necessary. The Button constructor
can return the new button directly as a parameter to the add method (or any other
method) as shown in the following:

```
public void init()
{
resize(320, 240);
add(new Button("Push me!"));
}
```

Public Button Methods

In addition to its constructors and to the methods available to it as a subclass of Component, the Button class provides the public member methods shown in Table 5.3.

Table 5.3. Public member methods of the Button class.

Method	Purpose
addNotify()	Creates a peer for the component.
getLabel()	Returns the button's current label.
paramString()	Returns the button's parameter string.
SetLabel(String)	Sets the button's label to the specified string.

EX05B is a more involved example of how to use the Button class and is shown in Listing 5.2. In this example, two buttons are created, one of which is disabled. This is shown in Figure 5.3.

Listing 5.2. EX05B.java.

```java
import java.applet.*;
import java.awt.*;

public class EX05B extends Applet
{
    int count = 0;
    Button button2 = new Button("Now push me");

    public void init()
    {
        resize(320, 240);

        add(new Button("Push me!"));

        button2.disable();
        add(button2);
    }

    public boolean action(Event evt, Object obj)
    {
        boolean result=false;

        if("Push me!".equals(obj)) {
            count++;

            switch(count)
            {
            case 1:
                button2.setLabel("almost");
                break;
```

continues

Listing 5.2. continued

```
            case 2:
                button2.setLabel("Now push me");
                button2.enable();
                break;
            }
            result = true;
        }
        else if("Now push me".equals(obj)) {
            getGraphics().drawString("Thank you", 20, 60);
            result = true;
        }
        return result;
    }
}
```

Figure 5.3.

EX05B before any buttons are pushed.

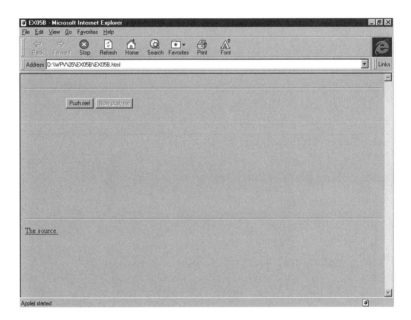

When EX05B starts running only the button labeled Push me! is enabled. Pushing this button will invoke the applet's action method, which keeps track of how many times the button has been pushed. If it has been pushed once, the second button's label is changed to Almost. If it has been pushed twice, the second button's label is reset to Now push me, and the button is enabled. Once the Now push me button is pushed, it displays a Thank you message as shown in Figure 5.4.

Figure 5.4.

EX05B after pushing
the Now push
me button.

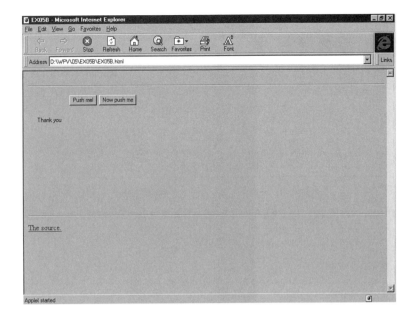

Text Fields and Areas

A text field is a one-line area for data-entry. A text area is multiline text field that includes scrollbars. There are various ways of constructing a text field or text area, as can be seen in the following examples:

```
TextField tf1 = new TextField(25);
TextField tf2 = new TextField("This is a TextField");
TextArea ta1 = new TextArea(10, 50);
TextArea ta2 = new TextArea("This is a 10 x 50 TextArea", 10, 50);
```

In this example, tf1 is constructed as a 25-column, 1-row text field; tf2 is constructed as a text field wide enough to hold the string "This is a TextField". Both text areas ta1 and ta2 will be 10 rows by 50 columns, but ta2 will contain the initial text shown. There are additional constructors for text field and text area beyond those demonstrated in these examples. Tables 5.4 and 5.5 show the constructors available for TextField and TextAreaField, respectively.

Table 5.4. Constructors for the TextField class.

Constructor	Purpose
TextField()	Creates a new, empty text field.
TextField(int)	Creates a new text field with the specified number of columns.
TextField(String)	Creates a new text field containing the specified String.
TextField(String, int)	Creates a new text field with the specified number of columns and containing the specified string.

85

Table 5.5. Constructors for the TextAreaField class.

Constructor	Purpose
TextArea()	Creates a new, empty text area.
TextArea(int, int)	Creates a new text area with the specified number of rows and columns.
TextArea(String)	Creates a new text area containing the specified String.
TextArea(String,int,int)	Creates a new text area with the specified number of rows and columns and containing the specified string.

Both TextField and TextArea are subclasses of the TextComponent class. This common base class provides the public methods listed in Table 5.6.

Table 5.6. Public members of TextComponent.

Method	Purpose
getSelectedText()	Returns the currently selected text.
getSelectionEnd()	Returns the ending column number of the selected text.
getSelectionStart()	Returns the starting column number of the selected text.
getText()	Returns the text in TextComponent.
isEditable()	Returns true if TextComponent is editable.
paramString()	Returns a parameter string for TextComponent.
removeNotify()	Removes TextComponent's peer.
select(int, int)	Selects the text between the specified columns.
selectAll()	Selects all of the text.
setEditable(boolean)	Indicates whether TextComponent is editable by the user.
setText(String)	Sets TextComponent to contain the specified string.

Beyond the methods shared through the TextComponent class, TextField and TextArea each implements its own additional member methods. These are listed in Tables 5.7 and 5.8.

Table 5.7. Public members of TextField.

Method	Purpose
addNotify()	Creates a peer for the component.
echoCharIsSet()	Returns true if an echo character has been set.
getColumns()	Returns the number of columns for TextField.
getEchoChar()	Returns the echo character that will be used.
minimumSize(int)	Returns the minimum dimensions for TextField with the specified number of columns.
minimumSize()	Returns the minimum dimensions for TextField.
paramString()	Returns a parameter string for TextField.
preferredSize(int)	Returns the preferred dimensions for TextField with the specified number of columns.
preferredSize()	Returns the preferred dimensions for TextField.
setEchoCharacter(char)	Sets the echo character to the specified character.

Table 5.8. Public members of TextArea.

Method	Purpose
addNotify()	Creates a peer for the component.
appendText(String)	Appends the specified string to TextArea.
getColumns()	Returns the number of columns for TextArea.
getRows()	Returns the number of rows for TextArea.
insertText(String, int)	Inserts the specified String at the specified column.
minimumSize(int, int)	Returns the minimum dimensions for TextArea with the specified number of rows and columns.
minimumSize()	Returns the minimum dimensions for TextArea.
paramString()	Returns a parameter string for TextArea.
preferredSize(int, int)	Returns the preferred dimensions for TextArea with the specified number of rows and columns.
preferredSize()	Returns the preferred dimensions for TextArea.
ReplaceText(String, int, int)	Uses the specified string to replace text between the specified columns.

A Text Field and Text Area Example

Listing 5.3 contains the EX05C class, which is a demonstration of using text fields and text areas. In this case, two text fields and two text areas are created. In the init method, each of these components is resized to its preferred size and then added to the applet. The first text field, tf1, uses setEchoCharacter to set the asterisk character as the character that will appear on the display regardless of what is typed. A button is created that, when pushed, will copy the text from each of the text fields into the text areas.

Listing 5.3. EX05C.java.

```java
import java.applet.*;
import java.awt.*;

public class EX05C extends Applet
{
    TextField tf1 = new TextField(25);
    TextField tf2 = new TextField("This is a TextField");
    TextArea ta1 = new TextArea(10, 50);
    TextArea ta2 = new TextArea("This is a 10 x 50 TextArea", 10, 50);

    public void init()
    {
        resize(320, 400);

        tf1.resize(tf1.preferredSize());
        tf1.setEchoCharacter('*');
        add(tf1);

        ta1.resize(ta1.preferredSize());
        add(ta1);

        tf2.resize(tf2.preferredSize());
        add(tf2);

        ta2.resize(ta2.preferredSize());
        add(ta2);

        add(new Button("Update"));
    }

    public boolean action(Event evt, Object obj)
    {
        boolean result=false;

        if("Update".equals(obj)) {
            ta1.appendText(tf1.getText() + "\r\n");
            ta2.insertText(tf2.getText() + "\r\n", 0);
```

```
                tf1.setText("");
                tf2.setText("");

                result = true;
                return result;
        }
}
```

The action method of EX05C checks to see whether the action was generated by the Update button. If so, tf1.getText and ta1.appendText are used to copy the text from the first text field, tf1, into the first text area, ta1. Similar operations are performed on the second fields except that the text is inserted into the beginning of the second text area, ta2, instead of appended to its end. After the text has been copied from the two TextField objects, each is set to an empty string. The results of running EX05C are shown in Figure 5.5. Notice that even though tf1 uses an echo character, the underlying text and not the echo character is copied to ta1.

Figure 5.5.

EX05C after
several updates.

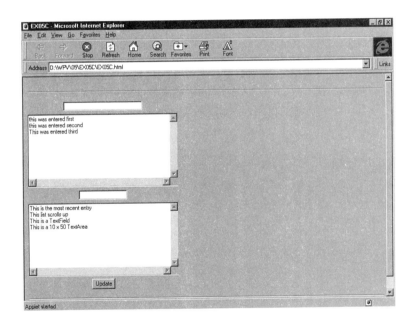

Labels

Of course, if you put a text field or text area on the screen, you should probably tell your user what you expect him to enter. You may have noticed that there is no capability to associate a prompt directly with a text field or text area. Instead, in Java, you use a different user interface class to create prompts: Label. The Label class contains three constructors as shown in Table 5.9.

Table 5.9. Constructors for the Label class.

Constructor	Purpose
Label()	Creates a label without a name.
Label(String)	Creates a new label with the specified String.
Label(String, int)	Creates a new label using the specified String and alignment value.

The alignment values specify how the text on the label should appear. Your choices are Label.LEFT, Label.RIGHT, and Label.CENTER. The following two lines will create two new labels:

```
add(new Label("Social Security Number:", Label.RIGHT);
add(new Label("First Name:"));
```

In addition to its constructors, the Label class provides the public methods shown in Table 5.10. Among other things, these methods enable you to change a label's text and alignment while the applet is running. As an example of this, look at class EX05D shown in Listing 5.4.

Table 5.10. Public methods of the Label class.

Method	Purpose
addNotify()	Creates a peer for the component.
getAlignment()	Returns the alignment value for the label.
getText()	Returns the text on the label.
paramString()	Returns a parameter string for the label.
setAlignment(int)	Sets the alignment value for the label.
setText(String)	Sets the text of the label to the specified String.

An Example

EX05D is an applet that could be the front end of a database program that lets users search for people in the database by Social Security number or name. When first loaded, the applet is ready to search by Social Security number, as shown in Figure 5.6.

Figure 5.6.
Searching EX05D by Social
Security number.

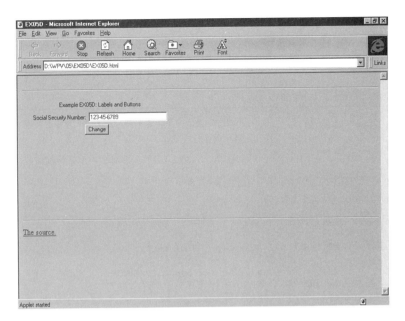

However, if the user doesn't know the Social Security number of the person he is searching for, he can select the Change button. This will change the search to be a name search, as shown in Figure 5.7.

Figure 5.7.
In EX05D, selecting Change
enables you to search by
name.

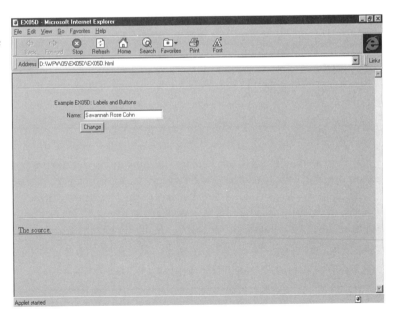

In class EX05D, a label displaying the applet's name is constructed and added to the applet. In the init method, an eponymously named label is constructed with the text Social Security Number. After the label is added to the applet, a text field and button are also added.

Listing 5.4. EX05D.java.

```
import java.applet.*;
import java.awt.*;

public class EX05D extends Applet
{
    Label label;

    public void init()
    {
        resize(320, 240);

        add(new Label("Example EX05D: Labels and Buttons"));

        label = new Label("Social Security Number:", Label.RIGHT);
        add(label);
        add(new TextField(25));
        add(new Button("Change"));
    }

    public boolean action(Event evt, Object obj)
    {
        boolean result=false;

        if("Change".equals(obj)) {
            if(label.getText().equals("Name:"))
                label.setText("Social Security Number:");
            else
                label.setText("Name:");
        }
            result = true;
        return result;
    }
}
```

The action method looks to see whether the Change button has been pressed. If so, it toggles the text on the label between "Name:" and "Social Security Number:". When label was constructed, its alignment was set as Label.RIGHT. Because of this, the shorter "Name:" label will be right-aligned in the space initially used by "Social Security Number:". This can be seen in Figure 5.8. If label had been constructed without specifying an alignment, the text would have been left-aligned.

Checkboxes and Checkbox Groups

Java checkboxes come in two varieties: grouped and ungrouped. Instances of the Java Checkbox classes are grouped using the CheckboxGroup class. If a CheckboxGroup contains more than one checkbox, only one of the checkboxes in the group can be set at any given time. In other programming environments, you may be used to referring to grouped checkboxes as radio buttons. You can see an example of a CheckboxGroup in Figure 5.8. The Male and Female buttons are grouped together and are therefore mutually exclusive.

Figure 5.8.

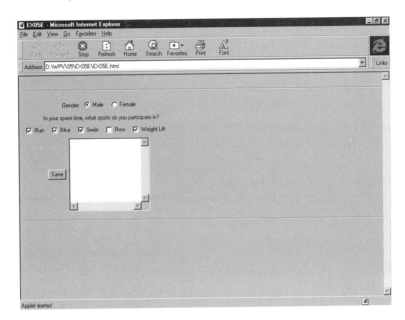

Grouped and ungrouped checkboxes in action.

Ungrouped checkboxes, on the other hand, can be checked or unchecked without regard to other checkboxes. In Figure 5.9 each of the sports is associated with an ungrouped checkbox because a user may need to mark more than one box.

There are three constructors for the Checkbox class, as shown in Table 5.11. Only one of the constructors assigns the new Checkbox object to a CheckboxGroup. The CheckboxGroup class has a single constructor that requires no parameters. The easiest way to assign a Checkbox to a CheckboxGroup is with the appropriate constructor. In the following code, a two-item group is created and then three ungrouped items are created:

```
CheckboxGroup genderGroup = new CheckboxGroup();
add(new Checkbox("Male",   genderGroup, false));
add(new Checkbox("Female", genderGroup, true));

add(new Checkbox("Option 1"));
add(new Checkbox("Option 2"));
add(new Checkbox("Option 3"));
```

Table 5.11. Constructors for the Checkbox class.

Constructor	Purpose
Checkbox()	Creates a checkbox without a label.
Checkbox(String)	Creates a checkbox using the specified String.
Checkbox(String, CheckboxGroup, boolean)	Creates a checkbox in the specified group, using the specified String and set to the specified default value.

In addition to their constructors, the Checkbox and CheckboxGroup classes offer additional public methods, as shown in Tables 5.12 and 5.13.

Table 5.12. Public methods of the Checkbox class.

Method	Purpose
addNotify()	Creates a peer for the component.
getCheckboxGroup()	Returns the checkbox group to which the checkbox belongs.
getLabel()	Returns the text on the checkbox.
getState()	Returns true if the checkbox is selected.
paramString()	Returns a parameter string for the label.
setCheckboxGroup(CheckboxGroup)	Assigns the checkbox to the specified CheckboxGroup.
setLabel(String)	Sets the text on the checkbox.
setState(boolean)	Checks or unchecks the checkbox.

Table 5.13. Public methods of the CheckboxGroup class.

Method	Purpose
getCurrent()	Returns the currently selected checkbox.
SetCurrent(Checkbox)	Makes the specified checkbox the current selection for the group.
toString()	Returns a String showing the current values of the CheckboxGroup. Useful for debugging.

An Example

As an example of using Checkboxes and CheckboxGroups, consider class EX05E as shown in Listing 5.5. This class creates the applet shown in Figure 5.8. The init method adds two checkboxes to the gender CheckboxGroup, five ungrouped checkboxes, a Save button, and a text area. When the Save button is pushed, the value in each of the checked checkboxes will be written to the text area.

Listing 5.5. EX05E.java.

```java
import java.applet.*;
import java.awt.*;

public class EX05E extends Applet
{
    CheckboxGroup genderGroup = new CheckboxGroup();
    Checkbox runCheckbox  = new Checkbox("Run");
    Checkbox bikeCheckbox = new Checkbox("Bike");
    Checkbox swimCheckbox = new Checkbox("Swim");
    Checkbox rowCheckbox  = new Checkbox("Row");
    Checkbox liftCheckbox = new Checkbox("Weight Lift");
    TextArea results = new TextArea(10, 25);


    public void init()
    {
        resize(320, 240);

        add(new Label("Gender: "));
        add(new Checkbox("Male",   genderGroup, false));
        add(new Checkbox("Female", genderGroup, true));

        add(new Label("In your spare time, what sports do you participate in?"));
        add(runCheckbox);
        add(bikeCheckbox);
        add(swimCheckbox);
        add(rowCheckbox);
        add(liftCheckbox);

        add(new Button("Save"));

        add(results);
    }

    public boolean action(Event evt, Object obj)
    {
        boolean result=false;

        if("Save".equals(obj)) {
            // clear the results area
            results.setText("");

            // display the gender
            Checkbox current = genderGroup.getCurrent();
            results.appendText(current.getLabel() + "\r\n");
```

continues

Listing 5.5. continued

```
            // check each of the sports
            if (swimCheckbox.getState() == true)
                results.appendText("Swim\r\n");
            if (bikeCheckbox.getState() == true)
                results.appendText("Bike\r\n");
            if (runCheckbox.getState() == true)
                results.appendText("Run\r\n");
            if (rowCheckbox.getState() == true)
                results.appendText("Row\r\n");
            if (liftCheckbox.getState() == true)
                results.appendText("Weight Lift\r\n");

            result = true;
        }
        return result;
    }
}
```

As you've seen in other examples in this chapter, the action method takes care of detecting when a button has been pushed. In this case the text area, results, is cleared. The current selection in genderGroup is then retrieved and the label on the current genderGroup checkbox is written to results. Finally, each of the ungrouped checkboxes is checked and text is appended to results for each that is checked. The results of this can be seen in Figure 5.9.

Figure 5.9.

The results of running EX05E.

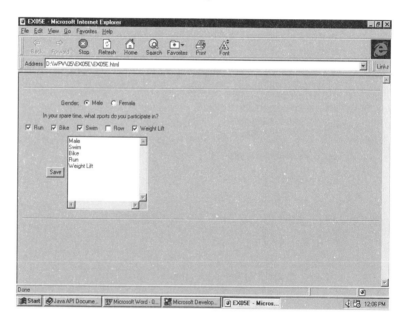

Lists and Choices

Checkboxes are not the only way to present options to your users. You can also use Java's Choice and List classes. In Java, a choice is a drop-down list from which the user may make a single selection. A list is a variable sized region from which the user may select one or more items. Figure 5.10 shows a screen that makes use of a choice to gather a person's gender and a list of sports, similar to what was done with Checkboxes in example EX04E.

Figure 5.10.

A Gender choice and a Sports list.

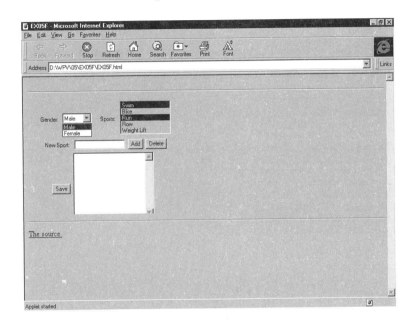

When you want to place a list or a choice onto an applet (or other Java container), you must take the following three steps:

1. Construct the new List or Choice object.

2. Add items to the List or Choice object.

3. Place the List or Choice object onto the applet.

The following code illustrates these steps in creating a new choice:

```
// create a Choice object
Choice genderChoice = new Choice();

// add items to the Choice
genderChoice.addItem("Male");
genderChoice.addItem("Female");

// then add the Choice to the applet
add(genderChoice);
```

The Choice class only has a single, no-parameter constructor. An object of the List class, however, can be created using either of the two constructors shown in Table 5.14. Usually you will use the second constructor in order to specify the number of visible rows and whether the user can select multiple items in the List.

Table 5.14. Constructors for the List class.

Constructor	Purpose
List()	Creates a new, empty list without any visible lines.
List(int, boolean)	Creates a new list with the specified number of visible lines. The boolean parameter specifies whether to allow multiple selections.

As an example of creating a new list and adding five items to it, consider the following:

```
// create a List object
List sportList = new List(5, true);

// add items to the List
sportList.addItem("Swim");
sportList.addItem("Bike");
sportList.addItem("Run");
sportList.addItem("Row");
sportList.addItem("Weight Lift");

// then add the List to the applet
add(sportList);
```

List and Choice Public Methods

Because of the many ways in which a user can interact with a list or a choice, these Java classes include many public member methods. The public methods of List are shown in Table 5.15, and the public methods of choice are shown in Table 5.16.

Table 5.15. Public methods of the List class.

Method	Purpose
addItem(String)	Adds the specified string to the bottom of the list.
addItem(String, int)	Adds the specified string at the specified index in the list.
addNotify()	Creates a peer for the component.
allowsMultipleSelection()	Returns true if the user can select multiple list items.

Method	Purpose
clear()	Removes all items from the list.
countItems()	Returns the quantity of items in the list.
delItem(int)	Deletes the item at the specified index.
delItems(int, int)	Deletes the specified range of items.
deselect(int)	Deselects the item at the specified index.
getItem(int)	Returns the item string at the specified index.
getRows()	Returns the number of visible rows.
getSelectedIndex()	Returns the index number of the selected item.
getSelectedIndexes()	Returns the index numbers of the selected items.
getSelectedItem()	Returns the item string of the selected item.
getSelectedItems()	Returns the item string of the selected items.
getVisibleIndex()	Returns the index of the last item passed to makeVisible.
isSelected(int)	Returns true if the specified item is selected.
makeVisible(int)	Makes the specified item visible in the list.
minimumSize(int)	Returns the minimum dimensions for a list with the specified number of rows.
minimumSize()	Returns the minimum dimensions for the list.
paramString()	Returns a parameter string for the list.
preferredSize(int)	Returns the preferred dimensions for a list with the specified number of rows.
preferredSize()	Returns the preferred dimensions for the list.
removeNotify()	Remove the list's peer.
replaceItem(String, int)	Replaces the item at the specified index with the specified string.
select(int)	Selects the specified item.
setMultipleSelection(boolean)	Enables or disables the selection of multiple items in the list.

Table 5.16. Public methods of the Choice class.

Method	Purpose
addItem(String)	Adds the specified string to the bottom of the choice.
addNotify()	Creates a peer for the component.
countItems()	Returns the quantity of items in the choice.
getItem(int)	Returns the item string at the specified index.
getSelectedIndex()	Returns the index number of the selected item.
getSelectedItem()	Returns the item string of the selected item.
paramString()	Returns a parameter string for the choice.
select(int)	Selects the specified item.
Select(String)	Selects the specified string in the choice.

An Example

To see the use of the List and Choice classes and some of their public member methods, consider EX05F, shown in Listing 5.6. This example creates the applet window shown in Figure 5.11.

Listing 5.6. EX05F.java.

```
import java.applet.*;
import java.awt.*;

public class EX05F extends Applet
{
    Choice genderChoice = new Choice();
    List sportList = new List(5, true);
    TextArea results = new TextArea(10, 25);
    TextField newSport = new TextField(15);

    public void init()
    {
        add(new Label("Gender: "));

        genderChoice.addItem("Male");
        genderChoice.addItem("Female");
        add(genderChoice);

        add(new Label("Sports: "));
        sportList.addItem("Swim");
        sportList.addItem("Bike");
        sportList.addItem("Run");
```

```
            sportList.addItem("Row");
            sportList.addItem("Weight Lift");
        add(sportList);

        add(new Label("New Sport: "));
        add(newSport);
        add(new Button("Add"));
        add(new Button("Delete"));

        add(new Button("Save"));

        add(results);

        resize(320, 240);
    }

    public boolean action(Event evt, Object obj)
    {
        boolean result=false;
        int i;

        if("Save".equals(obj)) {
            // clear the results area
            results.setText("");

            // display the gender
            String gender = genderChoice.getSelectedItem();
            results.appendText(gender + "\r\n");

            for(i=0;i<sportList.countItems();i++) {
                if(sportList.isSelected(i))
                    results.appendText(sportList.getItem(i) + "\r\n");
            }

            result = true;
        }
        else if("Add".equals(obj)) {
            String sport = newSport.getText();
            if(sport.length() > 0) {
                sportList.addItem(sport);
                newSport.setText("");
            }
        }
        else if("Delete".equals(obj)) {
            for(i=sportList.countItems()-1; i>=0; i--) {
                if(sportList.isSelected(i))
                    sportList.delItem(i);
            }
        }
        return result;
    }
}
```

EX05F is similar to EX05E except that it uses List and Choice objects instead of checkboxes, and it supports the capability to add and delete sports. After the user interface components are created in the init method, they are manipulated by the action method whenever the Save, Add, or Delete buttons are pushed. If the Save button is pushed, a string indicating if the user is male or female is created with genderChoice.getSelectedItem. This string is written to the results text area. Next, the code loops through the items in sportList. For each selected item that is found, the getItem method is used to retrieve the text of the selected item. This text is also added to the results text area.

If the Add button is pushed instead, the text in the newSport text field is retrieved. If this text field is not empty, sportList.addItem is used to add the new sport to the bottom of the list.

Finally, if Delete is pushed, the code loops through sportList using delItem to delete any selected items. Note that the loop counts down from sportList.countItems()-1 to 0. To have counted up would have possibly caused invalid numbers to be passed to delItem.

The result of EX05F after having added and deleted a few items is shown in Figure 5.11.

Figure 5.11.
EX05F after adding and deleting some sports.

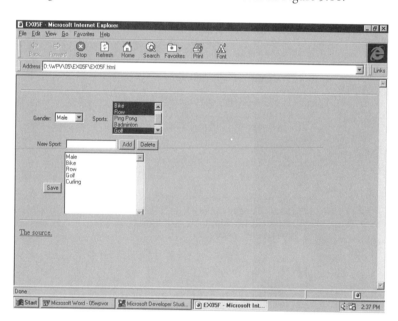

Scrollbars

Scrollbars can be used to satisfy a number of user interface goals. They are used on windows and lists to indicate that there is more to the object than meets the eye. They can also be used to allow a user to select a value from a range of values. For example, if you were designing a user interface that represented a home thermostat, a scrollbar would be an excellent choice. In Java, scrollbars can be created by using the Scrollbar class. The constructors for this class are shown in Table 5.17.

Table 5.17. Constructors for the Scrollbar class.

Constructor	Purpose
Scrollbar()	Creates a vertical scrollbar.
Scrollbar(int)	Creates a scrollbar in the specified orientation.
Scrollbar(int,int,int,int,int)	Creates a scrollbar in the specified orientation, initial value, visible area, minimum, and maximum value.

As you can see from Table 5.17, it is possible to construct a scrollbar in more than one screen orientation. The values Scrollbar.HORIZONTAL and Scrollbar.VERTICAL are defined in java.awt.Scrollbar. By default, a scrollbar will be positioned vertically. To create scrollbars using these constructors, consider the following examples:

```
Scrollbar bar1 = new Scrollbar(Scrollbar.HORIZONTAL, 50, 10, 0, 100);
Scrollbar bar2 = new Scrollbar();
Scrollbar bar3 = new Scrollbar(Scrollbar.VERTICAL);
```

In this case, bar1 is created as a horizontal bar that can accept values from 0 to 100. Initially, it will hold a value of 50. The visible portion of bar1 will be 10. In the second example, bar2 is created using the default constructor, which means it will be oriented vertically. Finally, bar3 is created using the constructor that requires only a parameter for the orientation. Because Scrollbar.VERTICAL is passed, a vertical scrollbar will be created.

The Scrollbar class offers a number of public methods. These are shown in Table 5.18.

Table 5.18. Public methods of the Scrollbar class.

Method	Purpose
addNotify()	Creates a peer for the component.
getLineIncrement()	Returns the amount by which the scrollbar will change when moving one line.
getMaximum()	Returns the maximum value for the scrollbar.
getMinimum()	Returns the minimum value for the scrollbar.
getOrientation()	Returns the orientation of the scrollbar.
getPageIncrement()	Returns the amount by which the scrollbar will change value when moving by a page.
getValue()	Returns the current value of the scrollbar.
getVisible()	Returns a value indicating how much of the scrollbar is visible.
paramString()	Returns a parameter string for Choice.

Table 5.18. continued

Method	Purpose
setLineIncrement()	Sets the amount by which to change the current value when moving one line.
setPageIncrement()	Sets the amount by which to change the current value when moving one page.
setValue()	Sets the current value of the scrollbar.
setValues(int,int,int,int)	Sets the current value, visible amount, minimum, and maximum values of the scrollbar.

An Example

As an example of using the Scrollbar class in the user interface of an applet, EX05G was created and is shown in Listing 5.7. In this example, the user is asked to enter his score for a round of golf using a scrollbar. The scrollbar is associated with a read-only text field that displays the value of the scrollbar. This can be seen in Figure 5.12.

Listing 5.7. EX05G.java.

```java
import java.applet.*;
import java.awt.*;

public class EX05G extends Applet
{
    Scrollbar scoreBar = new Scrollbar(Scrollbar.HORIZONTAL, 72, 10, 50, 120);
    TextField score = new TextField(5);

    public void init()
    {
        resize(320, 240);

        add(new Label("Score: "));

        score.setText("72");
        score.setEditable(false);
        add(score);

        add(scoreBar);
    }

    public boolean handleEvent(Event evt)
    {
        boolean result=false;
        int i;
```

```
        if(evt.target == scoreBar) {
            int value = scoreBar.getValue();
            String str = String.valueOf(value);

            score.setText(str);

            result = true;
        }
        return result;
    }
}
```

Figure 5.12.

Entering a golf score of 79
in EX05G by using the
scrollbar.

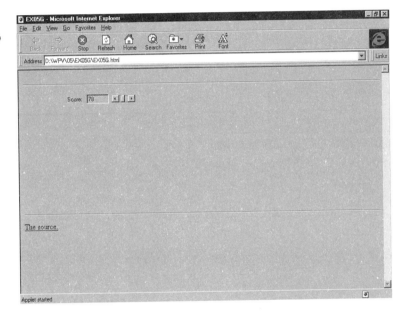

The member variable scoreBar is used to represent the scrollbar. Its constructor specifies horizontal alignment, an initial value of 72, a visible region of 10, a minimum value of 50, and a maximum value of 120. If you can shoot better than 50 for a round of golf, you're too busy golfing to enter your scores in my applet and if your score is over 120, I don't want to bother tracking it. (Sorry, Ken.) The TextField score will be used to always display the current value of the scrollbar.

In the init method, the components are added to the applet, the initial text is written to the text field, and score.setEditable(false) is used so that the user cannot change his score without using the scrollbar.

In the previous examples in this chapter, event handling was performed in the action method of the applet. To handle scrollbar events, however, you can use handleEvent. In this example, evt.target == scoreBar is used to determine whether the event was generated by the scrollbar. If it was, getValue is used to retrieve the value and the TextField score is updated.

Laying Out Controls

You may have already noticed that you've been using the add method to place user interface components on the applet and that you've never had to tell Java where to place each component. Somehow Java knew where each component belonged and placed it there. It almost seems like magic but what was really happening was that Java was making use of a *layout manager* to know how to place each new component.

The Java Software Developer's Kit (SDK) supports five layout managers, and you can write your own. A layout manager can be used by each of the Java classes that can be used to hold user interface components: Applet, Panel, Frame, and Dialog. Each of these classes has a default layout manager associated with it, as shown in Table 5.19. However, any layout manager can be used with any of these classes.

Table 5.19. Default layout managers.

Class	Default Layout Manager
Applet	FlowLayout
Dialog	BorderLayout
Frame	BorderLayout
Panel	FlowLayout

Layout Managers and the Resource Wizard

Layout managers can be a hassle to deal with. They keep you from writing useful code and focus you on a boring, trivial aspect of your applet: writing the user interface code. Fortunately, the creators of Visual J++ noticed this and have provided a solution. In addition to the layout managers included with the Java SDK, Visual J++ provides you with a tool for visually designing and laying out your controls. This process is identical to creating a Windows resource file.

These controls are then processed by the Visual J++ Resource Wizard, which creates code to add user interface components to an applet, dialog, frame, or panel. Additionally, the Resource Wizard provides you with a custom layout manager that will position your controls for you in the locations you indicated while visually designing your interface.

However, this doesn't mean you don't need to understand how the layout managers provided with Java work. Just because you have Visual J++ doesn't mean you can throw away the dozens of lines of legacy Java code already in use in your workplace that were written without Visual J++.

FlowLayout

The `FlowLayout` control is the default layout manager for the `Applet` class, so it has been used by default in all of the examples so far in this chapter. What `FlowLayout` does is to continue placing components on the same line until no more will fit. If a component won't fit on the current line, `FlowLayout` moves to the next line and places the component there. Components are placed on the screen in the order they are added to the applet.

Sometimes you can achieve desirable results this way, but you may have to work at it a bit. For example, look back at Figure 5.6. This example shows a text field above a text area and then another text field above another text area. I originally designed this screen to have the two text areas on top of two side-by-side text fields. Unfortunately, when I ran the applet, I discovered that because of the sizes of the components, they didn't line up the way I wanted them to. Although `FlowLayout` is not a great layout manager if you have more than a handful of components to display, it is an excellent choice for small quantities.

If you are working with a `Dialog` or `Frame` and want to create and use an instance of `FlowLayout` you can do so with the `setLayout` method as follows:

```
setLayout(new FlowLayout());
```

This will create a new instance of `FlowLayout` and will assign it to the object that executes this method.

BorderLayout

The `BorderLayout` class is very useful when you have a relatively small number of components to place and you want to have more control over how they are placed than is available with `FlowLayout`. A `BorderLayout` can control up to five components. Each component is placed in one of the following areas:

- ◯ North
- ◯ South
- ◯ East
- ◯ West
- ◯ Center

When you add a component using a `BorderLayout`, you specify the location in which to place the component. For example, the following code places a button in the North and a button in the South:

```
add("North", new Button("OK"));
add("South", new Button("Cancel"));
```

As you would expect, the North is the top of a container, the South is the bottom, the East is the right, and the West is the left. The Center is everything else. Usually this means that a component placed in the Center will be larger than other components. For example, look at Figure 5.13. This figure illustrates an applet that created five buttons, one in each position. Notice how the Center button grew to fill the available space in much the same manner as my waist grows to fill the last available hole in my belt.

Figure 5.13.

An applet using the BorderLayout layout manager.

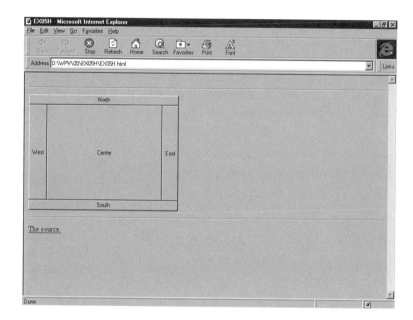

Listing 5.8 contains the code that created EX05H, which was shown in Figure 5.13. Notice that setLayout(new BorderLayout()) was used to assign the BorderLayout to the applet.

Listing 5.8. EX05H.java.

```
import java.applet.*;
import java.awt.*;

public class EX05H extends Applet
{
    public void init()
    {
        setLayout(new BorderLayout());

        add("North", new Button("North"));
        add("South", new Button("South"));

        add("East", new Button("East"));
        add("West", new Button("West"));
```

```
        add("Center", new Button("Center"));

        resize(320, 240);
    }

}
```

CardLayout

The CardLayout class is useful for presenting a user interface in which components can come and go. For example, you could use CardLayout to create an interface that included property pages or tabbed dialogs. Each page would be a separate card in this layout manager's lexicon. Using the methods of CardLayout, you can allow a user the freedom to switch between cards. As an example, consider the code in Listing 5.9.

Listing 5.9. EX05I.java.

```
import java.applet.*;
import java.awt.*;

public class EX05I extends Applet
{
    CardLayout layout;
    public void init()
    {
        resize(320, 240);
        layout = new CardLayout();
        setLayout(layout);
        add("Page1", new Button("Go to Page 2"));
        add("Page2", new Button("Go to Page 3"));
        add("Page3", new Button("Go to Page 4"));
        add("Page4", new Button("Go to Page 1"));
    }


    public boolean action(Event evt, Object obj)
    {
        boolean result=false;

        if("Go to Page 1".equals(obj)) {
            layout.show(this, "Page1");
            result = true;
        }
        else if("Go to Page 2".equals(obj)) {
            layout.next(this);
            result = true;
        }
        else if("Go to Page 3".equals(obj)) {
            layout.show(this, "Page3");
            result = true;
        }
```

continues

Listing 5.9. continued

```
        else if("Go to Page 4".equals(obj)) {
            layout.last(this);
            result = true;
        }
        return result;
    }
}
```

In this example, the goal is to create an applet that displays a page with a button on it. Pressing the button will move the user to another page with another button. When the user reaches the final page, he or she can press a button that will return him or her to the first page where it all starts again. Hopefully, the user will figure out that the cycle is repeating itself and, unlike Sisyphus, will stop before repeating the process too many times. An example of the first page of the example is shown in Figure 5.14.

Figure 5.14.

An example of the first page of a CardLayout.

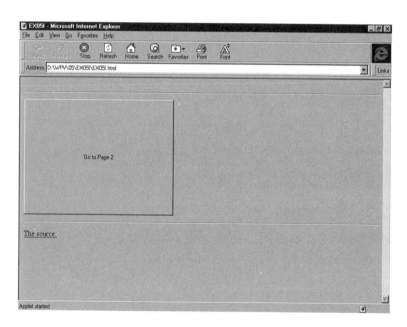

In EX05I, an instance of a CardLayout is created and stored in layout. This is assigned as the applet's layout manager using setLayout. Next, four buttons are created and added to the applet. As each button is added, it is given a name; for example, Page1 is the name given to the first button.

The action method takes care of displaying the proper page. If the button labeled Go to Page 1 is pushed, the layout.show method is passed the name (Page1) of the page to display. This updates the display with the appropriate button. A similar piece of code switches from page two to three. However, to demonstrate an alternate approach, the move from page one to two is done using layout.next, and layout.last is used to move to the fourth page.

NOTE:

One potentially disconcerting fact about CardLayout is that each card, or page, can contain only one component. This is the reason why only a single button was placed on each card in class EX05I. However, this limitation is not a real concern because Java includes a Panel class. You can place multiple components on an instance of Panel and then place a single Panel on a card. The Panel class is described in the next chapter, and an example is given of how to manipulate Panels on a CardLayout.

GridLayout

The GridLayout class is useful when you have a set of controls you want to place that are all the same size. For example, Figure 5.15 shows class EX05J, which has created a three-row by three-column grid. Each of the grid's components—eight buttons and a text field—are made the same size by GridLayout.

Figure 5.15.
Using GridLayout
in EX05J.

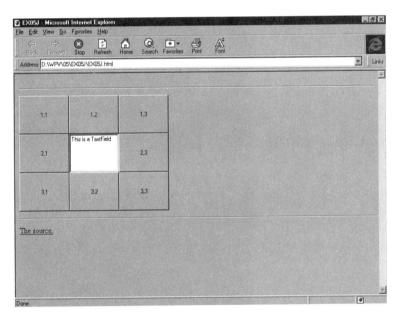

As you can see in Listing 5.10, using GridLayout is as simple as using FlowLayout. In creating a new instance of GridLayout, you can specify the number of desired rows and columns as in new GridLayout(3,3). As with the other layout managers, you then use setLayout to associate the layout manager with the applet. Finally, you can use add to assign new components to the applet.

Listing 5.10. EX05J.java.

```java
import java.applet.*;
import java.awt.*;

public class EX05J extends Applet
{
    public void init()
    {
        resize(320, 240);

        setLayout(new GridLayout(3,3));

        add(new Button("1,1"));
        add(new Button("1,2"));
        add(new Button("1,3"));
        add(new Button("2,1"));
        add(new TextField("This is a TextField"));
        add(new Button("2,3"));
        add(new Button("3,1"));
        add(new Button("3.2"));
        add(new Button("3,3"));

    }
}
```

GridBagLayout

The final layout manager, GridBagLayout, is the most involved to use but also gives you the most flexibility in placing your components. When using this layout manager, you also create an instance of GridBagConstraints. You then repeat a pattern of defining constraints ("this component should be the last one on the line," "this component should be twice as tall as other components," and so on), constructing a new component, and then applying the constraints to the component. The results can be worth the effort as this enables you to create complex screens, as shown in Figure 5.16.

Figure 5.16.

GridBagLayout can be used
to create complex screens.

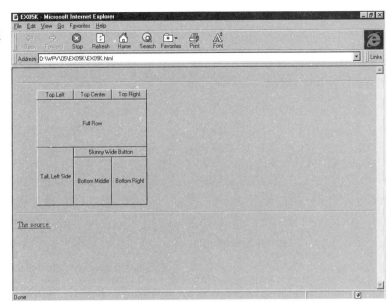

The code that creates the screen shown in Figure 5.17 is from example EX05K given in Listing 5.11.

Listing 5.11. EX05K.java.

```java
import java.applet.*;
import java.awt.*;

public class EX05K extends Applet
{
    public void init()
    {
        GridBagLayout layout = new GridBagLayout();
        GridBagConstraints gbc = new GridBagConstraints();

        setLayout(layout);

        // add the first button
        gbc.fill = GridBagConstraints.BOTH;
        Button button = new Button("Top Left");
        layout.setConstraints(button, gbc);
        add(button);

        // add a button to the same row
        gbc.gridwidth = GridBagConstraints.RELATIVE;
        button = new Button("Top Center");
        layout.setConstraints(button, gbc);
        add(button);
```

continues

Listing 5.11. continued

```
            // place a final button on the first row
            gbc.gridwidth = GridBagConstraints.REMAINDER;
            button = new Button("Top Right");
            layout.setConstraints(button, gbc);
            add(button);

            // create a  button the width of the applet
            gbc.weighty = 1.0;
            button = new Button("Full Row");
            layout.setConstraints(button, gbc);
            add(button);

            // create a tall button along the left side
            gbc.gridwidth = 1;
            gbc.gridheight = 2;
            gbc.weighty = 1.0;
            button = new Button("Tall, Left Side");
            layout.setConstraints(button, gbc);
            add(button);

            // create a skinny button to the right edge
            gbc.weighty = 0.0;
            gbc.gridwidth = GridBagConstraints.REMAINDER;
            gbc.gridheight = 1;
            button = new Button("Skinny Wide Button");
            layout.setConstraints(button, gbc);
            add(button);

            // create a button in the middle of the bottom
            gbc.gridwidth = GridBagConstraints.RELATIVE;
            button = new Button("Bottom Middle");
            layout.setConstraints(button, gbc);
            add(button);

            // create a button at the bottom right
            gbc.gridwidth = GridBagConstraints.REMAINDER;
            button = new Button("Bottom Right");
            layout.setConstraints(button, gbc);
            add(button);

            resize(320, 240);
        }
    }
```

In this example, new layout and constraint objects are constructed. The first button to be added to the screen is then created with the following code:

```
gbc.fill = GridBagConstraints.BOTH;
Button button = new Button("Top Left");
layout.setConstraints(button, gbc);
add(button);
```

The fill member of the GridBagConstraints object, gbc, is set to BOTH, which means the component will stretch both vertically and horizontally to fill the display area of the applet. Next the button is created, and layout.setConstraints is used to apply the constraints in gbc to the newly constructed button.

The second button is created by using the same GridBagConstraints object, gbc, so the same constraints will apply. Additionally, a new constraint, gbc.gridwidth = GridBagConstraints.RELATIVE, is added. This means that the component will be the next to the last component on a line. Similarly, when the third component is added the constraint gbc.gridwidth= GridBagConstraints.REMAINDER is used. This will make that component the last component on the line. The next item after an item with the REMAINDER constraint will begin a new line in the layout.

Other buttons are added in similar manners. Throughout the rest of EX05K, other member values of the constraint instance are set to demonstrate their effects.

Summary

This chapter covered a lot of territory. Along the way, you learned that the Component class is the base class for many of the Java user interface classes. You learned about the Button, TextField, TextArea, Label, Checkbox, List, Choice, and Scrollbar classes and how you can use them to create an applet's user interface. You were also introduced to layout manager and saw how to use a layout manager to control the placement of components. In the next chapter, you will continue learning about Java user interface programming by looking at windows, frames, dialogs, and menus.

Working with Frames, Dialogs, and Menus

In the prior chapter you learned all about the individual components that make up a Java applet's user interface. In this chapter you see how to effectively combine these components and place them on panels, frames, and dialogs. Using a panel gives you more control over how a group of components is placed on the screen. Frames and dialogs enable you to display freestanding windows from within an applet. Finally, you learn all about Java menus and how to add a menu to a frame.

Containers

There are many occasions when it would be convenient to treat more than one component (for example, a label and a set of checkboxes) as a group. For example, instead of placing each component onto the user interface one at a time, it would be nice to be able to create a group of components and then place the group on the user interface. Not only would this be convenient, it is necessary due to some of the built-in limitations of some of Java's layout managers.

As an example, think about the `BorderLayout` layout manager that was introduced in Chapter 5, "Java's User Interface Components." This layout manager enables you to place a component in the `North`, `South`, `East`, `West`, or `Center`. If there are only five locations you can put a component, where do you put a sixth?

Fortunately, Java provides a solution in the form of its `Container` classes. A `Container` class can be used to hold components. And because `Container` is a subclass of `Component`, you can place a container on the user interface just like you'd place a check box, text field, or any other component.

`Container` serves as a superclass for a number of other classes, one of which is the familiar `Applet` class. Each of the other subclasses of `Container` will be described in the following sections.

The `Panel` Class

The `Panel` class is the simplest of the Java `Container` classes. When an applet creates a panel, no new window is created and the panel is unseen by the user. However, by using panels you can exert more explicit control over the placement of components in an applet's user interface. A new panel is created using a simple constructor, as follows:

```
Panel myPanel = new Panel();
```

After a panel is created, you can add components to it. You then add the panel to another container. Because `Applet` is a container, you can add the panel directly to the `Applet`. This is demonstrated in the following code:

```
public class PanelSample extends Applet
{
    public void init()
    {
        Panel myPanel = new Panel();
        myPanel.add(new Button());
        add(myPanel);
    }
}
```

After the new panel is created, a button is placed on the panel. Finally, add is used to place the panel on the applet's user interface.

Each panel uses its own layout manager that is independent of the container on which the panel is placed. By default, Panel uses the FlowLayout manager. Because a panel can have a different layout manager than its parent Container, this enables you to create user interfaces that are as complex and precise as you want.

A Panel Example

As an example of how you can use panels, class EX06A is shown in Listing 6.1. This class illustrates a couple of important concepts related to the use of panels, including the use of different layout managers.

Listing 6.1. EX06A.java.

```
import java.applet.*;
import java.awt.*;

public class EX06A extends Applet
{
    public void init()
    {
        resize(320, 240);

        setLayout(new GridLayout(2,2));

        Panel p1 = new Panel();
        p1.add(new Button("Panel 1"));
        add(p1);

        Panel p2 = new Panel();
        p2.add(new Button("Panel 2-1"));
        p2.add(new TextField(8));
        add(p2);

        Panel p3 = new Panel();
        p3.setLayout(new GridLayout(2,2));
        p3.add(new Button("Panel 3-1"));
        p3.add(new Button("Panel 3-2"));
        p3.add(new Button("Panel 3-3"));
        p3.add(new Button("Panel 3-4"));
        add(p3);
```

continues   **119**

Listing 6.1. continued

```
        add(new Button("No Panel"));
    }
}
```

When run, example EX06A creates the screen shown in Figure 6.1. To create this interface the applet uses setLayout(new GridLayout(2, 2)) to create a two-row by two-column layout. The top two cells in the grid and the bottom, left cell are each displaying a panel. These panels are displaying the components placed on them.

Figure 6.1.

Running EX06A creates three panels and a panel-less area with a large button.

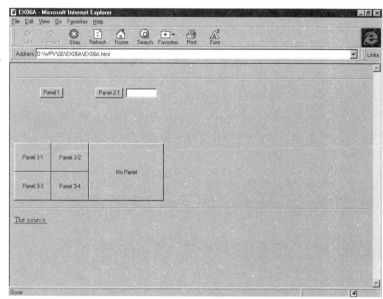

Panel p1 is created, and a new button is placed on it. The statement add(p1) is then used to place the panel onto the applet. Because no explicit layout manager was specified for panel p1, the default FlowLayout will be used. Next, a second panel, p2, is created. After adding a button and a TextField to this panel, it is added to the applet.

The third panel, p3, appears a little more complicated. However, this is only because it does not use the default layout manager. For p3 a new GridLayout object is created and four buttons are added to the panel. Then add(p3) is used to add this panel to the applet.

Finally, another button is created. This last button is added directly to the apple and is not first placed on a panel. Because the applet is using a GridLayout layout manager, the size of the button is increased so that it fills the entire grid cell, as shown in Figure 6.2.

You should take a moment to think about the different layout managers that are in use in EX06A. The applet itself is being laid out under the control of GridLayout. The first two cells in this grid are using FlowLayout, because it is the default for Panel. The third cell is again using GridLayout. This means the third cell is placed on the applet as part of a grid and that it will lay out its components as part of a grid within the grid. Finally, the fourth cell of the applet's GridLayout does not use a panel at all and its button is placed directly on the applet.

Placing a Panel on a Panel

What if instead of the screen shown in Figure 6.1, you wanted to create the screen shown in Figure 6.2? The only change here is in the top right cell. Here, a label is displayed in the top of the panel and a label and TextField are displayed in the bottom of the panel. How can you create this look?

Figure 6.2.

EX06B illustrates the placement of a panel on a panel.

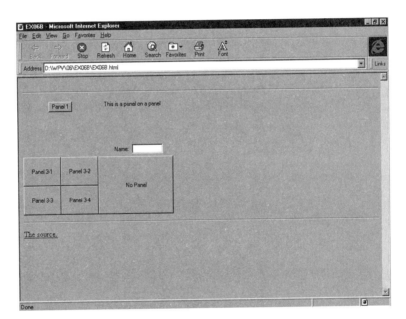

It's actually fairly simple. The answer lies in the capability to put a panel on another panel, as shown in class EX06B in Listing 6.2.

Listing 6.2. EX06B.java.

```java
import java.applet.*;
import java.awt.*;

public class EX06B extends Applet
{
    public void init()
    {
        resize(320, 240);

        setLayout(new GridLayout(2,2));

        Panel p1 = new Panel();
        p1.add(new Button("Panel 1"));
        add(p1);

        Panel p2 = new Panel();
        p2.setLayout(new BorderLayout());
        p2.add("North", new Label("This is a panel on a panel"));

        Panel subPanel = new Panel();
        subPanel.add(new Label("Name:"));
        subPanel.add(new TextField(8));
        p2.add("South", subPanel);
        add(p2);

        Panel p3 = new Panel();
        p3.setLayout(new GridLayout(2,2));
        p3.add(new Button("Panel 3-1"));
        p3.add(new Button("Panel 3-2"));
        p3.add(new Button("Panel 3-3"));
        p3.add(new Button("Panel 3-4"));
        add(p3);

        add(new Button("No Panel"));
    }
}
```

EX06B creates a new GridLayout instance and creates the first cell in the same way as was done in EX06A. The second panel, p2, is created and assigned a new instance of BorderLayout. A label, "This is a panel on a panel," is created and placed in the North of the panel.

Here is where things get interesting. A new panel, subPanel, is created. No layout manager is specified so subPanel will use the default FlowLayout. The Label and TextField are added to subPanel and then subPanel is added to the South of panel p2, creating the desired look.

Using Panels with CardLayout

In Chapter 5, you learned about the CardLayout layout manager. One shortcoming of this layout manager that was pointed out then is that it only allows you to place a single component on it. This sounds like the type of layout manager the federal government would buy: a layout manager so powerful it can lay out one component. Actually, CardLayout does serve a very useful purpose, but normally only when combined with panels.

The code for class EX06C, shown in Listing 6.3, uses CardLayout to enable the user to page between a sequence of four panels. If you recall example EX05I from Chapter 5, one of the problems with it was that it is difficult for the user to know which page he is currently on. Because CardLayout allows only one component to be added to each card, it was impossible to add both a label saying "You're on page one" and a button saying "Press here to go to page two." This problem is solved using panels in EX06C, as you can see in Figure 6.3.

Listing 6.3. EX06C.java.

```java
import java.applet.*;
import java.awt.*;

public class EX06C extends Applet
{
    CardLayout layout;
    public void init()
    {
        resize(320, 240);
        layout = new CardLayout();
        setLayout(layout);

        Panel panel1 = new Panel();
        panel1.setLayout(new BorderLayout());
        panel1.add("North", new Label("This is page 1"));
        panel1.add("Center", new Button("Go to Page 2"));
        panel1.add("South", new Label("This entire card is a panel."));
        add("Page1", panel1);

        Panel panel2 = new Panel();
        panel2.setLayout(new BorderLayout());
        panel2.add("North", new Label("This is page 2"));
        panel2.add("Center", new Button("Go to Page 3"));
        add("Page2", panel2);

        Panel panel3 = new Panel();
        panel3.setLayout(new BorderLayout());
        panel3.add("North", new Label("This is page 3"));
        panel3.add("Center", new Button("Go to Page 4"));
        add("Page3", panel3);

        Panel panel4 = new Panel();
        panel4.setLayout(new BorderLayout());
        panel4.add("North", new Label("This is page 4"));
        panel4.add("Center", new Button("Go to Page 1"));
        add("Page4", panel4);
    }

    public boolean action(Event evt, Object obj)
    {
        boolean result=false;
```

continues

Listing 6.3. continued

```
        if("Go to Page 1".equals(obj)) {
            layout.show(this, "Page1");
            result = true;
        }
        else if("Go to Page 2".equals(obj)) {
            layout.show(this, "Page2");
            result = true;
        }
        else if("Go to Page 3".equals(obj)) {
            layout.show(this, "Page3");
            result = true;
        }
        else if("Go to Page 4".equals(obj)) {
            layout.show(this, "Page4");
            result = true;
        }
        return result;
    }
}
```

In EX06C, a new instance of CardLayout is created and assigned to the applet using setLayout. Next the first panel, panel1, is created and is assigned to use BorderLayout. Two labels and a button are then added to panel1, and panel1 is added to the applet under the name "Page1" with add("Page1", panel1).

Figure 6.3.

EX06C shows how to combine panels with CardLayout.

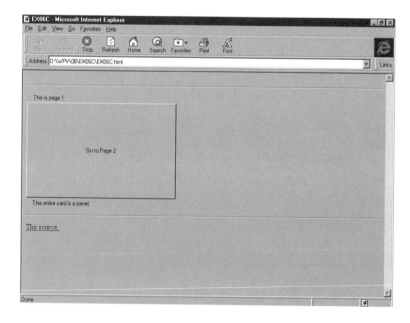

Three other panels are created in a similar manner, and the applet's action method is written to catch the button presses and to display the appropriate card.

The Window Class

Java's Window class is also a subclass of Container; however, you will probably never use the Window class directly. Instead, when you want to add a free-standing window to your applet, use either Frame or Dialog. These classes extend Window, and each adds unique functionality.

Frames

The Frame class extends Window and provides a class that can be used whenever you want to create a free-standing window that is not part of the browser in which the applet is being run. Figure 6.4, for example, illustrates a simple frame that has been moved outside the browser's borders.

Figure 6.4.

A frame exists outside the browser window.

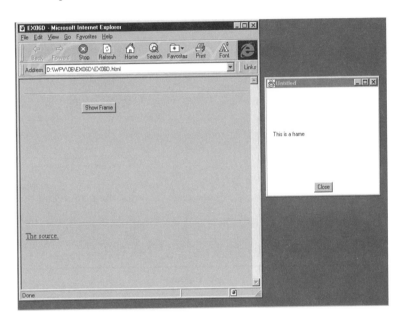

Creating a frame is as simple as using one of the constructors shown in Table 6.1. If you use the Frame() constructor, a default title of "Untitled" will be used. So, unless the frame will be used to display untitled books, you probably want to use the Frame(String) constructor. As examples of constructing new frames, consider the following:

```
Frame untitledFrame = new Frame();
Frame noTitleFrame = new Frame("");
Frame titledFrame = new Frame("Hi Mom, Send Cash");
```

Table 6.1. Constructors for the `Frame` class.

Constructor	Purpose
Frame()	Creates a frame with no title.
Frame(String)	Creates a frame with the specified title.

Once a frame is constructed you can treat it like any other container. By default, a frame uses the `BorderLayout` layout manager. You can specify a different layout manager and can add components, including `Panels`, using `add`. Of course `Frame` offers its own features beyond those available to other containers. A frame can have a menu, can use a variety of different cursors, and can have an icon placed on its title bar. In addition to the menu that can be added to the frame, each frame has a control menu located in the top left of the frame, as shown in Figure 6.5.

<u>Figure 6.5.</u>

A frame with its control menu dropped down.

To support these features, the `Frame` class includes the nonprivate member methods shown in Table 6.2.

Table 6.2. Nonprivate methods of the `Frame` class.

Method	Purpose
addNotify()	Creates a peer for the component.
dispose()	Disposes of resources (for example, menu bars) in use by the frame.
getCursorType()	Returns the cursor type that is displayed when the mouse pointer is over the frame.
getIconImage()	Returns the image used as the frame's icon.
getMenuBar()	Gets the frame's menubar.
getTitle()	Returns the frame's title.
isResizable()	Returns `true` if the frame is resizable.
paramString()	Returns the frame's parameter string.
remove(MenuComponent)	Removes the specified item from the frame's menu.

Method	Purpose
setCursor(int)	Sets the cursor that will be displayed when the mouse pointer is over the frame.
setIconImage(Image)	Sets the image to use as the frame's icon.
setMenuBar(MenuBar)	Sets the frame's menubar.
setResizable(boolean)	Makes the frame resizable or not, depending on the specified parameter.
setTitle(String)	Sets the dialog's title.

When using a frame, you should take the following steps:

1. Create the frame using new.
2. Place components (buttons, text fields, and so on) on the frame.
3. Use resize to set the frame to the correct dimensions.
4. When done with the frame, call dispose to release resources.

A Frame Example

Listing 6.4 creates the sample frame that was shown in Figure 6.4. The EX06D class is derived from Applet. In the init method, an instance of a new class called MyFrame is allocated but not displayed. A button labeled Show Frame is then added to the applet, and the action method looks for a push of this button. If the button push is detected, frame.show is used to display the instance.

Listing 6.4. EX06D.java.

```java
import java.applet.*;
import java.awt.*;

public class EX06D extends Applet
{
    MyFrame frame;

    public void init()
    {
        frame = new MyFrame();
        add(new Button("Show Frame"));
    }

    public boolean action(Event evt, Object obj)
    {
        boolean result = false;
```

continues

Listing 6.4. continued

```
            if ("Show Frame".equals(obj)) {
                frame.show();
                result = true;
            }
            return result;
        }
}

class MyFrame extends Frame {
    public MyFrame()
    {
        add("Center", new Label("This is a frame"));

        Panel p = new Panel();
        p.add(new Button("Close"));
        add("South", p);

        resize(250, 250);
    }

    public boolean action(Event evt, Object arg)
    {
        boolean result = false;

        if("Close".equals(evt.arg)) {
            dispose();
            result = true;
        }
        return result;
    }
}
```

The MyFrame class is defined as a subclass of Frame. The constructor for MyFrame places a label on the frame and then constructs a new panel. A Close button is then constructed and placed on the panel, and the panel is added to the frame. The frame is then resized. Don't forget to resize the frame, or it will be made only large enough to display the title bar. The action method of MyFrame watches for the Close button and then calls dispose to tell the Java Virtual Machine that the applet is done with this frame.

Controlling a Frame at Runtime

As Table 6.2 shows, there are a number of ways you can control the appearance of a frame at runtime. EX06E, shown in Listing 6.5, illustrates some of these.

Listing 6.5. EX06E.java.

```
import java.applet.*;
import java.awt.*;

public class EX06E extends Applet
{
    MyFrame frame;
```

```java
    public void init()
    {
        frame = new MyFrame();
        add(new Button("Show Frame"));
    }

    public boolean action(Event evt, Object obj)
    {
        boolean result = false;

        if ("Show Frame".equals(obj)) {
            frame.show();
            result = true;
        }
        return result;
    }
}

class MyFrame extends Frame {
    TextField title;
    Choice cursor;

    public MyFrame()
    {
        setLayout(new GridLayout(3,1));

        // create a panel and controls for
        // setting the frame's title
        Panel panel1 = new Panel();
        panel1.add(new Label("Title:"));
        title = new TextField(10);
        panel1.add(title);
        add(panel1);

        // create a panel and controls for
        // setting the frame's cursor
        Panel panel2 = new Panel();
        panel2.add(new Label("Cursor:"));
        cursor = new Choice();
        cursor.addItem("Default");
        cursor.addItem("Crosshair");
        cursor.addItem("Hand");
        cursor.addItem("Move");
        cursor.addItem("Text");
        cursor.addItem("Wait");
        panel2.add(cursor);
        add(panel2);

        // create a panel with two buttons
        Panel panel3 = new Panel();
        panel3.add(new Button("Apply"));
        panel3.add(new Button("Close"));
        add(panel3);

        resize(250, 250);
    }
```

continues

Listing 6.5. continued

```java
public boolean action(Event evt, Object arg)
{
    boolean result = false;

    if("Close".equals(evt.arg)) {
        dispose();
        result = true;
    }
    else if("Apply".equals(evt.arg)) {
        setTitle(title.getText());

        int Cursors[]={DEFAULT_CURSOR, CROSSHAIR_CURSOR,
            HAND_CURSOR, MOVE_CURSOR, TEXT_CURSOR,
            WAIT_CURSOR };

        setCursor(Cursors[cursor.getSelectedIndex()]);
    }
    return result;
}
}
```

In this example, a frame is created that can be customized by the user. The user can enter a string into a text field, select a cursor type from a choice, and then select the Apply button to see the results of his selections. This can be seen in Figure 6.6.

Figure 6.6.

Controlling the appearance of a frame at runtime.

To achieve this, the MyFrame constructor in EX06E constructs a text field and a choice, and adds them to panels to create a pleasant user interface. The action method of MyFrame then traps for a press on the Apply button. When that is detected, setTitle(title.getText) takes the string entered by the user and makes it the title of the frame. Similarly, a call to setCursor causes the frame to use the cursor selected by the user in the cursor Choice member.

Dialogs

The Java Dialog class is similar to the Frame class. Just like a frame, a dialog can hold components and accept user input. A dialog can be constructed using either of the constructors shown in Table 6.3.

Table 6.3. Constructors for the `Dialog` class.

Constructor	Purpose
`Dialog(Frame, boolean)`	Creates a dialog with the specified parent frame and modality.
`Dialog(Frame, String, boolean)`	Creates a dialog with the specified parent frame, title `String`, and modality.

Unfortunately, you cannot just construct a dialog and toss it directly onto the screen as you can with a frame. Every dialog must have a frame as its parent. Because an applet is not a frame, you cannot create a dialog with an applet as its parent. This isn't much of an inconvenience, however, because it is simple to create a frame, and you don't really need to do anything with the frame other than use it as the dialog's parent in the dialog constructor. For example, you can create and use a dummy frame as follows:

```
Frame dummyFrame = new Frame();
dummyFrame.resize(250, 250);
Dialog d = new Dialog(dummyFrame, false);
```

A key difference between a frame and a dialog is found in the final parameter to each of the `Dialog` constructors. This `boolean` parameter specifies the modality of the dialog. A dialog can be either *modal* or *modeless*. A modal dialog forces users to respond to it before they can continue working with other parts of the applet. Because of this, a modal dialog is perfect for displaying error messages or for gathering user input that is necessary before continuing further. A modeless dialog does not require that the user close the dialog before continuing.

Another difference between a frame and a dialog is that a menu can only be attached directly to a frame. Later in this chapter you learn how to attach a menu to a frame.

Because a dialog is closely related to a frame, a dialog's set of nonprivate methods should be familiar. These are shown in Table 6.4.

Table 6.4. Nonprivate methods of the `Dialog` class.

Method	Purpose
`addNotify()`	Creates a peer for the component.
`getTitle()`	Returns the dialog's title.
`isModal()`	Returns `true` if the dialog is modal.
`isResizable()`	Returns `true` if the dialog is resizable.
`paramString()`	Returns the dialog's parameter string.
`setResizable(boolean)`	Makes the dialog resizable or not, depending on the specified parameter.
`setTitle(String)`	Sets the dialog's title.

A Dialog Example

Class EX06F is an example of how to use a dialog in an applet. It is similar to EX06E in that the applet's main screen includes a button that activates the main part of the applet. In the prior example, a frame was displayed. In EX06F, pressing the Show Dialog button on the applet's main screen will create and display the dialog shown in Figure 6.7.

Figure 6.7.

An initially unresizable dialog.

The dialog, as shown in Figure 6.7, includes a label telling us that it cannot be resized, a Toggle button, and a Close button. Selecting the Toggle button enables resizing for the dialog and changes the label at the top of the dialog. Once the dialog is resizable, it can be stretched along any of its sides as shown in Figure 6.8.

Figure 6.8.

The same dialog after the Toggle button was pushed and the dialog was resized.

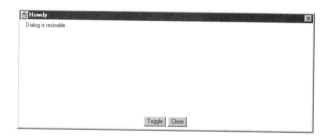

The code that creates this dialog is shown in Listing 6.6. This class includes two classes: the applet class (EX06F) and MyDialog, which extends Dialog. In the EX06F class member dlg of MyDialog is stored. In the init method for this class, you can see that a frame is constructed, resized, and then passed to the constructor for MyDialog. Notice that although the frame is constructed, it is never displayed. A button labeled Show Dialog is created. The action method looks for a push of this button and then calls dlg.show to display the dialog.

Listing 6.6. EX06F.java.

```
import java.applet.*;
import java.awt.*;

public class EX06F extends Applet
{
    MyDialog dlg;
```

```java
    public void init()
    {
        Frame f = new Frame();
        f.resize(250, 250);
        dlg = new MyDialog(f, "Howdy");
        add(new Button("Show Dialog"));
    }

    public boolean action(Event evt, Object obj)
    {
        boolean result = false;

        if ("Show Dialog".equals(obj)) {
            dlg.show();
            result = true;
        }
        return result;
    }
}

class MyDialog extends Dialog {
    Label resizeLabel;
    String labelText [] = {
        "Dialog is NOT resizable",
        "Dialog is resizable"
    };

    public MyDialog(Frame parent, String title)
    {
        super(parent, title, false);
        setResizable(false);

        resizeLabel = new Label(labelText[0]);
        add("North", resizeLabel);

        Panel p = new Panel();
        p.add(new Button("Toggle"));
        p.add(new Button("Close"));
        add("South", p);

        pack();
        resize(250, 250);
    }

    public boolean action(Event evt, Object arg)
    {
        boolean result = false;

        if("Toggle".equals(evt.arg)) {
            if (isResizable())
                resizeLabel.setText(labelText[0]);
            else
                resizeLabel.setText(labelText[1]);

            setResizable(!isResizable());
            result = true;
        }
```

continues

Listing 6.6. continued

```
        else if("Close".equals(evt.arg)) {
            dispose();
            result = true;
        }
        return result;
    }
}
```

The MyDialog class declares a label, resizeLabel, and an array of strings that will be displayed in the label so the user knows whether or not the dialog is currently resizable. The constructor for MyDialog uses super to construct the actual dialog. This is passed the undisplayed parent frame, the title of the dialog, and false to indicate that the dialog will be modeless.

Next, setResizable(false) is used to prevent the user from resizing the dialog initially. The label indicating this is constructed and placed on the dialog. The user interface is completed by placing the Toggle and Close buttons on a panel, which is then placed on the dialog.

The action method looks for a push of either the Toggle or the Close button. If Close is pushed, dispose is used to release the dialog. If Toggle is pushed, isResizable determines the current state of the dialog and the text of the label is changed appropriately. The code setResizable(!isResizable()) is used to toggle the resizable state of the dialog.

FileDialog

The final subclass of Container is the FileDialog class. This class can be used for creating File Save or File Open dialogs, as shown in Figure 6.9. This class is not available when programming applets. Because applets cannot access files, there is no need to open or close them. However, to complete this chapter's coverage of the Java Container classes, a brief overview of FileDialog is presented.

Figure 6.9.

The FileDialog in save mode under Windows 95.

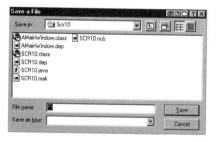

An instance of FileDialog can be constructed using either of two constructors, as shown in the following three examples:

```
FileDialog dlg1 = new FileDialog(frame, "Save");
FileDialog dlg2 = new FileDialog(frame, "Save", FileDialog.SAVE);
FileDialog dlg3 = new FileDialog(frame, "Open", FileDialog.OPEN);
```

Each `FileDialog` is created in either open or save mode, depending on whether it will be used to open an existing file or write to a file. These modes are identified by `FileDialog.SAVE` and `FileDialog.OPEN`. By default, a new instance of `FileDialog` is created in save mode. Therefore, `dlg1` and `dlg2` will be in save mode but `dlg3` will be in open mode.

Because `FileDialog` is a subclass of `Dialog`, it is necessary for each `FileDialog` to have a parent frame. The parent frame is passed as the first parameter to either `FileDialog` constructor. As with other dialogs, it is not necessary for the frame to be displayed.

Once constructed, a `FileDialog` is displayed with the `show` method. Usually, the entire purpose of displaying a `FileDialog` is to get a filename from the user. Naturally, there are member methods in `FileDialog` that enable you to retrieve this information after the user has entered it. The `getDirectory` method can be used to retrieve the directory name selected by the user. Similarly, `getFile` will return the filename. Combined, they give you the fully qualified filename.

As an example, the following code creates a `FileDialog` in save mode, displays it, and then prints the full path and filename entered by the user:

```
Frame f = new Frame();
f.resize(250, 250);

FileDialog d = new FileDialog(f, "Save a File", FileDialog.SAVE);
d.show();

System.out.println("Picked: " + d.getDirectory() + d.getFile());
```

Menus

The final subject in this chapter's discussion on user interface programming is menus. The hierarchy of Java classes involved in creating menus is shown in Figure 6.10. The `MenuComponent` class serves as an abstract base class for `MenuBar` and `MenuItem`; as such, you will never construct an actual instance of `MenuComponent`.

Figure 6.10.

The Java Menu classes.

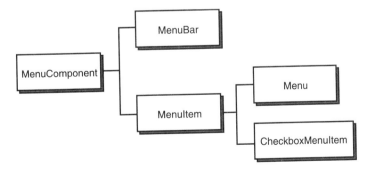

Menus in Java are created by combining three items: a menubar, one or more menus, and one or more menu items on each of the menus. Each of these items is labeled in Figure 6.11, which is a sample menu that will be built in the next section.

Figure 6.11.

The items which comprise a Java menu.

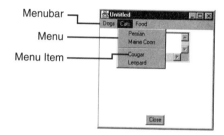

The MenuBar Class

The MenuBar class represents the top-most level of a menu. After creating a menubar, you can create Menu objects and assign the Menu objects to the menubar. A menubar is created as follows:

```
MenuBar bar = new MenuBar();
```

In addition to its constructor, the MenuBar class includes the methods listed in Table 6.5.

Table 6.5. Nonprivate methods of the MenuBar class.

Method	Purpose
add(Menu)	Adds a menu to this menubar.
addNotify()	Creates a peer for the object.
countMenus()	Returns the number of menus on this menubar.
getHelpMenu()	Returns the menu that has been identified as the Help menu for this menubar.
getMenu(int)	Returns the menu at the specified index.
remove(int)	Removes the menu at the specified index.
remove(MenuComponent)	Removes the specified menu component from this menubar.
removeNotify()	Removes the object's peer.
setHelpMenu(Menu)	Indicates the Help menu for this menubar.

In Java, menus are added to a class that implements the MenuContainer interface. In most cases this will be a class you define and base on Frame because Frame is the only Java container to implement MenuContainer. The following code adds a menubar to a frame:

```
MenuBar bar = new MenuBar();
// add menus to the MenuBar
myFrame.setMenuBar(bar);
```

The Menu Class

A menubar without any menus is as worthless as a pizza without any pepperoni. This can be easily rectified by creating Menu objects. To create a new menu, simply provide the name of the menu to the constructor, as follows:

```
Menu catMenu = new Menu("Cats");
Menu dogMenu = new Menu("Dogs");
```

After creating a menu, you must add it to the menubar. Menus will be displayed across the menubar in the order they are added to it. For example, the following code will create a Cats menu followed by a Dogs menu:

```
Menu catMenu = new Menu("Cats");
menuBar.add(catMenu);
Menu dogMenu = new Menu("Dogs");
menuBar.add(dogMenu);
```

A second Menu constructor is provided that is passed a string and a Boolean value indicating whether the menu is a tear-off menu. In addition to these constructors, the Menu class includes the methods listed in Table 6.6.

Table 6.6. Nonprivate methods of the Menu class.

Method	Purpose
add(MenuItem)	Adds the specified menu item to the menu.
add(String)	Adds an item with the specified label to the menu.
addNotify()	Creates a peer for the object.
addSeparator()	Adds a separator line to the menu.
countItems()	Returns the number of items in the menu.
getItem(int)	Returns the menu item at the specified index.
isTearOff()	Returns true if the menu can be torn off.
remove(int)	Removes the menu item at the specified index.
remove(MenuComponent)	Removes the specified menu component from the menu .
removeNotify()	Removes the object's peer.

The MenuItem Class

The menu still isn't useful, however, because no menu items have been added. A new menu item can be created by passing a string to the menu item constructor. For example, the following code illustrates all that is needed to create a menubar, a Dogs menu on the menubar, and three items on the Dogs menu:

```
MenuBar menuBar = new MenuBar();
Menu dogMenu = new Menu("Dogs");
dogMenu.add(new MenuItem("Labrador"));
dogMenu.add(new MenuItem("Poodle"));
dogMenu.add(new MenuItem("Spaniel"));
menuBar.add(dogMenu);
myFrame.setMenuBar(menuBar);
```

By default, MenuItems are *enabled*. This means that the user can select them from the menu on which they appear. It is possible to disable a MenuItem. This can be done using either the disable method or by passing false to the enable method. A MenuItem can be enabled by passing true to enable or by using enable without any parameters. These methods are illustrated in the following:

```
MenuItem item = new MenuItem("Big Dog");
item.disable();        // disable the MenuItem
item.enable();         // enable the MenuItem
item.enable(false);    // disable the MenuItem
item.enable(true);     // enable the MenuItem
```

The enable and disable methods are not the only ones available for a MenuItem. Table 6.7 describes each of the nonprivate members of MenuItem.

Table 6.7. Nonprivate methods of the MenuItem class.

Method	Purpose
addNotify()	Creates a peer for the object.
disable()	Disables selection of this menu item.
enable()	Enables selection of this menu item.
enable(boolean)	Enables or disables selection of the menu item based on the specified Boolean.
getLabel()	Returns the label for this menu item.
isEnabled()	Returns true if the menu item is selectable.
paramString()	Returns a parameter string for this menu item.
setLabel(String)	Sets the label of the menu item to the specified string.

The `CheckboxMenuItem` Class

The `CheckboxMenuItem` class is a subclass of `MenuItem` that can be used to display a check mark next to the item when desired. A `CheckboxMenuItem` is used almost identically to a regular `MenuItem`. It provides the additional `getState` and `setState(boolean)` methods, but is constructed and added to a menu as though it were a `MenuItem`. For example, the following code will create a new `CheckboxMenuItem` with the menu text `"Checkbox"`, set it to its checked state, and then add it to the menu:

```
CheckboxMenuItem checkbox = new CheckboxMenuItem("Checkbox");
checkbox.setState(true);
menu.add(checkbox);
```

In addition to its constructor, the `CheckboxMenuItem` class includes the methods listed in Table 6.8.

Table 6.8. Nonprivate methods of the `CheckboxMenuItem` class.

Method	Purpose
addNotify()	Creates a peer for the object.
getState()	Returns `true` if the `CheckboxMenuItem` is checked or `false` otherwise.
paramString()	Returns a parameter `String` for this menu item.
SetState(boolean)	Checks or unchecks the `CheckboxMenuItem` depending on the specified Boolean.

An Example of Adding a Menu to a Frame

In this example you will create a frame and attach a menubar to it. The menubar includes menus for Dogs, Cats, and Food. These menus are created by EX06G, which is shown in Listing 6.7. The `Applet` class in this example simply displays a button and waits for the user to push the button before displaying the frame with the menu on it.

Listing 6.7 EX06G.java.

```
import java.applet.*;
import java.awt.*;

public class EX06G extends Applet
{
    MyFrame frame;

    public void init()
    {
```

continues

Listing 6.7 continued

```java
        frame = new MyFrame();
        add(new Button("Show Frame"));
    }

    public boolean action(Event evt, Object obj)
    {
        boolean result = false;

        if ("Show Frame".equals(obj)) {
            frame.show();
            result = true;
        }
        return result;
    }
}

class MyFrame extends Frame {
    TextArea info;

    public MyFrame()
    {
        MenuBar menuBar = new MenuBar();

        // create a menu of dog breeds
        Menu dogMenu = new Menu("Dogs");
        dogMenu.add(new MenuItem("Labrador"));
        dogMenu.add(new MenuItem("Poodle"));
        dogMenu.add(new MenuItem("Spaniel"));
        // add the menu to the menu bar
        menuBar.add(dogMenu);

        // create a menu of cat breeds
        Menu catMenu = new Menu("Cats");
        catMenu.add(new MenuItem("Persian"));
        catMenu.add(new MenuItem("Maine Coon"));
        // separate house cats from wild cats
        catMenu.addSeparator();
        catMenu.add(new MenuItem("Cougar"));
        catMenu.add(new MenuItem("Leopard"));
        // add the menu to the menu bar
        menuBar.add(catMenu);

        // create a menu of pet foods
        Menu foodMenu = new Menu("Food");
        // create a CheckboxMenuItem for dog food
        CheckboxMenuItem dogFood = new CheckboxMenuItem("Dog Chow");
        dogFood.setState(true);
        foodMenu.add(dogFood);
        // there are two types of cat food so
        // create a sub menu
        Menu catFoodMenu = new Menu("Cat Food");
        catFoodMenu.add(new MenuItem("Tuna"));
        catFoodMenu.add(new MenuItem("Cat Chow"));
        // add the sub menu to the menu
        foodMenu.add(catFoodMenu);
        // add the menu to the menu bar
        menuBar.add(foodMenu);
```

```
        // add a Close button on a panel
        Panel p = new Panel();
        p.add(new Button("Close"));
        add("South", p);

        Panel p2 = new Panel();
        info = new TextArea(3, 20);
        p2.add(info);
        add("Center", p2);

        // set the frame's menu bar to the new menu
        setMenuBar(menuBar);

        resize(250, 250);
    }

    public boolean action(Event evt, Object arg)
    {
        boolean result = false;

        if("Close".equals(evt.arg)) {
            dispose();
            result = true;
        }
        else if ("Persian".equals(evt.arg)) {
            info.setText("A big furry cat\r\n");
            info.appendText("that I'm allergic to.");
            result = true;

        }
        else if ("Maine Coon".equals(evt.arg)) {
            info.setText("A really ferocious cat that\r\n");
            info.appendText("my Grandmother thinks is\r\n");
            info.appendText("a house cat.");
            result = true;

        }
        return result;
    }
}
```

The class MyFrame is where all the action is. In the constructor for this class, you can see that first a menubar, menuBar, is constructed. Next, dogMenu is constructed and three MenuItems are added to dogMenu before dogMenu is added to the menubar.

The second menu, catMenu, is created in a similar manner except that the addSeparator method is used to create a separating line between the first two domestic cats and the later two wild cats. Figure 6.11 shows the effect of adding the separator.

A third menu, foodMenu, is constructed. This menu is more involved than the first two menus because it includes both a CheckboxMenuItem and a submenu. This can be seen in Figure 6.12. After the CheckboxMenuItem is constructed and added to foodMenu, a new menu, catFoodMenu, is constructed. The Tuna and Cat Chow items are added to this menu. Then foodMenu.add(catFoodMenu) is used to add the catFoodMenu submenu to the Food menu. This is possible because Menu is a subclass of MenuItem.

Figure 6.12.

The Food menu has a
CheckboxMenuItem and a
submenu.

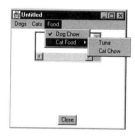

After the menus are created, a Close button and a text area are placed on panels on the frame. The text area will be used to display information about items from the Cat menu if they are selected by the user. Finally, the menubar is attached to the frame with setMenuBar(menuBar).

Of course, just putting a menu on a frame doesn't do anything unless you also trap the events generated by a user selecting the menu items. In this example, this is done in the action method. The only events handled are when the user selects Persian or Maine Coon from the Cats menu. Whenever one of these items is selected, an appropriate informational message about the selected breed of cat is written to the text area on the frame. This can be seen in Figure 6.13.

Figure 6.13.

Selecting Maine Coon from
the Cats menu displays
information about this
breed.

Summary

This chapter presented you with a lot of information about Java's Container classes Panel, Frame, Dialog, and FileDialog. You learned how to create and place panels on other containers in order to group components. You saw how panels can be combined with the CardLayout class to create a dynamic user interface. You learned how to use the Frame and Dialog classes to create windows that are not part of the browser's window. Additionally, you saw how to control a frame's cursor. Finally, you learned about Java's menu classes: MenuBar, Menu, MenuItem, and CheckboxMenuItem. You learned how to combine these to create menus and submenus that can be attached to a frame.

In the next chapter you will see how to simplify some of work involved in these tasks by using the Resource Wizard of Visual J++.

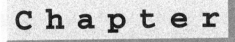

Chapter 7

Saving Time with the Resource Wizard

In the previous two chapters you learned about Java's user interface classes and how to use them. You learned how to combine layout managers and panels to position components at the right place on the screen. You also learned how to write code that would create menus. In this chapter you will take a detour. Instead of learning how to write Java code to solve a specific problem, you will learn how to avoid writing code by using another of the wizards built into Visual J++. In this chapter you are introduced to the Resource Wizard. The Resource Wizard enables you to visually design your screens and menus, thereby avoiding some of the work you went through in the preceding chapters.

The Easy Way

In college I had a math professor who would teach by filling a blackboard with complicated formulas and rules for solving a type of problem. He'd then work through a sample problem that took the entire class session and involved a seemingly infinite number of steps. If you forgot a step, you could forget getting the right answer. Invariably, after a couple of days of this the professor would start the next class session by announcing, "We've been doing it the hard way so far; now I'll show you the easy way." In this chapter you will learn the easy way of designing dialogs and menus.

Overview of the Resource Wizard

The Resource Wizard enables you to visually lay out and design your dialogs, frames, panels, and menus. Rather than having to worry about Java's layout managers and how to combine them to place components on the screen, you use a simple drag-and-drop editor. This enables you to see what you are creating as you create it. For example, Figure 7.1 shows a screen that has had OK and Cancel buttons already placed on it and a List is being positioned over the dialog.

To use the Resource Wizard you first create a *resource template* file, which will hold the container and menu resources used by your applet. You use the Visual J++ Dialog Editor to edit container resources (for example, panels, frames, and dialogs) and the Visual J++ Menu Editor to create and edit menus.

A resource template file (which ends with the .RCT extension) is then processed by the Resource Wizard. The Resource Wizard generates Java code that you can add to your project workspace, which enables you to use the dialogs and menus you designed.

Figure 7.1.

Dragging a List onto a dialog in the Dialog Editor.

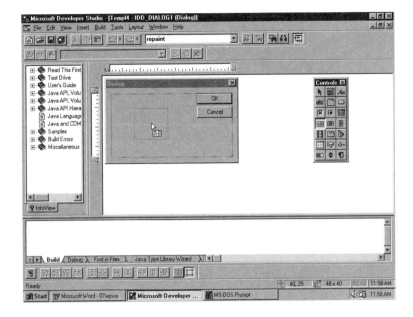

Using the Resource Wizard to Create Containers

Because a typical applet usually has more user interface components (such as text fields, buttons, and lists) than menus, the most common use of the Resource Wizard will be to assist in creating these components. If you are coming to Visual J++ from a Windows programming background, the way you think about dialog-like resources will have to change. In Windows programming, a program's resources are stored in a *resource file* that is compiled and linked into the program. In Java, this is not the case. Java dialogs are created at runtime using code such as the following:

```
Button okButton = new Button("OK");
TextField firstName = new TextField(15);
```

The Resource Wizard acts as a bridge between these two approaches. The Resource Wizard can read a resource template file and will generate the Java code necessary to display the components as designed in the Dialog Editor.

NOTE:

The resource template files (*.RCT) created by Visual J++ are stored in the same format as the files written by Visual C++. If you are converting a program from Visual C++ to Visual J++, you can take advantage of this and not have to re-create existing dialogs.

The Control Creator Class

The Resource Wizard creates a *control creator* class for each Dialog resource. A control creator class is used to place controls on any Java Container class. Controls are sometimes called components, but are always subclasses of the Java Component class that was introduced in Chapter 5, "Java's User Interface Components." A control creator class is a very flexible idea and can be used to place controls on any Java Container—not just Dialog. You can use a control creator class to place controls on a Panel, Frame, Applet, or Dialog.

TIP:

The naming of some of the components in Visual J++ is unfortunate. This is a legacy that results from Visual J++ sharing so much of the Developer Studio with Visual C++. Although it is called the Dialog Editor and it works on Dialog resources, the classes generated by the Resource Wizard based on these resources do not need to be used in Java dialogs. Remember, the control creator classes made by the Resource Wizard can be used to place Java components on any Container class, including Applet, Dialog, Panel, and Frame.

Each control creator class has two public methods: a constructor and CreateControls. The constructor is passed a Container onto which the controls will be placed. The CreateControls method takes care of actually placing the controls on the Container.

The DialogLayout Class

When you place controls in the Dialog Editor, you do not need to worry about which Java layout manager to use. You simply place the control where you want it and move on to placing the next control. How then does Java know where to place the controls?

The answer is in the second class created by Resource Wizard, DialogLayout. The DialogLayout class is created whenever you run Resource Wizard and have one or more dialog resources in the resource template file. The DialogLayout class implements the Java LayoutManager interface. It positions components on a container based on their size and the position in which they were placed in the Dialog Editor.

It is possible to use more than one resource template file to create a single Java applet. In fact, it is a common practice to keep commonly used or shared dialog resources in a file separate from applet-specific dialog resources. When you run Resource Wizard to convert each resource template, you will create multiple copies of the DialogLayout class. If this happens, don't worry about it. You need to add only one copy of DialogLayout to your project workspace and all copies of this class are identical.

One-Way Code Generation

The Resource Wizard is a one-way tool. Changes propagate from the resource template file into the generated Java source code. Changes do not flow in the opposite direction. You cannot, for example, edit a Resource Wizard–generated Java file and expect to see the changes appear in the Dialog Editor.

To make a change to a dialog resource, use File | Open to open the resource template file. Make the changes, save the file, and then re-execute the Resource Wizard. If you make changes directly to code generated by Resource Wizard, your changes will be overwritten the next time you run Resource Wizard.

A Step-by-Step Example

Enough theory, it's time for an example. This section presents an example of using the Dialog Editor to create a dialog resource, running the Resource Wizard to convert the resource into usable Java class code, and then modifying an applet to make use of the new classes. Each of the steps necessary to do this will be described in detail but the following is an overview of the steps necessary to use a dialog resource in an applet:

1. Create a new resource template.
2. Insert a dialog resource.
3. Set the dialog properties.
4. Place the components.
5. Run the Resource Wizard.
6. Add files to the project.
7. Write code to use the classes.

Example EX07A, described at the end of this section, illustrates how to use Resource Wizard–generated classes to simplify user interface development. Each of these steps will be discussed in relation to how it was performed in creating EX07A. To follow along through each of the steps, use the Applet Wizard to create a new applet. Before generating the applet, turn off comments and multithreading.

Step 1: Create a New Resource Template

First, you need to create a new resource template file. This can be done by selecting New from the File menu and selecting Resource Template. Your project workspace will show the new, empty resource template.

Step 2: Insert a Dialog Resource

Next, select Resource from the Insert menu. This will display the Insert Resource dialog as shown in Figure 7.2. Select Dialog and press OK to continue.

Figure 7.2.

The Insert Resource dialog.

At this point the Dialog Editor will be displayed and will contain a dialog ready for editing. Your screen should look similar to Figure 7.3.

Figure 7.3.

A new dialog resource ready for editing.

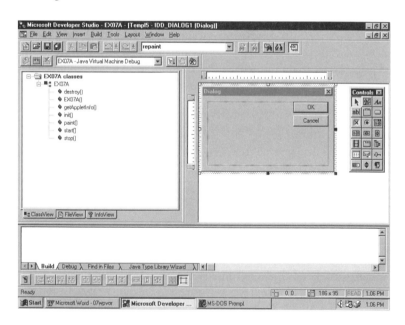

Step 3: Set the Dialog Properties

Each dialog resource has a set of properties you can set from within the Dialog Editor. To view the Dialog Properties dialog, double-click on the dialog or press Alt+Enter. You should see a Dialog Properties dialog similar to the one shown in Figure 7.4.

Figure 7.4.

The Dialog Properties dialog.

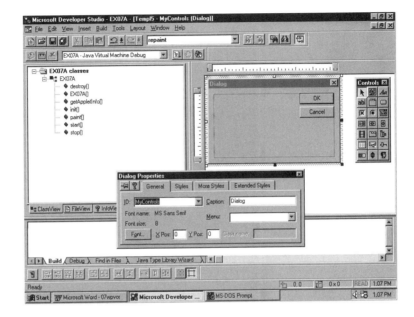

Here you need to set the ID of the dialog resource you are creating. The ID will be used as the name of the control creator class that Resource Wizard will generate based on this dialog resource. For example, in Figure 7.5 the ID is set to MyControls. This means that a class named MyControls in MyControls.java will be created by the Resource Wizard.

Step 4: Place the Components

Next, place the components on the dialog resource. To do this, select an item in the Controls toolbox and drag it over the dialog. Release it when it is in the proper position. To create example EX07A, drag an Edit Box, a Button, and a List Box onto the resource as shown in Figure 7.5.

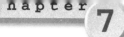
Figure 7.5.

An Edit Box, Static Text,
and a Button have been
placed on the dialog
resource.

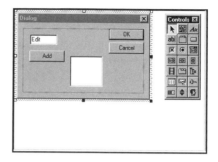

As you place each control, set its properties by double-clicking on it. An Edit Box control in the Dialog Editor corresponds to a Java TextField or TextArea. When you place the Edit Box control on the resource, set its ID to NewText, as shown in Figure 7.6. This will be the name given to the member variable in the control creator class.

Figure 7.6.

Setting properties for the
Edit Box control.

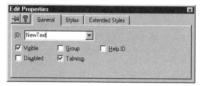

Similarly, the Button should be given an ID of AddButton and the List Box should be given an ID of ItemList, as shown in Figures 7.7 and 7.8, respectively. After adding these controls, delete the OK and Cancel buttons that were provided by default. When done adding controls, save the resource template. It does not need to be saved in the same directory as your other project files but doing so is usually more convenient. After saving, you can close the Dialog Editor.

Figure 7.7.

Setting properties for the
Button control.

Figure 7.8.

Setting properties for the
List Box control.

Because the Dialog Editor has its origins in Microsoft's Visual C++ product it contains controls that cannot be used in Visual J++. You should be careful to use only controls that can be converted into Visual J++ components, as shown in Table 7.1.

Table 7.1. Supported Java components and their Dialog Editor equivalents.

Java Component	Dialog Editor Control
Button	Button
Checkbox (ungrouped)	Check Box
Checkbox (grouped)	Radio Button
Choice	Combo Box
Label	Static text
List	List Box
Scrollbar	Horizontal or vertical scrollbars
TextField	Edit Box (with multiline set to false)
TextArea	Edit Box (with multiline set to true)

Step 5: Run the Resource Wizard

By now you have created a new resource template file, added controls to it, and saved the file. You are ready to run the Resource Wizard to convert your work into Java source code. Run the Resource Wizard by selecting Java Resource Wizard from the Tools menu. You will be presented with the first of two Resource Wizard screens, as shown in Figure 7.9. On this screen, enter the name of the resource file you saved in the prior step and select the Next button.

Figure 7.9.

Enter the resource template filename in the first step of the Resource Wizard.

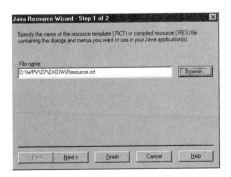

After pressing the Next button you see the second and final page of the Resource Wizard, as shown in Figure 7.10. This screen summarizes the dialog and menu resources that were found in the resource template file. Additionally, it enables you to modify the name of each class that will be generated if you don't like the names you gave on the properties pages in the Dialog Editor.

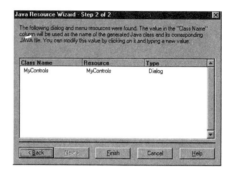

Figure 7.10.

You can change class names on step 2 of the Resource Wizard.

Selecting Finish will display a summary screen and then generate the necessary classes. In this example, `MyControls.java` will be generated as a control creator class for the dialog resource you designed and the standard `DialogLayout.java` will also be generated.

Step 6: Add Files to the Project

Before you can use the classes that Resource Wizard has generated, you must add them to your project. Do so by selecting Files into Project from the Insert menu.

Step 7: Write Code to Use the Classes

At this point you're ready to use the generated code. The complete EX07A class is shown in Listing 7.1. The lines of code needed to use the generated code are shown in bold. First, you must use `import` to make this class aware of the new Java class.

Listing 7.1. EX07A.java.

```java
import java.applet.*;
import java.awt.*;
import MyControls;

public class EX07A extends Applet
{
    MyControls ctrls;

    public void init()
    {
        ctrls = new MyControls(this);
        ctrls.CreateControls();
    }
```

```
    public boolean action(Event evt, Object obj)
    {
        if("Add".equals(obj))
        {
            String str = ctrls.NewText.getText();
            ctrls.ItemList.addItem(str);
            return true;
        }
        return false;
    }
}
```

Next, a member instance variable, MyControls ctrls, is declared. This variable is constructed in the init method by passing this to the MyControls constructor. Doing so creates an instance of MyControls that will place its components directly on the applet. This is possible because Applet is a subclass of Container. If, instead, you wanted to place the components on a frame, you could have passed a Frame object to the MyControls constructor. Finally, ctrls.CreateControls is used to actually create the controls.

You should also notice that it was not necessary to use resize to set the size of the applet. Because the control creator class sizes itself to the size of the dialog resource as drawn in the Dialog Editor, it is not necessary to explicitly resize the applet.

The action method is provided to illustrate how to access the individual components. It checks for a push of the Add button. If detected, it gets the text out of the text field named ctrls.NewText and adds this text as an item in the List named ctrls.ItemList. When run, the applet will appear as shown in Figure 7.11.

Figure 7.11.

Example EX07A after adding five items.

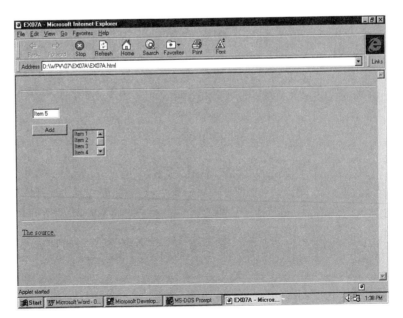

Using Control Creator Classes on Dialogs

In example EX07A you learned how to place Resource Wizard–generated controls onto an applet. You learned that you should add code to the applet's init method to create an instance of the control creator class and then call CreateControls. This works great for placing controls on an applet; however, how do you place controls on a Dialog or Frame because there is no init method in these classes?

Fortunately, placing Resource Wizard–generated controls on a Dialog or Frame is even easier than placing them on an applet. Rather than adding code to the init method of the applet, you can create the controls in the constructor of the class you've derived from Dialog or Frame. This can be seen in example EX07B, shown in Listing 7.2.

Listing 7.2. EX07B.java.

```java
import java.applet.*;
import java.awt.*;

public class EX07B extends Applet
{
    public void init()
    {
        resize(320, 240);

        // create a frame for the dialog
        // the frame isn't used but is the
        // parent of the dialog
        Frame frame = new Frame();

        // create the dialog and show it
        TestDialog dlg = new TestDialog(frame);
        dlg.show();
    }
}


class TestDialog extends Dialog
{
    MyControls ctrls;

    public TestDialog(Frame parent)
    {
        // invoke the Dialog constructor
        super(parent, "Test Dialog", false);

        // set an appropriate font
        setFont(new Font("Dialog", Font.BOLD, 12));

        // create the controls made by Resource Wizard
        ctrls = new MyControls(this);
        ctrls.CreateControls();
    }
```

```
public boolean action(Event evt, Object arg)
{
    boolean result = false;

    // when the Close button is pressed, close the dialog
    if("Close".equals(evt.arg)) {
        dispose();
        result = true;
    }
    return result;
}
}
```

In this example, the class EX07B extends Applet and creates a Frame to serve as the dialog's parent. Next, an instance of the TestDialog class is created and the show method is used to display it. The TestDialog constructor is where all the action is. This method uses super to construct the dialog, setFont to set an appropriate font for the dialog, and then creates the controls. An action method is provided for the TestDialog class that disposes of the dialog when its Close button is pressed.

It is important that you set the font the dialog will use. Normally it isn't necessary to set the font. However, the DialogLayout class generated by Resource Wizard uses the size of the current font to help determine where to place controls. Because of this, you should always use setFont when placing Resource Wizard–generated controls on a Frame or Dialog. For more information on fonts, see Chapter 16, "Sprucing Things Up with Colors and Fonts."

TIP:

Remember, you need to use setFont on a Dialog or Frame that will use a Resource Wizard–generated control creator class. Forgetting to do so will cause the dialog to be displayed without its controls.

Using the Resource Wizard to Create Menus

The process of visually designing menus in Visual J++ is completely analogous to the process you just followed to visually create and use a dialog resource. Instead of the Dialog Editor you use the Menu Editor, but after designing and saving menu resources, you still use the Resource Wizard to generate Java code. Because menus do not use layout managers, you do not need to use the DialogLayout class if you use only menus generated by Resource Wizard.

TIP:

In most cases, you should keep your menu and dialog resources in the same resource template file. Doing so reduces the number of times you will have to run Resource Wizard to generate code.

A Step-by-Step Menu Example

Because much of what you'll do to create a menu with the Resource Wizard is similar to what you've already done with dialogs, let's dive right in with an example. This section presents an example of using the Menu Editor to create a menu resource, running the Resource Wizard to convert the resource into usable Java code, and then modifying an applet to make use of the generated code. Each of the steps necessary to do this will be described in detail but the following is an overview of the steps necessary to use a menu resource in an applet:

1. Create a new resource template.
2. Insert a menu resource.
3. Set the menu properties.
4. Design the menu.
5. Run the Resource Wizard.
6. Add the menu class to the project.
7. Write code to use the menu.

Example EX07C, which is also included on the CD-ROM, will be built by following these steps. Before getting started, create a new applet with the Applet Wizard. Before generating the applet, turn off comments and multithreading.

Step 1: Create a New Resource Template

After selecting New from the File menu, you will be presented with a list of new file types. Select Resource Template and press OK.

Step 2: Insert a Menu Resource

Next, select Resource from the Insert menu. This displays the Insert Resource dialog that was shown in Figure 7.3. Select Menu and press OK to continue. At this point, the Menu Editor will be displayed and will contain a dialog ready for editing. Your screen should look similar to Figure 7.12. In this example, the Menu Editor is shown at the right of the Visual J++ desktop with an empty menu item highlighted and ready to be edited.

Figure 7.12.

A new menu resource
ready for editing.

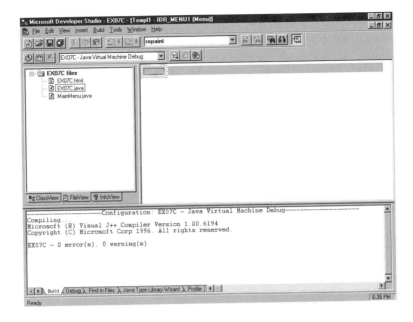

Step 3: Set the Menu Properties

As with dialog resources, you can set the properties of a menu resource. To set the menu's properties, double-click over the menu or press Alt+Enter. The Menu Properties dialog, as shown in Figure 7.13, is displayed. The only property you can set for a menu is its ID. The name you enter here will be the name of the class generated by the Resource Wizard.

Figure 7.13.

The Menu Properties
dialog.

Step 4: Design the Menu

In the Menu Editor you start with an empty menu with an outline border where the first menu item should be, as shown in Figure 7.13. You can double-click the mouse in that outline and create a menu item by settings its properties, as shown in Figure 7.15. After you create a menu item on the menu bar, you will have an outline border below the menu bar (indicating a true Java MenuItem) and another outline border on the menu bar adjacent to the first menu name. These can also be seen in Figure 7.14.

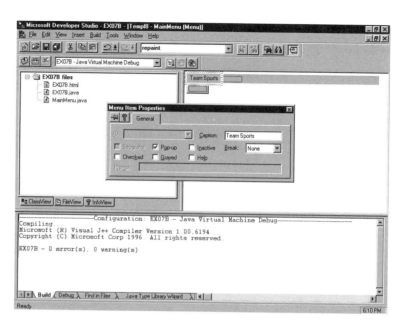

In the Menu Editor you can create two types of menu item: a pop-up menu item and a regular menu item. A pop-up menu item does not necessarily pop up; this is a generic term for any menu item that is really the top level of another menu. Therefore, the menu items across a menu bar are pop-up menu items and the items that drop down beneath these are not pop-up menu items. Figure 7.14 illustrated the creation of a pop-up menu item that will appear across the top menu bar. By comparison, Figure 7.15 shows the properties that may be set for a normal menu item.

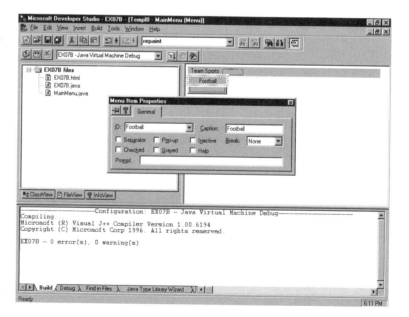

For all menu items you set a caption that will appear as the text on the screen. For regular menu items you may also specify a value for the ID field. This value will be used to assign a name to the member variable that Resource Wizard will create based on the menu item.

You can create a submenu by indicating that a menu item that is dropped down from the menu bar is a pop-up menu. This is done for the Racquet Sports menu item in Figure 7.16.

Figure 7.16.

Setting pop-up on a menu item creates a submenu.

To create example EX07C, create a Team Sports menu that includes Football and Baseball as menu items. Also, create an Individual Sports menu on the menu bar that includes a Swimming menu item and a Racquet Sports pop-up menu item. Beneath the Racquet Sports submenu create menu items for Tennis and Racquetball.

When finished, save the resource template file.

Step 5: Run the Resource Wizard

Select Java Resource Wizard from the Tools menu. Select the newly saved resource template and press Finish to generate your menu class file. For each menu resource in the resource template, the Resource Wizard will create a single Java class. In this example, the menu was named MainMenu, so MainMenu.java will be created.

Step 6: Add the Menu Class to the Project

Select Files into Project from the Insert menu to add the menu class to the project.

Step 7: Write Code to Use the Menu

The last step is to write code to make use of the generated classes. Listing 7.3 shows the contents of EX07C.java, a class that uses the menu resource that was created during the preceding steps. The lines of code needed to use the generated code are shown in bold. As with all external classes in Java, you must first use import to make this class aware of the new Java class.

Listing 7.3. EX07C.java.

```java
import java.applet.*;
import java.awt.*;
import MainMenu;

public class EX07C extends Applet
{
    MainMenu mainMenu;
    MenuFrame frame;

    public void init()
    {
        resize(320, 240);

        frame = new MenuFrame();
        frame.resize(300, 200);
        mainMenu = new MainMenu(frame);
        mainMenu.CreateMenu();
        frame.show();
    }
}

class MenuFrame extends Frame
{
    String text = new String("You selected: Nothing");

    MenuFrame()
    {
        super("Select a Sport");
    }

    public void paint(Graphics g)
    {
        g.drawString(text, 10, 10);
    }

    public boolean action(Event evt, Object obj)
    {
        boolean result = false;

        if(evt.target instanceof MenuItem)
        {
            text = "You selected: " + (String)obj;
            repaint();
            result = true;
        }

        return result;
    }
}
```

In the EX07C class, two member variables are declared. The first is an instance of the `MainMenu` class created by Resource Wizard. The second is an instance of a class called `MenuFrame`. This class is defined later in the file and is necessary because menus cannot be attached directly to an applet. In the `init` method, the frame is constructed and resized. The variable `mainMenu` is then constructed as an instance of the `MainMenu` class. The variable `frame` is passed to the `MainMenu` constructor indicating that the menu will be displayed within `frame`.

Next, `mainMenu.CreateMenu` is used to create the menu and all its menu items. This method is analogous to the `CreateControls` method used with dialog resources. Finally, `show` is used to display the frame.

The `MenuFrame` class is a simple extension of `Frame`. Its `paint` method is used to display the contents of a string and the string is set whenever the user selects a different menu item. The results of executing this applet can be seen in Figure 7.17.

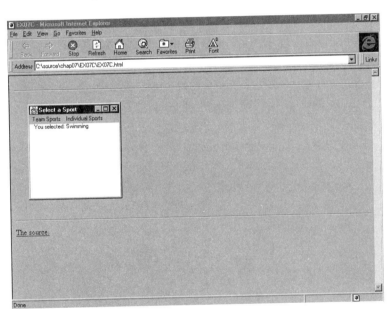

Figure 7.17.

Executing an applet with a menu created by the Resource Wizard.

Summary

In this chapter you learned about the Resource Wizard and how it can free you from some of the difficulties of hand-coding your user interface. You learned how the Resource Wizard is a one-way tool that turns your visual designs into Java classes that can be used in your projects. In this chapter you also worked through two examples: one using Resource Wizard with dialog resources and a second using Resource Wizard with menu resources. In the next chapter you will turn your attention to another time-saving feature of Visual J++, the debugger.

Debugging with the Visual J++ Debugger

Because the majority of us write perfect code on our first attempt, you probably won't need this chapter. But, just in case there is a late night where a couple of those pesky bugs slip into your code, this chapter explains some of the features of the Visual J++ Debugger, including controlling the flow of your application line-by-line, inspecting variables in various ways, and covering how the debugger can help when exceptions are thrown and when dealing with multithreaded applications.

Controlling the Execution

One of the most important aspects of debugging a program is getting a successful build. From there you can start setting breakpoints to instruct the debugger where you want to walk through your code. Finally, you have control of where you are walking.

Successful Build

Before you even think about debugging an application, you must first successfully build your application. When a compile-time error is encountered while building your applications, Visual J++ places all the necessary information into the Build tab of the output window. Each error line shows the location in the file where the error occurred, the line and column, and the error found. Figure 8.1 shows a sample compile-time error.

Figure 8.1.

Output window showing a compile error.

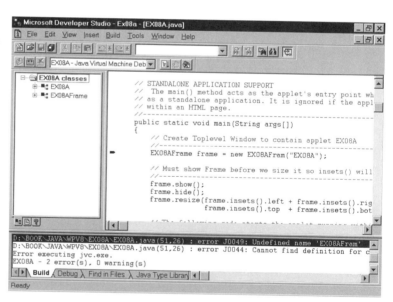

The example EX08A shown was created using the AppletWizard with all the bells and whistles turned on. For more information on creating applications and using the Applet Wizard, see Chapter 2, "Creating Your First Applet with Applet Wizard," and Chapter 3, "Using the Developer Studio."

While reviewing the code that was generated by the Applet Wizard, a character in the file was inadvertently deleted. When the application was then built, Visual J++ showed the compile-time errors in the Output window. By highlighting the line in the Output window, Visual J++ shows the source code line in error in the right pane of the Project Workspace and places a small blue arrow next to the line in error. In addition, the full error message is displayed in the status bar. For this example, it is clear that the name of the class is EX08AFrame, not EX08AFram.

Once you have successfully built your application free of compile-time errors, you are ready to start debugging. The next section covers how to set breakpoints.

Breakpoints

The first step in debugging your application is being able to start and stop execution of the source. To stop the execution of the application at a particular location in your program you must set a breakpoint. Breakpoints can be set on a specific source code line, at the entrance to or exit from a method, by examining the call stack, or at a specific memory address.

One of the most useful places to set a breakpoint is at a particular line of source code. To do this, simply place the cursor in the right pane of the Project View on the line of source where you want to stop. Then, use the Edit | Breakpoints command to bring up the Breakpoints dialog of Figure 8.2.

Figure 8.2.

Setting a breakpoint using the Breakpoints dialog.

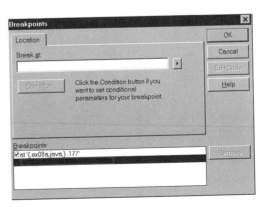

You can easily set a breakpoint on the source code line by pressing the button to the right of the edit box and selecting the choice displayed. Once you have set the breakpoint at the line, you can conditionally stop execution based on an expression. Pressing the Condition button brings up the dialog shown in Figure 8.3.

Figure 8.3.

Adding conditions to the breakpoint.

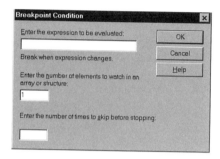

The breakpoint will not stop execution until the expression entered into the first edit evaluates to true (if a Boolean expression is entered), or when the expression changes.

Some pesky bugs have a habit of hiding the first time (or several times) around during execution. The last edit on the Breakpoint Condition dialog enables the user to specify the number of times for which the expression evaluates to true before the execution stops. In this way, the user does not have to keep track of the number of times a breakpoint has stopped if he or she knows the error does not surface until the tenth iteration through a loop.

The list at the bottom of the Breakpoints dialog shows all current breakpoints for the project. You will notice that that there is a check mark in a small box next to each breakpoint. This indicates that the breakpoint is enabled. If you want to leave a breakpoint in the project but don't stop on it because you may have debugged that section of code, simply disable the breakpoint. To do this, click the small check mark next to the breakpoint. This disables the breakpoint, while leaving it in the system. The Remove button to the right of the list enables the user to delete the currently selected breakpoint from the list.

As a visual indication of the breakpoint, you will notice that a small red dot is placed next to the line of source in the right pane of the Project Workspace. When the breakpoint is disabled, the dot is changed to a red circle.

Where Do You Go from Here?

Once you have established your breakpoints, you need to actually start debugging. To start the execution of a program in the debugger, use the Build | Debug | Go command. This will start executing the program. Make sure that the application will run in the stand-alone interpreter using the Debug tab of the Build | Settings dialog.

Once a breakpoint is encountered, Visual J++ stops execution of the program and displays Project Workspace with an arrow showing where the current execution point is in the source code. Figure 8.4 shows an example of this.

Figure 8.4.
Current execution point of a stopped application.

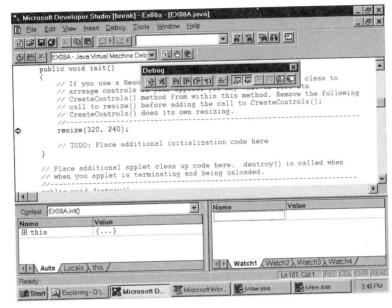

The Debug toolbar shown in Figure 8.4 contains a number of options at your disposal. Table 8.1 contains a listing of the commands available on the Debug toolbar.

Table 8.1. Debug toolbar command descriptions.

Command	Description
Restart	Restart the application, clearing the values of all variables.
Stop Debugging	Stop running the application in the debugger.
Step Into	Execute the current instruction, stepping into any methods encountered.

continues

Table 8.1. continued

Command	Description
Step Over	Execute the current instruction, without stepping into any methods encountered.
Step Out	Execute instructions until the first instruction is encountered after the call to the current method.
Run to Cursor	Execute instructions until the line with the cursor is encountered.
QuickWatch	Display the QuickWatch window.
Watch	Display the Watch window.
Variables	Display the Variables window.
Registers	Display the Registers window.
Memory	Display the Memory window.
Call Stack	Display the Call Stack.
Disassembly	Display the current source in the disassembled bytecode instructions.

Starting Program Execution

Let's stop for a second and go back to how to start the execution of the application. There are three processes involved and they all have shortcut keys associated with F5.

When in the debugger, you can just start the application executing instructions from the current instruction until a breakpoint is encountered using the Debug | Go command or by using F5. This is basically letting the program execute because you either want to see how the program completes execution or you have a breakpoint set somewhere later in the flow of execution.

Alternatively, you might want to restart the execution of the application from the start. Debug | Restart, or Shift+F5 clears all the contents of the variables, resets the current instruction to the start of the application, and executes a Go command. Again, this assumes that breakpoints have been set and enabled to stop the execution of the application at the appropriate locations.

Lastly, if you have seen what you were looking for, Debug | Stop Debugging, or Alt+F5, terminates the application and stops the execution of the debugger.

Watch Your Step

When you have stopped at a breakpoint, you are likely to want to see or control the flow of execution of instructions in your application. This is commonly referred to as stepping through your application. There are several possibilities when stepping.

Consider the following line of code:

```
double classicPrice = myClassic.CalculateSalePrice();
```

This line calls the `CalculateSalePrice` method of the `myClassic` instance of the `ClassicCar` class and stores the result in `classicPrice`. For this example, the definition of the class is irrelevant, but a possible definition can be found in Appendix A, "A Whirlwind Tour of the Java Language."

Assume this line is contained in the current method of an executing application and is the current instruction. Using the Debug | Step Into command, or F8, the current instruction will be the first line of the `CalculateSalePrice` method. In other words, you are stepping into the contents of the function being called. This is quite useful when the function being called is yours and you want to see how the function behaves when it is being called from different sources or you want to see which class is being called for an overridden function.

When stepping into functions, remember that flow of control is passed to the next logical method called. Therefore, if there are embedded method calls, the first one executed will be stepped into first. What if the calculated sales price of the car is no longer based on the car but is instead based on the markup of the dealership selling the car? The following line of code might be encountered:

```
double classicPrice = myClassic.CalculateSalePrice(myDealer.GetMarkup());
```

If this is the current line and F8 is pressed, the first method stepped into would be the call to `GetMarkup`. If F8 is pressed on the return of that method, `CalculateSalePrice` would then be entered.

If you are not interested in stepping into a function, you should use Debug | Step Over or F10. This steps over the call to the function and simply executes the current instruction and moves to the next instruction in the current method. For this command, it makes no difference the number of functions being called in the current instruction. Therefore, in both of the previous examples, the next instruction will always be the next instruction in the current method.

You might find yourself in a method where only the initial instructions of the method are in question and you really want to know how the result of this method affects the calling method. To step out of the current method, use the Debug | Step Out command (or Shift+F7). This command moves the currently executing instruction to the instruction immediately following the call to the current method.

The Debug | Run to Cursor command, or F7, is used to start execution and break when the line with the cursor is encountered. The same effect can be accomplished by setting a breakpoint on the current line, using the Debug | Go command to start execution and removing the breakpoint once the execution has stopped on the current line. Obviously, F7 is much easier to use.

Interrupting Your Program

A nice little feature of Visual J++ is the capability to stop the execution of your application. The Debug | Break command stops the execution of the application. This is very useful for those situations where you either forgot to set a breakpoint and started executing a long series of steps to get to a piece of code intended to be debugged, or your application slipped into an infinite loop.

CAUTION:

While the ability to interrupt your application is quite nice, it can also be very dangerous. The interruption occurs at a very low level. Therefore, where it will be interrupted is unpredictable. The best way to use this capability is to do the following:

1. Interrupt the application being debugged using the Debug | Break command.
2. Once the application has stopped, set a breakpoint where it will be encountered when the application is started back up.
3. Start the application back up with the Debug | Go command and let the breakpoint stop execution at a known location.

What Do You See?

So far, you have learned how to set breakpoints and control what is being executed. Although this accomplishes quite a bit, a much more useful tool is the capability to look at the state of the application. This section covers how to inspect the values of variables several different ways and how to take a look at the Call Stack of the application.

Variables

One the of the most useful features of a debugger is to look at the values of the variables in applications. The Visual J++ Debugger allows several different ways, including automatically displaying values using DataTips, an immediate inspection of variables using the QuickWatch dialog, placing variables on a Watch window which is automatically updated when values change, and by examining the Variables window which always contains variables at differing levels.

DataTips

A very quick and handy tool to use when inspecting values of variables is to simply place the mouse over the variable to be inspected. Figure 8.5 shows DataTips in action.

This is a quick and painless way to quickly glance at a value. Expressions can also be inspected by simply highlighting the expression and waiting for DataTips. Invalid expressions and variables not in the current scope will not bring up DataTips.

Figure 8.5.

Current execution point of
a stopped application.

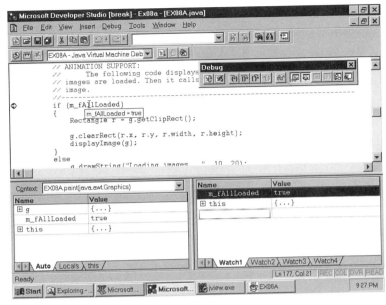

QuickWatch

A more thorough inspection of the value of a variable is handled with the QuickWatch window.
Figure 8.6 shows the QuickWatch window.

Figure 8.6.

Example of the
QuickWatch window.

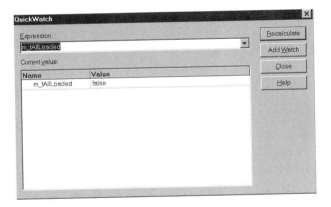

The first edit window lets the user type in the expression that is to be inspected. The bottom window shows the current value. The user can examine the value and modify any values available by
simply clicking the value next to the item to be modified.

The value being displayed may have a small plus symbol (+) next to the name in the name column. Visual J++ automatically detects whether the expression being inspected is an object that

contains objects in itself. By pressing the plus symbol, additional lines are added to the current value list representing the contained objects. Typical examples of this are when inspecting arrays or class instances. Figure 8.7 shows an example of inspecting the current class instance.

Figure 8.7.

Inspecting the current instance.

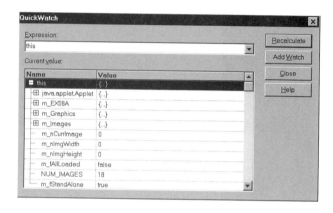

You can change the expression and repopulate the current value list by pressing the Recalculate button.

If the expression is a good one, you can add the expression as a Watch by using the Watch button.

Watch

The Watch window is used to monitor values. The values of the items being watched are updated when the values change. Therefore, you can always see the current value of the item. Figure 8.8 shows the Watch window.

Again, Visual J++ detects objects that contain objects and indicates the expandability of the objects with a small plus (+) symbol. You can expand or collapse an item by pressing on the + or - symbols next to the items.

You might have noticed that there are four tabs on the Watch window. Watches can be logically collected together on each of the four tabs. In this way, you can inspect the group of variables that is most applicable to the area being debugged.

You can add a watch to the current table in a variety of ways:

○ Through the Watch button of the QuickWatch dialog.
○ Select the item to be watched in the source and use the right mouse button to drag the item to the Watch window.
○ Type the name of the item directly into the Watch window.

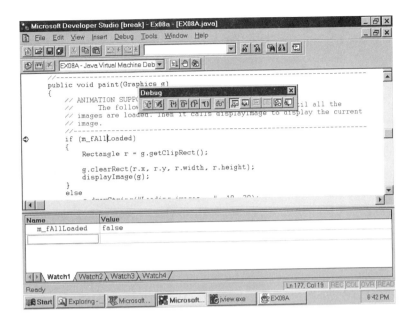

Figure 8.8.
The Project Workspace showing the Watch window.

Variables can be displayed using a variety of different formats when displayed in the Watch window. To specify the format to display a value, follow the name of the variable with a comma and a format specification from Table 8.2. (This table can also be found in the online Visual J++ documentation.)

Table 8.2. Format specifiers for displaying variables.

Specifier	Type of value displayed
d,i	Signed decimal integer
u	Unsigned decimal integer
o	Unsigned octal integer
x,X	Hexadecimal integer (non-numeric digits are displayed in the same case as the specifier)
l,h	Long or short prefix, respectively, for integer specifiers
f	Signed floating point
e	Signed scientific notation
g	Shorter version of either f or e
c	Single character
s	String
su	Unicode string

You can get additional information about a watched item by selecting that item in the Watch window. Use the right mouse button to display the pop-up menu and select the properties command. This will display the dialog of Figure 8.9 showing the name, type, and value of the item.

Figure 8.9.
The properties of a
watched item showing
the type of the item.

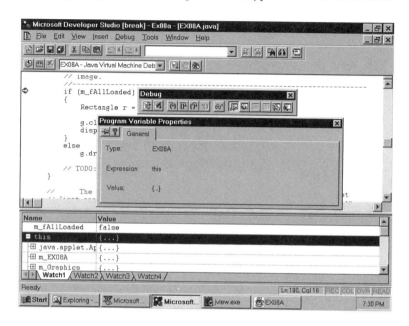

Variable Window

The Variable window is similar to the Watch window as seen in Figure 8.10.

The difference between the Variable window and the Watch window is that the user cannot add variables to this window. Instead, a variety of items are automatically added to various tabs as shown in Table 8.3.

Table 8.3. Variable window tab contents.

Tab	Contents of the tab
Auto	Variables referenced in the current or previously executed instruction
Local	All local variables defined in the current method
this	Object reference by this

The values for the items in the Variable window are displayed the same way as the Watch and QuickWatch windows. To modify the values, simply double-click the value to be modified and start typing. To show the type of an item, choose the item from the window and use the pop-up menu to select the Properties command.

Figure 8.10.
The Project Workspace
showing the Auto tab of
the Variable window.

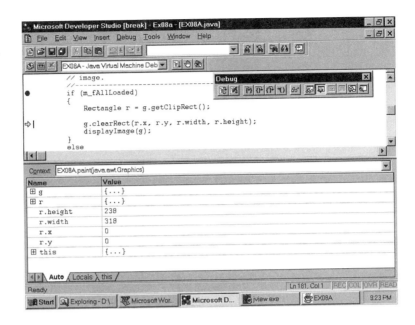

The context of the variables being displayed can be selected using the combobox at the top of the Variable window. The combobox contains the list of method calls that has led up to the execution of the current method. The content of context combobox is also contained in the Call Stack window.

Call Stack Window

The Call Stack window contains a logical mapping of the calls made to get to the currently executing method. Every time a call is made by a method, the calling method name is pushed onto the top of the stack. When the called method returns, the name is popped off the stack. The net result is a listing of methods called to get to the current method. Figure 8.11 shows an example of a Call Stack.

Figure 8.11.
The Project Workspace
showing the Call Stack
window.

```
Call Stack
⇨ EX08A.paint(java.awt.Graphics {...}) line 181
   sun.awt.win32.MComponentPeer.paint(java.awt.Graphics {...}) + 30 bytes
   sun.awt.win32.MComponentPeer.handleExpose(int 0, int 0, int 318, int 238) + 32
   sun.awt.win32.MToolkit.callbackLoop() address 0x00000000
   sun.awt.win32.MToolkit.run() + 68 bytes
   java.lang.Thread.run() line 292
```

TIP:

You can move the Call Stack window by simply dragging the title bar of the window—normal window functionality. However, because the window is a dockable window, if you move it to a dockable area, say the bottom of the dialog, it might try to dock, even if that is not your intention. To prevent the docking from taking place, press the Ctrl key before releasing the window.

Each line in the Call Stack contains the line used to call the method. In addition, the parameters types and value used in making the call to the method are displayed.

Exceptions

Visual J++ supports debugging into exceptions through the use of the Exceptions dialog of Figure 8.12.

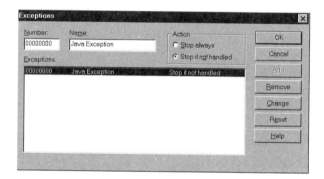

Figure 8.12.
Exceptions dialog.

To view the Exceptions dialog, execute the Debug | Exceptions command. This dialog enables the user to specify an exception and the action to be taken if the exception is thrown. Both system- and user-defined exceptions can be handled.

The two actions that can occur when an exception is thrown is to stop immediately or stop if the exception is not handled. One advantage of stopping immediately is that the debugger will stop as soon as the exception has been generated. The advantage of this is that the user has the chance to examine the source code in the state that caused the exception to occur and possibly fix the cause of the exception, if it can be fixed by modifying the value of a variable or a similar modification. Once the remedy is in place, the user can restart the application, at which point the user will be prompted if they would like the exception handlers to be called. If the problem has been remedied, the user should reply no.

The second action is notification that an exception was not handled by the exception-handling routines. With this option, the user will simply be notified that an unhandled exception occurred.

Threads

A thread is like a mini-process within an application. A process can be made up of one to many threads with each thread performing an individual task. The Visual J++ Debugger supports being able to choose the thread to be debugged using the dialog shown in Figure 8.13.

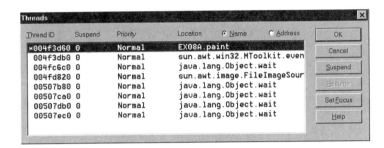

Figure 8.13.

Threads dialog.

This dialog shows that each thread in a process contains an identifying id, a suspend quantity, a priority (which for Java threads will always be normal), and the currently executing location. The location can be displayed either in terms of method currently being executed or in terms of address.

To learn more about multithreaded applications, see Chapter 12, "Moving Up to Multithreading."

Summary

Although you might possibly never read this chapter, it is nice to know that the Visual J++ Debugger enables the user extensive control over setting breakpoints to stop the execution of an application, lets the user to step in, and over, method calls, and allows for easy inspection and modification of all the variables being used by the application. In addition, support is provided to stop execution of the application when exceptions are thrown and to specify the thread that is to be debugged for multithreaded applications.

Chapter

9

Documenting Your Visual J++ Code

One of the problems that has faced maintenance programmers through the years has been the horrible documentation left behind by the original programmers. Usually the original programmers included comments in the source code but probably didn't comment as thoroughly as they should have. Then an ambitious project manager recognized the inadequacy of the in-line comments and forced the programmers to write a lengthy document about the software. This document was handed over to the maintenance programmers who used it to continue supporting and enhancing the software. Even if the maintenance programmers kept the in-line comments current, the other documentation fell out of date because it was just too hard to maintain. And, besides, the maintenance programmers ask, "Why should we keep the document up to date if we're also documenting the code?"

This is a very good question and one the Java developers must have asked themselves. Imagine yourself on the Java team. You've been working long hours writing the hundreds of classes that comprise Java and then you wake up one morning, hands still trembling from the previous night's caffeine excesses, and realize, "Darn! Now we've got to document all that code." The solution the Java developers came up with actually made it possible for them not to write a separate document describing each class, interface, and method. Instead, they wrote a program that would extract specially formatted source code comments and create class documentation from the embedded comments. The tool they developed to do this is called JavaDoc and is included in the Java Developer's Kit.

Overview

JavaDoc reads a .java file and creates a set of HTML files that can be read by a Web browser. As an example, consider the documentation for the Employee class that is shown in Figure 9.1. At the top of the documentation shown in this figure is an inheritance tree showing that Employee is a subclass of Person, which is a subclass of java.lang.Object.

In addition to the class' inheritance tree, Figure 9.1 shows that an overall class description can be provided as well as a Constructor Index. Figure 9.1 shows only one screen of the documentation that will be created for the Employee class in this chapter. There are many more areas and types of documentation that can be generated and are described in this chapter.

In addition to generating documentation for a single class, JavaDoc can generate system-level documentation. For example, Figure 9.2 shows an AllNames.html file generated by JavaDoc. This file lists all non-private members, both methods and variables, processed by JavaDoc.

Figure 9.1.

A sample documentation
page generated by
JavaDoc.

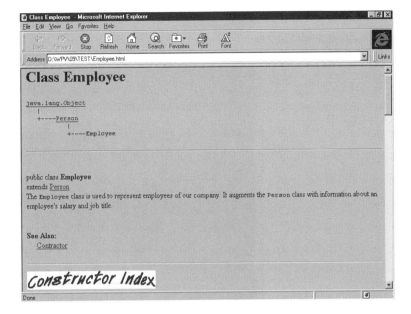

Figure 9.2.

Viewing the contents of
AllNames.html.

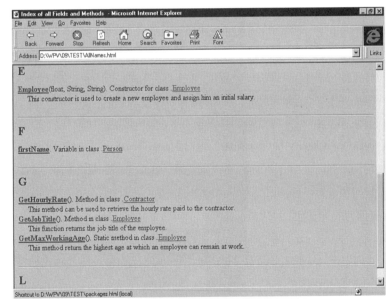

Similarly, JavaDoc can create `tree.html`. This file depicts the complete Java inheritance hierarchy, as shown in Figure 9.3.

Figure 9.3.

Viewing the Java class hierarchy in `tree.html` generated by JavaDoc.

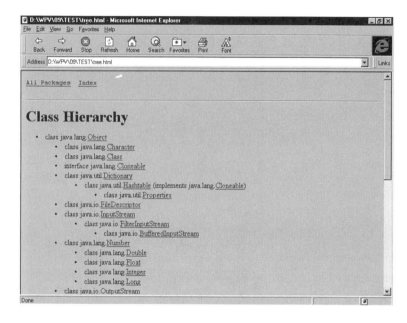

Running JavaDoc

JavaDoc is a command-line program that is supplied with the Java Developer's Kit. It can be invoked in the following manner:

```
javadoc [options] PackageName ¦ FileName.java
```

For example, to use JavaDoc to create documentation on a class named `Employee`, you would do the following:

```
javadoc employee.java
```

Command-Line Arguments and Environment Variables

The [options] parameter shown as part of the JavaDoc command line can be included if desired. It can be used to specify which directories should be searched for input files, the directory in which to put the generated HTML files, whether JavaDoc should run in a special verbose mode, and other options as summarized in Table 9.1.

Table 9.1. The JavaDoc command-line options.

Option	Description
-authors	An undocumented option that when specified will generate HTML based on the @author tag.
-classpath path	Specifies the path to be searched for files ending with the .java extension. If specified, it overrides the CLASSPATH environment variable.
-d directory	Specifies the target directory for writing HTML files.
-doctype [MIF | HTML]	An undocumented option that specifies the type of file to create. By default HTML files are created but FrameMaker MIF files can also be generated.
-noindex	An undocumented option that suppresses creation of the AllNames.html file.
-notree	An undocumented option that suppresses creation of the tree.html file.
-verbose	Instructs JavaDoc to run in a special mode that displays additional information as the files are parsed. This option is most useful if you have a class for which the documentation appears incorrect.
-version	An undocumented option that when specified will generate HTML based on the @version tag.

The only environment variable used by JavaDoc is CLASSPATH. This variable, if set in your environment, informs JavaDoc of the directories in which it should search for .java files. For example, to search the current directory, C:\VISUALJ\JAVA\SOURCE, and C:\MYJAVA\SOURCE, you would set CLASSPATH to the following:

```
.;C:\visualj\java\source;C:\myjava\source
```

NOTE:

JavaDoc is included as part of the Java Developer's Kit (JDK) as released by Sun Microsystems but is not included in Visual J++. To download the JDK, including JavaDoc, connect to http://java.sun.com.

Adding JavaDoc Comments

Unfortunately, JavaDoc is only as smart as the information you give to it. It gets its information by parsing source code files and looking for comments enclosed within the `/**` and `*/` delimiters. JavaDoc comments are placed immediately above the class or member that they are meant to describe. For example, consider the following class definition and associated comment:

```
/** This is a comment that describes MyClass in general. */
public class MyClass {
    /** The DoSomething method is used to do something. */
    public int DoSomething() {
        // method source goes here
    }
    // remaining class source code
}
```

In this example, JavaDoc comments have been placed above the class and above the `DoSomething` member method. Leading spaces and asterisk (*) characters are stripped from JavaDoc comment lines. This makes it possible for you to start each line with an asterisk, as shown in the following example:

```
/**
This is a comment that describes MyClass
in general. The leading * characters and
spaces will be removed. */
class Contractor extends Employee {
    // class body
}
```

Doing so is, of course, a matter of personal preference but this style is common among many Java programmers.

Documenting Classes

When documenting a class (in the comment immediately preceding the class definition), you can add class documentation tags to enhance the usability of the documentation. Class documentation tags each begin with an @ symbol to distinguish them. The following class documentation tags are available:

@author	author-name
@see	classname
@see	fully-qualified-classname
@see	fully-qualified-classname#method-name
@version	version-text

As an example of how these tags work, consider the following definitions of an Employee class and a Contractor class:

```
/**
 * The Employee class is used to represent employees
 * of our company. It augments the Person class with
 * information about an employee's salary and job
 * title.
 * @author Mike Cohn
 * @version 1.0.0
 * @see Contractor
 */
public class Employee extends Person {
    // class body
}

/**
 * The Contractor class is used to represent
 * contract employees. Contract employees are
 * paid by the hour.
 * @author Mike Cohn
 * @version 1.0.0
 */
class Contractor extends Employee {
    // class body
}
```

The comment preceding the Employee class describes the class and then shows the use of three of the class documentation tags. The author and version are only included in the generated documentation if you specify -authors and -version on the command line. The @see Contractor line in the Employee comment will inform readers that they may want to see a related class. Because the @see tag is used, JavaDoc will generate a link to the Contractor class documentation. This can be seen in Figure 9.4.

As you can see in Figure 9.4, a link is provided for all superclasses of Employee (java.lang.Object and Person) and the @see tag has created a link to Contractor in a "See Also" section. Following this link will jump directly to the Contractor documentation, as shown in Figure 9.5. The Contractor documentation does not need a @see tag back to Employee because Employee is a superclass of Contractor and already appears as a link in the inheritance hierarchy.

Figure 9.4.

Class documentation for Employee, including a link to Contractor.

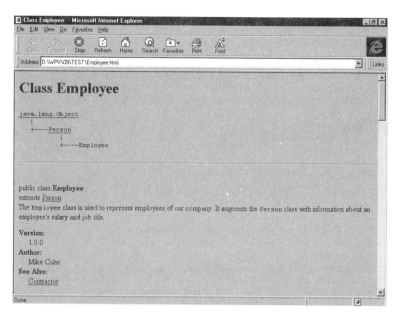

Figure 9.5.

Class documentation for Contractor.

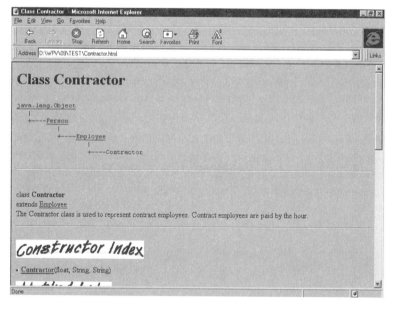

The link from Employee to Contractor positions your Web browser at the top of the documentation for the Contractor class. Sometimes you'd prefer to have a link jump to a specific place within the target class. You can link directly to a method by specifying the name of the method after the

target class. For example, the following tag would jump directly to the `GetHourlyRate` method in the `Contractor` class:

```
@see Contractor#GetHourlyRate
```

Documenting Methods

Like its class documentation tags, JavaDoc also supports method documentation tags. Method documentation tags are optional and can be placed in a JavaDoc comment directly above the method they describe. Like class documentation tags, method tags begin with the @ symbol. The following method documentation tags are available:

`@param`	parameter-name description
`@return`	description
`@exception`	fully-qualified-class-name description

To see how these tags can be used, consider the following definition of the `Contractor` class:

```java
class Contractor extends Employee {
    public Contractor(float sal, String fName, String lName) {
        super(sal, fName, lName);
    }
    private float hourlyRate;
/**
 * This method can be used to retrieve the hourly rate
 * paid to the contractor.
 * @return The contractor's hourly rate, excluding
 *         exceptional circumstances such as holidays
 *         and overtime.
 */
    public float GetHourlyRate() {
        return hourlyRate;
    }
/**
 * This method calculates how much is due to
 * a contractor based on how much he's worked
 * and his hourly rate.
 * @param hours The number of hours worked by the
 *         contractor during this pay period.
 * @return The amount of money due the contractor.
 */
    public float CalculatePayCheck(int hours) {
        return hours * hourlyRate;
    }
}
```

The `Contractor` class includes two non-constructor methods—`GetHourlyRate` and `CalculatePayCheck`. Each of these uses the `@return` tag to describe its return value. Additionally, `GetHourlyRate` uses `@param` to describe its input parameters. The results of this documentation can be seen in Figure 9.6.

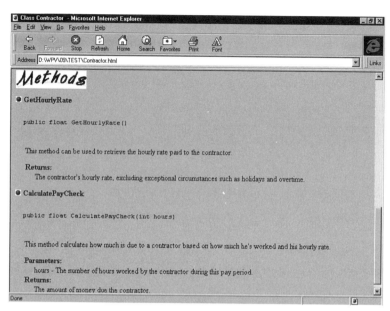

Figure 9.6.
Using @param and @return
to document Contractor.

As you can see from Figure 9.6, the @return and @param tags nicely format the descriptions entered in the JavaDoc comments. If a method receives more than one parameter, the @param tag can be repeated as often as necessary. Although the @exception tag is not shown in this example, it behaves identically to @return and @param.

Enhancing Your Documentation with HTML

By using the class and method documentation tags that you can embed within JavaDoc comments, you can take huge strides toward improving the way you document your code. However, because JavaDoc produces HTML files, you can go much further. By embedding HTML (Hypertext Markup Language) commands within your JavaDoc comments, you have almost infinite control over how your documentation will appear when viewed in a browser.

By using HTML tags, you can enhance your documentation by drawing attention to bold or italicized text, including numbered and bulleted lists, images, preformatted text, or even links to other documentation files or Web-based resources. Table 9.2 shows the HTML tags that you probably find most useful in documenting your Java code.

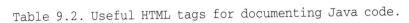

Table 9.2. Useful HTML tags for documenting Java code.

Tag	Purpose
`<A>...</A>`	Indicates a link anchor.
`<B>...</B>`	Format marked text with bold font.
`<BLOCKQUOTE>...</BLOCKQUOTE>`	Formats marked text as a lengthy quotation.
`<CITE>...</CITE>`	Format marked text as a citation.
`<CODE>...</CODE>`	Format marked text as source code.
`<EM>...</EM>`	Add emphasis to marked text.
`<I>...</I>`	Format marked text in italics.
`<IMG>`	Inserts a named image file.
`<LI>`	Indicates a list item with an ordered or unordered list.
`<OL>...</OL>`	Indicates an ordered (numbered) list.
`<P>`	Indicates the end of a paragraph.
`<PRE>...</PRE>`	Indicates preformatted text. Spacing and layout is preserved by using a monospaced font.
`<STRONG>...</STRONG>`	Adds maximum-strength emphasis to marked text.
`<TT>...</TT>`	Formats marked text in a typewriter font.
`<UL>...</UL>`	Indicates an unordered (bulleted) list.

CAUTION:

Because JavaDoc makes its own assumptions about how it will format text, you cannot use HTML tags like `<H1>` that are used to define headings.

An Example

This section demonstrates the use of JavaDoc including class documentation tags, method documentation tags, and embedded HTML tags. Assume you have the following class definition that you need to document:

```
public class Employee extends Person {
    private float salary;
    private String job;
```

```
    public Employee(float sal, String fName, String lName) {
        super(fName, lName);
        salary = sal;
    }
    public void AssignJob(String newJob) {
        job = newJob;
    }
    public String GetJobTitle() {
        return job;
    }
    public static int GetMaxWorkingAge() {
        return 64;
    }
    private float GetMaxSalary() {
        return 200000f;
    }
    public boolean ChangeSalary(float newSalary) {
        if (newSalary < salary)
            return false;
        if (newSalary > GetMaxSalary())
            return false;
        salary = newSalary;
        return true;
    }
}
```

First, you need to document the class itself. You do this with the following comment:

```
/**
 * The <tt>Employee</tt> class is used to represent
 * employees of our company. It augments the <tt>Person</tt>
 * class with information about an employee's salary and
 * job title.<p>
 * This class was written by:
 * <blockquote>
 * <img src=logo.gif width=300 height=100>
 * </blockquote>
 * @author Mike Cohn
 * @version 1.0.0
 * @see Contractor
 */
public class Employee extends Person {
```

This will create the documentation screen shown in Figure 9.7. You can see that the `<tt>`...`</tt>` tags were used to set the names of other classes in a distinctive typewriter-style font. The `<p>` tag is used to indicate the end of a paragraph. If this tag had not been used, the text on the following line would have merged with the text prior to the tag. The `<blockquote>` and `<img>` tags were used to include a graphics image indicating the author of the class.

Figure 9.7.

Class documentation for
`Employee`, including an
embedded graphic.

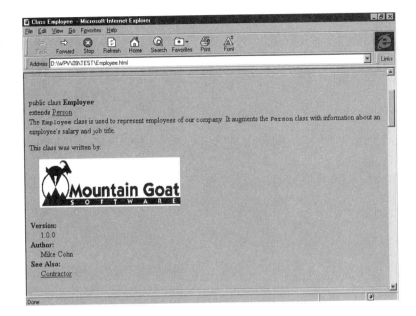

Next, you need to document the constructor. This is done with the following comment that will produce the documentation shown in Figure 9.8:

```
/** This constructor is used to create a new employee and
 * assign him an initial salary. <EM>It does not verify that
 * salary is less than the company's maximum salary.</EM>
 * You could use this method as follows:
 * <CODE><PRE>
 * Employee Emp = new Employee(35000f,"Mike","Cohn");
 * </PRE></CODE>
 * @param sal The starting salary of the new employee.
 * @param fName The employee's first name.
 * @param lName The employee's last name.
 */
public Employee(float sal, String fName, String lName) {
```

In this case the `<CODE>...</CODE>` and `<PRE>...</PRE>` tags were used to indicate a preformatted block of source code. Also, the `<EM>...</EM>` tags were used to apply emphasis to the statement that the employee's salary must be less than a company maximum. Finally, because this constructor is passed three parameters, each parameter is documented with the `@param` method tag.

Figure 9.8.

Documentation for the
Employee constructor.

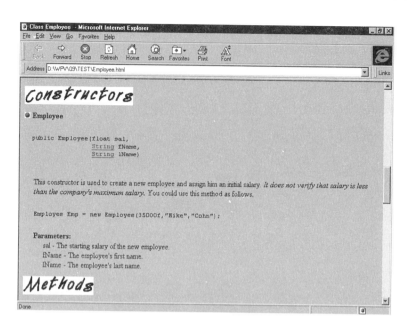

In addition to the full documentation shown in Figure 9.8, JavaDoc creates a constructor index and a method index for the class. The method index lists each of a class's nonprivate methods. These indexes appear as separate sections in the HTML document, as shown in Figure 9.9.

Figure 9.9.

The constructor and
method indexes for the
Employee class.

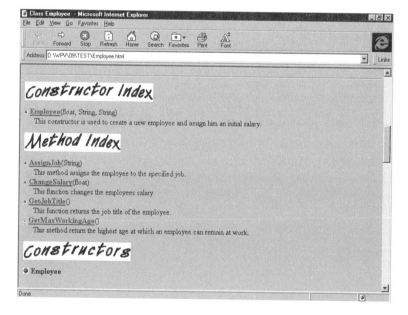

The `AssignJob` method is documented by adding the following comment:

```
/**
 * This method assigns the employee to the
 * specified job. This method does not verify the
 * <i>job title</i> against the list of <i>approved
 * job titles</i> created by <b>Human Resources</b>.
 * Likely job titles you may want to pass include:
 * <ul>
 * <li>Programmer
 * <li>Analyst
 * <li>QA
 * <li>Tech Writer
 * <li>Project Manager
 * <li>Database Administrator
 * <li>Database Engineer
 * </ul>
 * Reminder: All positions must be approved by the
 * <b>Manager of Human Resources</b> according to
 * the company's <CITE>Employee Hiring Guidelines.
 * </CITE>
 * @param newJob This is the new job title.
 * @see #GetJobTitle
 */
public void AssignJob(String newJob) {
```

The result of this documentation can be seen in Figure 9.10. This example demonstrates the use of `<B>...</B>` and `<I>...</I>` to bold and italicize text. Additionally, the use of an unordered (bulleted) list is demonstrated. The `<UL>...</UL>` tags indicate the start and end of the list and the `<LI>` tags indicate each of the list items. This example also demonstrates the use of `<CITE>...</CITE>` to indicate a citation. Finally, the `@see` method tag is used. In this example, no class name appears to the left of the #. This will create a link to a method within the current class.

Figure 9.10.

Documentation for the AssignJob method.

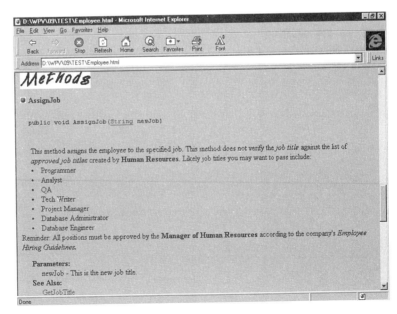

Next, the following comment is written for `GetJobTitle`:

```
/**
 * This function returns the job title of the employee.
 * @return A string representing the job title (for
 * example, "programmer").
 * @see #AssignJob
 */
public String GetJobTitle() {
```

The method `GetMaxWorkingAge` is defined as static, meaning that it is associated with the class itself, rather than with instances of the class. However, because it is a public method, it can be documented as shown in the following comment:

```
/**
 * This method returns the highest age at which
 * an employee can remain at work. <STRONG>
 * After this age, an employee must retire and
 * move to Florida.</STRONG>
 * @return The last allowable working year before
 * mandatory retirement.
 */
public static int GetMaxWorkingAge() {
```

The documentation for `GetJobTitle` and `GetMaxWorkingAge` will appear as shown in Figure 9.11. As you can see from this figure, the use of the `<STRONG>...</STRONG>` tag places heavy emphasis on the need for retirees to move to Florida.

Next, the method `GetMaxSalary` is documented, as follows:

```
/**
 * This comment will not show up in JavaDoc because
 * it is private.
 */
private float GetMaxSalary() {
```

However, `GetMaxSalary` is declared as `private`, so it will not be documented by JavaDoc. Because private functions are not usable outside the class in which they are declared, there is no need to document them for use by others in the same way that exists for externally visible methods.

At this point, the only method left to document is `ChangeSalary`, which is documented as follows:

```
/**
 * This function changes the employees salary.
 * A salary change can occur only after the two following
 * tests have been applied:
 * <ol>
 * <li>The new salary is higher than the current salary.
 * <li>The new salary is less than the maximum salary.
 * </ol>
 * @return <B>true</B> if the salary change is approved,
 *          <B>false</B> otherwise.
 * @param newSalary The proposed new salary.
 */
public boolean ChangeSalary(float newSalary) {
```

Figure 9.11.

Documentation for
GetJobTitle and
GetMaxWorkingAge.

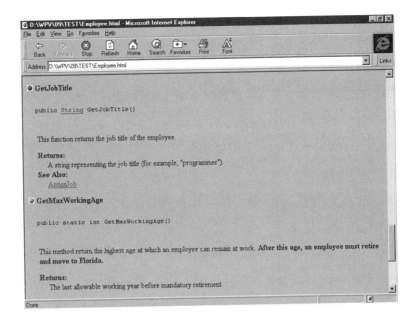

The documentation for ChangeSalary will appear as shown in Figure 9.12. This example demonstrates the use of <OL>...</OL> and <LI> to introduce an ordered list and its items. Ordered lists are like unordered lists except that instead of bullets, they have numbers to the left of each item. Additionally, this example shows that some HTML tags can be embedded with class or method documentation tags. In this case, <B>...</B> is embedded within the @return tag.

Figure 9.12.

Documentation for the
ChangeSalary method.

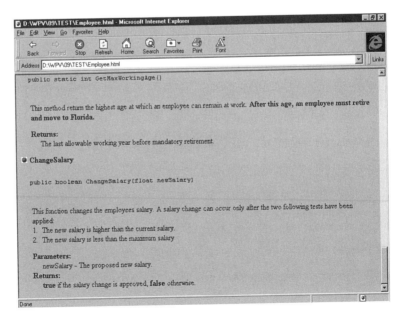

For clarity and completeness, Listing 9.1 shows the complete source to the Employee, Contract, and Person classes used throughout this example.

Listing 9.1. The Employee, Contractor, and Person classes.

```
/**
 * The <tt>Employee</tt> class is used to represent
 * employees of our company. It augments the <tt>Person</tt>
 * class with information about an employee's salary and
 * job title.<p>
 * This class was written by:
 * <blockquote>
 * <img src=logo.gif width=300 height=100>
 * </blockquote>
 * @author Mike Cohn
 * @version 1.0.0
 * @see Contractor
 */
public class Employee extends Person {
    private float salary;
    private String job;

    /** This constructor is used to create a new employee and
      * assign him an initial salary. <EM>It does not verify that
      * salary is less than the company's maximum salary.</EM>
      * You could use this method as follows:
      * <CODE><PRE>
      * Employee Emp = new Employee(35000f,"Mike","Cohn");
      * </PRE></CODE>
      * @param sal The starting salary of the new employee.
      * @param fName The employee's first name.
      * @param lName The employee's last name.
      */
    public Employee(float sal, String fName, String lName) {
        super(fName, lName);
        salary = sal;
    }

    /**
     * This method assigns the employee to the
     * specified job. This method does not verify the
     * <i>job title</i> against the list of <i>approved
     * job titles</i> created by <b>Human Resources</b>.
     * Likely job titles you may want to pass include:
     * <ul>
     * <li>Programmer
     * <li>Analyst
     * <li>QA
     * <li>Tech Writer
     * <li>Project Manager
     * <li>Database Administrator
     * <li>Database Engineer
     * </ul>
     * Reminder: All positions must be approved by the
     * <b>Manager of Human Resources</b> according to
     * the company's <CITE>Employee Hiring Guidelines.
     * </CITE>
```

```
 * @param newJob This is the new job title.
 * @see #GetJobTitle
 */
public void AssignJob(String newJob) {
    job = newJob;
}


/**
 * This function returns the job title of the employee.
 * @return A string representing the job title (for
 * example, "programmer").
 * @see #AssignJob
 */
public String GetJobTitle() {
    return job;
}


/**
 * This method returns the highest age at which
 * an employee can remain at work. <STRONG>
 * After this age, an employee must retire and
 * move to Florida.</STRONG>
 * @return The last allowable working year before
 * mandatory retirement.
 */
public static int GetMaxWorkingAge() {
    return 64;
}


  /**
   * This comment will not show up in JavaDoc because
   * it is private.
   */
private float GetMaxSalary() {
    return 200000f;
}


/**
 * This function changes the employees salary.
 * A salary change can occur only after the two following
 * tests have been applied:
 * <ol>
 * <li>The new salary is higher than the current salary.
 * <li>The new salary is less than the maximum salary.
 * </ol>
 * @return <B>true</B> if the salary change is approved,
 *         <B>false</B> otherwise.
 * @param newSalary The proposed new salary.
 */
public boolean ChangeSalary(float newSalary) {
    if (newSalary < salary)
        return false;
    if (newSalary > GetMaxSalary())
        return false;
    salary = newSalary;
    return true;
}
}
```

Listing 9.1. continued

```
/**
   * The Contractor class is used to represent
   * contract employees. Contract employees are
   * paid by the hour.
   * @author Mike Cohn
   * @version 1.0.0
   */
class Contractor extends Employee {
    public Contractor(float sal, String fName, String lName) {
        super(sal, fName, lName);
    }
    private float hourlyRate;
   /**
      * This method can be used to retrieve the hourly rate
      * paid to the contractor.
      * @return The contractor's hourly rate, excluding
      *          exceptional circumstances such as holidays
      *          and overtime.
      */
    public float GetHourlyRate() {
        return hourlyRate;
    }
   /**
      * This method calculates how much is due to
      * a contractor based on how much he's worked
      * and his hourly rate.
      * @param hours The number of hours worked by the
      *          contractor during this pay period.
      * @return The amount of money due the contractor.
      */
    public float CalculatePayCheck(int hours) {
        return hours * hourlyRate;
    }
}

class Person {
    protected String firstName;
    protected String lastName;
    Person() {}
    Person(String fName, String lName) {
        firstName = fName;
        lastName = lName;
    }
}
```

Summary

In this chapter, you learned how JavaDoc can simplify the job of documenting your classes. You saw how class documentation tags can be used to link classes by providing jumps between related classes. You also learned how to use method documentation tags to document the parameters, return values, and exceptions of each method. Even with this much power and flexibility, it only scratched the surface of what can be done. By embedding HTML commands directly into your comments, you learned how to enhance your documentation by using formatted text, numbered and bulleted lists, and embedded images. Finally, you saw an extensive example that put all of these pieces together to document a single class.

Useful Classes and Packages

Working with Java Strings

In this chapter you learn about the String and StringBuffer classes, two of the classes you will use most in your Java programming career. You learn how to convert other object types into strings so they can be displayed. You also learn how to perform a number of other operations on strings, including case conversion, searching for characters or substrings, and comparing strings. You learn how the StringBuffer class offers an alternative to the String class and is more useful when working with text that is likely to change. And finally, you learn how to use the many methods for appending or inserting into a StringBuffer.

The String Class

The Java String class, a part of the java.lang package, is used to represent strings of characters. Unlike C and C++, Java does not use an array of characters to represent a string. The String class is used to represent a string that is fairly static, changing infrequently if at all. This section describes how to use this class and includes examples of many of the nearly 50 methods or constructors that are a part of this important class.

Constructing New Strings

There are seven String constructors, as shown in Table 10.1. As examples of using these constructors, consider the following code:

```
String str1 = new String();
String str2 = new String("A New String");
char charArray[] = {'A', 'r', 'r', 'a', 'y' };
String str3 = new String(charArray);
String str4 = new String(charArray, 2, 3);
StringBuffer buf = new StringBuffer("buffer");
String str5 = new String(buf);
```

Table 10.1. Constructors for the String class.

Constructor	Purpose
String()	Creates an empty string.
String(String)	Creates a string from the specified string.
String(char[])	Creates a string from an array of characters.
String(char[], int, int)	Creates a string from the specified subset of characters in an array.
String(byte[], int)	Creates a string from the specified byte array and Unicode upper byte.
String(byte[],int,int,int)	Creates a string from the specified subset of bytes and Unicode upper byte.
String(StringBuffer)	Creates a string.

In the first example, str1 is created as an empty string. The second string, str2, will hold the text "A New String". The next two examples, str3 and str4, are constructed from a character array. In the case of str3, the entire array is placed in the string. For str4, three characters starting in array position two are copied into the string. Because Java arrays are zero-based, this results in str4 containing "ray". In the final example, the string str5 is constructed from a StringBuffer, buf. The StringBuffer class has much in common with String and is described in detail later in this chapter.

In addition to these constructors, there are other ways to get a String object. Many Java classes include a toString method that can be used to generate a string representation of the object. For example, consider the following:

```
Long myLong = new Long(43);
String longStr = myLong.toString();
g.drawString(longStr + myLong.toString(), 10, 20);
```

In this case, a Long object is created and set to hold the value 43. Note that this is an object of type Long, not a primitive of type long. Because myLong is an instance of a class, the toString method is used to place a string directly into longStr. The call to drawString illustrates that the converted string in longStr can be used as a regular string as can an inline use of myLong.toString.

Finally, Java supports the use of automatic strings, as follows:

```
g.drawString("This is an automatic string.", 10, 20);
```

In this case, the drawString method expects to be passed a string as its first parameter. To satisfy this expectation, a new String object is constructed using the quoted text. This happens behind the scenes automatically and requires no special attention on your part.

Basic String Methods

The basic methods for manipulating and examining a string are shown in Table 10.2. The Java String class is meant to hold text that does not change, so this table does not include a lot of methods for adding and inserting text. It does, however, include a simple concat method for adding one string to the end of another and a replace method for swapping one character for another.

Table 10.2. Basic string methods.

Method	Purpose
concat(String)	Concatenates one string onto another.
length()	Returns the length of the string.
replace(char, char)	Replaces all occurrences of one character with a different character.
toLowerCase()	Converts the entire string to lowercase.
toUpperCase()	Converts the entire string to uppercase.
trim()	Trims both leading and trailing whitespace from the string.

The concat method appends the specified string onto the current string and returns the result as a new string. This can be seen in the following, in which str3 will contain "Hello World":

```
String str1 = new String("Hello ");
String str2 = new String("World");
String str3 = str1.concat(str2);
```

The replace method can be used to change all occurrences of one character to a different character. The following example changes "Hi Mom" to "Hi Mum", allowing the program to be run in England:

```
String str = new String("Hi Mom ");
String newStr = str.replace('o', 'u');
```

Like concat, trim works by returning a new string. In this case, all leading and trailing whitespace characters are first removed from the returned string. The following example will remove the tabs, carriage return, new line, and space characters at both ends of the string:

```
String str = new String("\t\t In The Middle \r\n");
String newStr = str.trim();
```

The length method simply returns the number of characters in the string. In the following example, len will be set to 12:

```
String str = new String("Length of 12");
int len = str.length();
```

The toUpperCase and toLowerCase methods can be used to change the case of an entire string. Each works by returning a new string. In the following example, an uppercase version and a lowercase version of the same string are created:

```
String str = new String("This is MiXeD caSE");
String upper = str.toUpperCase();
String lower = str.toLowerCase();
```

Converting Variables to Strings

Because most of the display methods of Java's user interface classes use strings, it is important to be able to convert variables of other types into strings. Naturally, Java includes methods for doing this. The String class includes a set of static valueOf methods that can be used to create strings from other Java objects and primitive types. The valueOf methods are shown in Table 10.3.

Table 10.3. Useful methods for converting strings.

Method	Purpose
valueOf(char)	Returns a string containing the one specified character.
valueOf(char[])	Returns a string with the same text as the specified character array.
valueOf(char[], int, int)	Returns a string with the same text as a subset of the specified character array.

Method	Purpose
valueOf(boolean)	Returns a string containing either true or false.
valueOf(int)	Returns a string containing the value of the int.
valueOf(long)	Returns a string containing the value of the long.
valueOf(float)	Returns a string containing the value of the float.
valueOf(double)	Returns a string containing the value of the double.

Each of these methods is passed the variable to convert and returns a string representation of that variable. Because these methods are static, they are invoked using the name of the class rather than the name of an instance of the class. For example, consider the following uses of valueOf to create strings from numeric values:

```
String intStr = String.valueOf(100);
String floatStr = String.valueOf(98.6F);
String doubleStr = String.valueOf(3.1416D);
```

Each of these lines will result in the creation of a string containing the number specified. Consider also the following examples of non-numeric conversions:

```
String boolStr = String.valueOf(true);
String charStr = String.valueOf('Y');
char charArray[] = { 'A', 'r', 'r', 'a', 'y' };
String arrayStr1 = String.valueOf(charArray);
String arrayStr2 = String.valueOf(charArray, 2, 3);
```

In the first case, boolStr will be set to true. The variable charStr will be a string with a length of 1. The entire five-character array will be stored in arrayStr1, but only ray will be stored in arrayStr2.

Using Only Part of a String

Of course, sometimes the entire string is too much; you just need a portion of the string. Fortunately, the Java String class provides methods for accessing or creating a substring from a longer string. Each of the methods listed in Table 10.4 can be used to retrieve a portion of a string.

Table 10.4. Methods for using a substring.

Method	Purpose
charAt(int)	Returns the character at the specified location.
getBytes(int, int, byte[], int)	Copies the specified number of characters from the specified location into the byte array.
getChars(int, int, char[], int)	Copies the specified number of characters from the specified location into the char array.

continues

Table 10.4. continued

Method	Purpose
substring(int)	Returns a substring beginning at the specified offset of the current string.
substring(int, int)	Returns a substring between the specified offsets of the current string.

The charAt method retrieves the single character at the index given. For example, the following will place the character a in ch:

```
String str = new String("This is a String");
char ch = str.charAt(8);
```

The getBytes and getChars methods are similar. The first moves a substring into an array of bytes; the latter moves a substring into an array of characters. As an example, consider the following:

```
public void paint(Graphics g)
{
    String str = new String("Wish You Were Here");
    char charArray[] = new char[25];
    str.getChars(5, 13, charArray, 0);
    g.drawChars(charArray, 0, 8, 10, 10);
}
```

This code will extract You Were from str and move it into the charArray variable. It is then displayed using g.drawChars.

The two substring methods can be used to create new strings that are extracted from the current string. To create a substring from an offset to the end of the string, use the first version of substring, as follows:

```
String str = new String("This is a String");
String substr = str.substring(10);
```

In this case substr will hold String. To create a substring from the middle of a string, you can specify an ending offset as an additional parameter to substring. The following code will place You Were into substr:

```
String str = new String("Wish You Were Here");
String substr = str.substring(5, 13);
```

The character given by the beginning index will be included in the new string, but the character given by the ending index will not be.

Comparing Strings

As can be seen in Table 10.5, Java provides a number of methods for comparing one string to another. The compareTo method returns the difference between two strings by examining the first

two characters that differ in the strings. The difference between the characters is returned. For example, the character a differs from c by two characters, so 2 will be returned if these are the first two characters that differ. Depending on which string contains the higher valued character, the return value could be positive or negative. For example, in the following, result1 will equal –2 but result2 will be 2.

```
String str1 = new String("abc");
String str2 = new String("abe");

// compare str2 against str1
int result1 = str1.compareTo(str2);

// perform the same comparison but in the
// opposite direction (str1 against str2)
int result2 = str2.compareTo(str1);
```

Table 10.5. Methods for comparing strings.

Method	Purpose
compareTo(String)	Compares two strings. Returns 0 if they are equal, a negative value if the specified string is greater than the string, or a positive value otherwise.
endsWith(String)	Returns true if the string ends with the specified string.
equalIgnoreCase	Returns true if, ignoring differences in capitalization, the string matches the specified string.
equals(Object)	Returns true if the string matches the object.
equalTo(String)	Returns true if the string matches the specified string.
regionMatches(int,String,int,int)	Returns true if the specified region of the string matches the specified region of a different string.
regionMatches(boolean,int,String,int,int)	Returns true if the specified region of the string matches the specified region of a different string optionally considering the case of the strings.
startsWith(String)	Returns true if the string starts with the specified string.
startsWith(String, int)	Returns true if the string starts with the specified string at the specified offset.

The equals and equalTo methods perform similar comparisons; however, these each return a boolean value rather than a measure of how the strings differ. These can be used to compare one string against another string or against a string literal as shown in the following:

```java
public void paint(Graphics g)
{
    String str1 = new String("abc");

    // create str2 to have the same contents as str1
    String str2 = new String(str1);

    // compare str1 to the string made from it
    if (str1.equals(str2))
        g.drawString("str1 and str2 are equal", 10, 10);

    // compare str1 against a literal
    if (str1.equals("abc"))
        g.drawString("str1 equals abc", 10, 30);
}
```

In this case str1 is equal to both str2 and the literal abc. To perform a case-insensitive comparison use the equalIgnoreCase method, as follows:

```java
String str1 = new String("abc");
boolean result = str1.equalsIgnoreCase("ABC");
```

The endsWith method can be used to determine whether a string ends with a given string. Usually more useful are the two startsWith methods. These can be used to determine whether the string starts with a given string or whether that string appears at a specific location within the string. The endsWith and startsWith methods can be used as shown in the following:

```java
// create two Strings
String str1 = new String("My favorite language is Java");
String str2 = new String("I like the Java language");

// see if str1 ends with "Java"
boolean result1 = str1.endsWith("Java");        // true

// see if str1 starts with "My"
boolean result2 = str1.startsWith("My");        // true

// see if starting in offset 11 str2 starts with "Java"
boolean result3 = str2.startsWith("Java", 11);  // true
```

The two regionMatches methods can be used to see whether a region in one string matches a region in a different string. The second regionMatches method allows for case-insensitive comparisons of this nature. As an example of using regionMatches, consider the following:

```java
// create two longer Strings
String str1 = new String("My favorite language is Java");
String str2 = new String("I like the Java language");

// compare regions
// Start at offset 24 in str1 and compare against offset 11
// in str2 for 4 characters
boolean result = str1.regionMatches(24, str2, 11, 4);    // true
```

In this case the strings are compared for a length of four characters starting with index 24 in str1 and index 11 in str2. Because each of these substrings is "Java", result is set to true.

Searching Strings

In addition to comparing one string against another, you can also search a string for the occurrence of a character or another string. Unfortunately, you can do only a normal exact character search; no regular expression or wildcard searching is possible. The methods that can be used to search a string are shown in Table 10.6.

Table 10.6. Methods for searching a string.

Method	Purpose
indexOf(int)	Searches for the first occurrence of the specified character.
indexOf(int, int)	Searches for the first occurrence of the specified character following the given offset.
indexOf(String)	Searches for the first occurrence of the specified string.
indexOf(String, int)	Searches for the first occurrence of the specified string following the given offset.
lastIndexOf(int)	Searches backwards for the last occurrence of the specified character.
lastIndexOf(int, int)	Searches backwards for the last occurrence of the specified character preceding the given offset.
lastIndexOf(String)	Searches backwards for the last occurrence of the specified string.
lastIndexOf(String, int)	Searches backwards for the last occurrence of the specified string preceding the given offset.

As you can see from Table 10.6, the search methods have various signatures but are named either indexOf or lastIndexOf. The indexOf methods search forward from the start of a string to its end; the lastIndexOf methods search in the opposite direction.

To search for a character from the beginning of the string, use the indexOf(int) method. The following code illustrates searching for the character 'Y':

```
String str = new String("Wish You Were Here");
int index = str.indexOf('Y');
```

In this case, a 'Y' is found in index 5, so this value is placed in index. This works well for finding the first occurrence of a letter, but what if you need to find subsequent occurrences of the same letter? This can be done by using the indexOf(int, int) method. The additional parameter indicates the offset from which to start the search. By setting this value each time a matching character is found, a loop can be written to easily find all occurrences of a letter. As an example, consider the following code fragment:

```java
String str = new String("Wish You Were Here");

int fromIndex = 0;
while(fromIndex != -1)
{
    fromIndex = str.indexOf('W', fromIndex);
    if (fromIndex != -1)
    {
        // character was matched, use as desired
        fromIndex++;
    }
}
```

This example starts with str containing "Wish You Were Here" and uses a loop to find all 'W' characters. The variable fromIndex is initially set to 0. This causes the str.indexOf method call to start at the beginning of the string on the first pass through the loop. If fromIndex is not -1, this indicates that the character was found. The value is appended to a results string and fromIndex is incremented to move past the matching character. In this case a W is found at indexes 0 and 9.

Searching for a string is just as simple as searching for a character. The following example will search for the string "er":

```java
public void paint(Graphics g)
{
    String str = new String("Wish You Were Here");
    int count = 0;

    int fromIndex = 0;
    while(fromIndex != -1)
    {
        fromIndex = str.indexOf("er", fromIndex);
        if (fromIndex != -1)
        {
            count++;
            fromIndex++;
        }
    }
    g.drawString(String.valueOf(count), 10, 10);
}
```

This string will be found twice, once in Were and once in Here.

TIP:

The StringTokenizer class provides a very powerful mechanism for parsing a string. This class is fully described in Chapter 11, "The Java Utility Classes."

The StringBuffer Class

The primary limitation of the string class is that once the string is created you cannot change it. If you need to store text that may need to be changed you should use the StringBuffer class. The StringBuffer class includes methods for inserting and appending text. Additionally, a StringBuffer object may be easily converted into a String class when necessary.

To create a new string buffer, you can use any of the three constructors shown in Table 10.7. Examples of using these constructors are as follows:

```
StringBuffer buf1 = new StringBuffer(25);
StringBuffer buf2 = new StringBuffer();
StringBuffer buf3 = new StringBuffer("This is a StringBuffer");
```

In the first case, buf1 will be an empty StringBuffer with an initial length of 25. Similarly, buf2 will be an empty StringBuffer but buf3 will contain "This is a StringBuffer".

Table 10.7. StringBuffer constructors.

Constructor	Purpose
StringBuffer()	Creates an empty StringBuffer.
StringBuffer(int)	Creates an empty StringBuffer with the specified length.
StringBuffer(String)	Creates a StringBuffer based on the specified string.

Useful StringBuffer Methods

In addition to the methods for inserting and appending text, the StringBuffer class contains other methods you will need to be familiar with. These are shown in Table 10.8. The capacity method can be used to determine the storage capacity of the string buffer. Because each string buffer can grow as text is appended or inserted, the capacity of the string buffer can exceed the length of the text currently stored in it. While capacity returns the amount of text that could be stored in the currently allocated space of the string buffer, length returns how much of that space is already used. As an example, consider the following:

```
StringBuffer buf = new StringBuffer(25);
buf.append("13 Characters");
int len = buf.length();
int cap = buf.capacity();
```

In this case, the constructor specifies a capacity of 25 for buf. However, only thirteen characters are placed in it with the append method. Because of this, the length of buf is 13 while its capacity is 25. These values will be stored in len and cap, respectively.

Table 10.8. Useful methods of the `StringBuffer` class.

Method	Purpose
`capacity()`	Returns the current capacity of the `StringBuffer`.
`charAt(int)`	Returns the character located at the specified index.
`ensureCapacity(int)`	Ensures the capacity of the `StringBuffer` is at least the specified amount.
`getChars(int,int,char[],int)`	Copies the specified characters from the `StringBuffer` into the specified array.
`length()`	Returns the length of the `StringBuffer`.
`setCharAt(int, char)`	Sets the value at the specified index to the specified character.
`setLength(int)`	Sets the length of the `StringBuffer` to the specified value.
`toString`	Returns a string representing the text in the `StringBuffer`.

The `ensureCapacity` method can be used to increase the capacity of the string buffer and the `setLength` method can be used to set the length of the buffer. If `setLength` is used to reduce the length, the characters at the end of the buffer are lost. If, instead, `setLength` is used to increase the length of a string buffer, null characters are used to fill the additional space at the end. This can be seen in the following code:

```
StringBuffer buf = new StringBuffer("0123456789");
buf.setLength(5);
// buf now contains "01234"
buf.setLength(10);
// buf now contains "01234" followed by five null characters
```

The `toString` method will be one of the `StringBuffer` methods you will use most frequently. This method creates a string representation of the text in the string buffer. This is useful because so many of the Java library methods expect a string as a parameter. For example, the following code illustrates how to display the contents of a string buffer in an applet's `paint` method:

```
public void paint(Graphics g)
{
    StringBuffer buf = new StringBuffer("Hello, World");
    g.drawString(buf.toString(), 10, 10);
}
```

The `charAt` and `setCharAt` methods can be used to retrieve the character at a specific index and to set the character at a specific index, respectively. This can be seen in the following:

```
StringBuffer buf = new StringBuffer("Hello");
char ch = buf.charAt(1);
buf.setCharAt(1, 'a');
```

Because StringBuffers are zero-based, ch will contain 'e'. The setCharAt method replaces this 'e', changing the string buffer to say "Hallo". The getChars method can be used to retrieve characters from a string buffer and place them into a character array. The getChars method has the following signature:

```
public synchronized void getChars(int srcBegin, int srcEnd,
        char dst[], int dstBegin) ;
```

The srcEnd parameter indicates the first character after the desired end of the text. It will not be placed in the destination array, so you should be careful to specify the proper value. In the following example, getChars is used to place the characters of String into the array:

```
StringBuffer buf = new StringBuffer("A String Buffer");
char array[] = new char[10];
buf.getChars(2,8, array, 0);
```

CAUTION:

The getChars method will throw a StringIndexOutOfBoundsException if any of the parameters represents an invalid index.

Appending

Because the main distinction between the String and StringBuffer classes is the capability of a StringBuffer instance to increase in size, methods are provided for appending to a StringBuffer. Each of the following methods can be used to append to a StringBuffer:

- ○ append(Object)
- ○ append(String)
- ○ append(char)
- ○ append(char[])
- ○ append(char[], int, int)
- ○ append(boolean)
- ○ append(int)
- ○ append(long)
- ○ append(float)
- ○ append(double)

Use of these methods is demonstrated by the following:

```
StringBuffer buf = new StringBuffer("Hello");
buf.append(", World");
```

```
StringBuffer buf2 = new StringBuffer("Revolution #");
buf2.append(9);

StringBuffer buf3 = new StringBuffer("My daughter is ");
float ageSavannah = 10F/12F;
buf3.append(ageSavannah);
buf3.append(" years old");
```

In the first case buf is set to contain "Hello" and then append(String) is used to create "Hello, World". The second case illustrates append(int) to create the text "Revolution #9". Finally, buf3 illustrates the use of append(float) combined with append(String).

Inserting

Of course, sometimes the text you want to add to a string buffer needs to go somewhere other than at the end. In these cases, append is of no use and you need to use one of the provided insert methods. A variety of insert methods is provided, as follows:

- ○ insert(int, Object)
- ○ insert(int, String)
- ○ insert(int, char[])
- ○ insert(int, boolean)
- ○ insert(int, char)
- ○ insert(int, int)
- ○ insert(int, long)
- ○ insert(int, float)
- ○ insert(int, double)

Each of these methods is passed the index at which to insert the text and then an object to be inserted. For example, the following code inserts the all-important half month into a child's age:

```
StringBuffer buf = new StringBuffer("My daughter is 10 months old");
buf.insert(17, "-and-a-half");
```

Summary

In this chapter, you learned about the String and StringBuffer classes, two of the most commonly used classes in Java programming. You learned that the String class is intended to hold nonchanging text. You saw many examples of using the member methods of the String class, including changing the case of a string, trimming whitespace, and accessing substrings. You learned how to convert variables of other types into strings and how to search and compare strings. Finally, you saw how the StringBuffer class is a more useful class for dynamic strings because text can be inserted and appended.

The Java Utility Classes

- The BitSet Class

- The Date Class

- The Hashtable Class

- The Properties Class

- The Random Class

- Observers and Observables

- The Vector Class

- The Stack Class

- The StringTokenizer Class

In this chapter you learn about the java.util package. This package provides some of the most useful Java classes that you will come to rely on. It introduces the following nonabstract classes:

```
BitSet
Date
Hashtable
Properties
Observable
Random
Vector
Stack
StringTokenizer
```

The BitSet class is useful for storing and manipulating arbitrarily long sets of bits. The Date class can be used to represent dates and times, and provides methods for converting dates to and from strings. The Hashtable class can be used for creating an array of keys and values and allowing elements to be looked up by either key or value. The Properties class extends Hashtable by allowing elements to be streamed into or out of the class. The Observable class can be extended, and enables you to create new classes that will notify other classes when they change. It works in conjunction with the Observer interface, which is also part of the java.util package.

The Random class is a pseudo-random number generator that can return integer, floating-point, or Gaussian-distributed values. The Stack class is an extension of Vector and supplies a last-in-first-out (LIFO) data structure. The Vector class can be used for storing any objects and can store objects of more than one type in the same vector. The StringTokenizer class provides a flexible mechanism for parsing strings.

The BitSet Class

The BitSet class represents a dynamically sized set of bits. Two constructors are provided, one that creates an empty set of unspecified size and one that creates a set of a specified size. The set method can be used to set an individual bit or clear can be used to clear an individual bit. The first bit in a BitSet is the zero bit so that myBitset.set(0) is a valid statement.

The logical functions and, or, and xor are all supported and will combine the BitSet with another set. BitSets can be compared for equality using equals and can be converted to strings using toString. For the purpose of converting a BitSet to a string, a set bit is represented by the value 1 and a clear bit is represented by 0.

The available constructor and nonprivate methods for BitSet are shown in Table 11.1.

Table 11.1. Public constructors and methods of `BitSet`.

Member	Purpose
`BitSet()`	Constructs an empty bit set.
`BitSet(int)`	Constructs an empty bit set with the specified number of bits.
`and(BitSet)`	Logically ANDs two bit sets.
`clear(int)`	Clears the specified bit.
`clone()`	Creates a duplicate copy of the `BitSet`.
`equals(Object)`	Returns true if two `BitSet`s are equal.
`get(int)`	Returns the value of the specified bit.
`hashCode()`	Returns a hash code for the bit set.
`or(BitSet)`	Logically ORs two bit sets.
`set(int)`	Sets the specified bit.
`size()`	Returns the size of the bit set in bits.
`toString()`	Formats the `BitSet` as a string.
`xor(BitSet)`	Logically XORs two bit sets.

An Example

As an example of how to use `BitSet` consider class EX11A, shown in Listing 11.1. In this example, the method `BitSetTest` is invoked as the result of the user pressing a button. As various operations on `BitSet`s are performed, a `TextArea` is updated to display the results of the operations.

Listing 11.1. EX11A.java.

```java
import java.applet.*;
import java.awt.*;
import java.util.*;

public class EX11A extends Applet
{
    TextArea results = new TextArea(10, 20);

    public void init()
    {
        add(new Button("Start"));
        add(results);

        resize(320, 240);
    }
```

continues

Listing 11.1. continued

```java
public boolean action(Event evt, Object obj)
{
    boolean result=false;

    if("Start".equals(obj)) {
        BitSetTest();
        result = true;
    }
    return result;
}

void BitSetTest()
{
    // create a BitSet and set items 1 and 4
    BitSet bits1 = new BitSet(10);
    bits1.set(1);
    bits1.set(4);

    // create a BitSet and set items 4 and 5
    BitSet bits2 = new BitSet(10);
    bits2.set(4);
    bits2.set(5);

    // display the contents of these two BitSets
    results.appendText("Bits 1=" + bits1.toString() + "\r\n");
    results.appendText("Bits 2=" + bits2.toString() + "\r\n");

    // test for equality of the two BitSets
    if(bits1.equals(bits2))
        results.appendText("bits1 == bits2\r\n");
    else
        results.appendText("bits1 != bits2\r\n");

    // create a clone and then test for equality
    BitSet clonedBits = (BitSet)bits1.clone();
    if(bits1.equals(clonedBits))
        results.appendText("bits1 == clonedBits\r\n");
    else
        results.appendText("bits1 != clonedBits\r\n");

    // logically AND the first two BitSets
    bits1.and(bits2);
    results.appendText("ANDing bits1 and bits2\r\n");
    // and display the resulting BitSet
    results.appendText("bits1=" + bits1.toString() + "\r\n");
}
}
```

In the BitSetTest method, two BitSets are constructed. The first, bits1, has bits 1 and 4 set. The second, bits2, has bits 4 and 5 set. The toString method is used to display the contents of the BitSets. The BitSets are then compared using equals. Next, a clone of bits1 is created. To show that the clone method was successful, the BitSets are compared and a message is displayed. Finally, the and method is used to logically AND two BitSets and the result is displayed using toString.

The Date Class

The Date class stores a representation of a date and time, and provides methods for manipulating the date and time components. As summarized in Table 11.2, constructors are provided that will create a new Date instance based on the current date and time, the number of milliseconds since midnight on January 1, 1970, a string, or from integers representing the year, month, day, hours, minutes, and seconds.

Table 11.2. Constructors for the Date class.

Constructor	Purpose
Date()	Creates a Date using today's date.
Date(long)	Creates a Date using the specified number of milliseconds since January 1, 1970.
Date(int,int,int)	Creates a Date using the specified year, month, and day.
Date(int,int,int,int,int)	Creates a Date using the specified year, month, day, hours, and minutes.
Date(int,int,int,int,int,int)	Creates a Date using the specified year, month, day, hours, minutes, and seconds.
Date(String)	Creates a Date using the specified string.

As examples of how these constructors can be used to create new Date objects, consider the following:

```
Date date1 = new Date();
Date date2 = new Date(95, 10, 14);
Date date3 = new Date(95, 10, 14, 13, 16, 45);
Date date4 = new Date("14 November 1995 13:16:45");
```

In this case, date1 will be set to the current date and time. The date2 variable will be set to November 14, 1995. Months are zero-based in the Date class, so 10 is passed as a parameter to indicate the eleventh month. The third example adds more exactness to the second example. While date2 will represent the stroke of midnight on November 14, 1995, date3 is explicitly set to 13:16: 45 (45 seconds after 1:16 p.m.). Finally, date4 creates the same time as date3, but does so from a string.

Many methods are also provided for manipulating Date instances. For example, dates can be compared with the before, after, and equals methods. Methods are also provided for converting a Date into various formatted strings. The nonprivate instance methods of the Date class are shown in Table 11.3.

Table 11.3. Nonprivate instance methods of the Date class.

Method	Purpose
after(Date)	Returns true if the Date occurs after the specified Date.
before(Date)	Returns true if the Date occurs before the specified Date.
equals(Object)	Returns true if two Dates are equal.
getDate()	Returns the day (1–31) portion of the Date.
getDay()	Returns the day of the week (Sunday is 0)indicated by the Date.
getHours()	Returns the hours (0–23) portion of the Date.
getMinutes()	Returns the minutes (0–59) portion of the Date.
getMonth()	Returns the month (0–11) portion of the Date.
getSeconds()	Returns the seconds (0–59) portion of the Date.
getTime()	Returns the number of milliseconds since midnight on January 1, 1970.
getTimezoneOffset()	Returns the offset in minutes for the current timezone from UTC (Coordinated Universal Time, similar to GMT, Greenwich Mean Time).
getYear()	Returns the year after 1900.
hashCode()	Returns a hash code for the Date.
setDate(int)	Sets the day of the month.
setHours(int)	Sets the hours.
setMinutes(int)	Sets the minutes.
setMonth(int)	Sets the month.
setSeconds(int)	Sets the seconds.
setTime(long)	Sets the time to the specified number of milliseconds since midnight January 1, 1970.
setYear(int)	Sets the year after 1900.
toGMTString()	Returns a formatted string of the Date in the GMT time zone.
toLocaleString()	Returns a formatted string of the Date in the current time zone.
toString()	Returns a formatted string of the Date including the day of the week.

In addition to the instance methods shown in Table 11.3, the Date class includes two static methods. Static methods can be invoked without an instance of the class. The static methods of the Date class can be used to determine the number of seconds since midnight on January 1, 1970 based on a string or integer values representing the date and time. These are summarized in Table 11.4; examples of their use are as follows:

```
long temp = Date.parse("14 November 1996");
Date date1 = new Date(temp);
temp = Date.UTC(96, 10, 14, 13, 16, 45);
Date date2 = new Date(temp);
```

Table 11.4. Static methods of the Date class.

Method	Purpose
UTC(int,int,int,int,int,int)	Returns the milliseconds since midnight January 1, 1970 based on the year, month, day, hours, minutes, and seconds parameters.
parse(String)	Returns the milliseconds since midnight January 1, 1970 based on parsing the supplied string.

As an example of the use of the Date class, consider example EX11B, as shown in Listing 11.2. The init method of this class displays a TextArea and then creates a Date object based on the current date. The toString, toLocaleString, and toGMTString methods are used to display the current date in various formats. An instance named BastilleDay is then constructed using the date of that holiday. Next, the year value for BastilleDay is set to the current year using the setYear and getYear methods. Finally, after is used to determine whether Bastille Day has already occurred this year, or if there is still time to shop for presents for your French friends. The results of executing this class are shown in Figure 11.1.

Listing 11.2. EX11B.java.

```
import java.applet.*;
import java.awt.*;
import java.util.*;

public class EX11B extends Applet
{
    TextArea results = new TextArea(10, 50);

    public void init()
    {
        add(results);

        Date today = new Date(); // today
```

continues

Listing 11.2. continued

```
        // display the current date in a couple of different formats
        results.appendText("Today is:" + today.toString() + "\r\n");
        results.appendText("Locale Time:" + today.toLocaleString() + "\r\n");
        results.appendText("GMT:" + today.toGMTString() + "\r\n");

        // store Bastille Day (July 14th) in an instance
        Date BastilleDay = new Date(96, 6, 14);       // 7-14-96

        // set Bastille Day to be in the current year
        BastilleDay.setYear(today.getYear());

        // see if we've already missed Bastille Day
        if (today.after(BastilleDay))
            results.appendText("You missed Bastille Day!\r\n");
        else
            results.appendText("Bastille Day is coming!\r\n");

        resize(320, 240);
    }
}
```

Figure 11.1.

The results of executing
EX11B after Bastille Day.

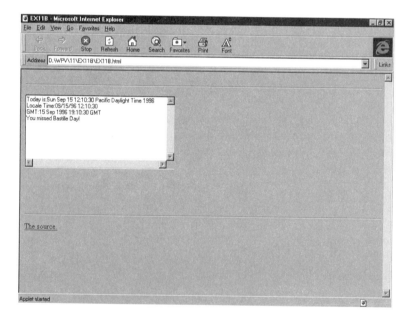

The Hashtable Class

The Hashtable class extends the abstract Dictionary class that is also defined in the java.util package. A Hashtable is used for mapping keys to values. For example, it could be used to map names to ages, programmers to projects, job titles to salaries, and so on.

A `Hashtable` will expand in size as elements are added to it. When creating a new `Hashtable` you can specify an initial capacity and a load factor. The `Hashtable` will increase in size whenever adding a new element would move the `Hashtable` past its threshold. A `Hashtable`'s threshold is its capacity multiplied by its load factor. For example, a `Hashtable` with a capacity of 100 and a load factor of 0.75 would have a threshold of 75 items. The constructors for `Hashtable` are shown in Table 11.5.

Table 11.5. Constructors for the `Hashtable` class.

Constructor	Purpose
Hashtable(int)	Constructs a new `Hashtable` with the specified initial capacity.
Hashtable(int, float)	Constructs a new `Hashtable` with the specified initial capacity and load factor.
Hashtable()	Constructs a new `Hashtable` using default values for initial capacity and load factor.

As an example of how to construct a new `Hashtable`, consider the following:

```
Hashtable hash1 = new Hashtable(500, .80);
```

In this case a `Hashtable` is constructed that will hold 500 elements. When the `Hashtable` becomes 80 percent full (a load factor of .80), its maximum size will be increased.

Each element in a `Hashtable` consists of a key and value. Elements are added to a `Hashtable` using the `put` method and are retrieved using `get`. Elements may be deleted from a `Hashtable` with `remove`. The `contains` and `containsKey` methods can be used to look up a value or key in the `Hashtable`. These and other `Hashtable` methods are summarized in Table 11.6.

Table 11.6. Nonprivate methods of the `Hashtable` class.

Method	Purpose
clear()	Removes all elements from the `Hashtable`.
clone()	Creates a clone of the `Hashtable`.
contains(Object)	Returns true if the `Hashtable` contains the specified object.
containsKey(Object)	Returns true if the `Hashtable` contains the specified key.
elements()	Returns an enumeration of the elements in the `Hashtable`.
get(Object)	Retrieves the object associated with the specified key.
isEmpty()	Returns true if the `Hashtable` is empty.
keys()	Returns an enumeration of the keys in the `Hashtable`.

continues

Table 11.6. continued

Method	Purpose
put(Object, Object)	Adds a new element to the Hashtable using the specified key and value.
rehash()	Rehashes the Hashtable into a larger Hashtable.
remove(Object)	Removes the object given by the specified key.
size()	Returns the number of elements in the Hashtable.
toString()	Returns a formatted string representing the Hashtable.

Class EX11C, shown in Listing 11.3, demonstrates how to use the Hashtable class. In this example a new Hashtable, ht, is constructed and is used to store the five best albums released by Pink Floyd. The Hashtable is displayed to a TextArea using toString.

Listing 11.3. EX11C.java.

```
import java.applet.*;
import java.awt.*;
import java.util.*;

public class EX11C extends Applet
{
    TextArea results = new TextArea(10, 75);

    public void init()
    {
        add(results);

        // create a new Hashtable
        Hashtable ht = new Hashtable();

        // add Pink Floyd's best albums
        ht.put("Pulse", new Integer(1995));
        ht.put("Dark Side of the Moon", new Integer(1973));
        ht.put("Wish You Were Here", new Integer(1975));
        ht.put("Animals", new Integer(1977));
        ht.put("Ummagumma", new Integer(1969));

        // display the Hashtable
        results.appendText("Initailly: "+ht.toString() + "\r\n");

        // test for any album from 1969
        if (ht.contains(new Integer(1969)))
            results.appendText("An album from 1969 exists\r\n");

        // test for the Animals album
        if (ht.containsKey("Animals"))
            results.appendText("Animals was found\r\n");
```

```
        // find out what year Wish You Were Here was released
        Integer year = (Integer)ht.get("Wish You Were Here");
        results.appendText("Wish You Were Here was released in " +
                year.toString() + "\r\n");

        // remove an album
        results.appendText("Removing Ummagumma\r\n");
        ht.remove("Ummagumma");

        // move through an enumeration of all keys in the table
        results.appendText("Remaining:\r\n");
        for (Enumeration enum=ht.keys(); enum.hasMoreElements() ;)
            results.appendText((String)enum.nextElement()+"\r\n");

        // and resize the applet window
        resize(500, 240);
    }
}
```

In this Hashtable, the names of the albums are the keys and the years are the elements. Therefore, contains is used to look up the integer element 1969 to see whether the list contains any albums from 1969. Similarly, containsKey is used to search for the key "Animals" to see if that album made the list. Next, the get method is used to see whether "Wish You Were Here" is in the Hashtable. Because get returns the element associated with the key, both the name and year are displayed at this point. This can be seen in Figure 11.2.

Figure 11.2.

The results of executing EX11C.

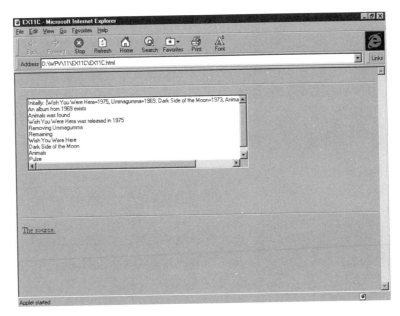

Next, I had some second thoughts about including "Ummagumma" in a list of best albums and used `remove` to delete it from the `Hashtable`. Finally, the `keys` method is used to create an Enumeration of the keys stored in the `Hashtable`. The applet then iterates through the enumeration using `enum.hasMoreElements` and `enum.nextElement`.

The Properties Class

The `Properties` class extends `Hashtable` and adds the capability to read and write a `Hashtable` to a stream. Because an applet cannot access files, the `Properties` class is useful only for applications.

Like `Hashtable`, this class can be used to store keys and associated values. Through its save and load methods, `Properties` can be written to disk. This makes this class an excellent mechanism for storing configuration information between runs of a program. An example of a `Properties` file written by the save method is as follows:

```
#This is a header comment
#Sat Sep 14 15:55:15 Pacific Daylight Time 1996
prop3=put three
prop2=put two
prop1=put one
```

Because `Properties` is a subclass of `Hashtable`, new key/value pairs are added using the `put` method of `Hashtable`. The constructors and nonprivate methods of `Properties` are shown in Table 11.7.

Table 11.7. Nonprivate constructors and methods of `Properties` class.

Member	Purpose
`Properties()`	Creates a new `Properties` object.
`Properties(Properties)`	Creates a new `Properties` object based on the specified default values.
`getProperty(String)`	Returns the property value associated with the specified key.
`getProperty(String,String)`	Returns the property value associated with the specified key. If the key is not found, the specified default is returned.
`list(PrintStream)`	Lists all of the properties to the specified `PrintStream`.
`load(InputStream)`	Reads a set of properties from the specified `InputStream`.
`propertyNames()`	Returns an Enumeration of all property names.
`save(OutputStream, String)`	Saves the `Properties` and a header string to the specified `OutputStream`.

Example EX11D, shown in Listing 11.4, shows how to create an instance, put three properties into it, save it, and then reload the keys and values into a different instance.

Listing 11.4. EX11D.java demonstrates the Properties class.

```java
import java.awt.*;
import java.io.*;
import java.util.*;

public class EX11D
{
    public static void main(String[] args)
    {
        // create a new instance
        Properties props1 = new Properties();

        // put three properties into it
        props1.put("prop1", "put one");
        props1.put("prop2", "put two");
        props1.put("prop3", "put three");

        // retrieve each of the three properties
        String prop1 = props1.getProperty("prop1", "one");
        String prop2 = props1.getProperty("prop2", "two");
        String prop3 = props1.getProperty("prop3");

        // save the properties to a file
        try
        {
            props1.save(new FileOutputStream("test.ini"), "My header");
        }
        catch (IOException e) {
            return;
        }

        // create a new instance and read the file in from the file
        Properties props2 = new Properties();
        try
        {
            FileInputStream inStr = new FileInputStream("test.ini");
            props2.load(inStr);
        }
        catch (IOException e) {
            return;
        }

        // retrieve a property from the second instance
        String prop = props2.getProperty("prop2", "two");
    }
}
```

The Random Class

This class represents a pseudo-random number generator. Two constructors are provided, one taking a seed value as a parameter and the other taking no parameters and using the current time as a seed. Constructing a random number generator with a seed value is a good idea unless you want the random number generator to always generate the same set of values. On the other hand, sometimes it is useful to generate the same sequence of "random" numbers. This is frequently useful while debugging a program.

Once the random number generator is created, a value can be retrieved from it using any of the following methods:

```
nextDouble
nextFloat
nextGaussian
nextInt
nextLong
```

The constructors and methods of Random are summarized in Table 11.8. Use of the Random class is very simple, so no example is presented here. However, example EX11E, shown in the following discussion of the Observer class, also uses Random.

Table 11.8. Nonprivate constructors and methods of Random class.

Method	Purpose
Random()	Creates a new random number generator.
Random(long)	Creates a new random number generator based on the specified seed value.
nextDouble()	Returns the next double value between 0.0D and 1.0D from the random number generator.
nextFloat()	Returns the next float value between 0.0F and 1.0F from the random number generator.
nextGaussian()	Returns the next Gaussian-distributed double from the random number generator. Generated Gaussian values will have a mean of 0 and a standard deviation of 1.0.
nextInt()	Returns the next integer value from the random number generator.
nextLong()	Returns the next long value from the random number generator.
setSeed(long)	Sets the seed value for the random number generator.

Observers and Observables

An Observable class is a class that may be watched or monitored by another class that implements the Observer interface. Associated with each Observable instance is a list of Observers. Whenever the Observable instance changes it can notify each of its Observers. By using Observable and Observer classes you can achieve a better partitioning of your code by decreasing the reliance of one class or another.

The Observable Class

The Observable class includes a single constructor that takes no parameters. It also includes a number of methods for managing its list of Observers. These are summarized in Table 11.9.

Table 11.9. Nonprivate constructors and methods of Observer class.

Member	Purpose
Observable()	Creates a new Observable instance.
addObserver(Observer)	Adds an Observer to the list of objects observing this instance.
clearChanged()	Clears the internal flag used to indicate that an Observable object has changed.
countObservers()	Returns the number of Observers of this object.
deleteObserver(Observer)	Deletes an Observer from the list of Observers of this object.
deleteObservers()	Deletes all Observers of this object.
hasChanged()	Returns true if the object has changed.
notifyObservers()	Notifies all Observers that a change has occurred in the Observable object.
notifyObservers(Object)	Notifies all Observers that a change has occurred and passes them the specified argument.
setChanged()	Sets the internal flag to indicate that a change has occurred.

The Observer Interface

The Observer interface defines an update method that is invoked by an Observable object whenever the Observable object has changed and wants to notify its Observers. The signature of update is as follows:

```
public abstract void update(Observable o, Object arg);
```

This method is called whenever an Observable instance that is being observed invokes either of its notifyObservers methods. It is passed the Observable object that changed and an optional additional parameter.

An Example

As an example of how Observable can be used, consider the declaration of the Obsable class in Listing 11.5. The Obsable class stores a secret number that is generated by a random number generator. Whenever the secret number changes, all Observers are notified.

Listing 11.5. EX11E.java demonstrates Observable and Observer.

```
import java.applet.*;
import java.awt.*;
import java.util.*;

// define a class that stores a secret number
class Obsable extends Observable {
    private int secretNumber;
    private Random generator;

    public Obsable(int seed) {
        // create a random number generator that will
        // make the "secret numbers"
        generator = new Random(seed);
    }

    public void GenerateNumber() {
        // generate a new secret number
        secretNumber = generator.nextInt();
        // indicate to Observable that the instance has changed
        setChanged();
        // notify all of the observers and pass the new number
        notifyObservers(new Integer(secretNumber));
    }
}

public class EX11E extends Applet implements Observer
{
    Integer secretNumber;
    Obsable obs;
    TextField tf;
```

```
public EX11E()
{
    // create a new instance of the observable class
    obs = new Obsable(12);
    // indicate that "this" is an observer
    obs.addObserver(this);

    // create a read-only TextField
    tf = new TextField(10);
    tf.setEditable(false);
}

public void init() {
    add(new Label("Secret Number:"));
    add(tf);
    add(new Button("Change"));
    resize(320, 240);
}

// this method is invoked when the observable object
// notifies its observers
public void update(Observable o, Object arg) {
    // store the secret number and display it
    secretNumber = (Integer)arg;
    tf.setText(String.valueOf(secretNumber));
}

public boolean action(Event evt, Object obj)
{
    boolean result=false;

    if("Change".equals(obj)) {
        obs.GenerateNumber();
        result = true;
    }
    return result;
}
}
```

No Observable class is complete without an Observer, so Listing 11.5 also includes class EX11E, which extends Applet and implements the Observer interface. The results of executing this applet are shown in Figure 11.3. The constructor for EX11E creates an instance of Obsable, the Observable class defined previously and adds the applet as an observer of the Observable object. The init method places a label, TextField, and button on the screen. The TextField will be used to display the current value of the secret number.

The EX11E class contains an update method that is part of the Observer interface. This method is passed an Observable item and an Object as parameters. As shown in the declaration of Obsable, the Object is an integer. Therefore, update casts the Object into an Integer, stores it in the instance variable secretNumber, and then updates the TextField.

Figure 11.3

The result of executing EX11E.

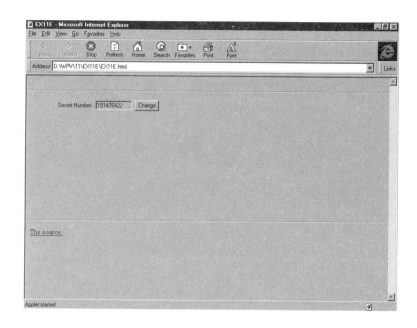

The action method traps pushes of the Change button and then calls obs.GenerateNumber to generate a new random number. Each time GenerateNumber changes the secret number, the update method in the observer will be called. In this case, this will update the display with each newly generated random number.

The Vector Class

One of the problems with an array is that you must know how big it must be when you create it. This is not always practical and is rarely easy. Imagine what would have happened if the founding fathers of the United States were programmers and they used a 13-element array to hold the names of all the states. Even if the lead programmer on this project (Thomas Jefferson, if I remember my eighth grade history correctly) had the foresight to double or triple the array size to allow for future growth, it still would not have been enough.

The Java Vector class solves this problem by providing a form of resizable array that can grow as more elements are added to it. A Vector stores items of type Object so that it can be used to store instances of any Java class. A single Vector may store different elements that are instances of different classes.

At any point in time a Vector has the capacity to hold a certain number of elements. When a Vector reaches its capacity, its capacity is incremented by an amount specific to that Vector. The Vector class provides three different constructors that enable you to specify the initial capacity and increment quantity of a Vector when it is created. These constructors are summarized in Table 11.10.

Table 11.10. Constructors for the Vector class.

Constructor	Purpose
Vector(int)	Creates a new Vector with the specified initial capacity.
Vector(int, int)	Creates a new Vector with the specified initial capacity and increment quantity.
Vector()	Creates a new Vector with defaults for the initial capacity and increment quantity.

An item is added to a Vector using addElement. Similarly, an element can be replaced using setElementAt. A Vector can be searched using the contains method, which simply looks for an occurrence of an Object. The elements method is useful because it returns an enumeration of the Objects stored in the Vector. These and other member methods of Vector are summarized in Table 11.11.

Table 11.11. Nonprivate methods of the Vector class.

Method	Purpose
addElement(Object)	Inserts the specified element into the Vector.
capacity()	Returns the number of elements that will fit into the currently allocated portion of the Vector.
clone()	Clones the vector, but not its elements.
contains(Object)	Returns true if the Vector contains the specified Object.
copyInto(Object [])	Copies the elements of the Vector into the specified array.
elementAt(int)	Retrieves the element located at the specified index.
elements()	Returns an enumeration of the elements in the Vector.
ensureCapacity(int)	Ensures that the Vector can hold at least the specified minimum capacity.
firstElement()	Returns the first element in the Vector.
indexOf(Object)	Searches the Vector and returns the zero-based index of the first matching Object.
indexOf(Object, int)	Searches the Vector beginning at the specified index number and returns the zero-based index of the next matching Object.
insertElementAt(Object, int)	Adds the specified Object at the specified index.
isEmpty()	Returns true if the Vector has no elements.
lastElement()	Returns the last element in the Vector.

continues

Table 11.11. continued

Method	Purpose
lastIndexOf(Object)	Searches the Vector and returns the zero-based index of the last matching Object.
lastIndexOf(Object, int)	Searches the Vector beginning at the specified index number and returns the zero-based index of the prior matching Object.
removeAllElements()	Removes all elements from the Vector.
removeElement(Object)	Removes the specified Object from the Vector.
removeElementAt(int)	Removes the Object at the specified index.
setElementAt(Object, int)	Replaces the Object at the specified index with the specified Object.
setSize(int)	Sets the size of the Vector to the specified new size.
size()	Returns the number of elements currently in the Vector.
toString()	Returns a formatted string representing the contents of the Vector.
trimToSize()	Removes any excess capacity in the Vector by resizing it.

As an example of using Vector consider example class EX11F, shown in Listing 11.6. This example again uses a TextArea to display the results of various operations. In this example, a Vector, v1, is constructed. Initially, enough space is reserved for 10 elements and the Vector will increase its capacity by four whenever there is no room for a new element.

Listing 11.6. EX11F.java demonstrates the Vector class.

```java
import java.applet.*;
import java.awt.*;
import java.util.*;

public class EX11F extends Applet
{
    TextArea results = new TextArea(10, 75);

    public void init()
    {
        resize(500, 240);
        add(results);

        // create a new Vector to hold 10 elements
        // and to increase by 4 each time it's necessary
        Vector v1 = new Vector(10, 4);

        // add elements, both Integer and String, to the Vector
        v1.addElement(new Integer(1));
```

```
v1.addElement(new Integer(2));
v1.addElement(new Integer(3));
v1.addElement("Four");
v1.addElement(new Integer(5));

// display the entire Vector
results.appendText(v1.toString() + "\r\n");

// see if the Vector contains this Integer
if (v1.contains(new Integer(2)))
    results.appendText("It contains 2\r\n");

// see if the Vector contains this String
if (v1.contains("Four"))
    results.appendText("It contains Four\r\n");

// Display the capacity of the Vector
int capacity = v1.capacity();
results.appendText("Can hold " +
        String.valueOf(capacity) + "\r\n");

// Display the element at index number 3
results.appendText("ElementAt 3 = " +
        (String)v1.elementAt(3) + "\r\n");

// clear out the Vector
v1.removeAllElements();

// add the names of Pink Floyd's first five albums
v1.addElement("Piper At The Gates of Dawn");
v1.addElement("Saucerful of Secrets");
v1.addElement("Ummagumma");
v1.addElement("Meddle");
v1.addElement("The Dark Side of the Moon");

// use an enumeration to display each of the album titles
for (Enumeration enum = v1.elements();
        enum.hasMoreElements(); )
    results.appendText((String)enum.nextElement()+"\r\n");
    }

}
```

Initially, five elements—four integers and one string—are added to the Vector. This illustrates the capability to store objects of different types in the same Vector. Next, the toString method is used to display the entire Vector. This, along with the other messages displayed by EX11F, can be seen in Figure 11.4.

Next, the contains method is used to determine if the Vector contains the Integer 2 and the string "Four". The capacity of the Vector is then displayed and the item at index number three is retrieved and displayed. Because Vector is zero-based this will retrieve the fourth element in the Vector.

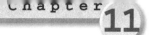

Figure 11.4.

The result of executing
EX11F.

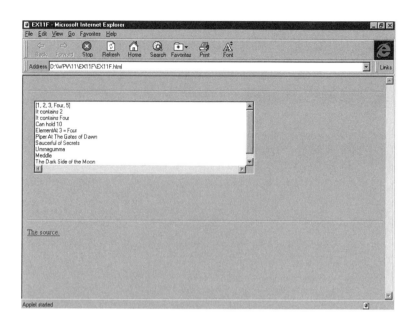

The method `removeAllElements` is then used to remove the current elements. The names of Pink Floyd's first five albums are then added to the `Vector`. Finally, the `elements` method is used to return an Enumeration of the elements. The `hasMoreElements` and `nextElement` method are used in a loop that displays each of the album titles.

The Stack Class

The `Stack` class extends `Vector` and implements a simple last-in-first-out stack. An item is stored on a stack by "pushing" it onto the stack. An item may subsequently be "popped" off the stack and used. The item popped off a stack will always be the most recently pushed item.

Because `Stack` extends the `Vector` class, no size is associated with a `Stack` instance. The `Stack` will continue to grow in size as new items are pushed onto it. In addition to methods to push and pop items, a `peek` method is provided for looking at the next item, a `search` method is provided for scanning the `Stack` for a specific item, and an `empty` method is provided determining whether more items are stored in the `Stack`.

The single constructor as well as the nonprivate methods of `Stack` are summarized in Table 11.12.

Table 11.12. Constructors and nonprivate methods of the Stack class.

Member	Purpose
Stack()	Creates a new Stack.
empty()	Returns true if the Stack is empty.
peek()	Returns the last Object added to the Stack but does not remove it from the Stack.
pop()	Returns the last Object added to the Stack and removes it.
push(Object)	Adds the specified Object to the Stack.
search(Object)	Searches for the specified Object in the Stack.

An example of using Stack is provided in example EX11G, shown in Listing 11.7. In this example a Stack is created and three items are added to it. The toString method is used to display the Stack's initial contents. The peek method is used to look at the last object added to the Stack but does not actually remove the object. Next, search is used to look for an occurrence of "2" within the Stack. Finally, pop is used to remove an object from the Stack and toString is used to redisplay its contents. The results of executing this applet are shown in Figure 11.5.

Listing 11.7. EX11G.java demonstrates the Stack class.

```java
import java.applet.*;
import java.awt.*;
import java.util.*;

public class EX11G extends Applet
{
    TextArea results = new TextArea(10, 30);

    public void init()
    {
        resize(320, 240);
        add(results);

        // create a new Stack
        Stack stk = new Stack();

        // add three items to the Stack
        stk.push("1");
        stk.push("2");
        stk.push("3");

        // display the entire Stack
        results.appendText("Stack=" + stk.toString() + "\r\n");

        // peek at what's next off the stack
        String str = (String)stk.peek();
        results.appendText("Peeked at: " + str + "\r\n");
```

continues

Listing 11.7. continued

```
        // see if there's a "2" anywhere in the Stack
        if (stk.search("2") != -1)
            results.appendText("Found 2\r\n");

        // pop an item off the Stack
        str = (String)stk.pop();
        results.appendText("Popped: " + str + "\r\n");

        // display the entire Stack
        results.appendText("Stack=" + stk.toString() + "\r\n");
    }
}
```

Figure 11.5.

The result of executing
EX11G.

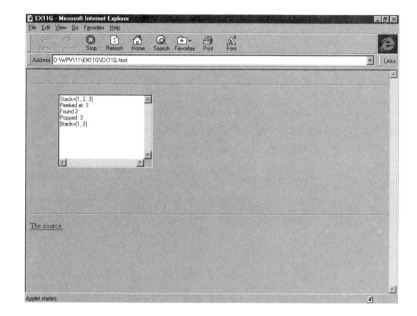

The StringTokenizer Class

A StringTokenizer can be used to parse a string into its constituent tokens. For example, each word in a sentence could be considered a token. However, the StringTokenizer class goes beyond the parsing of sentences. You can create a fully customized tokenizer by specifying the set of token delimiters when the StringTokenizer is created. For parsing text, the default whitespace delimiters are usually sufficient. However, you could use the set of arithmetic operators (+, *, /, and -) if parsing an expression.

The delimiter characters can be specified when a new StringTokenizer object is constructed. Table 11.13 summarizes the three available constructors. Examples of using these constructors are the following:

```
StringTokenizer st1 = new StringTokenizer("A stream of words");
StringTokenizer st2 = new StringTokenizer("4*3/2-1+4", "*+/-", true);
StringTokenizer st3 = new StringTokenizer("aaa,bbbb,ccc", ",");
```

In the first example, the st1 StringTokenizer will be constructed using the supplied string and the default delimiters. The default delimiters are the space, tab, newline, and carriage return characters. These delimiters are useful when parsing text, as with st1. The second example constructs a StringTokenizer for tokenizing arithmetic expressions using the *, +, /, and - symbols as supplied. Finally, the third StringTokenizer, st3, will tokenize the supplied string using only the comma character as a delimiter.

Table 11.13. Constructors for the StringTokenizer class.

Constructor	Purpose
StringTokenizer(String)	Creates a new StringTokenizer based on the specified string to be tokenized.
StringTokenizer(String, String)	Creates a new StringTokenizer based on the specified string to be tokenized and set of delimiters.
StringTokenizer(String,String,boolean)	Creates a new StringTokenizer based on the specified string to be tokenized, set of delimiters, and a flag that indicates if delimiters should be returned as tokens.

Because StringTokenizer implements the enumeration interface it includes the hasMoreElements and nextElement methods. Additionally, the methods hasMoreTokens and nextToken are provided and perform the same operations. The nonprivate methods of StringTokenizer are summarized in Table 11.14.

Table 11.14. Nonprivate methods of the StringTokenizer class.

Method	Purpose
countTokens()	Returns the number of remaining tokens.
hasMoreElements()	Returns true if there are more elements in the string being tokenized. It is identical to hasMoreTokens.
hasMoreTokens()	Returns true if there are more tokens in the string being tokenized. It is identical to hasMoreElements.

continues

Table 11.14. continued

Method	*Purpose*
nextElement()	Returns the next element in the string. It is identical to nextToken.
nextToken()	Returns the next token in the string. It is identical to nextElement.
nextToken(String)	Changes the set of delimiters to the specified string and then returns the next token in the string.

Class EX11H is an example of how to use the StringTokenizer class and is shown in Listing 11.8. In this example two StringTokenizer objects are created. The first, st1, is used to parse an arithmetic expression. The second, st2, parses a line of comma-delimited fields. For both tokenizers, hasMoreTokens and nextToken are used to iterate through the set of tokens, displaying each token in a TextArea. The results of executing EX11H are shown in Figure 11.6.

Figure 11.6.

The result of executing EX11H.

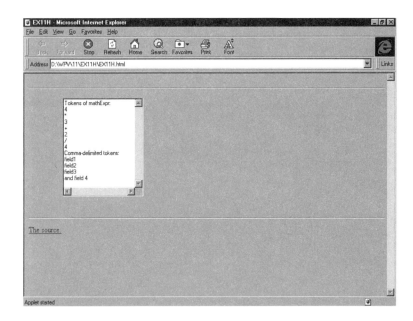

Listing 11.8. EX11H.java demonstrates the StringTokenizer class.

```
import java.applet.*;
import java.awt.*;
import java.util.*;

public class EX11H extends Applet
{
    TextArea results = new TextArea(14, 25);
```

```
public void init()
{
    resize(320, 240);
    add(results);

    // put an arithmetic expression in a string
    // and create a tokenizer for the string
    String mathExpr = "4*3+2/4";
    StringTokenizer st1 = new StringTokenizer(mathExpr,
            "*+/-", true);

    // while there are tokens left, display each token
    results.appendText("Tokens of mathExpr:\r\n");
    while (st1.hasMoreTokens())
        results.appendText(st1.nextToken() + "\r\n");

    // create a String of comma-delimited fields
    // and create a tokenizer for the string
    String commas = "field1,field2,field3,and field 4";
    StringTokenizer st2=new StringTokenizer(commas,",",false);

    // while there are tokens left, display each token
    results.appendText("Comma-delimited tokens:\r\n");
    while (st2.hasMoreTokens())
        results.appendText(st2.nextToken() + "\r\n");
    }
}
```

Summary

This chapter gave you a thorough overview of the classes in the java.util package. You learned how to use the BitSet class to store large amounts of Boolean data, how to manipulate dates and times with the Date class, how to generate random numbers, and how to tokenize strings. You learned how the Observable class works in conjunction with the Observer interface to allow you to decouple your code. The Hashtable class was described and you learned how the Properties class can be used in applications to stream data to and from files. Finally, you learned how the Vector class can be used as a resizable array and how the Stack class extends Vector.

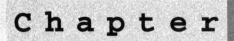

Chapter

12

Moving Up to Multithreading

- Threads
- ThreadGroups

Multithreading means that a program is divided into separate processes, each of which is then executed individually, but simultaneously. Operating systems use multiprocessing, wherein each program being executed can be thought of as an individual process. When a program is divided, each process is commonly referred to as a thread. The difference between multiprocessing on an operating system level and multiprocessing on a program level is that threads of a program are executed in the same program space. Thus, all threads of a program have access to the same variables and memory space.

This chapter covers how to use the Thread class to execute tasks simultaneously by declaring threads that perform specific tasks. The task executed by the thread can either be part of the applet, with the implementation of the run method, or by declaring a Thread-derived class. This chapter shows how these tasks can communicate effectively with each other. In addition, threads can be grouped and prioritized using the ThreadGroup class.

Threads

Threads are very useful in doing a number of tasks simultaneously. Long or involved processing is typically off-loaded to a thread so that the normal processing can occur with the user. This off-loaded processing can include loading an image into memory to be displayed immediately, queuing up potentially displayable images, playing audio, or any other task that can happen asynchronously to the user's actions. In fact, among other system threads is the garbage collecting thread that takes care of freeing unused memory.

Threads are implemented in Java using the Runnable interface. One of the most difficult concepts to handle when working with threaded applications is to control access to critical sections of code. With Java, this support is built directly into the language with synchronization. Since synchronization is a blocking process, additional functionality is provided to control the locks implemented by the synchronization.

Runnable and Threads

The basis for threads in Java is the Runnable interface, which simply consists of a single method:

```
public interface Runnable
{
    public abstract void run();
}
```

There are two ways to create user-defined threads in an applet: implementing the Runnable interface in a class and passing an instance of the Runnable object to an instance of the Thread class, or deriving from the Thread class. Deriving from the Thread class is a viable option because the Thread class is itself a Runnable object.

Implementing the Runnable interface requires the addition of a single function to a class. Consider the following class implementing the Runnable interface:

```
class MyApplet extends Applet implements Runnable
{
    protected Thread myOtherPersonality;

    public void init()
    {
        myOtherPersonality = new Thread(this);
    }

    public void run()
    {
        // this is where my other personality takes over
        ...
    }
}
```

This Applet-derived class creates a new thread in the init method, passing the instance of the applet to the thread. Therefore, the thread will use the run method of the applet.

Alternately, deriving from the Thread class involves overriding the run method. Here is the same example implemented with a class derived from Thread:

```
class MyApplet extends Applet
{
    protected MyThread myOtherPersonality;

    public void init()
    {
        myOtherPersonality = new MyThread();
    }
}

class MyThread extends Thread
{
    public void run()
    {
        // this is where my other personality takes over
        ...
    }
}
```

The run method was moved from the Applet class to the MyThread class.

These classes show only the basic differences between the two implementations. However, this example does use the Thread constructor that takes a Runnable object as a parameter. Table 12.1 shows all of the Thread constructors that do not take a ThreadGroup instance in the constructor. Constructors involving ThreadGroups will be covered in a later section.

Table 12.1. Public constructors of the Thread class callable without a ThreadGroup.

Member	Purpose
Thread()	Creates a thread with a default name.
Thread(Runnable)	Creates a thread, with a default name, that will call the Runnable object's run method.
Thread(Runnable, String)	Creates a named thread that will call the Runnable object's run method.
Thread(String)	Creates a named thread.

The execution of a thread consists of three distinct parts: start, run, and stop. Every thread must be started using the Thread.start method. Once this method is called, the Java Virtual Machine calls the appropriate run method. The intent of the run method is that it will run until either the thread is interrupted, or the thread runs to completion. Thread.stop is used to stop a thread. Table 12.2 shows the methods used to control the execution of a thread.

Table 12.2. Thread methods used to control execution.

Member	Purpose
resume()	Resumes execution of a thread after it has been suspended.
run()	Contains the code to be executed while the thread is running.
start()	Starts execution of a thread.
stop()	Stops execution of a thread.
stop(Throwable)	Uses the throwable object to stop the execution of a thread.
suspend()	Momentarily stops the execution of a thread. To restart the thread, call the resume method.

The typical methods in which threads are started and stopped are Applet.start and Applet.stop. Threads should be started and stopped in these locations so that when a page is exited, the threads associated with the applet are also stopped.

Additional functionality can also be found in the Thread class. Table 12.3 shows the remainder of the public methods of the Thread class.

Table 12.3. Additional public methods of the `Thread` class.

Member	Purpose
activeCount()	Returns the number of active threads in the current thread's `ThreadGroup` instance.
checkAccess()	Checks that permissions are granted for the current thread to modify this thread.
countStackFrames()	Returns the number of stack frames associated with this thread.
currentThread()	Returns the currently active thread.
destroy()	A destructive way to destroy the thread.
dumpStack()	Dumps the stack trace for the thread.
enumerate(Thread [])	Copies the currently active threads of the group the thread is part of to the array.
getName()	Returns the name of the thread.
getPriority()	Returns the current priority of the thread.
getThreadGroup()	Returns the `ThreadGroup` instance associated with the thread.
interrupt()	Sends an interrupt to the thread.
interrupted()	Returns if the thread has been interrupted.
isAlive()	Returns if the thread is active (that is, has not been stopped).
isDaemon()	Returns if the thread has the `Daemon` flag set.
isInterrupted()	Returns if the thread has been interrupted.
join()	Waits for the termination of the thread.
join(long)	Waits for the termination of the thread, but waits only for the specified number of milliseconds.
join(long, int)	Waits for the termination of the thread, but waits only for the specified number of milliseconds plus an additional number of nanoseconds.
setDaemon(boolean)	Marks the thread as a `Daemon` thread. When there are only `Daemon` threads running, Java will exit.
setName(String)	Sets the name of the thread.
setPriority(int)	Attempts to set the priority of the thread, making sure permissions are correct and that the `ThreadGroup` allows it.
sleep(long)	Causes the current thread to sleep for the specified number of milliseconds.
sleep(long, int)	Causes the current thread to sleep for the specified number of milliseconds plus an additional number of nanoseconds.
toString()	Returns a string representation of the thread.
yield()	Yields execution to other waiting threads.

A Runnable Object Example

Figure 12.1 shows EX12A, an example of using the Runnable implementation.

Figure 12.1.

EX12A.

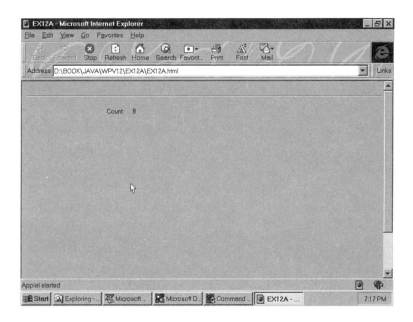

This example uses a thread to count from 10 down to 0 at one-second increments, resets the count, and repeats this cycle. Listing 12.1 shows the code for EX12A.

Listing 12.1. Listing of EX12A.

```java
import java.applet.*;
import java.awt.*;

public class EX12A extends Applet implements Runnable
{
    protected Thread CounterThread;
    protected Label CountLabel;
    protected int count = 10;

    public void init()
    {
        // provide something to look at
        add(new Label("Count:"));
        CountLabel = new Label(Integer.toString(count));
        add(CountLabel);
    }

    public void start()
    {
```

```
        if (CounterThread == null) {
            // allocate the thread, using the local run method
            CounterThread = new Thread(this);
            CounterThread.start();
        }
    }

    public void stop()
    {
        if (CounterThread != null) {
            // stop the thread
            CounterThread.stop();
            CounterThread = null;
        }
    }

    public void run()
    {
        while (true) {
            try {
                Thread.sleep(1000);
            }
            catch (InterruptedException e) {}

            CountDown();
        }
    }

    protected void CountDown()
    {
        count--;

        CountLabel.setText(Integer.toString(count));

        if (count == 0)
            // reset to 11 since the first call will move it back
            //    down to 10 and then display
            count = 11;
    }
}
```

In this example, the init method adds a label that acts as a prompt and a label that will hold the decrementing count.

The Applet.start method, which is called by the browser to tell the applet to start executing, checks to see if a thread has been allocated. If it hasn't, the thread is allocated, passing the applet instance in the constructor so that the local run method will be called and started.

Once the thread is started, the run method will be called. The run method consists of an infinite loop. The first step inside the loop is a little nap. The Thread.sleep method stops execution of the thread for the specified number of milliseconds. Passing a value of 1000 thus produces a delay of one second. During this time, the thread is simply stopped. Note that because the sleep method has the potential of causing a deadlock situation, because no locks are released for the thread while sleeping, this function has the potential of throwing InterruptedException. The next step inside the run method is to call CountDown().

CountDown() decrements the applet's count variable, displays the count in the label, and resets the count if necessary.

Lastly, the stop method takes care of stopping the thread. A check is done to make sure that the thread was allocated. If successful, the thread is stopped and the thread set back to null. Setting of the thread to null accomplishes two things: It allows the garbage collector to free the unused memory and it allows the start method to start another thread the next time the page is activated.

NOTE:

Java actually guarantees that the start and stop methods of Applet will be called in the proper order. Therefore the checking of the existence of the thread in EX12A is unnecessary, but is included to show code completeness.

Suspend and Resume

Another option, instead of having the Thread instances come and go, is to use the suspend and resume methods of the Thread class:

```
public final void suspend()
public final void resume()
```

These methods provide the same effect as starting and stopping the thread, but do not incur the overhead of creating and destroying the Thread instance. Example EX12B extends the EX12A example by placing two buttons on the applet that gives the user the ability to suspend the countdown and then resume it. Figure 12.2 shows the new example.

Only two methods were modified to create EX12B. Listing 12.2 shows the init method of the applet.

Listing 12.2. init method of EX12B.

```
public void init()
{
    // gives us some control over where the controls are
    //    to be placed
    setLayout(new BorderLayout());

    // provide some control over the count
    Panel p = new Panel();
    p.add(SuspendButton);
    p.add(ResumeButton);
    add("North", p);

    // provide a visual of the count
```

```
    p = new Panel();
    p.add(new Label("Count:"));
    CountLabel = new Label(Integer.toString(count));
    p.add(CountLabel);
    add("Center", p);
}
```

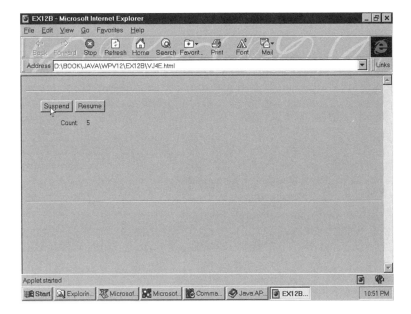

This method now uses a BorderLayout instance so that the buttons and labels will be located next to each other. To support this, the buttons and labels were each added to a panel, which is then added to the applet. For more information about layout managers, see Chapter 5, "Java's User Interface Components."

Listing 12.3 shows the action method of EX12B, which shows what occurs when the buttons are pressed.

Listing 12.3. action method of EX12B.

```
public boolean action(Event evt, Object arg)
{
    boolean retval = false;             // assume event not processed

    if (evt.target == SuspendButton) {
        if (CounterThread != null)
            CounterThread.suspend();

        retval = true;
    }
    else if (evt.target == ResumeButton) {
```

Listing 12.3. continued

```
        if (CounterThread != null)
            CounterThread.resume();

        retval = true;
    }

    return retval;
}
```

If the suspend button is pressed and the thread exists, the suspend method is called. This stops the execution of the run method and thus the countdown. If the resume button is then pressed, resume is called for the thread and execution will continue.

CAUTION:

Be careful and courteous when using the suspend and resume methods of the Thread class instead of allocating and destroying a Thread instance. If you only suspend a thread when leaving a Web page, the thread is still in existence, just not being used. And, in fact, you may never get back to the page with the suspended thread. This is essentially a memory leak that takes processing capabilities away from subsequent operations.

Synchronization

So far, problems with accessing the data in the various threads have not been discussed. And, in fact, the examples have not been thread-safe. Every function that has been called has made the modifications to the variables as needed, without regard to the possibility that another thread may be in the process of changing the values too. To solve this problem, Java has built into the language synchronization support.

Java's Synchronization

Synchronization is the capability of a thread to provide a locking mechanism on an object so that a critical section of code can be executed without the fear of being interrupted, or interleaved with another thread making modifications to the same data. Every object in Java has a built-in lock. This is used by the synchronized keyword to provide access to code by only a single thread.

synchronized can be used in two different ways. The first is around a block of code. The syntax of a synchronized block takes the form

```
synchronized(object_reference) {
    code_block
}
```

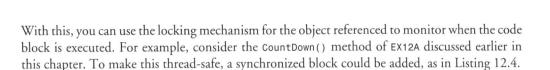

With this, you can use the locking mechanism for the object referenced to monitor when the code block is executed. For example, consider the CountDown() method of EX12A discussed earlier in this chapter. To make this thread-safe, a synchronized block could be added, as in Listing 12.4.

Listing 12.4. The CountDown() method from EX12A with a synchronized block.

```
protected void CountDown()
{
    // use the lock in the EX12A class to control access
    synchronized(this) {
        count--;

        CountLabel.setText(Integer.toString(count));

        if (count == 0)
            // reset to 11 since the first call will move it back
            //    down to 10 and then display
            count = 11;
    }
}
```

The second form of synchronization is applied to entire methods. This is accomplished by placing the synchronized modifier in the method declaration. Listing 12.5 shows the same method as a synchronized method.

Listing 12.5. A synchronized CountDown() method from EX12A.

```
protected synchronized void CountDown()
{
    count--;
z
    CountLabel.setText(Integer.toString(count));

    if (count == 0)
        // reset to 11 since the first call will move it back
        //    down to 10 and then display
        count = 11;
}
```

This method of synchronization is probably more common due to its ease of readability.

Synchronization Example

To make use of the synchronization method, the working example will be extended so that the maximum value of the countdown can be modified by the user. Figure 12.3 shows the interface to example EX12C.

To accomplish the transition to a thread-safe applet, only a couple of modifications had to be made to the code of EX12B to produce EX12C.

A new control, MaxCountTextField, was added to the applet to collect the new starting point for the count. This field was added, along with the prompt for the field in the init method:

```
protected TextField MaxCountTextField;
protected int maxCount = 10;
protected int count = maxCount;

public void init()
{

    ...

    // let the user set the max count
    p = new Panel();
    p.add(new Label("Enter the starting point:"));
    MaxCountTextField = new TextField(Integer.toString(maxCount), 3);
    p.add(MaxCountTextField);
    add("South", p);
}
```

Figure 12.3.

EX12C.

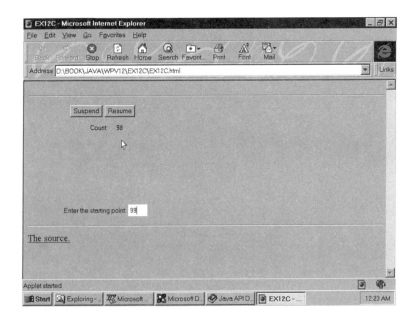

A new else clause was added to the action method to handle when the user pressed Return after entering a new maximum value. This handler calls SetMaxCount to read that information and reset the count. These methods are shown in Listing 12.6.

Listing 12.6. action and SetMaxCount methods of EX12C.

```
public boolean action(Event evt, Object arg)
    {
```

```
        boolean retval = false;           // assume event not processed

    if (evt.target == SuspendButton) {
        if (CounterThread != null)
            CounterThread.suspend();

        retval = true;
    }
    else if (evt.target == ResumeButton) {
        if (CounterThread != null)
            CounterThread.resume();

        retval = true;
    }
    else if (evt.target == MaxCountTextField) {
        SetMaxCount();

        retval = true;
    }

    return retval;
}

protected synchronized void SetMaxCount()
{
    try {
        maxCount = Integer.parseInt(MaxCountTextField.getText());

        count = maxCount + 1;
    }
    catch (NumberFormatException e)
    {
        // reset the contents back to the current max
        MaxCountTextField.setText(Integer.toString(maxCount));
    }
}
```

Because both the countdown thread of the applet and the user portion of the applet modify the contents of the count variable, it is very important that the program blocks simultaneous modifications of count. Therefore CountDown is now a synchronized method:

```
protected synchronized void CountDown()
{
    count--;

    CountLabel.setText(Integer.toString(count));

    if (count == 0)
        // reset to maxCount + 1 since the first call will
        //    move it back down to maxCount and then display
        count = maxCount + 1;
}
```

In addition, since the SetMaxCount resets the current count, it is also a synchronized method, as shown in Listing 12.6.

Wait and Notify

Synchronization provides a mechanism to lock execution of a single thread through a critical section. However, there are times when a thread is in a critical section but control needs to be given up for other threads to process, even though the critical section has not been completed. This can be accomplished with the wait and notify methods. These methods are not in the Thread class, as you might suspect. Instead, they are in the Object class. This is because they deal directly with the locking mechanism, which also happens to be in the Object class.

There are three versions of the wait method:

```
public final void wait()
public final void wait(long)
public final void wait(long, int)
```

The first version waits until the thread is interrupted or until a notify method is called for the object. The next version is similar to the first in that it waits, but will be automatically notified if the specified time-out elapses before the thread is notified. The last version is very similar to the second, except that the time-out period can be specified in finer increments. These functions must be called in a synchronized block or method that has previously obtained a lock on the object. If that is not the case, an exception of the type IllegalMonitorStateException will be thrown. Note that all three of these functions release the lock on the object before going to sleep. Therefore, if the thread is notified, the lock must be re-obtained on the object before the thread continues.

To wake a waiting object, one of the two notify methods should be called:

```
public final void notify()
public final void notifyAll()
```

notify wakes up a single thread that is waiting on an object. However, if there is more than a single thread waiting on an object, there is no guarantee that the first object that called wait will be the first object notified. In cases where there are more than a single thread waiting on an object, notifyAll can be used to wake up all of the threads waiting. Once a thread is awakened, processing resumes at the point immediately after the point where the wait method was called.

CAUTION:

When using the wait and notify methods, make sure to take into account that the object locks are released while the thread is waiting. Therefore, another thread can easily modify class variables before the thread is notified. Consider the following simple example:

```
class BadAssumption
{
    int n;

    public synchronized void DoSomething()
    {
        n = 5;

        // do other processing here
```

```
        wait();

        // do other processing here

        // allocate 5 strings
        Strings [] myStrings = new Strings[n];
    }
}
```
Even though the DoSomething is a synchronized method, there is no guarantee that n will still contain a value of 5 when myStrings is allocated.

ThreadGroups

Threads allow programs to be separated into processes. To add a little control to the creation of processes, Java provides the ability to group threads. This functionality is contained in the ThreadGroup class. In addition to the basic grouping ability, the ThreadGroup class provides functionality to set priorities and is the basis for the security concepts of Java programming.

Using ThreadGroups

ThreadGroups are used to group related threads together. They also have the ability to group threads with other ThreadGroups. The net result is that hierarchical trees can be generated with ThreadGroups.

There are two constructors for the ThreadGroup class:

```
public ThreadGroup(String)
public ThreadGroup(ThreadGroup, String)
```

Because an instance of the ThreadGroup is a node of a tree, every node has a parent ThreadGroup. The first constructor creates a named ThreadGroup, whose parent is the ThreadGroup of the currently executing thread. The second constructor creates a named ThreadGroup, setting the parent to be the passed-in ThreadGroup.

To create a thread in a ThreadGroup, one of the Thread constructors shown in Table 12.4 must be used.

Table 12.4. Public constructors of the Thread class used to place a thread into a ThreadGroup.

Member	Purpose
Thread(ThreadGroup, Runnable)	Creates a thread in the ThreadGroup, with a default name, that will call the Runnable object's run method.

continues

Table 12.4. continued

Member	Purpose
Thread(ThreadGroup, Runnable, String)	Creates a named thread in the ThreadGroup that will call the Runnable object's run method.
Thread(ThreadGroup, String)	Creates a named thread in the ThreadGroup.

One advantage of using a ThreadGroup is that there are several functions that can be called for the ThreadGroup that are recursively applied to all threads contained within the ThreadGroup. Table 12.5 contains a summary of these methods.

Table 12.5. Public methods of ThreadGroup that are applied recursively to contained threads.

Member	Purpose
resume()	Resumes all processes in the ThreadGroup.
stop()	Stops all processes in the ThreadGroup.
suspend()	Suspends all processes in the ThreadGroup.

Table 12.6 contains other public methods of the ThreadGroup class.

Table 12.6. Additional public methods of the ThreadGroup class.

Member	Purpose
activeCount()	Returns the number of active threads in the current ThreadGroup and all offspring.
activeGroupCount()	Returns the number of active ThreadGroups in the current ThreadGroup and all offspring.
checkAccess()	Determines whether the current thread has permissions to modify this ThreadGroup.
enumerate(Thread [])	Returns a list of the active threads in the ThreadGroup.
enumerate(Thread [], boolean)	Returns a list of the active threads in the ThreadGroup; optionally traverses ThreadGroup tree recursively.
enumerate(ThreadGroup [])	Returns a list of active groups.
enumerate(ThreadGroup [], boolean)	Returns a list of active groups; optionally traverses ThreadGroup tree recursively.
getMaxPriority()	Returns the highest priority in group.
getName()	Returns the name.

Member	Purpose
getParent()	Returns parent ThreadGroup.
isDaemon()	Returns Daemon flag.
parentOf(ThreadGroup)	Returns if the current ThreadGroup is an ancestor of the argument.
setDaemon(boolean)	Sets the Daemon flag.
setMaxPriority()	Sets the highest possible priority this ThreadGroup can have.
toString()	Returns a string representation of this ThreadGroup.
uncaughtException(Thread, Throwable)	Called by Java Virtual Machine when an exception does not get caught by a contained thread.

Priority

Every thread can have an associated priority. This priority determines how often the thread gets serviced. To set the priority, the following method in Thread is used:

```
public void setPriority(int)
```

The parameter of this function can be one of the following three values defined in Thread:

```
MAX_PRIORITY
NORM_PRIORITY
MIN_PRIORITY
```

In general, threads within ThreadGroups will all have the same priority, since similar tasks will normally have the same priority. The following methods in ThreadGroup support this functionality:

```
public int getMaxPriority()
public void setMaxPriority(int)
```

ThreadGroups Example

Figure 12.4 shows a sample program using ThreadGroups.

This example uses two ThreadGroups; each of them has a number of threads drawing a polygon on the applet. Additional support is provided to start and stop the drawing via buttons on the applet. Listing 12.6 shows the DrawThread class used in example EX12D.

Figure 12.4.

EX12D.

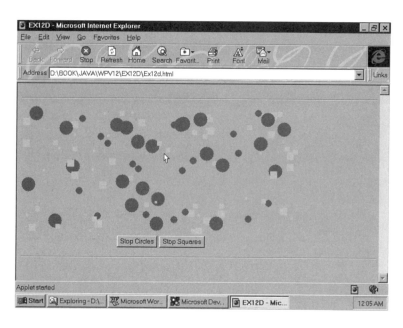

Listing 12.6. DrawThread class of EX12D.

```java
class DrawThread extends Thread
{
    protected static Graphics g;
    protected static Random r = new Random();
    protected int totalWidth, totalHeight;
    protected int count;

    public static void SetGraphics(Graphics _g)
    {
        g = _g;
    }

    public DrawThread(ThreadGroup group, int totalWidth,
            int totalHeight, int count)
    {
        super(group, Integer.toString(count));

        this.totalWidth = totalWidth;
        this.totalHeight = totalHeight;
        this.count = count;
    }

    public void run()
    {
        while (true) {
            try {
                sleep(GetNextRandom(4, 1) * 1000);
            }
            catch (InterruptedException e) {}

            if (g != null)
```

```
                    Draw(g, GetNextRandom(totalWidth, 0),
                            GetNextRandom(totalHeight, 0));
        }
    }

    protected synchronized int GetNextRandom(int range, int offset)
    {
        return (int)(r.nextDouble() * (double)range) + offset;
    }

    protected void Draw(Graphics g, int x, int y)
    {
    }
}
```

DrawThread is the superclass for two classes: DrawCircleThread and DrawSquareThread. The classes do what their names imply.

The base class takes a ThreadGroup in the constructor. This ThreadGroup is used to hold common threads drawing similar polygons. In addition, the constructor takes some configuration parameters for where the polygon can be drawn. run is overridden in the Thread class and contains an infinite loop. Inside the loop, the thread first goes to sleep for 1 to 5 seconds. Notice that all threads use the same random number generator. Therefore, GetNextRandom is a synchronized method. The last step in the run method is to call Draw to draw a polygon at a random location on the applet.

The DrawCircleThread and DrawSquareThread classes exist only to draw their respective polygons. Notice again that since the Graphics instance is being changed by the Draw methods, these methods must be synchronized:

```
class DrawCircleThread extends DrawThread
{
    protected final static int graphicsSize = 30;

    public DrawCircleThread(ThreadGroup group, int totalWidth,
            int totalHeight, int count)
    {
        super(group, totalWidth - graphicsSize,
                totalHeight - graphicsSize, count);
    }

    protected synchronized void Draw(Graphics g, int x, int y)
    {
        g.setColor(Color.red);
        g.fillOval(x, y, graphicsSize / count, graphicsSize / count);
    }
}

class DrawSquareThread extends DrawThread
{
    protected final static int graphicsSize = 5;

    public DrawSquareThread(ThreadGroup group, int totalWidth,
            int totalHeight, int count)
    {
```

```
        super(group, totalWidth - graphicsSize,
                totalHeight - graphicsSize, count);
    }

    protected synchronized void Draw(Graphics g, int x, int y)
    {
        g.setColor(Color.green);
        g.fillRect(x, y, graphicsSize * count, graphicsSize * count);
    }
}
```

Listing 12.7 shows the applet using the above threads.

Listing 12.7. Applet class of EX12D.

```
import java.applet.*;
import java.awt.*;
import java.util.*;

public class EX12D extends Applet
{
    protected Panel p = new Panel();
    protected Button CircleButton = new Button("Stop Circles");
    protected Button SquareButton = new Button("Stop Squares");
    protected ThreadGroup Circles = new ThreadGroup("Circles");
    protected ThreadGroup Squares = new ThreadGroup("Squares");

    public void init()
    {
        setLayout(new BorderLayout());

        p.add(CircleButton);
        p.add(SquareButton);
        add("South", p);
    }

    public boolean action(Event evt, Object obj)
    {
        boolean result = false;          // asume no action

        if ("Start Circles".equals(obj)) {
            Circles.resume();
            CircleButton.setLabel("Stop Circles");

            result = true;
        }
        else if ("Stop Circles".equals(obj)) {
            Circles.suspend();
            CircleButton.setLabel("Start Circles");

            result = true;
        }
        else if ("Start Squares".equals(obj)) {
            Squares.resume();
            SquareButton.setLabel("Stop Squares");

            result = true;
        }
```

```
        else if ("Stop Squares".equals(obj)) {
            Squares.suspend();
            SquareButton.setLabel("Start Squares");

            result = true;
        }

        return result;
    }

    public void start()
    {
        DrawThread.SetGraphics(getGraphics());

        // add two circle threads
        for (int count = 1; count <= 2; count++)
            (new DrawCircleThread(Circles, size().width,
                    size().height - p.size().height,
                    count)).start();

        // add three square threads
        for (int count = 1; count <= 3; count++)
            (new DrawSquareThread(Squares, size().width,
                    size().height - p.size().height,
                    count)).start();
    }

    public void stop()
    {
        Circles.stop();
        Squares.stop();
    }
}
```

The init method of the applet places the components needed onto the applet. action takes care of processing the button clicks. ThreadGroup.suspend and ThreadGroup.resume are used to start and stop the display of all of the same types of polygons at once.

start allocates all of the threads being used in the applet, adding them to the appropriate ThreadGroups. stop simply calls the ThreadGroup function to stop all threads.

Summary

In this chapter, threads were explored. Threads can be created by either implementing the Runnable interface or by deriving a class from the Thread class. Once the threads are created, synchronization issues need to be addressed. This is accomplished by using synchronized blocks or synchronized methods around critical sections that modify class variables. ThreadGroups can then be used to logically group threads together to form logical groupings and later will be used to create hierarchical trees that help with Java security.

Chapter 13

Using Java Streams

- What Is a Stream?

- Abstract Stream Classes—InputStream and OutputStream

- Byte Array and String Streams

- File Streams

- Filter Streams

- Pipe Streams

Java includes a well-designed collection of stream classes and interfaces that make up most of the java.io package. This chapter describes several uses for streams and how to take advantage of them in your Java applets and applications. Because streams in Java are an integral part of network programming, this chapter will establish a foundation that is built upon in Part IV, "Networking with Java."

What Is a Stream?

At the heart of every computer program is the concept of exchanging data between two or more sources. This can be as simple as reading data from or writing data to a buffer within the same program or as seemingly complex as transferring data between two different processes running on different systems located on opposite sides of the world. The sources and destinations of data transfer are also diverse. On the typical personal computer, input devices include the keyboard and mouse, whereas output devices include the monitor and printer. Devices capable of both input and output include the disk drive, modem, and network interface card.

Streams were created to abstract the concept of exchanging information between these various devices and provide a consistent interface for programmers to interact with different sources of I/O in their programs. The basic idea of a stream is that data enters one end of a data channel in a particular sequence and comes out the other end in the same sequence—a first-in-first-out (FIFO) scheme. The very nature of streams is a perfect match for an object-oriented language such as Java. In addition, the built-in Java stream classes can be extended through inheritance to provide the same operations as those used for the primitive data types for your own user-defined types.

NOTE:

Depending on the capability of the source or destination of a stream to process the data being requested or written in a timely manner, your program might encounter situations where it has to wait for a device to process a request. This side effect of stream processing is known as blocking and most often occurs when hardware devices are involved, such as disk drives or network connections. The good news is that Java's stream classes and methods were designed with blocking in mind. The effects of blocking are mitigated by checking the stream for blocking before reading or writing, using buffers or caches, or running stream I/O requests in threads so that blocking does not affect the rest of your program.

Abstract Stream Classes—InputStream and OutputStream

Java's implementation of streams begins with two abstract classes: InputStream and OutputStream. All specialized streams for input and output operations are derived from these two classes. In addition, java.io includes a few interfaces and support classes that as a group provide a powerful framework for your streaming needs.

InputStream

InputStream includes several methods that provide the basic input needs for all the input streams to come. Each of the read() methods extract one or more bytes of data from the stream and move the current position in the stream along according to how many bytes are read. Each read() and skip() method will also block until at least some data is available to process. Table 13.1 lists the name and a brief description of each public method.

Table 13.1. Public methods of InputStream.

Method	Description
int read()	Reads a single byte of data from the stream. The return value is the byte read as an int or –1 if the end of the stream was reached.
int read(byte[])	Reads data into an array of bytes. The number of bytes read is determined by the length of the byte array passed as an argument. The return value is the number of bytes read or –1 if the end of the stream was reached.
int read(byte[], int, int)	Reads data into an array of bytes starting at a specific location in the array for a certain number of bytes. The return value is the number of bytes read or –1 if the end of the stream was reached.
long skip(long)	Jumps over the specified number of bytes in the stream. The actual number of bytes skipped is returned from this method. Note that this implementation of skip() casts the long passed as a parameter to an int before the skip is performed. It is the job of derived classes to override the default implementation to support skipping larger increments.

continues

Table 13.1. continued

Method	Description
int available()	Returns the number of bytes that can be read without blocking.
mark(int)	Positions a placeholder at the current position in the stream that can be returned to later by calling reset() and sets the maximum number of bytes that can be read before the mark is invalidated. Because not all input streams support marking, markSupported() should be called first to determine whether marking is supported by the current input stream if the type of stream is unknown at runtime.
boolean markSupported()	Returns an indication of the current input stream's capability to support marking.
reset()	Returns the current position in the stream to the location set in the previous call to mark(). If the number of bytes read since the last mark() has exceeded the limit, an IOException is thrown.
close()	Closes the input stream and releases any resources allocated by the stream.

NOTE:

Many of the methods in the java.io package throw exceptions when problems arise. Most stream exceptions are of the IOException variety, a class derived from Exception, which is used exclusively by java.io. Four other exception classes derived from IOException provide more specific types of exceptions. All the InputStream methods except mark() and markSupported() throw an IOException when I/O errors occur.

OutputStream

Like InputStream, the abstract class OutputStream provides the fundamental methods used by all its derived stream classes. Also like the InputStream read() methods, the write() methods will block until the data is actually written to the output object or device. An IOException is thrown if any of the OutputStream methods encounter an error. Table 13.2 lists the name and a brief description of each public method.

Table 13.2. Public methods of OutputStream.

Method	Description
write(int)	Writes a single byte to the stream.
write(byte[])	Writes the entire length of an array of bytes to the stream.
write(byte[], int, int)	Writes a portion of an array of bytes starting at a specific location in the array for a certain number of bytes.
flush()	If the output stream is buffered, this method will force any bytes in the buffer to be written to the stream.
close()	Closes the output stream and releases any resources allocated by the stream.

Byte Array and String Streams

Now that we have covered the primary base classes used by input and output streams, let's cover some concrete stream classes. First we'll discuss the input and output streams that can be used with objects in memory, byte arrays, and String objects.

ByteArrayInputStream

Derived from InputStream, a ByteArrayInputStream object allows you to perform input stream style operations on an ordinary byte array. This can be valuable when you are working with a sequence of data in the form of a byte array and want to read single or multiple bytes, skip, or jump around within the array. Using streams in this fashion extends the built-in array access methods of subscripting by providing a more powerful and flexible framework.

ByteArrayInputStream offers two constructors: one that takes a byte array as a parameter and the other that accepts a byte array, an offset to the first byte to start reading, and the length of the byte array as parameters.

> **NOTE:**
>
> ByteArrayInputStream internally stores a reference to the byte array passed to the constructor as well as the length of the array. Therefore, the byte array is not duplicated within ByteArrayInputStream. However, be aware that any changes made directly to the byte array used by the ByteArrayInputStream will also affect the stream. Also, marking is not supported by this class, but the reset() method will reposition the stream to the beginning of the array.

The sample Java application found in Listing 13.1 illustrates how a byte array can be accessed as an input stream and the effect of manipulating the byte array after the ByteArrayInputStream object has been created.

Listing 13.1. EX13A.java.

```java
import java.io.*;

class EX13A
{
    void printInputStream(InputStream s)
    {
        try
        {
            System.out.print("[");
            while (s.available() > 0)
            {
                System.out.print(s.read());
            }
            System.out.println("]");
            s.reset();
        }
        catch (Exception e)
        {
            System.err.println("Error displaying array: " + e);
        }
    }

    public static void main(String args[])
    {
        byte buf1[] = { 1, 2, 3, 4, 5 };
        // Create an input stream based on buf1.
        InputStream is1 = new ByteArrayInputStream(buf1);
        EX13A example = new EX13A();
        example.printInputStream(is1);   // Print the stream as is.
        buf1[0] = 0;                      // Modify the array outside of the stream.
        example.printInputStream(is1);   // Print it again.
        byte buf2[] = { 6, 7, 8, 9 };    // Create another array...
        buf1 = buf2;                      // ... and assign it to buf1.
        example.printInputStream(is1);   // Print it one last time.
        // Create another input stream based on buf2 that works with
        // the last two bytes of the array only.
        InputStream is2 = new ByteArrayInputStream(buf2, 2, buf2.length - 2);
        example.printInputStream(is2);   // Finally, print is2.
    }
}
```

This application produces the following output:

```
[12345]
[02345]
[02345]
[89]
```

Notice that when the array used by the stream is modified after the stream is created, the change is reflected the next time the stream is printed. However, also note that when the array used by the stream is assigned to another array, the internal reference to the original array is unaffected.

ByteArrayOutputStream

This class is the complement of `ByteArrayInputStream` in that it allows you to write data into an array of bytes. Except with this output version, the class internally creates and maintains the byte array for you. In fact, it even will expand the byte array as needed. Of course, it also has methods to retrieve the internal byte array at any point as a byte array, string, or Unicode string.

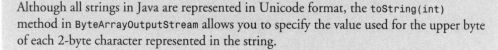

> NOTE:
>
> Although all strings in Java are represented in Unicode format, the `toString(int)` method in `ByteArrayOutputStream` allows you to specify the value used for the upper byte of each 2-byte character represented in the string.

The following simple code segment illustrates how to create, write to, and retrieve the contents of a `ByteArrayOutputStream`:

```
// Create a stream with a starting internal buffer size of 1 byte.
ByteArrayOutputStream os = new ByteArrayOutputStream(1);
try
{   // Overflow initial allocated buffer size.
    os.write(72);      // "H"
    os.write(105);     // "i"
}
catch (IOException e)
{
    System.err.println("Error writing to byte stream: " + e);
}
// Retrieve stream's internal buffer as a byte array.
byte buf[] = os.toByteArray();
// See how it grew...
System.out.println("Length of array is " + buf.length + "\n" + os.toString());
```

StringBufferInputStream

Like `ByteArrayInputStream`, `StringBufferInputStream` allows you to interact with a memory-based object, namely a string, in the context of a stream. However, because the `String` class already provides a wealth of access methods, the use of `StringBufferInputStream` solely for working with strings does not add much value. But if your program is expected to handle data from conventional stream sources (for example, files or network connections) as well as strings, `StringBufferInputStream` provides the necessary abstraction.

File Streams

Although file I/O in Java applets is usually denied or restricted due to security constraints imposed by browsers, the java.io package includes a complete set of stream classes for dealing with disk files. Indeed, Java applications are not subject to the same security constraints as applets and can include sophisticated file I/O functionality.

FileInputStream

From the input side, FileInputStream provides basic input stream capabilities for dealing with files. A FileInputStream object can be created using one of three constructors that accept the name of a file, a File object, or a FileDescriptor object, respectively.

> ### NOTE:
>
> Although File and FileDescriptor are classes within the java.io package, they will not be discussed in detail here because they are not part of the stream family of classes. Suffice it to say that the File class is used to represent a file in terms of the notation used by the host file system and provides basic file and directory functions such as making directories, enumerating files in a directory, deleting files, and renaming files. The FileDescriptor class is simply used to represent a handle to an open file or socket. Sockets and their integration with streams will be covered in detail in Part IV, "Networking with Java."

The example in Listing 13.2 prints the contents of a text file named somefile.dat to the console.

Listing 13.2. EX13B.java.

```
import java.io.*;

class EX13B
{
    public static void main(String args[])
    {
        try
        {
            // Create a simple file input stream.
            FileInputStream fis = new FileInputStream("somefile.dat");

            // Read the entire contents of the file.
            while (fis.available() > 0)
            {
                System.out.print((char)fis.read());
            }
        }
        catch (Exception e)
        {
```

```
                System.err.println("Error reading file: " + e);
        }
    }
}
```

FileOutputStream

The FileOutputStream class is very similar to FileInputStream in that it can be created by either
a filename passed as a string, File object, or FileDescriptor.

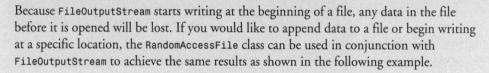

NOTE:

Because FileOutputStream starts writing at the beginning of a file, any data in the file
before it is opened will be lost. If you would like to append data to a file or begin writing
at a specific location, the RandomAccessFile class can be used in conjunction with
FileOutputStream to achieve the same results as shown in the following example.

The example in Listing 13.3 opens a file for reading and writing using a RandomAccessFile object,
binds an output stream to it, and writes a string to the end of the file.

Listing 13.3. EX13C.java.

```java
import java.io.*;

class EX13C
{
    public static void main(String args[])
    {
        RandomAccessFile rf;
        try
        {
            // Open a file for read and write access.
            rf = new RandomAccessFile("outfile.dat", "rw");
            // Use the just opened file as the destination for a stream.
            of = new FileOutputStream(rf.getFD());
            // Attach a print stream to output stream.
            PrintStream pos = new PrintStream(new FileOutputStream(rf.getFD()));
            // Go to the end of the file...
            rf.seek(rf.length());
            // ... and write a string.
            pos.print("Tack this to the end of the file.");
        }
        catch (IOException e)
        {
            System.err.println("Error writing to file: " + e);
        }
    }
}
```

Filter Streams

As mentioned earlier, streams are simply a metaphor for data entering one end of a data channel and exiting the other end in the same order. What if you would like to modify the data as it travels in or out of the data channel, without having to extend Java's input and output streams? Filter streams not only provide the capability to manipulate data as it passes through a stream but they can also be chained together to create a combined effect of several filters. This is perhaps the most powerful aspect of Java's streams.

There are two base classes that input and output filter classes are derived from: `FilterInputStream` and `FilterOutputStream`.

FilterInputStream

On the input stream side, `FilterInputStream` is the base class for all the input stream filters. This class does not make any modifications to the attached stream, but merely provides the chaining functionality that will be exploited by its subclasses. The `FilterInputStream` is attached to an input stream by passing the input stream to the filter stream's constructor.

```
InputStream is = new FileInputStream("somefile.dat");
FilterInputStream fis = new FilterInputStream(is);    // Meaningless filter attached.
```

BufferedInputStream

The `BufferedInputStream`'s contribution to its attached stream is the addition of a buffer, or cache, to the stream. This has the effect of improving the performance of some input streams, especially those bound to slower sources like a file or network connection.

NOTE:

The C++ stream library uses the subclasses of the abstract `streambuf` class to provide buffering to its streams. However, buffered streams in C++ encapsulate a pointer to a `streambuf` object rather than using Java's filter approach.

You can specify the size of the buffer used by `BufferedInputStream` when it is created or accept the default of 2048 bytes. It then intercepts your calls to the `read` methods and attempts to satisfy your request with data in its buffer. If the data in the buffer is not sufficient, a read to the next input stream in the chain is done to fill the buffer and return the data requested. Anytime a read request can be satisfied from the buffer, you have saved a potentially slow read from the attached stream. `BufferedInputStream` also supports marking and ensures that the mark limit set remains valid.

Because file access can sometimes be quite slow, let's enhance the example in Listing 13.2 to use a `BufferedInputStream`. The improved version is shown in Listing 13.4.

Listing 13.4. EX13D.java.

```java
import java.io.*;

class EX13D
{
    public static void main(String args[])
    {
        try
        {
            // Create and attach a simple file input stream to a
            // buffered filter, using the default buffer size of 2048 bytes.
            BufferedInputStream bis = new BufferedInputStream(new
            ➡FileInputStream("somefile.dat"));

            // Now read the buffered stream.
            while (bis.available() > 0)
            {
                System.out.print((char)bis.read());
            }
        }
        catch (Exception e)
        {
            System.err.println("Error reading file: " + e);
        }
    }
}
```

Although it might not be obvious from this example, when the first call to `read()` is made, the `BufferedInputStream` reads in 2048 bytes (the default size of the buffer) and simply returns 1 byte at a time from the buffer for subsequent reads. There are certainly hardware and operating system caches involved as well, but it is always going to be faster to satisfy a read request from a memory location within the program than it is to make a system call to the operating system. It would also be more efficient to read more than one byte at a time from the stream, especially if it is unbuffered, but as we will see in the next section, some data types within a stream are only made up of a few bytes, so the value of `BufferedInputStream` still exists.

DataInputStream

A stream of data, especially if it contains primitive data types, is of little use unless it can be converted from a sequence of bytes into its native type. Indeed, all the examples we have looked at thus far have dealt with streams of text data that required nothing more than casting each `int` returned to a character before it was used.

```java
char c = (char)someinputstream.read();
```

In real programs, the data being transferred through streams is certainly going to be more complex and made up of several different types. And for most primitive data types such as long, float, and double, casting is not appropriate. The task of converting data to its native type as it is received is the perfect job for a filter stream. DataInputStream is a subclass of FilterInputStream and is responsible for filtering primitive data types from an input stream.

DataInput Interface

Because translating unknown pieces of machine-independent data into primitive data types has meaning outside of input streams, the DataInput interface was developed to create a generic connection to its translation methods. DataInputStream implements the DataInput interface.

Table 13.3 lists the name and description of each method of the DataInput interface.

Table 13.3. Public methods of the DataInput interface.

Method	Description
readFully(byte[])	Like read(byte[]), this method reads data into an array of bytes. The number of bytes read is determined by the length of the byte array passed as an argument.
readFully(byte[], int, int)	Like read(byte[], int, int), this method reads data into an array of bytes starting at a specific location in the array for a certain number of bytes.
int skipBytes(int)	Like skip(long), this method jumps over the specified number of bytes in the stream. The actual number of bytes skipped is returned from this method. Note that this skip() takes an int rather than a long as a parameter.
boolean readBoolean()	Reads and returns a Boolean.
byte readByte()	Like read(), this method reads and returns a single byte of data but returns the byte as a byte rather than an integer.
int readUnsignedByte()	Reads and returns an unsigned byte cast as a 32-bit integer to prevent possible truncation.
short readShort()	Reads and returns a 16-bit short.
int readUnsignedShort()	Reads and returns an unsigned short cast as a 32-bit integer to prevent possible truncation.

Method	Description
char readChar()	Reads and returns a 16-bit character.
int readInt()	Reads and returns a 32-bit integer.
long readLong()	Reads and returns a 64-bit long.
float readFloat()	Reads and returns a 32-bit float.
double readDouble()	Reads and returns a 64-bit double.
String readLine()	Reads a line of text until a \r, \n, or \r\n is found. The text is returned as a string.
String readUTF()	Like readLine(), this method reads a line of text from the stream. However, the text is read as a UTF-8 encoded string.

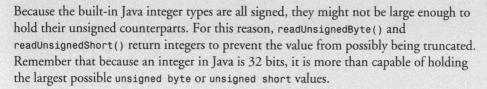

NOTE:

Because the built-in Java integer types are all signed, they might not be large enough to hold their unsigned counterparts. For this reason, readUnsignedByte() and readUnsignedShort() return integers to prevent the value from possibly being truncated. Remember that because an integer in Java is 32 bits, it is more than capable of holding the largest possible unsigned byte or unsigned short values.

Rather than include an example of how to use DataInputStream here, let's see how it works in conjunction with some of the other filter streams. The example for LineNumberInputStream (discussed next) and DataOutputStream both use DataInputStream.

LineNumberInputStream

The LineNumberInputStream is another input stream filter, except its task is to count the number of lines that have been read. It is most useful when you are reading several lines of text from a source, typically a file, and want to keep track of the current line number or total number of lines in a stream. The methods setLineNumber() and getLineNumber() enable you to set and get the internal line number count maintained by LineNumberInputStream.

Consider the example in Listing 13.5 that implements a simple text search program similar to UNIX's grep command.

Listing 13.5. EX13E.java.

```java
import java.io.*;

class EX13E
{
    public static void searchFile(String criteria, File file)
    {
        try
        {
            // Create a buffered line-number stream based on the target file.
            LineNumberInputStream linestream =
                new LineNumberInputStream
                (new BufferedInputStream(new FileInputStream(file)));
            DataInputStream dis = new DataInputStream(linestream);

            while (dis.available() > 0)
            {
                String line = dis.readLine();
                if (line.indexOf(criteria) != -1)
                {   // Found a match!
                    System.out.println("File " + file.getName() + ", line " +
                            linestream.getLineNumber() + ":\n" + line);
                }
            }
        }
        catch (IOException e)
        {
            System.err.println("Error reading " + file.getName() + ": " + e);
        }
    }

    private static void usage()
    {
        System.err.println("Usage: grep searchtext target");
        System.err.println("Where target is a file or directory.");
    }

    public static void main(String args[])
    {
        if (args.length != 2)
        {
            System.err.println("Invalid number of arguments.");
            usage();
            return;
        }

        File target = new File(args[1]);

        if (target.isDirectory())
        {   // Retrieve a list of the files in the directory...
            String[] list = target.list();

            // ... and search each file for the search text.
            for (int i = 0; i < list.length; i++)
```

```
                {
                    searchFile(args[0], new File(target, list[i]));
                }
            }
            else if (target.isFile())
            {
                // Just one file so just pass it to the search routine.
                searchFile(args[0], target);
            }
            else
            {
                System.err.println("Target is not a file or directory.");
                usage();
            }
        }
    }
}
```

Notice how a `BufferedInputStream` is sandwiched between the `LineNumberInputStream` and the `FileInputStream` to provide I/O buffering for each file. It is critical that the `BufferedInputStream` be attached first so that all the other filter streams will leverage the buffering. It is also important that the `LineNumberInputStream` be attached before the `DataInputStream` so that calls to the `DataInputStream` are sent through the `LineNumberInputStream`. Otherwise, if `LineNumberInputStream` is attached to the `DataInputStream`, each line will not be counted as it is read. Because we want to read text from each file one line at a time, `DataInputStream` was used for its `readLine()` method.

PushbackInputStream

This input filter stream is somewhat unusual in that it puts a character back into an input stream. It can be used if you are expecting a certain sequence of characters and want to test the next byte in the stream to see whether it maintains the sequence. If the sequence is broken, `PushbackInputStream` has an `unread()` method that stages a byte to be returned as part of the next read of the stream. The `readLine()` method of `DataInputStream` uses a `PushbackInputStream` (if the host stream is not already a `PushbackInputStream`) if the carriage-return line-feed (\r\n) sequence is broken.

> **NOTE:**
>
> The `PushbackInputStream` filter functions similar to the `peek()` member function of the `iostream` class in the C++ stream library. However, the `PushbackInputStream` returns a byte to the stream whereas the `peek()` member function in `iostream` allows you to preview the next character in the stream without removing it.

FilterOutputStream

On the output stream side, FilterOutputStream forms the basis for the output stream filters. Like FilterInputStream, it does not make any modifications to stream data as it passes by but only provides the chaining used by its subclasses. The FilterOutputStream is attached to an output stream by passing the output stream to the filter stream's constructor.

BufferedOutputStream

BufferedOutputStream provides the same performance gains that BufferedInputStream does for input streams, but its buffer is used for an output stream. The basic concept is the same. Requests to write to an output stream are cached in an internal buffer. When the internal buffer reaches capacity it is flushed from the buffer to the output stream. The size of the internal buffer defaults to 512 bytes but can be overridden by calling the appropriate constructor with the desired size.

Because the use of a BufferedOutputStream is so similar to that of BufferedInputStream, an example will not be presented.

DataOutputStream

This filter provides methods that write primitive data types to an output stream. Primitive data types are most often used when working with files or network connections. Like DataInputStream, this class implements the methods of an interface, DataOutput.

DataOutput Interface

The DataOutput interface defines the methods to write Java's primitive data types to a source. Within the java.io package, DataOutput is implemented by DataOutputStream and RandomAccessFile. As already mentioned, DataOutputStream implements DataOutput to write primitive types to an output stream. RandomAccessFile implements DataOutput to write primitive types solely to a disk file. Although a member of the java.io package, RandomAccessFile will not be discussed here because it is not a part of the stream hierarchy.

Table 13.4 lists the name and description of each method of the DataOutput interface as it relates to DataOutputStream.

Table 13.4. Public methods of the `DataOutput` interface.

Method	Description
`write(int)`	Writes 1 byte as a 32-bit integer.
`write(byte[])`	Writes an entire byte array. The number of bytes written is determined by the length of the byte array passed as an argument.
`write(byte[], int, int)`	Writes the portion of a byte array starting at a specific location in the array for a certain number of bytes.
`writeBoolean(boolean)`	Writes an 8-bit `Boolean`.
`writeByte(int)`	Like `write(int)`, this method writes a single byte as a 32-bit integer.
`writeShort(int)`	Writes a `short` as a 32-bit integer.
`writeChar(int)`	Writes a `char` as a 32-bit integer.
`writeInt(int)`	Writes a 32-bit integer.
`writeLong(long)`	Writes a 64-bit `long`.
`writeFloat(float)`	Writes a 32-bit `float`.
`writeDouble(double)`	Writes a 64-bit `double`.
`writeBytes(String)`	Writes a `String` as bytes.
`writeChars(String)`	Writes a `String` as chars.
`writeUTF(String)`	Writes a `String` as a UTF-8 encoded sequence of characters.

NOTE:

The C++ stream library uses operator overloading to write primitive data types to a stream. Although the syntax of operator overloading may appear more elegant, it can be difficult to program correctly and can be confusing to users of your classes. The creators of Java felt that this was too much of a price to pay.

The example shown in Listing 13.6 ties together several of the stream classes and stream filters that we have already discussed into one program. The basic idea of the program is to read statistics about itself when it is started, update the statistics, and write them back out. The statistics are stored in a file with the same name as the class and the extension .dat.

Listing 13.6. EX13F.java.

```java
import java.io.*;
import java.util.Date;

class EX13F
{
    private Date dateLastUpdated;    // Date the last time the stats for this program
    ➥were written.
    private String userLastUpdated; // User's name that performed the last update.
    private int executionCount;      // The number of times this program has been run.

    // This method reads the program stats from a file by the same name as the class.
    public void retrieveStats() throws IOException
    {
        try
        {
            // Create a data stream filter with a file input stream as the host
            ➥stream.
            DataInputStream dis = new DataInputStream(new
            ➥FileInputStream(getClass().getName() + ".dat"));

            // Initialize the data members with the values in the stat file.
            dateLastUpdated = new Date(dis.readLong());
            userLastUpdated = dis.readUTF();
            executionCount = dis.readInt();
        }
        catch (FileNotFoundException e)
        {
            // Eat this exception since the file won't exist initially.
        }
    }

    // This method writes the program stats back out to the same file.
    public void saveStats() throws IOException
    {
        // Update date is now.
        Date today = new Date();

        // This time create an output data filter attached to a file output stream.
        DataOutputStream dos = new DataOutputStream(new
        ➥FileOutputStream(getClass().getName() + ".dat"));

        // Write each value back out to the file.
        dos.writeLong(Date.parse(today.toGMTString()));
        if (userLastUpdated.length() == 0)
            userLastUpdated = "Ace Programmer";
        dos.writeUTF(userLastUpdated);
        dos.writeInt(++executionCount);
    }
```

```java
    public static void main(String args[])
    {
        EX13F example = new EX13F();  // Create an instance.

        try
        {   // Read the stats in from the last run.
            example.retrieveStats();

            // And print them out.
            System.out.println("Program last update date: " +
            ➡example.dateLastUpdated);
            System.out.println("Last updated by: " + example.userLastUpdated);
            System.out.println("Execution count: " + example.executionCount);

            // Now prompt the user for their name to update the stat file.
            System.out.print("\nWhat is your name: ");
            System.out.flush();

            // Use a data stream again so we can use readLine()
            // to read from the console.
            DataInputStream stdin = new DataInputStream(System.in);
            example.userLastUpdated = stdin.readLine();

            // Finally, save the stats back out to the file.
            example.saveStats();
        }
        catch (Exception e)
        {
            System.err.println("Error processing stats file: " + e);
        }
    }
}
```

In this example, primitive data types are read and written from a disk file using `DataInputStream` and `DataOutputStream` filters. The current date is converted to a `long` before being written to the file and is read back in as a `long` and converted back into a date. The user's name is written out as a `String` using `writeUTF()` to take advantage of the fact that this method writes the string's length to the stream prior to the actual characters. The `readUTF()` method then reads the stream for the size of the string first to determine the length of the string—a built-in variable length string handler. Finally, the execution count of the program is written and read as an integer.

This program also illustrates how to prompt for and retrieve user input from the keyboard using a text-based application. The `java.lang.System` class has three `public static` stream objects representing the standard input, output, and error for the system. The file system reserves file descriptors 0, 1, and 2 for standard input, output, and error, respectively. Although these three file descriptors are used most of the time for interacting with the keyboard and console, they can also be redirected to files and the standard input and output of other programs via unnamed pipes. Therefore, the `System.in` object is a buffered input file stream while `System.out` and `System.err` are buffered print output file streams. The host operating system's command interpreter, or shell, takes care of redirecting the standard input, output, and error in the appropriate context each time a program is run.

PrintStream

We have actually been using the PrintStream filter in every sample program in this chapter. As mentioned in the previous paragraph, the System.out and System.err objects are FileOutputStreams that use a PrintStream filter. This filter adds the capability to force the attached stream to be flushed every time a newline (\n) character is written. It also provides several overloaded versions of print() and println() that write each of the primitive data types to the attached stream as strings. In addition, each of the println() methods also append a newline to each object written.

Pipe Streams

Pipes have been an integral part of several operating systems for many years. In general, pipes are used to provide a one-way communication link between two processes. In Java, pipes can be used to connect two threads or two applets. And since pipes were implemented as streams, any of the stream filters can be attached to a pipe to provide the same effects that we have already seen. If a two-way communications link is needed, two pairs of pipes can be constructed that flow in opposite directions.

Pipes are supported by two classes: PipedInputStream and PipedOutputStream. They must be created in pairs and connected to each other by using either class's connect() method.

PipedInputStream

The receiving end of a piped stream is supported by PipedInputStream. It contains a 1024-byte internal ring buffer that is used to hold incoming data as it is received from its connected PipedOutputStream.

NOTE:

Physically, a ring buffer is like any other buffer in memory. However, where it differs from other buffers is in how it is used. Two offsets are used to manage a ring buffer: one represents the position of the last byte written to the buffer and the other represents the position of the last byte read. Once either offset reaches the end of the buffer, it is moved back to the beginning. As long as the write offset stays equal to or ahead of the read offset, a ring buffer maintains the illusion of an endless piece of memory. However, if the write offset wraps around and passes the read offset, data can be lost. Fortunately, PipedInputStream will block further writes to its ring buffer by PipedOutputStream until data is read.

When data is written to an output pipe, PipedOutputStream calls the receive() method of its attached PipedInputStream to send data down the pipe. The receive() method will write the data to its buffer if there is room. Otherwise, it will block the output pipe until there is space in the buffer or the pipe is broken. Likewise, when a read is performed on PipedInputStream it will return data if it exists in the buffer. Otherwise, it will block the caller to the read() method until the data requested is received, the pipe is closed, or the pipe is broken.

> **NOTE:**
>
> A pipe is determined to be broken when the thread of either end of a pipe terminates.

PipedOutputStream

The PipedOutputStream has an easier job. As described above, once connected to a PipedInputStream object, it simply calls the input pipe's receive() method to send data down the pipe. One point to keep in mind is that calls to the write() methods will block if the input pipe does not have enough room in its internal buffer to hold the data being sent. However, if you run your pipe I/O in separate threads, blocking will not affect the responsiveness of your program.

The following example illustrates the use of pipes to communicate between two applets running on the same Web page. One applet sits in a loop spinning an animated globe. It also creates a thread that is responsible for monitoring an input pipe for commands from another applet that change the manner in which the globe is animated. The second applet displays six pushbuttons that enable the user to start and stop the animation, change the rotation of the globe, and increase or decrease the speed of the animation. When one of the buttons is pressed, a command is sent to the animation applet through an output pipe. Figure 13.1 displays the Web page and the two applets in action.

Listing 13.7 includes a portion of the source code for the first applet and the thread class used to monitor the input pipe. The basis for the animation in the applet may look familiar to you because it is the default animation created by the Visual J++ Applet Wizard. A few enhancements were made to integrate the pipe monitor thread and the custom animation. The complete source listing can be found on the accompanying CD-ROM.

Figure 13.1.

The pipe stream example.

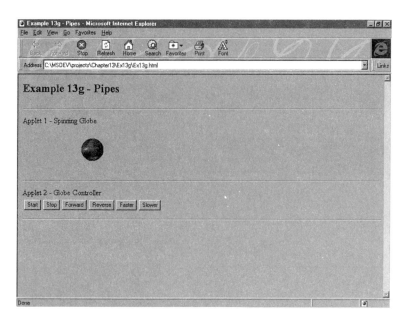

Listing 13.7. EX13G.java.

```java
import java.applet.*;
import java.awt.*;
import java.io.*;

public class EX13G extends Applet implements Runnable
{
    //...
    private PipedInputStream inputPipe;
    private PipeMonitor monitor;

    public EX13G()
    {   // Create input pipe and share with pipe monitor.
        inputPipe = new PipedInputStream();
        monitor = new PipeMonitor(inputPipe);
    }


    //...

    public void run()
    {
        if (!m_fAllLoaded)
        {   // Load all images first.
            if (!loadImages())
                return;
        }

        while (true)
```

```
    {   // Check to see if globe should be animated.
        if (monitor.isAnimated())
        {
            try
            {   // Display image and move on to next image.
                displayImage(m_Graphics);
                if (monitor.getRotation() == monitor.FORWARD)
                {   // Move forward through image array.
                    if (++m_nCurrImage == NUM_IMAGES)
                        m_nCurrImage = 0;
                }
                else
                {   // Move backwards through image array.
                    if (--m_nCurrImage < 0)
                        m_nCurrImage = NUM_IMAGES - 1;
                }

                // Rate of animation is controlled by sleep time.
                Thread.currentThread().sleep(monitor.getSleepTime());
            }
            catch (InterruptedException e)
            {
                stop();
                monitor.stop();
            }
        }
    }
}


    //...

    public void connectPipes(PipedOutputStream out) throws IOException
    {   // Called by controller applet to connect input & output pipes.
        inputPipe.connect(out);
        // Only start pipe monitor if necessary.
        if (!monitor.isAlive())
            monitor.start();    // Waits for commands sent through pipe.
    }
}

class PipeMonitor extends Thread
{
    public final int FORWARD = 1;
    public final int REVERSE = 2;

    // Setup attributes with default values.
    private int rotation = FORWARD;
    private int sleepTime = 50;
    private boolean animated = true;
    private DataInputStream inputPipe;

    private PipeMonitor() {} // Hide default ctor.

    public PipeMonitor(PipedInputStream pi)
    {
```

continues

Listing 13.7. continued

```
        inputPipe = new DataInputStream(pi);
    }

    // Access methods.
    public synchronized int getRotation() { return rotation; }
    public synchronized int getSleepTime() { return sleepTime; }
    public synchronized boolean isAnimated() { return animated; }

    public void run()
    {
        String cmd;
        while (true)
        {
            try
            {   // Wait for a ('\n' terminated) command from the pipe.
                do
                    cmd = inputPipe.readLine();
                while (cmd == null);

                // Interpret command and change settings.
                if (cmd.equalsIgnoreCase("FORWARD"))
                    rotation = FORWARD;
                else if (cmd.equalsIgnoreCase("REVERSE"))
                    rotation = REVERSE;
                else if (cmd.equalsIgnoreCase("START"))
                    animated = true;
                else if (cmd.equalsIgnoreCase("STOP"))
                    animated = false;
                else if (cmd.equalsIgnoreCase("FASTER"))
                    sleepTime -= (sleepTime == 10 ? 0 : 10);
                else if (cmd.equalsIgnoreCase("SLOWER"))
                    sleepTime += 10;
            }
            catch (IOException e) {}
        }
    }
}
```

The source code for the second applet is shown in Listing 13.8. The command() method is where the connection is made with the animation applet and the commands are sent down the output pipe. A DataOutputStream filter is attached to the pipe to allow strings to be sent across the connection.

Listing 13.8. EX13G2.java.

```
import java.applet.*;
import java.awt.*;
import java.io.*;
import EX13G;

public class EX13G2 extends Applet
{
```

```java
private DataOutputStream outputPipe = null;

    public void init()
    {   // Add control buttons to manipulate globe.
        add(new Button("Start"));
        add(new Button("Stop"));
        add(new Button("Forward"));
        add(new Button("Reverse"));
        add(new Button("Faster"));
        add(new Button("Slower"));
    }

    public boolean action(Event event, Object obj)
    {
        boolean retval = false;

        if (event.target instanceof Button)
        {
            try
            {   // Send the appropriate command based
                // on the label of the button pressed.
                command(((Button)event.target).getLabel());
            }
            catch (IOException e)
            {
                // Add your exception logic here.
            }
            retval = true;
        }

        return retval;
    }

    public void command(String cmd) throws IOException
    {
        if (outputPipe == null)
        {   // Pipe needs to be created and connected to
            // the animated globe applet.

            // Get a reference to the animated globe applet.
            EX13G ex13g;
            ex13g = (EX13G)getAppletContext().getApplet("globe");

            if (ex13g == null)
            {
                throw new IOException("globe applet could not be found.");
            }

            // Setup output pipe.
            PipedOutputStream p = new PipedOutputStream();
            ex13g.connectPipes(p);
            outputPipe = new DataOutputStream(p);
        }

        outputPipe.writeBytes(cmd + "\n");
    }
}
```

The HTML used to run the two applets is shown in Listing 13.9. It is critical that the name of the first applet be set correctly so that the command applet can make the connection.

Listing 13.9. EX13G.html.

```
<HTML>
<HEAD>
<TITLE>Example 13g - Pipes</TITLE>
</HEAD>
<BODY>
<H2>Example 13g - Pipes</H2>
<HR>
Applet 1 - Spinning Globe<BR>
<APPLET CODE=EX13G.class WIDTH=300 HEIGHT=100 NAME=globe></APPLET>
<HR>
Applet 2 - Globe Controller<BR>
<APPLET CODE=EX13G2.class WIDTH=300 HEIGHT=30 NAME=controller></APPLET>
<HR>
</BODY>
</HTML>
```

Summary

Java's stream classes provide a flexible and powerful framework for transferring data between objects. Receivers and senders of data across a stream can range from in-memory byte arrays to files on a disk drive. And as we will see in Part IV, streams serve as the foundation for Java's impressive and easy-to-use networking features.

Part III

Beyond Buttons and Bars: Improving the User Interface

Chapter

14

Incorporating Graphics

In this chapter you will learn how to augment the appearance of your Java program by using graphics. Java provides a complete set of classes for drawing lines and geometric shapes such as arcs, ovals, rectangles, and polygons. You will also learn how to display and manipulate images. You will learn about Java's classes for filtering, cropping, and modifying images. You will also learn about the ImageObserver interface that allows an applet to monitor the progress of an image that is being retrieved for display.

Drawing Filled and Outlined Shapes

In this section you will learn about the Graphics class that is included in the java.awt package. You've already seen the Graphics class used in many of the examples in this book. For example, in Chapter 2, "Creating Your First Applet with Applet Wizard," the following code was used to display "Hello, World" on the screen:

```
public void paint(Graphics g)
{
    g.drawString("Hello, World", 10, 10);
}
```

As you would expect of a class named Graphics, it can be used to do much more than draw strings. The Graphics class can be used to draw a variety of shapes. Figure 14.1 illustrates a very simple screen that was created with member methods of the Graphics class.

Figure 14.1.

A very simple example of drawing filled and outlined shapes.

The Graphics class includes methods for drawing both filled and outlined shapes. An outlined shape is just the outline of the shape; a filled shape is the outline plus the area bounded by the outline. The bounded area is filled by painting it with the current color.

> **NOTE:**
>
> The use of color is discussed in Chapter 16, "Sprucing Things Up with Colors and Fonts."

A variety of shapes can be drawn using the Graphics class, as shown in Table 14.1. As you can see from this table, all shapes except a line can be drawn both filled and outlined. Because a line always has a width of one, there is no need to draw filled lines.

Table 14.1. Shapes that can be drawn by the Graphics class.

Shape	Filled	Outlined
Arc	Yes	Yes
Line	No	Yes
Oval	Yes	Yes
Polygon	Yes	Yes
Rectangle	Yes	Yes
Round Rectangle	Yes	Yes
3-D Rectangle	Yes	Yes

When you use any of these methods to draw a shape, you pass it the coordinates at which the shape is to be drawn. As far as the Graphics class is concerned, coordinate numbering starts at 0,0 in the top left and increases down and to the right. This can be seen in Figure 14.2.

Lines

One of the simplest shapes to draw is a line. A line can be drawn using the drawLine member of the Graphics class. The signature of drawLine is as follows:

```
public abstract void drawLine(int x1, int y1, int x2, int y2);
```

This method will draw a line between the points given by (x1, y1) and (x2, y2). As an example, imagine you have been asked to display the image shown in Figure 14.3. This drawing can be created with the code shown in Listing 14.1.

Figure 14.2.

The Graphics coordinate system places 0,0 in the top left and increases down and to the right.

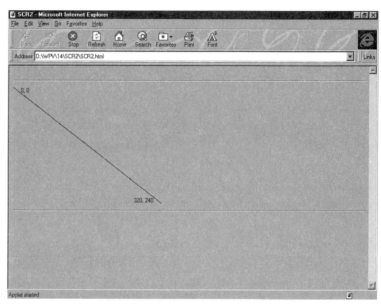

Figure 14.3.

A simple figure created with drawLine.

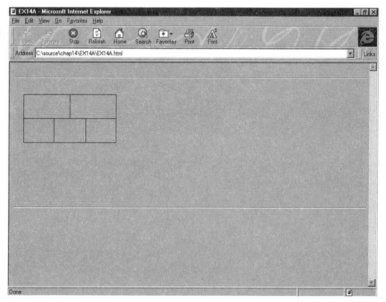

Listing 14.1. EX14A.java.

```
import java.applet.*;
import java.awt.*;

public class EX14A extends Applet
{
```

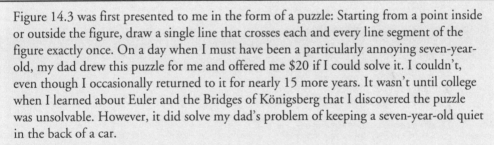

```
public void init()
{
    resize(320, 240);
}

public void paint(Graphics g)
{
    // draw the three horizontal lines
    g.drawLine(20,  20, 220,  20);
    g.drawLine(20,  70, 220,  70);
    g.drawLine(20, 120, 220, 120);

    // draw the vertical lines at each end
    g.drawLine(20,  20,  20, 120);
    g.drawLine(220, 20, 220, 120);

    // draw the vertical line in the top half
    g.drawLine(120, 20, 120, 70);

    // draw two vertical lines in the bottom half
    g.drawLine( 86, 70,  86, 120);
    g.drawLine(154, 70, 154, 120);
}
}
```

NOTE:

Figure 14.3 was first presented to me in the form of a puzzle: Starting from a point inside or outside the figure, draw a single line that crosses each and every line segment of the figure exactly once. On a day when I must have been a particularly annoying seven-year-old, my dad drew this puzzle for me and offered me $20 if I could solve it. I couldn't, even though I occasionally returned to it for nearly 15 more years. It wasn't until college when I learned about Euler and the Bridges of Königsberg that I discovered the puzzle was unsolvable. However, it did solve my dad's problem of keeping a seven-year-old quiet in the back of a car.

Rectangles

There are more methods for drawing rectangles than I have fingers on one hand. There are six. Fortunately, I could count them all on two hands and didn't need to use my toes or this book would have had an unpleasant odor. Of the six methods for drawing rectangles, three draw filled rectangles and three draw outlined rectangles. Methods whose names begin with draw are used to create outlined rectangles; methods whose names begin with fill are used to create filled rectangles. The following methods are available:

```
public void drawRect(int x, int y, int width, int height);
public abstract void fillRect(int x, int y, int width, int height);
```

```
public void draw3DRect(int x, int y, int width, int height,
        boolean raised);
public void fill3DRect(int x, int y, int width, int height,
        boolean raised);
public abstract void drawRoundRect(int x, int y, int width,
        int height, int arcWidth, int arcHeight);
public abstract void fillRoundRect(int x, int y, int width,
        int height, int arcWidth, int arcHeight);
```

A simple rectangle, as drawn by drawRect and fillRect, requires only parameters for the starting x and y coordinates and the width and height of the rectangle. A three-dimensional rectangle can be painted with draw3DRect or fill3DRect by specifying an additional parameter that indicates whether the rectangle should appear raised or lowered. The three-dimensional effect is achieved by brightening or darkening the color of the rectangle when it is drawn. Because of this, you must use setColor prior to painting the rectangle or the three-dimensional effect will not be apparent.

Finally, a rectangle with rounded corners can be painted with drawRoundRect or fillRoundRect. These methods require two additional parameters that specify the width and height of the arc that is used to draw the corners. Larger values for these parameters will create more rounded corners.

As an example of how these methods may be used, consider the code in Listing 14.2. This code will create the screen shown in Figure 14.4.

Listing 14.2. EX14B.java illustrates how to draw rectangles.

```java
import java.applet.*;
import java.awt.*;

public class EX14B extends Applet
{
    public void paint(Graphics g)
    {
        // draw an outlined rectangle
        g.drawRect(10, 10, 200, 200);
        g.drawString("drawRect", 10, 225);

        // draw a filled rectangle
        g.fillRect(15, 15, 30, 60);
        g.drawString("fillRect", 15, 90);

        // set a color so that the 3D rectangles
        // are displayed as raised or indented
        g.setColor(Color.cyan);

        // draw an outlined 3D rectangle
        g.draw3DRect(60, 15, 40, 10, false);
        g.drawString("draw3DRect", 60, 40);

        // draw a filled 3D rectangle
        g.fill3DRect(140, 15, 30, 20, true);
        g.drawString("fill3DRect", 140, 50);

        // draw an outlined round rectangle
        g.drawRoundRect(20, 110, 40, 60, 20, 40);
        g.drawString("drawRoundRect", 20, 185);
```

```
        // draw a filled round rectangle
        g.fillRoundRect(120, 110, 60, 60, 20, 20);
        g.drawString("fillRoundRect", 120, 185);
    }

    public void init()
    {
        resize(320, 240);
    }
}
```

Figure 14.4.

Examples of the various
rectangle methods.

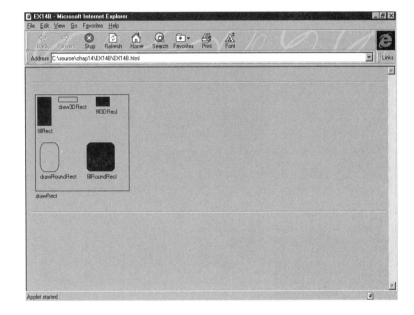

Arcs

You've already used arcs to create the rounded corners of a rectangle drawn with drawRoundRect
or fillRoundRect. You can also create an arc on its own. Arcs are created with the drawArc or fillArc
methods whose signatures are the following:

```
public abstract void drawArc(int x, int y, int width, int height,
        int startAngle, int arcAngle);
public abstract void fillArc(int x, int y, int width, int height,
        int startAngle, int arcAngle);
```

As with the rectangle methods, the method whose name begins with draw will paint an outlined
shape, and the method whose name begins with fill will paint a filled shape. To paint an arc you
specify the position and size of an imaginary rectangle that bounds the arc. You also specify the
starting angle of the arc and the number of degrees in the arc. This can be seen in Figure 14.5.

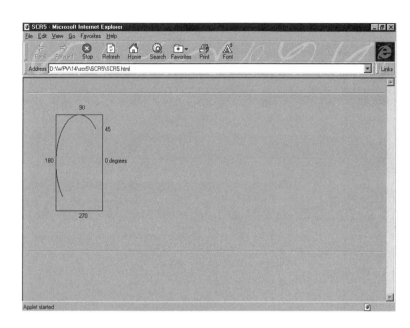

Figure 14.5.

An arc is specified by
describing an imaginary
rectangle surrounding it.

Figure 14.5 shows an arc and also uses drawRectangle to explicitly paint the invisible rectangle that surrounds the arc. The rectangle and arc of this example were created with the following two statements:

```
g.drawArc(60, 30, 100, 200, 45, 180);
g.drawRect(60, 30, 100, 200);
```

The first four parameters to drawArc indicate a rectangle that starts at (60, 30) is 100 pixels wide, and 200 pixels high. These same four values are passed to drawRect to explicitly draw the rectangle. The final two parameters to drawArc indicate that the arc should begin at 45 degrees and end 180 degrees later (at 225 degrees). As you can see in Figure 14.5, the 0 degree position is at three o'clock. Because the final parameter is a positive number, the arc will be drawn in a counterclockwise direction. A negative number causes the arc to be drawn in a clockwise direction. This can be seen in Figure 14.6, which shows the same arc when drawn in the opposite direction with the following code:

```
g.drawArc(60, 30, 100, 200, 45, -180);
```

Class EX14C, shown in Listing 14.3, demonstrates how to use drawArc and fillArc. Three rows of arcs are painted, as can be seen in Figure 14.7. The first row shows four arcs drawn with counterclockwise angles. The second row shows the same four arcs drawn in a clockwise direction. The final row shows two filled arcs with starting angles other than 0.

Figure 14.6.

The same arc when drawn in a clockwise direction.

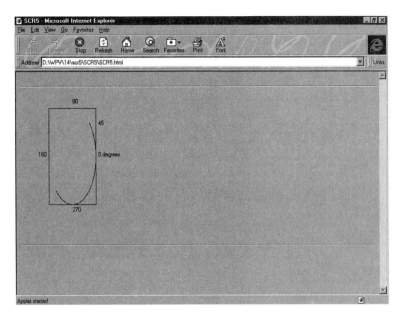

Listing 14.3. EX14C.java.

```java
import java.applet.*;
import java.awt.*;

public class EX14C extends Applet
{
    public void init()
    {
        resize(320, 240);
    }

    public void paint(Graphics g)
    {
        // draw arcs with counterclockwise angles
        g.drawArc(10, 60, 20, 50, 0, 90);
        g.drawArc(60, 60, 20, 50, 0, 180);
        g.drawArc(110, 60, 20, 50, 0, 270);
        g.drawArc(160, 60, 20, 50, 0, 360);

        // draw arcs with clockwise angles
        g.drawArc(10, 120, 20, 50, 0, -90);
        g.drawArc(60, 120, 20, 50, 0, -180);
        g.drawArc(110, 120, 20, 50, 0, -270);
        g.drawArc(160, 120, 20, 50, 0, -360);

        // draw filled arcs that don't start at 0
        g.fillArc(10, 180, 20, 50, 45, 180);
        g.fillArc(60, 180, 20, 50, 0, 135);
    }
}
```

303

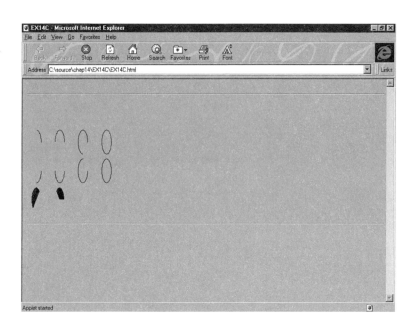

Figure 14.7.

Sample arcs painted with
drawArc and fillArc.

Ovals

Drawing an oval is very similar to drawing a regular rectangle. An oval can be painted using either
of the following methods:

```
public abstract void drawOval(int x, int y,int width,int height);
public abstract void fillOval(int x, int y,int width,int height);
```

As is consistent with the other member methods of Graphics, drawOval paints an outlined oval
and fillOval paints a filled oval. As with arcs, the parameters passed to these methods describe an
imaginary rectangle surrounding the oval. As an example of painting ovals, consider class EX14D,
shown in Listing 14.4. This class paints a large outlined oval and then paints a smaller filled oval
inside the larger oval. The results of executing this class can be seen in Figure 14.8.

Listing 14.4. EX14D.java.

```
import java.applet.*;
import java.awt.*;

public class EX14D extends Applet
{
    public void init()
    {
        resize(520, 400);
    }

    public void paint(Graphics g)
    {
```

```
// draw an outlined oval
g.drawOval(10, 10, 225, 300);
g.drawString("drawOval", 102, 323);

// draw a filled oval within the outlined oval
g.fillOval(73, 120, 100, 100);
g.drawString("fillOval", 105, 233);
    }
}
```

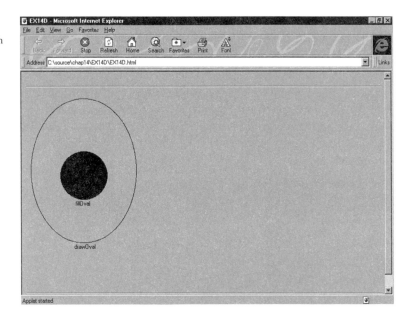

Figure 14.8.

Sample ovals painted with drawOval and fillOval.

Polygons

If what you really want to draw is a non-standard shape that can't be painted with one of the methods described so far, you may be able to use the polygon drawing methods. As usual, methods are provided for painting outlined and filled shapes. The following four methods can be used to paint polygons:

```
public abstract void fillPolygon(int xPoints[], int yPoints[],
        int nPoints);
public abstract void drawPolygon(int xPoints[], int yPoints[],
        int nPoints);
public void fillPolygon(Polygon p);
public void drawPolygon(Polygon p);
```

The first two of these methods are each passed two arrays that represent the x and y positions of the points on the polygon and an integer. As an example of how this works, consider the following:

```
int xPoints[] = new int[4];
int yPoints[] = new int[4];
```

```
xPoints[0] = 150;
xPoints[1] = 150;
xPoints[2] = 250;
xPoints[3] = 150;

yPoints[0] = 150;
yPoints[1] = 250;
yPoints[2] = 250;
yPoints[3] = 150;

g.fillPolygon(xPoints, yPoints, 4);
```

In this case two arrays are allocated to hold four items each. The corners of the polygon are given by the matched pairs of the arrays. For example, (xPoints[0], yPoints[0]) and (xPoints[1], yPoints[1]) identify the first two of four corners on the polygon.

The other two methods for drawing polygons are passed a polygon as their lone parameter. These methods are more convenient if you already have a Polygon object. The following code is equivalent to the prior example but passes a Polygon to fillPolygon instead of passing the arrays:

```
int xPoints[] = new int[4];
int yPoints[] = new int[4];

xPoints[0] = 150;
xPoints[1] = 150;
xPoints[2] = 250;
xPoints[3] = 150;

yPoints[0] = 150;
yPoints[1] = 250;
yPoints[2] = 250;
yPoints[3] = 150;

Polygon p = new Polygon(xPoints, yPoints, 4);
g.fillPolygon(p);
```

As a further example of how the fillPolygon and drawPolygon methods may be used, consider example EX14E, which is shown in Listing 14.5. This example draws three shapes, a four-sided polygon, and two triangles, as shown in Figure 14.9.

Listing 14.5. EX14E.java.

```
import java.applet.*;
import java.awt.*;

public class EX14E extends Applet
{
    public void init()
    {
        resize(520, 400);
    }

    public void paint(Graphics g)
    {
```

```
    drawFirstPolygon(g);
    drawSecondPolygon(g);
    drawThirdPolygon(g);
}

private void drawFirstPolygon(Graphics g)
{
    int xPoints[] = new int[5];
    int yPoints[] = new int[5];

    xPoints[0] = 60;
    xPoints[1] = 100;
    xPoints[2] = 150;
    xPoints[3] = 110;
    xPoints[4] = 60;

    yPoints[0] = 10;
    yPoints[1] = 70;
    yPoints[2] = 30;
    yPoints[3] = 170;
    yPoints[4] = 10;

    g.drawPolygon(xPoints, yPoints, 5);
}

private void drawSecondPolygon(Graphics g)
{
    int xPoints[] = new int[4];
    int yPoints[] = new int[4];

    xPoints[0] = 150;
    xPoints[1] = 150;
    xPoints[2] = 250;
    xPoints[3] = 150;

    yPoints[0] = 150;
    yPoints[1] = 250;
    yPoints[2] = 250;
    yPoints[3] = 150;

    g.fillPolygon(xPoints, yPoints, 4);
}

private void drawThirdPolygon(Graphics g)
{
    int xPoints[] = new int[4];
    int yPoints[] = new int[4];

    xPoints[0] = 250;
    xPoints[1] = 300;
    xPoints[2] = 200;
    xPoints[3] = 250;

    yPoints[0] = 300;
    yPoints[1] = 350;
    yPoints[2] = 350;
    yPoints[3] = 300;
```

continues

Listing 14.5. continued

```
        Polygon p = new Polygon(xPoints, yPoints, 4);

        g.drawPolygon(p);
    }
}
```

Figure 14.9.

Sample polygons painted with drawPolygon and fillPolygon.

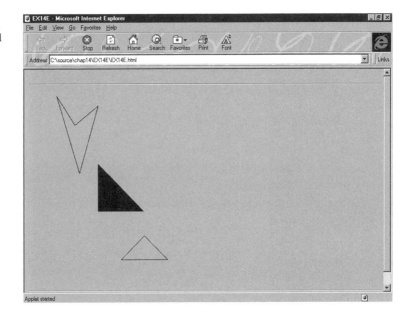

Images

In addition to geometric shapes and lines, you can also display graphics images, such as JPG or GIF files. To do this you use any of the four provided drawImage methods whose signatures are as follows:

```
public abstract boolean drawImage(Image img, int x, int y,
    ImageObserver observer);
public abstract boolean drawImage(Image img, int x, int y,
    int width, int height, ImageObserver observer);
public abstract boolean drawImage(Image img, int x, int y,
    Color bgcolor, ImageObserver observer);
public abstract boolean drawImage(Image img, int x, int y,
    int width, int height,Color bgcolor,ImageObserver observer);
```

The first of these methods is passed the image itself, the coordinates of its top-left corner, and an ImageObserver. ImageObserver is an interface that is implemented by the Component class. Because Applet is a subclass of Component you can use any class you derive from Applet as an ImageObserver. ImageObservers are useful because they can be sent information about the image as it is being loaded. Because `Applet` implements the ImageObserver interface, you can pass `this` as the ImageObserver parameter. This can be seen in the following code fragment:

```
public class MyClass extends Applet
{
    // ...other methods here
    public void paint(Graphics g)
    {
        g.drawImage(myImage, 100, 100, this);
    }
}
```

The second `drawImage` method is passed parameters for width and height. This causes the image to be scaled so that it appears in the specified rectangle. The final two `drawImage` methods are the same as the first two with the addition of being able to specify a background color for the image.

However, before you can use `drawImage` you must have an `Image` object to draw. As you already learned in Chapter 4, "Applet Programming Fundamentals," this can be done with the `getImage` method of the `Applet` class. Typically, this is done in the `init` method of the applet, as follows:

```
public class MyClass extends Applet
{
    Image myImage;

    // ...other methods here

    public void init()
    {
        myImage = getImage(getDocumentBase(), "savannah.jpg");
    }
}
```

As an example of displaying images, consider EX14F, as shown in Listing 14.6. Note that since the `Image` class is in `java.awt.image`, this package must be imported. In the `init` method of EX14F, `getImage` is used to create the `Image` object, `myImage`. In the `paint` method this image is displayed twice. The first use of `drawImage` specifies a square from point (0, 0) to point (150, 150). The image will be resized and displayed in this area. This can be seen in Figure 14.10. The second use of `drawImage` specifies only the coordinates of the top left of the image.

Listing 14.6. EX14F.java displays a simple image.

```
import java.applet.*;
import java.awt.*;
import java.awt.image.*;

public class EX14F extends Applet
{
    private Image myImage;

    public void init()
    {
        resize(620, 470);
```

continues

Listing 14.6. continued

```
        // create the image
        myImage = getImage(getDocumentBase(), "savannah.jpg");
    }

    public void paint(Graphics g)
    {
        // paint the image in the specified rectangle
        g.drawImage(myImage, 0, 0, 150, 150, this);

        // paint the image on the screen
        g.drawImage(myImage, 160, 0, this);
    }
}
```

Figure 14.10.

The same image displayed
with two different
drawImage methods.

Filtering Images

It is also possible to create and use filters on images before they are displayed. The class
CropImageFilter is provided in the java.awt.image package and is a useful filter that enables you
to display only a portion of the image. Class EX14G, shown in Listing 14.7, illustrates how to use
CropImageFilter.

Listing 14.7. EX14G.java.

```java
import java.applet.*;
import java.awt.*;
import java.awt.image.*;

public class EX14G extends Applet
{
    private Image myImage;
    private Image croppedImage;

    public void init()
    {
        resize(630, 470);

        myImage = getImage(getDocumentBase(), "savannah.jpg");

        // create a filter that will crop the image to the
        // area starting at point (195, 0) with a width of 140
        // and a height of 150
        CropImageFilter myCropFilter = new CropImageFilter(195,0,
                140, 150);

        // create a new image source based on the original image
        // and using the newly created filter
        FilteredImageSource imageSource = new
                FilteredImageSource(myImage.getSource(),
                myCropFilter);

        // create the cropped image
        croppedImage = createImage(imageSource);
    }

    public void paint(Graphics g)
    {
        // paint the cropped image
        g.drawImage(croppedImage, 0, 0, this);

        // paint the original image to the right of the cropped one
        g.drawImage(myImage, 160, 0, this);
    }
}
```

After using getImage to create the Image object, the init method of EX14G constructs a new CropImageFilter object named myCropFilter. This constructor is passed the x and y coordinates, and the width and height of where to start cropping the image. In this case, a rectangle 140 pixels wide and 150 high will be cropped beginning at point (195, 0). Next, the constructor for FilteredImageSource is used to create a new image source. The image source is based on the original image and myCropFilter. Finally, createImage is used to return the actual Image object.

This work is put to use in the paint method. This method uses drawImage first to display the cropped image and then to display the original image for comparison. The results can be seen in Figure 14.11.

Figure 14.11.

The CropImageFilter can be used to crop images.

Writing Your Own Image Filter

It is also possible to create your own filter. To do so you create a subclass of either ImageFilter or RGBImageFilter and override methods to provide the filtering you want. The RGBImageFilter class is a subclass of ImageFilter and makes it very easy to write a filter that manipulates the colors of the individual pixels in an image.

As an example of how you can create your own filter based on RGBImageFilter, imagine you needed to write a filter that will remove part of an image. This could be very useful in a litigation support system for processing documents. In this type of system it is important to be able to redact, or black out, text. Or, as you'll see in this example, a redaction filter is useful for hiding the eyes of a Mafia informant.

Listing 14.8 shows EX14H. This example illustrates the use of a redaction filter, as shown in Figure 14.12. The class RedactFilter is defined as a subclass of RGBImageFilter. Its constructor is passed values that indicate the area to be redacted.

Listing 14.8. EX14H.java illustrates the creation of a custom filter.

```
import java.applet.*;
import java.awt.*;
```

```java
import java.awt.image.*;

class RedactFilter extends RGBImageFilter
{
    int startX, startY, endX, endY;

    // the constructor is passed the coordinates of the area
    // to redact and stores these values
    public RedactFilter(int x, int y, int width, int height)
    {
        startX = x;
        startY = y;
        endX   = startX + width;
        endY   = startY + height;
    }

    public int filterRGB(int x, int y, int rgb)
    {
        // if the (x,y) position is in the redacted area
        // return red, otherwise return the same color that
        // was passed in
        if (x >= startX && x <= endX && y >= startY && y <= endY)
            return 0xff0000ff;
        else
            return rgb;
    }
}

public class EX14H extends Applet
{
    private Image myImage;
    private Image redactedImage;

    public void init()
    {
        resize(570, 470);

        // get the original image
        myImage = getImage(getDocumentBase(), "savannah.jpg");

        // create a filter and specify the range to be redacted
        ImageFilter filter = new RedactFilter(220, 80, 80, 15);

        // create a new image source based on the original
        // image and the new filter
        FilteredImageSource imageSource=new FilteredImageSource(
                myImage.getSource(), filter);

        // create the redacted image from the image source
        redactedImage = createImage(imageSource);
    }

    public void paint(Graphics g)
    {
        // paint the redacted image
        g.drawImage(redactedImage, 0, 0, this);
    }
}
```

The method filterRGB is an overridden member of RGBImageFilter. This method is called once for each pixel in the image. Its x and y parameters indicate the location of the pixel being passed. Its rgb parameter indicates the current color of the pixel. The value returned by filterRGB is the color that will be displayed for this pixel. To alter the image, return something different from the current value in rgb. In this case, RedactFilter checks to see whether the pixel is within the specified area. If so, red is returned. If not, the unchanged rgb value is returned.

Figure 14.12.

The RedactFilter can be used to conceal the identity of a Mafia informant.

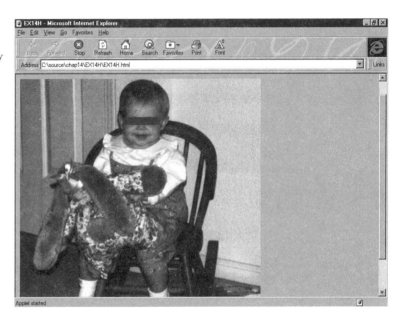

The RedactFilter is used very similarly to how CropImageFilter was used in the prior example. In the init method of EX14H, getImage is used to create the image. Next, a new instance of RedactFilter is constructed and a new image source is created based on the original image and the filter. Finally, createImage is used to create the redacted image from the image source. The paint method uses drawImage as it would with any other image.

The ImageObserver Interface

As you might recall, when the drawImage method was first introduced you needed to pass this as the final parameter to it, as in the following example:

```
g.drawImage(redactedImage, 0, 0, this);
```

This parameter represents an ImageObserver and since the Applet class implements the ImageObserver interface through the Component class, you can use the Applet this variable. So far you've been asked to take this parameter on faith. Now it's time to see what an ImageObserver can do.

The ImageObserver interface includes a single method. This method, `imageUpdate`, is called whenever additional information about an image becomes available. For example, it might take time to retrieve a large image across the Internet. The ImageObserver interface can monitor the progress of an image retrieval. An applet could then possibly display a progress message, an estimated time to complete, or take any other useful action. The signature of `imageUpdate` is as follows:

```
public abstract boolean imageUpdate(Image img, int infoflags,
        int x, int y, int width, int height);
```

The first parameter represents the image being updated. The second parameter represents a combination of various flags that give information about the image. These flags are described in Table 14.2. The remaining parameters usually represent a rectangle indicating the portion of the image that has been retrieved so far. Depending on the values in the `infoflags` parameter, some of these parameters might be invalid. The `imageUpdate` method should return `true` if you want to continue receiving updates, or `false` otherwise.

Table 14.2. Flags used in the `imageUpdate` method.

Flag	Description
ABORT	Retrieval of the image was aborted.
ALLBITS	All bits of the image have been retrieved.
ERROR	An error occurred while retrieving the image.
FRAMEBITS	A frame that is part of a multi-frame image has been completely retrieved.
HEIGHT	The `height` parameter now represents the final height of the image.
PROPERTIES	The properties of the image have been retrieved.
SOMEBITS	More bits have been retrieved.
WIDTH	The `width` parameter now represents the final width of the image.

As an example of how `imageUpdate` can be used, consider EX14I, as shown in Listing 14.9. In this example, a text area is created that will be used to display status messages. The `imageUpdate` method compares the value in the `infoflags` parameter against `ImageObserver.ERROR` and `ImageObserver.ALLBITS`. When one of these flags is set, a message is appended to the text area.

Listing 14.9. EX14I.java illustrates the use of the ImageObserver interface.

```
import java.applet.*;
import java.awt.*;
import java.awt.image.*;

public class EX14I extends Applet
{
```

continues

Listing 14.9. continued

```java
    private Image myImage;
    TextArea status;

    public void init()
    {
        resize(520, 470);

        // create the image
        myImage = getImage(getDocumentBase(), "savannah.jpg");

        // create a text area for displaying status information
        status = new TextArea(5, 20);
        add(status);
    }

    public void paint(Graphics g)
    {
        // paint the image in the specified rectangle
        g.drawImage(myImage, 0, 110, 350, 350, this);
    }


    public synchronized boolean imageUpdate(Image img,
            int infoflags, int x, int y, int width, int height)
    {
        // if an error occurs, display the message
        if ((infoflags & ImageObserver.ERROR) != 0)
            status.appendText("Error\r\n");

        // once all the bits have been received display
        // a message and repaint the applet
        if ((infoflags & ImageObserver.ALLBITS) != 0)
        {
            status.appendText("Allbits\r\n");
            repaint();
        }
        return true;
    }
}
```

Summary

This chapter gave you an in-depth look at the Graphics class and how you can use the methods of this class to enhance the appearance of your Java programs. In this chapter you learned how to draw outlined and filled shapes such as lines, arcs, ovals, rectangles, and polygons. You also learned about the Image class. You learned how to filter, crop, and modify images prior to display. Finally, you also saw how the ImageObserver interface allows an Applet to monitor the progress of an image that is being retrieved. In the next chapter you will learn how to further improve your Java programs by using animation and sound.

Multimedia Programming with Java

- Animation
- Sounds

Multimedia is a powerful technique that can be used to really intrigue your users into spending hours in front of their computers. With intense graphics and sounds, your users can be captivated.

The preceding chapter covered how to use the Graphics class to draw various shapes and images in programs. This chapter goes farther and discusses how to start to animate the graphics and images and how to add sound to your programs.

Animation

Animation is the process by which images are displayed over time, giving the appearance of movement. This task can be accomplished in several ways. This section covers using the MediaTracker class to load multiple images into a program, some techniques to polish animations, and an alternative method of animation using a single image.

Using the MediaTracker Class to Load Multiple Images

The MediaTracker class can be used to load various media. This sounds good, but, unfortunately, like most things in life, it sounds better than it is. Currently, the only media it tracks is images. It does a really good job, though.

Why would a MediaTracker instance be used? If you did not use MediaTracker, every program written would have to implement an ImageObserver. MediaTracker uses an internal ImageObserver to monitor the loading of images.

The MediaTracker Class

The MediaTracker constructor takes a single argument:

```
public MediaTracker(Component comp)
```

The Component parameter is the component for which the images are being loaded. Since Applet is derived from Component, this is typically passed to a MediaTracker instance inside of an Applet derived class.

After an instance has been allocated, images can be added. To add an image, one of the following methods is used:

```
public void addImage(Image, int)
public void addImage(Image, int, int, int)
```

Both addImage methods take an image and an identifier. The image is created via Applet.getImage. The following code illustrates the use of this method, which is a code fragment from the preceding chapter:

```
myImage = getImage(getDocumentBase(), "savannah.jpg");
```

The identifier passed as the second argument is used to identify and track either a single image or a group of images. The value of the identifier indicates the priority given to the loading of the images. Images with a lower value have a higher priority when loading. If several images are given the same identifier, all references to that identifier apply to all the images with that identifier. Therefore, when the status of the images is referred to, that is, by using statusID, the value returned should be applied to all images with that identifier.

After an image, or group of images, has been added, the status of the loading of the image can be monitored with the following methods:

```
public int statusID(int, boolean)
public int statusAll(boolean)
```

These methods both return a value that is the combination of the following flags found in the MediaTracker class:

    ABORTED
    COMPLETE
    ERRORED
    LOADING

statusID is used to return the status associated with a single identifier. Alternatively, statusAll is used to return the overall status of all the images being monitored. After adding an image, the MediaTracker class does nothing to initiate the actual loading of the images. Both of these methods, along with several other methods of the class, take an additional Boolean parameter. This parameter indicates that the images should be loaded, if they haven't been already.

Table 15.1 shows additional methods of the MediaTracker class that can be used to monitor the loading progress.

Table 15.1. MediaTracker class methods.

Member	Purpose
checkAll()	Returns TRUE if all images associated with the MediaTracker instance have been loaded.
checkAll(boolean)	Returns TRUE if all images associated with the MediaTracker instance have been loaded. Optionally initiates the loading of the images.
checkID(int)	Returns TRUE if all images associated with the identifier have been loaded.
checkID(int, boolean)	Returns TRUE if all images associated with the identifier have been loaded. Optionally initiates the loading of the images.
getErrorsAny()	Returns an array of objects associated with the MediaTracker instance that have encountered an error.

continues

Table 15.1. continued

Member	Purpose
getErrorsID()	Returns an array of objects associated with the identifier that have encountered an error.
isErrorAny()	Returns TRUE if there are any objects associated with the MediaTracker instance that encountered an error.
isErrorID(int)	Returns TRUE if there are any objects associated with the identifier that encountered an error.
statusID(int, boolean)	Returns a combined status of all of the objects associated with the identifier. Optionally initiates the loading of the images.
statusAll(boolean)	Returns a status of the load process for all objects associated with the identifier.
waitForAll()	Blocking method that waits for all images associated with the MediaTracker instance to be loaded.
waitForAll(long)	Blocking method that waits for all images associated with the MediaTracker instance to be loaded. Times out after the specified number of milliseconds.
waitForID(int)	Blocking method that waits for all images associated with the identifier to be loaded.
waitForID(int, long)	Blocking method that waits for all images associated with the identifier to be loaded. Times out after the specified number of milliseconds.

A MediaTracker Example

As an example of using the MediaTracker class, consider displaying several images. Listing 15.1 contains the Applet code used for example EX15A.

Listing 15.1. The Applet class used for example EX15A.

```
import java.applet.*;
import java.awt.*;
public class EX15A extends Applet implements Runnable
{
 protected ImageCanvas Images[];
 protected MediaTracker ImageTracker;
 protected Thread ImageThread;
 public void init()
 {
```

```
// If you use a ResourceWizard-generated "control creator" class to
// arrange controls in your applet, you may want to call its
// CreateControls() method from within this method. Remove the following
// call to resize() before adding the call to CreateControls();
// CreateControls() does its own resizing.
//-----------------------------------------------------------------------
resize(500, 300);
// create a tracker to monitor image loading
ImageTracker = new MediaTracker(this);
// create a place to put the image controls
Images = new ImageCanvas[3];
// add the images to be tracked
for (int index = 0; index < 3; index++) {
Images[index] = new ImageCanvas(ImageTracker,
getImage(getCodeBase(),
"images\\Christopher" +
Integer.toString(index + 1) + ".jpg"));
add(Images[index]);
}
}
public void start()
{
if (ImageThread == null) {
ImageThread = new Thread(this);
ImageThread.start();
}
}
public void stop()
{
if (ImageThread != null) {
ImageThread.stop();
ImageThread = null;
}
}

public void run()
{
// wait for all of the images to be loaded
for (int index = 0; index < 3; index++)
Images[index].WaitForImage();
}
}
```

The first step performed in the init method is to create the MediaTracker instance. Because Applet
is derived from Component, this is passed to the constructor. The next task performed is to add the
controls that will be used to display the images. A new class, ImageCanvas, is defined in this file,
which is used to do the actual displaying of the image. The following code fragment does several
things to instantiate an ImageCanvas for each image to be displayed:

```
Images[index] = new ImageCanvas(ImageTracker,
 getImage(getCodeBase(),
 "images\\Christopher" +
 Integer.toString(index + 1) + ".jpg"));
```

This code uses getImage to retrieve the image. The image's location can be found by using the code's URL and the string created, with the knowledge that the image is in an image subdirectory and is a JPEG file named *christopherx.jpg*, in which x indicates the image number. The image is then passed to the ImageCanvas constructor, along with the MediaTracker used to monitor the loading of the image.

The remaining code in the Applet class is concerned primarily with instantiating a thread that will be used with the MediaTracker instance to monitor the loading of the images. For more information on using threads, see Chapter 12, "Moving Up to Multithreading." Because monitoring the loading of images usually involves sleeping, this should always be in a user-allocated thread. This allows threads that are allocating and controlling the Applet classes to continue to do their jobs.

ImageCanvas was added to this example to show that you do not always have to handle displaying information in the Applet.paint method. Listing 15.2 shows the code for the ImageCanvas class.

Listing 15.2. The ImageCanvas class of example EX15A.

```java
class ImageCanvas extends Canvas
{
 // NextImageId is used to give each image a unique id
 protected static int NextImageId = 1;
 protected MediaTracker ImageTracker;
 protected Image TheImage;
 protected int LocalImageId;
 protected boolean ImageIsLoaded = false;
 protected boolean LoadError = false;
 ImageCanvas(MediaTracker ImageTracker, Image TheImage)
 {
 // use the next available image id and increment the next id
 LocalImageId = NextImageId;
 NextImageId++;
 // save the passed in info
 this.ImageTracker = ImageTracker;
 this.TheImage = TheImage;
 // resize the canvas to a known size
 resize(200, 140);
 // add the image to the media tracker
 ImageTracker.addImage(TheImage, LocalImageId,
 size().width, size().height);
 }
 public void paint(Graphics g)
 {
 if (ImageIsLoaded) {
 if (LoadError)
 g.drawString("Error loading image.", 10, 10);
 else
 g.drawImage(TheImage, 0, 0, this);
 }
 else {
 g.drawString("Loading", 10, 10);
 }
```

```
}
public void WaitForImage()
{
try {
ImageTracker.waitForID(LocalImageId);
}
catch (InterruptedException e) {}
// set state flags
ImageIsLoaded = true;
LoadError = ImageTracker.isErrorID(LocalImageId);
// force the component to be updated
repaint();
}
}
```

This class has several protected members used to hold information about the image it is displaying (ImageTracker, TheImage, LocalImageId, ImageIsLoaded, and LoadError).

The first step in the class constructor is to assign a unique ID for the current image, using the value of the static NextImageId and then incrementing the value for the next instance. Additionally, information is saved in the class, and the component is resized to a reasonable size. Finally, the image is added to the MediaTracker with the local identifier and the size of the Canvas on which the image will be displayed.

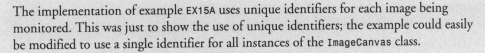

NOTE:

The implementation of example EX15A uses unique identifiers for each image being monitored. This was just to show the use of unique identifiers; the example could easily be modified to use a single identifier for all instances of the ImageCanvas class.

The paint method is straightforward, displaying a string if the image is being loaded or if there was an error loading the image, or displaying the image itself if it was successfully loaded.

Use WaitForImage if you want to wait until the image is loaded and ready to be displayed. MediaTracker.WaitForID is used to have the MediaTracker instance wait until the image is loaded. After the image is loaded, the state members are set to tell paint the appropriate action to take. Finally, repaint is called for the component to update the look of the component.

The result of running example EX15A is shown in Figure 15.1.

Note that the third image was intentionally named incorrectly on the disc to show the error condition being displayed.

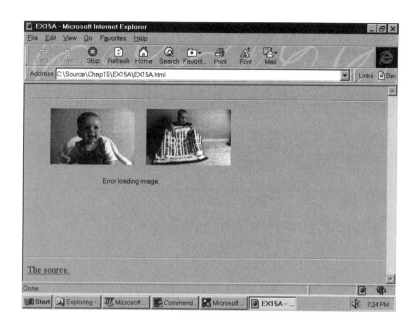

Figure 15.1.

Example EX15A.

Basic Animation

In the preceding section, it was shown how MediaTracker could be used to monitor the loading of multiple images. This mechanism can be used in creating animation. Animation can be performed by displaying an image, pausing, and then displaying the next image. If the images are closely related, movement can be successfully simulated.

A banner is the displaying of a message such that the image scrolls by a "window." It appears to be a continuous image. A banner is a good way to explore animation, because the implementation is easy to follow, and the same basic techniques can be applied to more complicated animation.

Creating a Banner

One type of animation is exemplified by the use of a banner. A banner gives the impression that a wide image is being shown to the user in a scrolling fashion. Because the banner repeats, it gives the impression that the image makes a big loop and one end is tied to the other. Figure 15.2 shows example EX15B displaying a banner.

The implementation of animation is straightforward. The process is to display an image, pause for a short amount of time (typical computer animation is 10 to 20 frames per second), and then display another image that is only slightly different from the preceding image. The quality of animation is determined by the quality of the images being displayed and the amount of delay between each image. That is, the smaller the differential between images, the faster they need to be displayed. Of course, you pay a price for having a large number of images. Download time must be considered, because all the images need to be downloaded, which can be quite costly when you are accessing a slow server or using a slower machine. A happy medium must be achieved for successful animation.

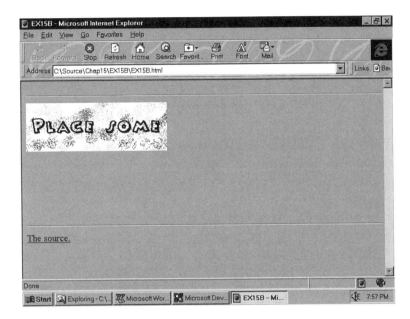

Figure 15.2.
A banner being displayed with example EX15B.

Twenty images are loaded with example EX15B. Six of those images are displayed at a time. The init method is very similar to the preceding example. Because the sole purpose of the applet is to display the banner, however, the images are loaded and monitored directly in the Applet derived class. Similarly, the monitoring of the loading of the images is done in a user-declared thread. The start and stop methods are used to allocate and stop the thread appropriately.

The heart of the applet is in the paint and run methods. Listing 15.3 shows the paint method.

Listing 15.3. The paint method of example EX15B.

```
public void paint(Graphics g)
{
// if all the images haven't been loaded, don't do anything
if (LoadedCount >= ImageCount) {
int currentId = CurrentImageId;
for (int index = 0; index < 6; index++) {
// assume images have a width of 50
g.drawImage(Images[currentId - ImageIdBase],
index * 50, 0, this);
currentId = GetNextId(currentId);
}
}
}
```

The first thing to notice is that the animation is not even started unless all images have been loaded. Because the amount of time required to download the images is potentially so much greater than the amount of time required to cycle through the animation, it is always a good idea to not start the animation until all the images have been loaded.

If the images have been loaded, paint simply draws six images using the Graphics instance, g. Using the assumption that all the images are the same width, the location for each image is calculated, based on the index of the image being drawn and its width. Because the banner will continue indefinitely, GetNextId is used to get the ID of the next image to display.

GetNextId is a simple, protected function used to cycle through the IDs of the images used for the banner:

```
protected int GetNextId(int currentId)
{
int nextId = currentId + 1;
if (nextId >= ImageCount + ImageIdBase)
nextId = ImageIdBase;
return nextId;
}
```

Listing 15.4 shows the next major player in this animation game.

Listing 15.4. The run method of example EX15B.

```
public void run()
{
int id = ImageIdBase;
while (id <= ImageIdBase + ImageCount - 1) {
if ((ImageTracker.statusID(id, true) & MediaTracker.COMPLETE)
== MediaTracker.COMPLETE) {
IncrementImageCount();
id++;
}
else {
try {
Thread.sleep(250);
} catch (InterruptedException e) {}
}
}
ProgressMessage.hide(); // don't show progress any more
while (true) {
repaint();
try {
Thread.sleep(750);
} catch (InterruptedException e) {}
CurrentImageId = GetNextId(CurrentImageId);
}
}
```

The thread used to monitor the loading of the images was passed this as the parameter to the constructor. Therefore, the run method of the applet is called when the thread is started. The first step in the thread is to cycle through the IDs of the images being loaded, checking for a completion status. If the image has completed the loading process, IncrementImageCount is called to increment LoadedCount and update the message being displayed. Listing 15.5 shows the implementation of the IncrementImageCount method. If the loading of the image has not completed, the thread sleeps for a quarter of a second.

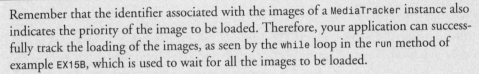

NOTE:

Remember that the identifier associated with the images of a MediaTracker instance also indicates the priority of the image to be loaded. Therefore, your application can successfully track the loading of the images, as seen by the while loop in the run method of example EX15B, which is used to wait for all the images to be loaded.

After all the images have been loaded, the label that is used to show the progress is hidden so that the banner can be displayed. The second while loop in this method is the typical endless loop found in user-defined threads. The loop consists of a call to the repaint method to paint the first, and subsequent, blocks of the banner. Because that was so hard, a little snooze is now in order. Finally, the current image ID is cyclically incremented using GetNextId.

Listing 15.5. The IncrementImageCount method of example EX15B.

```
protected synchronized void IncrementImageCount()
{
LoadedCount++;
// inform the user what is happening
ProgressMessage.setText("Loaded " +
Integer.toString(LoadedCount) + " of the " +
Integer.toString(ImageCount) + " images...");
ProgressMessage.resize(ProgressMessage.preferredSize());
// tell the layout manager to do its job
validate();
}
```

That covers the basics of animation. The techniques covered here are all that are needed to start investigating simple to complex animations. The following sections cover techniques that can be used to improve the look and performance of animations in general.

Improving the Paint

Due to the frequency with which animations are drawn, one of the biggest enemies of animations is flicker. A couple of things can be done to reduce the amount of flicker that occurs in the drawing of animations.

paint has to be a very generic method to handle the variety of tasks it might have to do. It has to be able to handle everything from drawing text to drawing like Gauguin. When repaint is called to update the screen, you are not really calling a method that calls paint, but telling the applet to paint the screen when it has time. Additionally, the function that really calls the paint method is update. The default implementation for update is something like:

```
public void update(Graphics g) {
  g.setColor(getBackground());
  g.fillRect(0, 0, width, height);
  g.setColor(getForeground());
  paint(g);
}
```

The first thing that happens is that the background color is selected into the Graphics and the background is filled. Guess where the main cause of the flicker is generated from. Because animations typically redraw the entire area that is being animated, a simple enhancement would be to override the update function and simply call the paint method. Here's an example:

```
public void update(Graphics g) {
  paint(g);
}
```

Consider the previous banner example. Because the same area is always rendered in the paint method, this simple update goes a long way to reduce the flicker. This new update method was added to example EX15B and is on the accompanying CD as example EX15C.

The second method to improve the painting of animations is to actually reduce the amount of what is being painted. This can be easily accomplished by letting the update method do a little more work and setting the clipping region in the Graphics instance that is passed to paint.

Due to the fact that the simplified update was so effective in the banner example, the clipping region does not have any effect for that example. Instead, consider a classic example of animation: the bouncing ball in front of a complicated background. Figure 15.3 shows a sketch of two sequential positions of the ball.

Assume that the circle labeled P1 in the figure was the original location of the ball and the circle labeled P2 in the figure is the current location of the ball. Realize that this is a very exaggerated diagram of two sequential positions of the ball, to illustrate what the clipping region is.

Up to this point, the approach would be to draw the entire background and then add the ball at the new position. Depending on the size of the graphics boundary, this might or might not be an acceptable approach. A larger area, however, would take quite a while to draw, and our friend flicker would be back. When the image is being updated, a large portion of the image will not change from one position to the next. What will change is mainly the area between the two positions of the ball. Therefore, if we restrict the painting to only the region defined by the perimeter of the balls, also known as the clipping region, the painting task becomes much simpler, based only on the amount of painting being done.

Figure 15.3.

A sketch of two sequential positions of a bouncing ball.

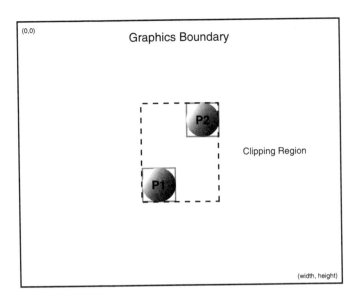

To determine the clipping region, the following function could be used:

```
Rectangle GetClippingRegion(int x1, int y1, int x2, int y2, int width, int height)
{
 int clipX, clipY, clipWidth, clipHeight;
 // determine the leftmost x coordinates and subsequently the
 // clipping region width
 clipX = min(x1, x2);
 clipWidth = abs(x2 - x1) + width;
 // determine the uppermost y coordinates and subsequently the
 // clipping region height
 clipY = min(y1, y2);
 clipHeight = abs(y2 - y1) + height;
 return new Rectangle(clipX, clipY, clipWidth, clipHeight);
}
```

This function assumes that the point (x1, y1) defines the origin of the rectangular region that completely encloses the ball at position P1 and that (x2, y2) defines the origin of the rectangular region that completely encloses the ball at position P2. Additionally, because the ball is theoretically the same ball, it will be the same size at P1 and P2.

The preceding clipping region could now be utilized in a new update method:

```
public void update(Graphics g) {
 Rectangle rect = GetClippingRegion(previousX, previousY,
 currentX, currentY, ballWidth, ballHeight);
 g.clipRec(rect.x, rect.y, rect.width, rect.height);
 paint(g);
 previousX = currentX;
 previousY = currentY;
}
```

This method determines the region that needs to be updated, based on the previous position and the current position, and then sets the clipping rectangle of the Graphics that is passed to the paint method. Finally, the current position is saved as the previous position.

You might wonder how we now utilize that clipping region in the paint function. Well, we don't have to worry about that. Because the paint method makes calls to the Graphics to do any type of output, the Graphics worries about the clipping regions and simply ignores any updates to the regions outside the clipping rectangle.

These methods will reduce the amount of flickering associated with animation to a somewhat reasonable amount. Eliminating the background redraw stops unnecessary updates while defining a clipping region localized to what is being redrawn.

Double Buffering

Perhaps one of the best general enhancements that can be done to animations and graphics renderings in general is to use a second buffer to draw the image. After the image is complete, it is copied to the main image in one fell swoop. This is commonly referred to as *double buffering*.

If the preceding clipping region example just showed how advantageous it is to reduce the area that is being rendered, how can double buffering help us, if we just have to copy the entire image at the end of the process? The answer is that the complicated images often are composed of several operations (that is, drawing the background images, drawing foreground images that were obscured by a main image, and then drawing a new version of the main image). By performing these drawing operations to an "in memory" buffer instead of the program's screen, you prevent the user from seeing the multiple operations. Additionally, when Java does perform the copy, the virtual machine can typically take advantage of block copy routines implemented in the native language that copies larger portions of images.

Let's revisit the banner example and add double buffering to help out the animation. The only difference between example EX15C and example EX15D is the update method found in Listing 15.6.

Listing 15.6. The double-buffering update method of example EX15D.

```
public void update(Graphics g)
{
  // create an off-screen image if there isn't one
  if (OffScreenImage == null)
  OffScreenImage = createImage(size().width, size().height);
  // get a graphics that can be used with the off-screen image
  Graphics offScreenGraphics = OffScreenImage.getGraphics();
  // use the paint method to draw to the off-screen image
  paint(offScreenGraphics);
  // splat!! the new image over the current image
  g.drawImage(OffScreenImage, 0, 0, this);
  // release the resources associated with the off-screen image
  offScreenGraphics.dispose();
}
```

This method first allocates a new image, if one has not been allocated, making it the size of the applet. Next, a Graphics instance is retrieved from the image to be used to draw to the image. Now comes the tricky part. Because you have likely developed the paint method to perform any drawing that needs to be done, simply call the paint method to draw to the off-screen image. When the painting is completed, do a mass copy to the existing Graphics and the image will be updated. Finally, release the graphics context, because most operating systems have limited resources for drawing among all of their processes.

Image Manipulation

As an alternative to displaying multiple images, you might want to consider the manipulation of a single image. This cannot, however, be applied to all animations. For example, consider the default animated program generated by the Visual J++ Applet Wizard. For more information on using the AppletWizard, see Chapter 2, "Creating Your First Applet with Applet Wizard."

The default example shows the Earth spinning on its normal North Pole to South Pole axis. This could not be replicated using a single image unless you could come up with a very odd perspective. If, however, you want to totally change the entire ecosystem, you could take a single view of the Earth and experiment with rotating it on an axis that runs through the equator. In terms of animation, this would mean taking a single image and spinning the image.

Another example using a single image is the banner example. Figure 15.4 shows the entire banner used in the previous examples.

Figure 15.4.
The full banner contents.

This image is used to display the banner in the applet by taking advantage of the clipping region and being able to specify a starting location of the image being drawn that is outside the area of the image. Listing 15.7 shows the relevant methods of example EX15E.

Listing 15.7. The scrolling-banner class EX15E methods using a single image.

```
public void paint(Graphics g)
{
// if the image hasn't been loaded, don't do anything
if (ImageLoaded) {
g.clipRect(0, 0, ImageDisplayWidth, ImageDisplayHeight);
// draw the first round of the image
g.drawImage(SingleImage, CurrentDisplayXValue, 0, this);
// calculate where the wrapping image starts
int wrapXLocation = CurrentDisplayXValue + ImageWidth;
```

continues

Listing 15.7. continued

```
// if the wrap image has started into the displayable
// range, draw the image again
if (wrapXLocation < ImageDisplayWidth)
g.drawImage(SingleImage, wrapXLocation, 0, this);
}
}
public void run()
{
try {
ImageTracker.waitForID(ImageId);
}
catch (InterruptedException e) {}
ImageLoaded = true;
ProgressMessage.hide(); // don't show progress any more
while (true) {
repaint();
try {
Thread.sleep(ImageDelay);
} catch (InterruptedException e) {}
CurrentDisplayXValue = GetNextXValue(CurrentDisplayXValue);
}
}
protected int GetNextXValue(int currentXValue)
{
int nextXValue = currentXValue - ImageXDecrement;
if (nextXValue < -ImageWidth)
nextXValue = -ImageXDecrement;
return nextXValue;
}
```

The paint method first clips the drawing region to the area that is being displayed. The first image is drawn in the graphics using CurrentDisplayXValue. This value is the key to the scrollability of the image, and it ranges from 0 to the negative width of the image (that is, −1000). Because the clipping rectangle starts at (0, 0), nothing is displayed to the left of the applet display area, as expected. The next operation determines where the second drawing of the image needs to take place to perform the wrapping function. This calculation is essentially determining whether the end of the first image is within the display area. If it is, the image is drawn for the second time within the display area.

The run method is not atypical and should be pretty familiar. GetNextXValue is used to determine the next starting location for the first image. Notice that if the first image is being drawn so that the entire image is outside the displayable area, the image is reset to "take over" the scrolling of the second image found in paint.

As you can see, this method is not applicable to every animation situation. If it can be used, however, the savings in not having to load multiple images will add up.

Sounds

Sounds can easily be added to your program through the use of the `AudioClip` class. The definition of `AudioClip` is simple:

```
public interface java.applet.AudioClip
{
 public abstract void loop();
 public abstract void play();
 public abstract void stop();
}
```

As you can see from the code, `AudioClip` is an interface and not a class. The reason for this is that an instance of this class cannot be instantiated. Instead, the user must call a function that will allocate a system-defined class that implements audio suitable for the device being used by the user.

To obtain an `AudioClip`, the `getAudioClip` methods of `Applet` can be called:

```
public AudioClip getAudioClip(URL);
public AudioClip getAudioClip(URL, String);
```

Both functions take URLs that indicate the location of the audio clip. For the first function, the audio clip has to be completely defined in the URL. The second function allows the additional specification of where the audio clip is located, relative to the URL.

Additionally, `Applet` provides "shortcuts" to playing audio with the following methods:

```
public void play(URL)
public void play(URL, String)
```

The parameters to these methods are the same as those for `getAudioClip`, mentioned previously.

The audio clips currently supported by Java are rather limited. The only supported format is 8-bit, μlaw, 8000 Hz, mono channel, Sun `.au` files. With a careful search on the Internet, however, you can find conversion utilities to convert from various types of audio files to .au files.

TIP:

To add personalized audio to your programs when using Microsoft Windows, you can use the Sound Recorder and your multimedia hardware to record just about anything. This recording produces a standard Windows `.wav` file. From here, you can use a conversion utility to convert this file from a `.wav` file to an `.au` file. A good shareware utility I found on the Internet is GoldWave, which can be found at

```
http://web.cs.mun.ca/~chris3/goldwave
```

This utility not only allows you to convert the file types, but also supports various audio manipulations, including echoing, creating distortion, and adjusting the volume, to name a few.

Figure 15.5 shows the interface for example EX15F. This interface allows the playing of three short audio clips and has a background clip that continually loops after it has been loaded.

Figure 15.5.

Example EX15F.

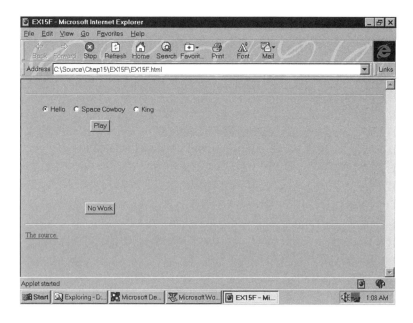

The background audio clip is rather lengthy, so it is loaded in a user-allocated thread. The run method of example EX15F is shown in Listing 15.8.

Listing 15.8. The run method of example EX15F.

```
public void run()
{
HiHoo = getAudioClip(getCodeBase(), "audio\\Heighho.au");
HiHoo.loop();
Work.setLabel("No Work");
}
```

HiHoo is an AudioClip instance of the EX15F class; it gets assigned using Applet.getAudioClip, using the relative location of the method. Then, loop is used to play the clip continuously.

NOTE:

If audio is being used to play longer selections, more than just warning beeps and whistles, the program should allow the user to disable the audio. Even the best sounds found by the programmer can be interpreted as annoying by others. Additionally, some user might be trapped with slow access connections and might not want to wait for the Internet traffic to download the audio.

Listing 15.9 shows how the action method of the EX15F class does double duty in starting and stopping the background clip, and it uses Applet.play to play the short clips.

Listing 15.9. The action method of example EX15F.

```
public boolean action(Event evt, Object obj)
{
boolean retval = false;
// check to see if the audio should be turned off or on
if ("Work".equals(obj)) {
HiHoo.loop(); // start the music
Work.setLabel("No Work");
retval = true;
}
else if ("No Work".equals(obj)) {
HiHoo.stop(); // stop the music
Work.setLabel("Work");
retval = true;
}
// check to see if one of the simple sounds should be played
else if ("Play".equals(obj)) {
Checkbox current = SimplerSounds.getCurrent();
play(getCodeBase(), "audio\\" + current.getLabel() + ".au");
retval = true;
}
return retval;
}
```

Summary

In this chapter, you learned that going from graphics to animation is a straightforward process. The MediaTracker class makes it easy to load multiple images without having to add ImageObserver overhead to every program. After images have been loaded, a thread can handle showing an image, pausing, and then showing another image to produce simple animation. A few techniques were introduced to prevent animation flicker, including reducing background draws, using clipping rectangles to reduce the overall amount of what is being drawn, and finally using an in-memory image buffer to implement image double buffering. As an alternative to using multiple images, a single image could also be used that contains all the images that contribute to the animation. Calculating drawing of this single image can produce effective animations in certain circumstances. Finally, Java's sound support was introduced, which rounds out the multimedia topics.

Chapter

16

Sprucing Things Up with Colors and Fonts

So far, we have been using components in their default configuration. We have moved them around, made them different sizes, and let the layout managers place them for us. One of the changes we can make to the components is to give them a little color and change the font. With Java and Visual J++, this is an easy task that you can use to dramatically change the look of your program.

In this chapter, a sample application that displays some text will be used to illustrate the use of color and font. In addition, two buttons will be added. The first button will bring up a dialog that lets the user set the color of text to display. With this dialog, the user will be able to use a preset default color, or set a custom color. The second button will bring up a dialog that lets the user select the font to be used for the text. This dialog allows the selection of the type of font, the size of the font, and optional attributes of bold and italic.

The Base Applet

The best way to explore this topic is to dive right in. The base application is shown in Figure 16.1.

Figure 16.1.

The base applet used to set the color and font.

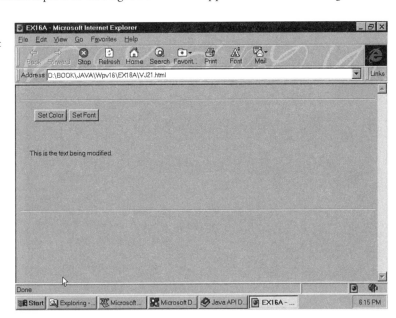

Listing 16.1 shows the source to this applet.

Listing 16.1. EX16A.java.

```java
import java.applet.*;
import java.awt.*;

public class EX16A extends Applet
{
```

```
    protected Button SetColorButton = new Button("Set Color");
    protected Button SetFontButton = new Button("Set Font");
    protected String MyText = new String("This is the text being modified.");

    public void init()
    {
        add(SetColorButton);
        add(SetFontButton);
    }

    public void paint(Graphics g)
    {
        g.drawString(MyText, 20, 100);
    }
}
```

The applet-derived class contains two buttons: SetColorButton and SetFontButton. The init method is straightforward and simply adds the components to the applet. In addition, MyText is displayed in the paint method to have something to operate on. Easy stuff.

Setting the Color

The basis for setting the color of a number of items is the Color class. This section covers the definition of the Color class, a generic dialog used to set the color, and an applet putting it to use.

The Color Class

The Color class is a simple class that can hold any color. It does this by storing a color based on the concentration of red, green, and blue.

To create a color, use one of the three Color constructors:

```
public Color(float r, float g, float b);
public Color(int rgb);
public Color(int r, int g, int b);
```

The first of these constructors takes the three parts in floating point format. The concentration of each element expressed with values ranging from 0 to 1.0. The next two constructors will probably be used more often because their values are expressed as integer values ranging from 0 to 255. The first of the integer constructors has the values encoded in a single integer—bits 16–23 represents red, 8–15 represents green, and 0–7 represents blue. The final integer constructor simply has the values separated into three manageable parts.

Here are some examples of declaring colors:

```
Color black = new Color(0, 0, 0);
Color white = new Color(255, 255, 255);
Color coolPurple = new Color(0.345, 0, 0.5);
```

The values for each color indicate the concentration of the color; therefore, the lower the number, the lower the concentration. And conversely, the higher the value, the higher the concentration. The examples express this with `black` being an absence of color, and `white` being a combination of all colors. The rest of the colors fall somewhere in between.

NOTE:

Remember that colors are only as good as the device displaying them. Therefore, the following two colors might or might not be the same.

```
Color coolPurple = new Color(102, 0, 128);
Color coolerPurple = new Color(68, 0, 128);
```

So that you are not completely on your own, the `Color` class provides the following predefined colors, which are instances of the `Color` class and can be used whenever a `Color` class is used:

black	magenta
blue	orange
cyan	pink
darkGray	red
gray	white
green	yellow
lightGray	

Once you have an instance of `Color`, there are a variety of things that can be done with the color. The public methods are described in Table 16.1.

Table 16.1. Public methods of the `Color` class.

Member	Purpose
brighter()	Returns a color brighter than the current color.
darker()	Returns a color darker than the current color.
equals(Object)	Compares two color objects for the same color.
getBlue()	Returns the blue component.
getColor(String)	Returns the color of the named system property.
getColor(String, Color)	Returns the color of the named system property, specifying a default if not found.
getColor(String, int)	Returns the color of the named system property, specifying a default if not found.
getGreen()	Returns the green component.
getHSBColor(float, float, float)	Returns a color with the given hue, saturation, and brightness.

Member	Purpose
getRed()	Returns the red component.
getRGB()	Returns the components combined in a single integer.
hashCode()	Returns a hash code representing the color.
HSBtoRGB(float, float, float)	Returns an RGB value for a color specified by hue, saturation, and brightness.
RGBtoHSB(int, int, int, float)	Returns values for hue, saturation, and brightness for a color specified by an RGB value.
toString()	Returns a string representation of the color.

Set Color Dialog

Given the knowledge of how to construct a color given the components, the task is to develop a dialog that enables the user to select his own color. Figure 16.2 contains the dialog at work.

<u>Figure 16.2.</u>
Set Color dialog of EX16B.

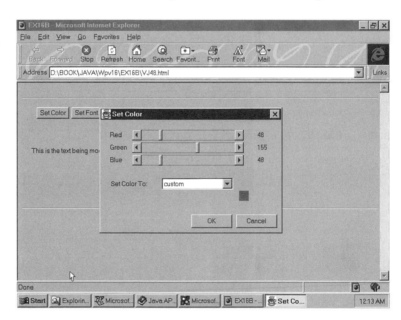

With the dialog, the user can select a custom color by specifying the color components using the scrollbars. Adjusting the scrollbars with the arrows or by dragging the thumbnail will automatically adjust the value to the right of each scrollbar. If the user selects a default color from the choice list, this automatically adjusts the scrollbar values to the appropriate values so that the user can see what components make up the default values. A sample swatch of the color is displayed in the box in the lower right of the dialog.

The first step in creating this dialog was to use the Resource Wizard to design and lay out the components of the class. For more information on using the Resource Wizard, refer to Chapter 7, "Saving Time with the Resource Wizard." This process produced the resource file `SetColor.rct`. We then used the Tools | Java Resource Wizard to produce the files `DialogLayout.java` and `SetColorControls.java`.

CAUTION:

When using the Dialog Editor, be sure to only place controls on your container classes that have a direct translation to Java components. Refer to Table 7.1, in Chapter 7, for a list of available controls and the corresponding Java components.

`DialogLayout` is a layout manager that is based on Dialog Logical Units (DLUs). This class is used by the `SetColorControls` class to place components at a specific location on the dialog using DLUs. To learn more about layout managers, see Chapter 5, "Java's User Interface Components."

Listing 16.2 shows the contents of the `SetColorControls` class generated by the Java Resource Wizard.

Listing 16.2. `SetColorControls.java`.

```
import java.awt.*;
import DialogLayout;

public class SetColorControls
{
    Container    m_Parent       = null;
    boolean      m_fInitialized = false;
    DialogLayout m_Layout;

    // Control definitions
    //-------------------------------------------------------------------
    Button        OkButton;
    Button        CancelButton;
    Scrollbar     RedScrollbar;
    Label         IDC_STATIC1;
    Label         IDC_STATIC2;
    Scrollbar     GreenScrollbar;
    Scrollbar     BlueScrollbar;
    Label         IDC_STATIC3;
    Label         IDC_STATIC4;
    Choice        StandardColorChoice;
    Label         RedValue;
    Label         GreenValue;
    Label         BlueValue;
```

```java
    // Constructor
    //----------------------------------------------------------------------
    public SetColorControls (Container parent)
    {
        m_Parent = parent;
    }

    // Initialization.
    //----------------------------------------------------------------------
    public boolean CreateControls()--
    {
        // CreateControls should be called only once
        //------------------------------------------------------------------
        if (m_fInitialized || m_Parent == null)
            return false;

        // m_Parent must be extended from the Container class
        //------------------------------------------------------------------
        if (!(m_Parent instanceof Container))
            return false;

        // Since a given font may not be supported across all platforms, it
        // is safe to modify only the size of the font, not the typeface.
        //------------------------------------------------------------------
        Font OldFnt = m_Parent.getFont();
        if (OldFnt != null)
        {
            Font NewFnt = new Font(OldFnt.getName(), OldFnt.getStyle(), 8);

            m_Parent.setFont(NewFnt);
        }

        // All position and sizes are in dialog logical units, so we use a
        // DialogLayout as our layout manager.
        //------------------------------------------------------------------
        m_Layout = new DialogLayout(m_Parent, 220, 116);
        m_Parent.setLayout(m_Layout);
        m_Parent.addNotify();

        Dimension size   = m_Layout.getDialogSize();
        Insets    insets = m_Parent.insets();

        m_Parent.resize(insets.left + size.width  + insets.right,
                        insets.top  + size.height + insets.bottom);

        // Control creation
        //------------------------------------------------------------------
        OkButton = new Button ("OK");
        m_Parent.add(OkButton);
        m_Layout.setShape(OkButton, 111, 98, 50, 14);

        CancelButton = new Button ("Cancel");
        m_Parent.add(CancelButton);
        m_Layout.setShape(CancelButton, 166, 98, 50, 14);
```

continues

Listing 16.2. continued

```
        RedScrollbar = new Scrollbar (Scrollbar.HORIZONTAL, 0, 1, 0, 99);
        m_Parent.add(RedScrollbar);
        m_Layout.setShape(RedScrollbar, 39, 10, 136, 11);

        IDC_STATIC1 = new Label ("Red", Label.LEFT);
        m_Parent.add(IDC_STATIC1);
        m_Layout.setShape(IDC_STATIC1, 10, 11, 28, 8);

        IDC_STATIC2 = new Label ("Green", Label.LEFT);
        m_Parent.add(IDC_STATIC2);
        m_Layout.setShape(IDC_STATIC2, 10, 24, 28, 8);

        GreenScrollbar = new Scrollbar (Scrollbar.HORIZONTAL, 0, 1, 0, 99);
        m_Parent.add(GreenScrollbar);
        m_Layout.setShape(GreenScrollbar, 39, 23, 136, 11);

        BlueScrollbar = new Scrollbar (Scrollbar.HORIZONTAL, 0, 1, 0, 99);
        m_Parent.add(BlueScrollbar);
        m_Layout.setShape(BlueScrollbar, 39, 36, 136, 11);

        IDC_STATIC3 = new Label ("Blue", Label.LEFT);
        m_Parent.add(IDC_STATIC3);
        m_Layout.setShape(IDC_STATIC3, 10, 37, 28, 8);

        IDC_STATIC4 = new Label ("Set Color To:", Label.LEFT);
        m_Parent.add(IDC_STATIC4);
        m_Layout.setShape(IDC_STATIC4, 11, 62, 50, 8);

        StandardColorChoice = new Choice ();
        m_Parent.add(StandardColorChoice);
        m_Layout.setShape(StandardColorChoice, 75, 60, 87, 52);

        RedValue = new Label ("0", Label.LEFT);
        m_Parent.add(RedValue);
        m_Layout.setShape(RedValue, 190, 11, 18, 8);

        GreenValue = new Label ("0", Label.LEFT);
        m_Parent.add(GreenValue);
        m_Layout.setShape(GreenValue, 190, 24, 18, 8);

        BlueValue = new Label ("0", Label.LEFT);
        m_Parent.add(BlueValue);
        m_Layout.setShape(BlueValue, 190, 37, 18, 8);

        m_fInitialized = true;
        return true;
    }
}
```

The member variable m_Parent holds the container class in which the controls are placed. m_Layout is the layout manager that is used to position the controls on the container. Additionally, there is a component instance for each of the controls placed on the dialog in the Dialog Editor.

The two member methods of this class are simple, yet effective. The constructor saves the parent of all of the components. CreateControls does some basic housekeeping to make sure the parent exists and that it is a type of container. It then sets up the layout manager for the parent. Finally, it places all the controls on the container, based on the designed DLUs.

The next step is examining the class used for the dialog. This dialog will contain an instance of the controls class mentioned above and the desired code necessary to coordinate the activities on the dialog. Listing 16.3 contains the SetColorDialog class of EX16B.

Listing 16.3. SetColorDialog class of EX16B.

```
class SetColorDialog extends Dialog
{
    protected Color selectedColor;
    protected ColorData cData;
    protected SetColorControls ctrls;
    protected Rectangle sampleRect;

    public SetColorDialog(Frame parent, ColorData cData)
    {
        super(parent, "Set Color", true);

        setFont(new Font("Dialog", Font.PLAIN, 16));

        // don't let the user change the size
        setResizable(false);

        resize(220, 116);

        // create the controls for the dialog
        ctrls = new SetColorControls(this);
        ctrls.CreateControls();

        FillSetColorTo();
        SetupScrollbars();

        // save the data and start off with the current color
        this.cData = cData;
        selectedColor = new Color(cData.GetColor().getRGB());
    }

    public boolean action(Event evt, Object arg)
    {
        boolean result = false;        // assume no action

        if ("OK".equals(evt.arg)) {
            cData.SetColor(selectedColor);
            dispose();                 // close the dialog
        }
        if ("Cancel".equals(evt.arg))
            dispose();                 // close the dialog

        return result;
    }
```

continues

. . . .

Listing 16.3. continued

```java
public boolean handleEvent(Event evt)
{
    boolean result = false;          // assume no action

    // call the superclass for normal processing
    result = super.handleEvent(evt);

    // process the event here if not handled yet
    if (!result) {
        if (evt.target == ctrls.RedScrollbar) {
            handleScrollbarEvent(ctrls.RedScrollbar, ctrls.RedValue);
            result = true;
        }
        else if (evt.target == ctrls.GreenScrollbar) {
            handleScrollbarEvent(ctrls.GreenScrollbar, ctrls.GreenValue);
            result = true;
        }
        else if (evt.target == ctrls.BlueScrollbar) {
            handleScrollbarEvent(ctrls.BlueScrollbar, ctrls.BlueValue);
            result = true;
        }
        else if (evt.target == ctrls.StandardColorChoice) {
            handleChoiceEvent();
            result = true;
        }
    }

    return result;
}

public void paint(Graphics g)
{
    super.paint(g);                  // let normal processing happen

    if (selectedColor != null) {
        if (sampleRect == null) {
            // determine where we can put the sample color
            sampleRect = ctrls.StandardColorChoice.bounds();
            sampleRect.x += sampleRect.width + 10;
            sampleRect.width = 20;
            sampleRect.height = 20;
        }

        g.setColor(selectedColor);

        g.drawRect(sampleRect.x, sampleRect.y,
                sampleRect.width, sampleRect.height);
        g.fillRect(sampleRect.x, sampleRect.y,
                sampleRect.width, sampleRect.height);
    }
}

protected void FillSetColorTo()
{
    ctrls.StandardColorChoice.addItem("black");
    ctrls.StandardColorChoice.addItem("blue");
    ctrls.StandardColorChoice.addItem("cyan");
```

```
    ctrls.StandardColorChoice.addItem("darkGray");
    ctrls.StandardColorChoice.addItem("gray");
    ctrls.StandardColorChoice.addItem("green");
    ctrls.StandardColorChoice.addItem("lightGray");
    ctrls.StandardColorChoice.addItem("magenta");
    ctrls.StandardColorChoice.addItem("orange");
    ctrls.StandardColorChoice.addItem("pink");
    ctrls.StandardColorChoice.addItem("red");
    ctrls.StandardColorChoice.addItem("white");
    ctrls.StandardColorChoice.addItem("yellow");
    ctrls.StandardColorChoice.addItem("custom");
}

protected void SetupScrollbars()
{
    ctrls.RedScrollbar.setValues(0, 10, 0, 255);
    ctrls.GreenScrollbar.setValues(0, 10, 0, 255);
    ctrls.BlueScrollbar.setValues(0, 10, 0, 255);
}

protected void handleScrollbarEvent(Scrollbar sBar, Label sBarValue)
{
    int value = sBar.getValue();

    // set the text value according to the scroll bar
    sBarValue.setText(String.valueOf(value));

    // reset the actual sample
    SetSampleColor();

    // changing of the scroll bar means it is custom
    ctrls.StandardColorChoice.select("custom");
}

protected void handleChoiceEvent()
{
    Color standardColor = null;     // holds found color
    String name = ctrls.StandardColorChoice.getSelectedItem();

    // check for each of the standard colors
    if (name == "black")
        standardColor = new Color(Color.black.getRGB());
    else if (name == "blue")
        standardColor = new Color(Color.blue.getRGB());
    else if (name == "cyan")
        standardColor = new Color(Color.cyan.getRGB());
    else if (name == "darkGray")
        standardColor = new Color(Color.darkGray.getRGB());
    else if (name == "gray")
        standardColor = new Color(Color.gray.getRGB());
    else if (name == "green")
        standardColor = new Color(Color.green.getRGB());
    else if (name == "lightGray")
        standardColor = new Color(Color.lightGray.getRGB());
    else if (name == "magenta")
        standardColor = new Color(Color.magenta.getRGB());
    else if (name == "orange")
        standardColor = new Color(Color.orange.getRGB());
```

Listing 16.3. continued

```
            else if (name == "pink")
                standardColor = new Color(Color.pink.getRGB());
            else if (name == "red")
                standardColor = new Color(Color.red.getRGB());
            else if (name == "white")
                standardColor = new Color(Color.white.getRGB());
            else if (name == "yellow")
                standardColor = new Color(Color.yellow.getRGB());

            // set the scrollbar if the color is not custom
            if (standardColor != null) {
                SetScrollbarValue(ctrls.RedScrollbar,
                        ctrls.RedValue, standardColor.getRed());
                SetScrollbarValue(ctrls.GreenScrollbar,
                        ctrls.GreenValue, standardColor.getGreen());
                SetScrollbarValue(ctrls.BlueScrollbar,
                        ctrls.BlueValue, standardColor.getBlue());

                // reset the actual sample
                SetSampleColor();
            }
    }

    protected void SetScrollbarValue(Scrollbar sBar,
            Label sBarValue, int value)
    {
        sBar.setValue(value);            // set the value

        // set the text value according to the new value
        sBarValue.setText(String.valueOf(value));
    }

    protected void SetSampleColor()
    {
        int red = ctrls.RedScrollbar.getValue();
        int green = ctrls.GreenScrollbar.getValue();
        int blue = ctrls.BlueScrollbar.getValue();

        selectedColor = new Color(red, green, blue);
        repaint();
    }
}
```

Let's take a look at the constructor. It takes as its parameter the parent frame, which is required by all dialogs, and a ColorData class instance. The next section will cover the ColorData class in detail. For now, it is enough to know that this is the mechanism used to pass the initial color to the dialog and the selected color back to the calling class.

Inside the constructor, the first step is to call the superclass constructor. This call is required to be the first line in the constructor. Next, the font is set for the dialog. This is always a good idea since the controls class is based on the current font of the container dialog. The call to setResizeable disables the user from changing the size of the dialog. This is important because a mechanism to resize the controls is not built into the dialog. Next, create the controls using the classes previously discussed. Finally, initialize some of the controls with `FillSetColorTo` and `SetupScrollbars` method calls, and set the starting color to the color passed in.

The `SetColorControls` class is concerned only with the actual placement of the components on the dialog. It does not take care of any configuration specific to the application or initialization. `FillSetColorTo` loads the choice box for the standard default colors. Notice how `ctrls`, the `SetColorControl` class instance, is used to reference the choice component. In addition to the standard colors, the choice of "custom" is used when the scrollbars are modified directly. `SetupScrollbars` is used to initialize the ranges for all the scrollbars from a range of 0 to 255, which corresponds to the integer ranges from the `Color` class.

The `paint` method is used to display the sample color in the lower right of the dialog, using the currently selected color. `SetColor`, of the `Graphics` instance g, is called to set the color. Because `Graphics` contains only a single color, that color is used for all subsequent drawings. Thus, the sample color rectangle is filled with the currently selected color. Later, you will see that when the color changes, the dialog forces a redrawing of the dialog, using `repaint`, to update the sample color.

The button presses are caught and acted upon in the `action` method. If the OK button is pressed, the currently selected color is saved in the `ColorData` class and the dialog resources are disposed of, causing the dialog to close. If the Cancel button is pressed, the dialog resources are also disposed of, once again causing the dialog to close.

Perhaps the busiest of the methods is the `handleEvent` method. The first thing this does is try to get out of doing anything by calling the superclass with the current event. This allows the `action` processing to occur. Then, if there is something left to do with the event, this method checks to see whether the event involves one of the scrollbars or the choice.

If the scrollbar was modified, `handleScrollbarEvent` updates the label next to the scrollbar with the current scrollbar value, updates the sample color being displayed by calling `SetSampleColor`, and forces the selected item in the choice to be "custom." `SetSampleColor` takes the values from the three scrollbars and creates a new color based on these values. It then forces the sample rectangle to be redrawn with the newly selected color by calling the `repaint` method of the dialog.

If a new item in the choice is selected, `handleChoiceEvent` is called. Unfortunately, since `switch` does not work on strings, the majority of this code is looking for the standard color that was selected. If a standard color is found, `SetScrollbarValue` is called for each of the components. In this way, the user can see exactly what goes into making the standard colors. Then, `SetSampleColor` is used to update the sample rectangle.

That wasn't too bad. You now have a reusable dialog that can be used in a variety of situations in which you want to let the user choose his own color. The next section covers how the dialog actually communicates with the instantiating class on what color was selected, using the `ColorData` class.

Communicating with the Set Color Dialog

One of the hardest aspects of using dialogs to collect information from users is relaying the collected information back to the calling class. One option is to pass the calling class into the dialog class and let the dialog call method(s) set the collected data in the calling class. Let's take a quick look and consider EX16C, shown in Listing 16.4.

Listing 16.4. EX16C.

```java
import java.applet.*;
import java.awt.*;

public class EX16C extends Applet
{
    protected InputDialog IDialog;
    protected TextField MyField = new TextField(20);

    public void SetMyFieldText(String str)
    {
        MyField.setText(str);
    }

    public void init()
    {
        add(new Button("Set Text"));
        add(MyField);

        // set up the frame for the dialog
        Frame frame = new Frame();
        frame.resize(250, 100);
        IDialog = new InputDialog(frame, this);
    }

    public boolean action(Event evt, Object obj)
    {
        boolean result = false;          // assume no action

        if ("Set Text".equals(obj)) {
            IDialog.show();
            result = true;
        }

        return result;
    }
}

class InputDialog extends Dialog
{
    protected TextField InputText;
    protected EX16C aplt;

    public InputDialog(Frame parent, EX16C aplt)
    {
        super(parent, "Input into my field please...", true);
```

```
        this.aplt = aplt;

        InputText = new TextField();
        add("North", InputText);

        Panel p = new Panel();
        p.add(new Button("OK"));
        p.add(new Button("Cancel"));
        add("South", p);

        pack();
        resize(250, 100);
    }

    public boolean action(Event evt, Object arg)
    {
        boolean result = false;          // asume no action

        if ("OK".equals(evt.arg)) {
            aplt.SetMyFieldText(InputText.getText());
            dispose();                   // close the dialog
        }
        if ("Cancel".equals(evt.arg))
            dispose();                   // close the dialog

        return result;
    }
}
```

When a button is pressed, this applet shows a dialog that gathers the text that is displayed in the text field of the applet. The importance of this applet is the fact that the dialog is passed the applet in the constructor. When the buttons on the dialog are pressed to close the dialog, the information collected is put back into the applet (see InputDialog.action). This concept is not very practical for generic dialogs because it has very high coupling between the classes involved.

An alternate approach would be to use Observer and Observable classes from the java.util package. For a complete description of these classes along with other classes found in the java.util package, see Chapter 11, "The Java Utility Classes."

Let's go back to the sample applet, EX16B. Listing 16.5 shows the observable data that is passed to the Set Color dialog.

Listing 16.5. Observable Color data class of EX16B.

```
class ColorData extends Observable
{
    protected Color clr = new Color(Color.black.getRGB());

    public Color GetColor()
    {
        return clr;
    }
```

continues

Listing 16.5. continued

```
    public void SetColor(Color clr)
    {
        this.clr = clr;                       // save the color

        // flag the change an notify the on-lookers
        setChanged();
        notifyObservers();
    }
}
```

The sole purpose of this class is to pass data from the applet to the Set Color dialog. The single piece of data is the color of the text. Obviously, more complicated dialogs would have more data.

GetColor is just an access method to the color. Both the applet and the dialog call this method—the applet to determine the color of the text to be displayed, while the Set Color dialog calls it to determine the starting color for the dialog. SetColor is called by the Set Color dialog when the user presses the OK button after making a selection. This method first saves the new color, then makes the Observable-specific calls that mark that the data has changed, then notifies all of the class's observers that the data has changed.

The only thing that the applet needs to do is to implement the Observer interface. Listing 16.6 shows the code from the EX16B applet pertinent to being an Observer.

Listing 16.6. Observer-specific code of EX16B applet.

```
public class EX16B extends Applet implements Observer
{
    ...
    protected ColorData cData = new ColorData();
    ...

    public void init()
    {
        ...
        // let the applet observe the color
        cData.addObserver(this);
        ...
    }
    ...

    public void update(Observable o, Object arg)
    {
        // since the paint method already looks at cData, simply
        //    force a repaint of the dialog to pick up the new color
        repaint();
    }
}
```

The applet instantiates an instance of the Observable color data that is used to paint the text. In init, it tells Observable that it is an observer by making a call to addObserver and passing the applet. update is the only method in the Observer interface and must be defined. This method is what gets notified when Observable changes. Since we are the only observer of the color, all we have to do is repaint the applet and the new color will take effect.

Why go through the overhead of using the Observer/Observable relationship? That's easy. One of the problems with showing a dialog is that the actual lifespan of the dialog is asynchronous with respect to the actions of the applet. Therefore, this interface is an easy way to get the dialog to tell the applet when it modifies the common data. And, more importantly, this process decouples the dialog and the applet so that the dialog can be used in any applet for a variety of different color settings. Now, let's look at the final part of the applet that uses the Set Color dialog.

Using the Set Color Dialog

To use the Set Color dialog, we go back to the basic applet with two buttons and some text that is being displayed. Listing 16.7 shows the applet class EX16B.

Listing 16.7. Applet class EX16B.
```
public class EX16B extends Applet implements Observer
{
    protected Button SetColorButton = new Button("Set Color");
    protected Button SetFontButton = new Button("Set Font");
    protected String MyText = new String("This is the text being modified.");
    protected Frame frame;
    protected ColorData cData = new ColorData();
    protected SetColorDialog SetColorDlg;

    public void init()
    {
        // set up the set color dialog frame
        frame = new Frame();
        frame.resize(1, 1);

        // let the applet observe the color
        cData.addObserver(this);

        // add the controls to the applet
        add(SetColorButton);
        add(SetFontButton);
    }

    public void paint(Graphics g)
    {
        // use the color data to set the text color
        g.setColor(cData.GetColor());

        g.drawString(MyText, 20, 100);
    }
```

continues

Listing 16.7. continued

```
public boolean action(Event evt, Object obj)
{
    boolean result = false;           // asume no action

    if ("Set Color".equals(obj)) {
        SetColorDlg = new SetColorDialog(frame, cData);
        SetColorDlg.show();

        result = true;
    }

    return result;
}

public void update(Observable o, Object arg)
{
    // since the paint method already looks at cData, simply
    //   force a repaint of the dialog to pick up the new color
    repaint();
}
}
```

The init method sets up the frame to use for the dialog, sets up the data used for the dialog, and places the buttons on the applet. paint actually uses the color by setting the color in the Graphics and then calls DrawString to do the drawing. Again, the Graphics instance will use the color to do all subsequent actions. action is a straightforward implementation of displaying the dialog in response to a button click.

In this section, you have learned how a color is created and stored. Along the way, a dialog that could be used in a number of situations to let that user set that color was created. Once a color was chosen, a Graphics instance used that color to change the color of text on the applet. This, however, is not the only location in which the resulting color can be used. Every component has a foreground color and background color associated with it. The following methods of Component can be used to access these colors.

```
public Color getBackground();
public void setBackground(Color);
public Color getForeground();
public void setForeground(Color);
```

Because everything that is displayed is a component, these methods can be used to change the color on virtually any item in your applet.

Setting the Font

The font selection is encapsulated with the Font class. Since fonts are very system-dependent, an additional class, FontMetrics is used to retrieve specifics about how the font is actually laid out on the output device. This section covers the Font and FontMetrics classes, goes over a dialog used to select a font, and puts that dialog to use in an extension of a previously defined example.

The `Font` and `FontMetrics` Classes

A font can be loaded by specifying a name and size of font desired. This information can be passed to the single `Font` class constructor:

```
Font(String, int, int)
```

This constructor takes a string that contains a name, such as "`Dialog`" or "`Helvetica`," an integer containing style indications, and a point size. The style can contain three values defined in the `Font` class:

```
PLAIN
BOLD
ITALIC
```

You can combine these values together by using a bitwise OR operation or by adding them together to form a compound style. Of course, PLAIN combined with anything has no effect (especially since it is defined as 0), but used alone, it indicates that the font will be displayed normally.

After you have created the font, Table 16.2 shows the public methods that can be used to retrieve some general information about the font.

Table 16.2. Public methods of the `Font` class.

Member	Purpose
`equals(Object)`	Compares two font objects for the same font.
`getFamily()`	Returns a platform-specific name.
`getFont(String)`	Returns the font of the named system property.
`getFont(String, Font)`	Returns the font of the named system property, returning the font as a default if not found.
`getName()`	Returns the font name.
`getSize()`	Returns the font point size.
`getStyle()`	Returns the font style.
`hashCode()`	Returns a hash code representing the color.
`isBold()`	Returns true if the bold style bit is set.
`isItalic()`	Returns true if the italic style bit is set.
`isPlain()`	Returns true if neither the bold nor italic style bits are set.
`toString()`	Returns a string representation of the font.

`FontMetrics` returns specific information about how a particular font is rendered on the output device. This information is typically used so that lines of text are properly spaced.

FontMetrics are based on a given Font. Therefore, the constructor takes the font being examined:

```
protected FontMetrics(Font)
```

Notice that the constructor is not public, so a program cannot instantiate an instance of this class. This is done because the information retrieved is very device-specific. Therefore, you must call a device-specific method, such as Component.getFontMetrics() or Graphics.getFontMetrics(), to retrieve the information about the font currently being rendered.

Table 16.3 shows the public methods of the FontMetrics class.

Table 16.3. Public methods of the FontMetrics class.

Member	Purpose
bytesWidth(byte [], int, int)	Returns the width of the array of bytes.
charsWidth(char [], int, int)	Returns the width of the array of characters.
charWidth(char)	Returns the width of the single character.
charWidth(int)	Returns the width of the single character.
getAscent()	Returns the standard distance from the baseline of the font to the top of the characters in the font.
getDescent()	Returns the standard distance from the baseline of the font to the bottom of the characters in the font.
getFont()	Returns the font being analyzed.
getHeight()	Returns the total size of a line; sum of leading, ascent, and descent.
getLeading()	Returns space required between lines.
getMaxAdvance()	Returns the maximum advance.
getMaxAscent()	Returns the maximum ascent.
getMaxDescent()	Returns the maximum descent.
getWidths()	Returns an array of the widths of the first 256 characters.
stringWidth(String)	Returns the width of the string.

You should never have to deal with FontMetrics unless your program is handling the display of text directly to the output devices. By using the components on your applets and dialogs, you let the Java packages deal with these specifics.

Set Font Dialog

Developing a dialog that allows the user to select the font he or she wants to use is an easy way to get familiar with the Font class. Figure 16.3 shows the dialog in action.

Figure 16.3.
Set Font dialog of EX16D.

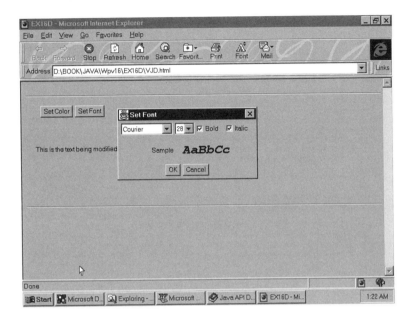

This dialog contains a choice for the font name and the font size. In addition, the user can select the bold and italic attributes of the font by using the appropriate checkboxes. As a courtesy, a sample of the selected font is displayed. Listing 16.8 shows the dialog class used for the Set Font dialog of example EX16D.

Listing 16.8. SetFontDialog class of EX16D.

```
class SetFontDialog extends Dialog
{
    protected Font selectedFont;
    protected FontData fData;
    protected Choice NameChoice = new Choice();
    protected Choice SizeChoice = new Choice();
    protected Checkbox BoldCheckbox = new Checkbox("Bold");
    protected Checkbox ItalicCheckbox = new Checkbox("Italic");
    protected Label SampleLabel = new Label("AaBbCc", Label.CENTER);

    public SetFontDialog(Frame parent, FontData fData)
    {
        super(parent, "Set Font", true);

        setFont(new Font("Dialog", Font.PLAIN, 12));
        setBackground(Color.lightGray);
```

continues

Listing 16.8. continued

```java
        // don't let the user change the size
        setResizable(false);

        resize(300, 150);

        setBackground(Color.lightGray);

        // create the controls for the dialog
        Panel fontSelectionPanel = new Panel();
        fontSelectionPanel.add(NameChoice);
        fontSelectionPanel.add(SizeChoice);
        fontSelectionPanel.add(BoldCheckbox);
        fontSelectionPanel.add(ItalicCheckbox);
        add("North", fontSelectionPanel);

        Panel fontSamplePanel = new Panel();
        fontSamplePanel.add(new Label("Sample"));
        fontSamplePanel.add(SampleLabel);
        add("Center", fontSamplePanel);

        Panel dialogClosePanel = new Panel();
        dialogClosePanel.add(new Button("OK"));
        dialogClosePanel.add(new Button("Cancel"));
        add("South", dialogClosePanel);

        // fill in the choice lists
        FillChoiceLists();

        // save the data and start off with the current font
        this.fData = fData;
        NameChoice.select(fData.GetFont().getName());
        SizeChoice.select(Integer.toString(fData.GetFont().getSize()));

        BoldCheckbox.setState(
                (fData.GetFont().getStyle() & Font.BOLD) == Font.BOLD);
        ItalicCheckbox.setState(
                (fData.GetFont().getStyle() & Font.ITALIC) == Font.ITALIC);

        GetSelectedFont(false);

        SampleLabel.setFont(selectedFont);
    }

    public boolean action(Event evt, Object arg)
    {
        boolean result = false;          // asume no action

        if ("OK".equals(evt.arg)) {
            fData.SetFont(selectedFont);
            dispose();                   // close the dialog
        }
        if ("Cancel".equals(evt.arg))
            dispose();                   // close the dialog

        return result;
    }
```

```java
    public boolean handleEvent(Event evt)
    {
        boolean result = false;          // assume no action

        // call the superclass for normal processing
        result = super.handleEvent(evt);

        // process the event here if not handled yet
        if (!result) {
            if ((evt.target == NameChoice) ||
                    (evt.target == SizeChoice) ||
                    (evt.target == BoldCheckbox) ||
                    (evt.target == ItalicCheckbox)) {
                GetSelectedFont(true);
                result = true;
            }
        }

        return result;
    }

    protected void FillChoiceLists()
    {
        String fonts[] = Toolkit.getDefaultToolkit().getFontList();

        for (int index = 0; index < fonts.length; index++)
            NameChoice.addItem(fonts[index]);

        // there is no way to get the font sizes that are available
        //    on the host, so just add some to the listbox
        for (int index = 8; index <= 36; index += 4)
            SizeChoice.addItem(Integer.toString(index));
    }

    protected void GetSelectedFont(boolean redisplay)
    {
        int style = Font.PLAIN;

        if (BoldCheckbox.getState())
            style |= Font.BOLD;

        if (ItalicCheckbox.getState())
            style |= Font.ITALIC;

        selectedFont = new Font(NameChoice.getSelectedItem(), style,
                Integer.parseInt(SizeChoice.getSelectedItem()));

        if (redisplay) {
            // apply the new font to the sample and make sure
            //    it fits in the dialog
            SampleLabel.setFont(selectedFont);
            SampleLabel.resize(SampleLabel.preferredSize());

            // tell the layout manager to do its job again
            validate();
        }
    }
}
```

The class contains several components that will be referenced later within the class to get the selected font and to set up the sample of this selected font. The constructor does some initial setting up of the dialog, including setting the dialog font to a standard font (which is in itself a good example of how to set the font directly) and the color of the background of the dialog to a calm color. Next, the controls are placed on the dialog. The controls are placed in three containers: One holds the selection of the font controls, one holds the sample font controls, and the last holds the controls used to get out of the dialog. All three of these containers are placed on the dialog using the default BorderLayout Manager. Finally, the possible choice values are populated with a call to FillChoiceLists and the controls are initialized with the font passed into the constructor via fData.

action and handleEvent are straightforward and are implemented very similar to the color dialog of EX16B, shown previously.

FillChoiceLists is used to populate the choices. The Toolkit class in java.awt contains a function that will retrieve a list of fonts available to the applet. getFontList was used to retrieve an array of strings containing the font names available. Unfortunately, currently there is not a way to get the font sizes available for each font. Therefore, this example simply puts a variety of numbers into the size choice. This is not a problem because fonts are similar to colors in that if a requested font does not exist, a similar font will be returned in its place.

GetSelectedFont is called to read the font currently selected and to allocate a new Font instance. After a new font has been generated, the sample is updated to use the new font. Because we have the potential of drastically changing the size required to display our sample string, resize is called with the preferredSize of the label. This will change the size of the label to accommodate the new string. Since the layout manager is like most managers and never does anything until told to do so, validate tells the dialog to reposition its controls.

Communicating with the Set Font Dialog

Communication between the Set Font dialog and the applet is once again utilizing the Observer/Observable approach. Listing 16.9 shows the data class used to hold the font information making the trip between the applet and the dialog.

Listing 16.9. FontData class of EX16D.

```
class FontData extends Observable
{
    protected Font fnt = new Font("Dialog", Font.PLAIN, 12);

    public Font GetFont()
    {
        return fnt;
    }

    public void SetFont(Font fnt)
    {
        this.fnt = fnt;                    // save the font
```

```
    I// flag the change and notify the on-lookers
    setChanged();
    notifyObservers();
  }
}
```

Using the Set Font Dialog

Using the Set Font dialog is very similar to using the Set Color dialog and the complete example using both dialogs can be found on the accompanying CD as example EX16D. Figure 16.4 shows the resulting applet using one of my favorite colored fonts.

Figure 16.4.

Applet from EX16D.

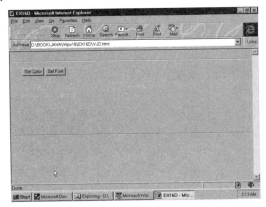

Summary

This chapter covered the elements of an example where a couple of very useful dialogs were created. The first dialog allowed the user to choose a color from either a standard set of colors, or allowed the user to create their own color by selecting the concentrations of red, green, and blue. Once the color was selected, this chapter showed how it was used to change the color of text being drawn in the applet. As an aside, this chapter showed a very useful example of the Observer and Observable utility classes. The second dialog allowed the user to select a font from one of the system fonts. This font was then applied to the text being drawn in the applet.

The next section covers the networking aspects of the Java language. Among other topics, accessing various URLs from within applets, communication using both datagrams and sockets, and Java security support are covered.

Part

IV

Networking with Java

Chapter 17

Accessing URLs

Uniform Resource Locators (URLs) are perhaps the most noticeable and least understood aspect of the Internet phenomenon. You would be hard-pressed to find a magazine or television program today that doesn't include the now familiar Web address of the company paying for an advertisement. It is not uncommon to hear a newscaster or radio personality confidently recite a URL on the air, "h-t-t-p-colon-slash-slash...." Fortunately, all the public needs to know is that if they type this odd-looking sequence of characters into their Web browser, graphically presented information and, thanks to Java, active content will fill the screen.

This chapter discusses the definition of a URL, tells how it can be used to locate Web and other resources, and shows what classes are provided by Java to allow you to seamlessly work with URLs in your programs.

What Is a URL?

Although the World Wide Web has dominated the Internet in recent years, there are many other types of resources that provide a diverse range of services on the Internet. For example, electronic mail, file transfer, and search tools were among the first services to be developed for the Internet. In fact, much of the success of the Web is due to its capability to bring together many of these resources into one interface. Indeed, the two most popular Web browsers available today are able to perform file transfers, send and receive electronic mail, and interact with news services in addition to their normal Web duties. The URL is the key to defining the method, location, and name of the many types of resources available on the Internet.

The general format of a URL is composed of a protocol name, a colon, and some protocol specific information about a resource:

`protocol name:protocol specific information`

A resource's protocol is the language used to interpret the data that is shared across a network connection about that resource. The protocol name portion is not case-sensitive and can include letters, numbers, a plus sign (+), period (.), and hyphen (-). The protocol-specific information portion can include any character. However, non-printable, reserved, and unsafe characters must be escaped, or encoded, to ensure the original meaning of the URL is maintained. Once received by the server, the URL is decoded before it is interpreted. Characters are escaped by replacing them with the percent (%) sign and their hexadecimal value. For example, if the less-than (<) character is to be used in a URL, it must be escaped to %3C because it is one of the unsafe characters. The unsafe group of characters includes <, >, ", #, %, {, }, [,], |, \, ^, ~, and '. These characters have special meaning as part of the URL itself or on the systems transporting or interpreting the URL. For example, the tilde (~) is commonly used in a Web URL to designate the path to a user's home directory on a server. A URL of `http://www.jory.com/~james/homepage.html` points to my personal home page on my server located in my user directory (`/james`). If I wanted to use a tilde as part of my home page filename (`home~page.html`), the tilde in the filename should be escaped to eliminate any confusion over the tilde used to designate my user directory. The correct URL would then be `http://www.jory.com/~james/home%7Epage.html`.

NOTE:

See Request for Comments (RFC) 1738 for more information on URLs. The current library of RFCs can be found on the accompanying CD-ROM.

Table 17.1 lists some of the more common URLs for resources found on the Internet.

Table 17.1. Common URLs found on the Internet.

Resource	Sample URL
Hypertext Transfer Protocol (HTTP)	`http://somehost.com`
Simple Mail Transfer Protocol (SMTP)	`mailto:someone@somehost.com`
File Transfer Protocol (FTP)	`ftp://somehost.com/someplace/somefile.ext`
Local file	`file:/c:/someplace/somefile.ext`
News (Usenet News)	`news:some.news.group`
Telnet (interactive session)	`telnet://somehost.com`
Wide Area Information Server (WAIS)	`wais://somehost.com/database?search`

The URLs with two slashes after the colon use a common syntax for the protocol-specific information. These types of URLs are used to access a resource on a specific host. The general format for host-based resources is defined like this:

`protocol name://user:password@host:port/path`

The *user*, *password*, and *port* fields are optional and if missing will cause the default behavior to be used. For example, FTP URLs found on Web pages typically do not include a user and password. In these cases, the Web browser attempts to initiate an anonymous FTP session by logging on to the FTP server on your behalf using anonymous as the user ID and your electronic mail address as the password. Likewise, if the port is missing from the URL, the default port is used based on the specified protocol. For example, the HTTP protocol uses port 80 by default.

NOTE:

A *port* represents the logical connection point between a client and server process communicating over a network connection. It is analogous to a channel on television or frequency on the radio. Port numbers up to and including 1024 are reserved for system use and when assigned are often referred to as well-known sockets, services, or ports. Port numbers above 1024 and below 65535 are unassigned and can be used for user applications. Ports and the underlying protocol suite used to transport data across the Internet are discussed in Chapter 18, "Networking with Datagrams and Sockets."

The URL Classes

Now that you have seen how URLs are used to identify resources on the Internet, take a look at the classes provided by Java to access them.

URL Class

Encapsulating the inherent complexity and flexibility of all known URL formats as well as those to come in a set of classes would certainly be a daunting task. Fortunately, the Java implementers have taken care of this for you. The java.net package includes four URL-related classes and one interface. The URL class drives the whole process and takes care of interacting with the other classes. Adding support for new or custom URL formats is also possible by subclassing the appropriate classes, which will be shown later in this chapter.

NOTE:

Unfortunately, security constraints imposed by Web browsers limit the type of URLs and the hosts that you can communicate with in your applets. In general, you are limited to communicating with the host serving your applet or the HTML page containing your applet and only then using protocols supported and allowed by the browser's Java Virtual Machine. The current implementations of Netscape's Navigator and Microsoft's Internet Explorer limit your applets to working with HTTP URLs only. However, there are a few ways to get around this restriction. Of course, Java applications are not bound by the same constraints.

As a result of the restriction placed on applets to have access only to Web URLs, the design of the URL classes were naturally slanted toward HTTP resources. The default behavior is to expect a

Web URL, but these effects can be overcome through subclassing and overriding the appropriate methods. Table 17.2 lists the methods of interest from the URL class.

Table 17.2. URL methods of interest.

Method	Description
URL(String, String, int, String)	Creates an absolute URL based on the protocol, host, port, and filename passed as parameters.
URL(String, String, String)	Creates an absolute URL based on the protocol, host, and filename passed as parameters. Because the port is not specified, the default port is used based on the protocol.
URL(String)	Creates an absolute URL based on the unparsed string passed as a parameter.
URL(URL, String)	Creates a new URL relative to the URL passed as a parameter using the filename parameter.
int getPort()	Returns the port number of the URL.
String getProtocol()	Returns the protocol name of the URL.
String getHost()	Returns the host name of the URL.
String getFile()	Returns the filename of the URL.
String getRef()	Returns the reference of the URL.
URLConnection openConnection()	Returns an instance of a URLConnection via an internal reference to a URLStreamHandler object. Depending on the protocol of the URL, an actual connection to the host may not be made at this time.
InputStream openStream()	Opens a connection and returns an InputStream to the URL. If an InputStream is not supported by the URL, an UnknownServiceException is thrown.
Object getContent()	Opens a connection and returns an object representing the contents of the URL.
setURLStreamHandlerFactory (URLStreamHandlerFactory)	A static method that sets the URLStreamHandlerFactory based on the parameter.

Each URL constructor will throw a `MalformedURLException` if a `URLStreamHandler` could not be found for the URL's protocol. Once constructed, access to the actual resource associated with the URL can be obtained through the `openConnection()`, `openStream()`, or `getContent()` methods. The method used depends on the nature of the resource to which you are connecting. If you need detailed information about the resource and want to perform input and output operations, use `openConnection()`, which provides the most control. The SMTP example applet discussed later in this chapter uses this type of access. However, if you just need read access to the resource (such as a text file), `openStream()` will do the job. Finally, if a content handler is available for the resource, `getContent()` will return an instance of an `Object` that represents the resource. The current implementation of Java includes content handlers for the following MIME types: `text/plain`, `image/gif`, `image/jpeg`, `image/x_xbitmap`, and `image/x_xpixmap`. Content handlers will be discussed again later in this chapter.

NOTE:

The Multipurpose Internet Mail Extensions (MIME) standard was created to expand the type of data that could be delivered with electronic mail. Under MIME, non-text–based attachments to electronic mail notes are preceded by header information capable of describing the type of data in the attachment, the encoding scheme used, and even the application that should be used to interpret the data. The Content-type header field is the key to interpreting the resource. In its basic form, the content-type is composed of a type and subtype in the form `type/subtype`. For example, a content-type of `text/html` defines a resource (such as a Web page) that is text-based and in HTML format.

Because the nature of the resources found on the Web are also as diverse as the types of attachments to electronic mail, MIME was adopted for the Web and thus is supported by Java.

CAUTION:

Unless you intend to open more than one connection to a resource, do not call `openConnection()`, `openStream()`, or `getContent()` more than once, because each call opens a new connection. Calling one of these methods and then another has the same effect because all three methods refer to the same resource.

URLStreamHandler Class

URLStreamHandler is an abstract base class used to create connections to URL resources as well as provide parsing functionality for URLs. To create handlers for new or currently unsupported URLs, this class must be subclassed. The current implementation of Java provides handlers for the HTTP, file, doc, and news URLs. However, as mentioned, only http resources can be used by applets. Table 17.3 lists the methods of interest for URLStreamHandler.

Table 17.3. URLStreamHandler methods of interest.

Method	Description
URLConnection openConnection(URL)	This abstract protected method is called by URL to create a connection to the specified URL. This method must be overridden by a subclass.
parseURL(URL, String, int, int)	URL objects created with and based on unparsed URLs will call this method to interpret the unparsed URL and give the URLStreamHandler an opportunity to interpret the URL based on its own format.

Remember from our discussion of the URL class that the URL class was designed primarily with the HTTP protocol and URL format in mind? Well, for protocols that have URL formats different from HTTP, the URL class will call parseURL() to give the URLStreamHandler an opportunity to parse the URL in its intended context. Once successfully parsed, URLStreamHandler sets the parsed URL values in the attached URL object through the protected setURL() method.

URLConnection Class

This is another abstract base class used in conjunction with the URL and URLStreamHandler classes. It provides more direct access to the resource than the URL class, as well as detailed MIME information about the resource. Table 17.4 lists several methods from URLConnection.

Table 17.4. URLConnection methods of interest.

Method	Description
connect()	This abstract protected method is called by URL to create a connection to the specified URL. This method must be overridden by a subclass.
URL getURL()	Returns the URL object associated with this connection.
int getContentLength()	Returns the length of the resource in bytes.
String getContentType()	Returns the content-type for the resource.
String getContentEncoding()	Returns the content-encoding for the resource.
long getExpiration()	Returns the expiration of the resource.
long getDate()	Returns the sending date of the resource.
long getLastModified()	Returns the date that the resource was last modified.
Object getContent()	Returns an instance of an object representing the contents of the resource.
InputStream getInputStream()	Returns an input stream to the resource.
OutputStream getOutputStream()	Returns an output stream to the resource.
setContentHandlerFactory (ContentHandlerFactory)	Sets the ContentHandlerFactory to the value passed as a parameter.

Depending on the type of resource and the level of detail available in the MIME header for the resource, some of the methods listed in Table 17.4 might not return valid information.

URLStreamHandlerFactory Interface

Recall from the URL class that when a URL object is created, a URLStreamHandler must be found that supports the protocol of the resource. If not, a MalformedURLException is thrown. Part of the process of finding a URLStreamHandler for the resource involves consulting a reference to an object that implements the URLStreamHandlerFactory interface. If the URLStreamHandlerFactory's createURLStreamHandler() method does not support the requested protocol or a URLStreamHandlerFactory was not set in URL via the URL.setURLStreamHandlerFactory() method, URL will check the protocol against Java's built-in protocol handlers as a last resort. Figure 17.1 illustrates the process that URL goes through to find a URLStreamHandler for a resource.

Figure 17.1.

URL's search for a
URLStreamHandler.

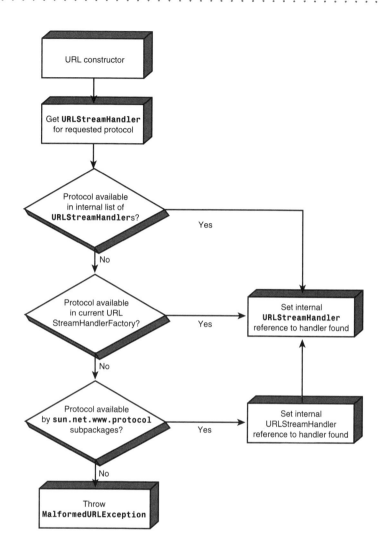

NOTE:

After the URL.setURLStreamHandlerFactory() has been called once, it cannot be changed again. For applets, a default URLStreamHandlerFactory that only supports HTTP URLs is set when the applet's frame is initialized. This is the reason support for new or unsupported URL formats cannot be added to applets. However, default URLStreamHandlerFactory is not set for Java applications, so you are free to set your own.

Now that we have covered the main URL-related classes, let's subclass them to create a basic Simple Mail Transfer Protocol (SMTP) client application.

Extending the URL classes—SMTP Client Application

To illustrate how new or unsupported URL formats can be added to Java applications, the following example will implement the `mailto` URL. Three utility classes will be constructed to complete the example: the `SmtpURLConnection`, `SmtpURLStreamHandler`, and `SmtpURLStreamHandlerFactory` classes.

Let's start with the `SmtpURLStreamHandlerFactory` class. Once it is set as the default `URLStreamHandlerFactory` for the URL class, its `createURLStreamHandler()` is called whenever a URL is created for a resource for which URL does not already have a `URLStreamHandler`. Our handler factory's job is to return an instance of `SmtpURLStreamHandler` when a `mailto` URL is requested. Otherwise `null` is returned, which causes URL to check the protocol against the built-in types. Listing 17.1 shows the source code for `SmtpURLStreamHandlerFactory`.

Listing 17.1. `SmtpURLStreamHandlerFactory.java`.

```java
import java.net.*;
import SmtpURLStreamHandler;

public class SmtpURLStreamHandlerFactory implements URLStreamHandlerFactory
{
    public URLStreamHandler createURLStreamHandler(String protocol)
    {
        if (protocol.equalsIgnoreCase("mailto"))
            return new SmtpURLStreamHandler();
        else
            return null;
    }
}
```

The next class, `SmtpURLStreamHandler`, is a subclass of `URLStreamHandler`. Its jobs are to parse the `mailto` URL for the receiver's electronic mail ID and create a new `SmtpURLConnection` object when the `openConnection()` method is called. Listing 17.2 lists the source code for this class.

Listing 17.2. `SmtpURLStreamHandler.java`.

```java
import java.net.*;
import java.io.*;

public class SmtpURLStreamHandler extends URLStreamHandler
{
    String to;

    protected URLConnection openConnection(URL u)
```

```
    {
        return new SmtpURLConnection(u, to);
    }

    protected void parseURL(URL u, String spec, int start, int limit)
    {
        String protocol = u.getProtocol();
        String host = u.getHost();

        int atSign = spec.indexOf('@', start);

        if (atSign == -1)
            to = "";
        else
        {
            to = spec.substring(start, atSign - 1);
            host = spec.substring(atSign + 1, limit);
        }

        setURL(u, protocol, host, 25, "", "");
    }
}
```

The last SMTP class is SmtpURLConnection and is a subclass of URLConnection. It provides methods to set the from and to address for the note as well as sending the note itself. An output stream can also be retrieved from SmtpURLConnection but not an input stream. The smtpClient private data member, borrowed from the sun.net.smtp package, actually takes care of reading and validating the responses from the SMTP server. Listing 17.3 lists the source code for SmtpURLConnection.

Listing 17.3. SmtpURLConnection.java.

```
import java.net.*;
import java.io.*;

public class SmtpURLConnection extends URLConnection
{
    private sun.net.smtp.SmtpClient smtpClient;
    protected String to;
    protected String from;
    protected String smtpServer;

    public SmtpURLConnection(URL u, String to)
    {
        super(u);
        this.to = to;
        smtpClient = null;
    }

    public void setFrom(String from)
    {
        this.from = from;
    }

    public void setTo(String to)
    {
        this.to = to;
```

continues

Listing 17.3. continued

```java
    }

    public void setSmtpServer(String smtpServer)
    {
        this.smtpServer = smtpServer;
    }

    public void sendIt() throws IOException
    {
        if (connected)
        {
            smtpClient.closeServer();
            connected = false;
        }
        else
            throw new IOException("nothing to send.");
    }

    public void closeServer() throws IOException
    {
        if (connected)
            smtpClient.closeServer();
    }

    protected void finalize()
    {
        try
        {
            closeServer();
        }
        catch (IOException e) {}
    }

    public void connect() throws IOException
    {
        if (!connected)
        {
            smtpClient = null;
            try
            {
                smtpClient = new sun.net.smtp.SmtpClient(smtpServer);
            }
            catch (Throwable e)
            {
                if (smtpClient != null)
                    smtpClient.closeServer();
                if (e instanceof SecurityException)
                {
                    throw (SecurityException)e;
                }
                throw (e instanceof IOException ? (IOException) e
                        : new IOException(e.toString()));
            }
            if (smtpClient == null)
                throw new IOException("Couldn't connect to " + smtpServer);
```

```
                    connected = true;
                    smtpClient.from(from);
                    smtpClient.to(to + "@" + url.getHost());
            }
    }

    public OutputStream getOutputStream() throws IOException
    {
        if (!connected)
            connect();
        return smtpClient.startMessage();
    }
}
```

Finally, the source for the SMTP client application is shown in Listing 17.4, and a screen shot is shown in Figure 17.2. The bulk of the code deals with setting up and managing the interface of the application. The critical sections are the last line of the constructor where the URL URLStreamHandlerFactory is set to SmtpURLStreamHandlerFactory, and the send() method where the mail is sent to the recipient.

Listing 17.4. EX17A.java.

```
import java.awt.*;
import java.net.*;
import java.io.*;
import SmtpURLConnection;
import SmtpURLStreamHandler;
import SmtpURLStreamHandlerFactory;

public class EX17A extends Frame
{
    TextField from, to, smtpServer, status;
    TextArea note;
    Button send, close;

    public EX17A(String caption)
    {
        super(caption);

        from = new TextField(20);
        to = new TextField(20);
        smtpServer = new TextField(40);
        note = new TextArea(10, 40);
        status = new TextField(40);
        status.setEditable(false);
        send = new Button("Send");
        close = new Button("Close");
        Label l;

        GridBagLayout gbag = new GridBagLayout();
        GridBagConstraints cons = new GridBagConstraints();
        cons.insets = new Insets(5, 5, 5, 5);

        setLayout(gbag);
```

continues

377

Listing 17.4. continued

```
cons.anchor = GridBagConstraints.NORTHWEST;
l = new Label("From:");
gbag.setConstraints(l, cons);
add(l);

cons.gridwidth = GridBagConstraints.REMAINDER;
cons.fill = GridBagConstraints.HORIZONTAL;
gbag.setConstraints(from, cons);
add(from);

cons.gridwidth = 1;
cons.fill = GridBagConstraints.NONE;
l = new Label("To:");
gbag.setConstraints(l, cons);
add(l);

cons.gridwidth = GridBagConstraints.REMAINDER;
cons.fill = GridBagConstraints.HORIZONTAL;
gbag.setConstraints(to, cons);
add(to);

cons.gridwidth = 1;
cons.fill = GridBagConstraints.NONE;
l = new Label("SMTP Server:");
gbag.setConstraints(l, cons);
add(l);

cons.gridwidth = GridBagConstraints.REMAINDER;
cons.fill = GridBagConstraints.HORIZONTAL;
gbag.setConstraints(smtpServer, cons);
add(smtpServer);

cons.fill = GridBagConstraints.NONE;
cons.insets.bottom = 0;
l = new Label("Note:");
gbag.setConstraints(l, cons);
add(l);
cons.insets.bottom = 5;

cons.weighty = 1.0;
cons.fill = GridBagConstraints.BOTH;
gbag.setConstraints(note, cons);
add(note);

cons.gridwidth = 1;
cons.fill = GridBagConstraints.NONE;
cons.weighty = 0;
l = new Label("Status:");
gbag.setConstraints(l, cons);
add(l);

cons.gridwidth = GridBagConstraints.REMAINDER;
cons.fill = GridBagConstraints.HORIZONTAL;
cons.weightx = 1.0;
gbag.setConstraints(status, cons);
add(status);
```

```
        Panel buttons = new Panel();
        buttons.setLayout(new FlowLayout(FlowLayout.CENTER, 20, 5));
        buttons.add(send);
        buttons.add(close);
        cons.gridwidth = GridBagConstraints.REMAINDER;
        cons.fill = GridBagConstraints.NONE;
        cons.anchor = GridBagConstraints.CENTER;
        gbag.setConstraints(buttons, cons);
        add(buttons);

        pack();
        show();

        URL.setURLStreamHandlerFactory(new SmtpURLStreamHandlerFactory());
    }

    public boolean handleEvent(Event evt)
    {
        if (evt.target == send)
        {
            if (to.getText().length() > 0 && smtpServer.getText().length() > 0)
                send();
            else
                status.setText("Enter destination address and SMTP Server.");
            return true;
        }
        else if (evt.target == close || evt.id == Event.WINDOW_DESTROY)
        {
            dispose();
            System.exit(0);
            return true;
        }
        else
            return super.handleEvent(evt);
    }

    protected void send()
    {
        SmtpURLConnection mailConn = null;
        status.setText("Sending note...");
        try
        {
            URL url = new URL("mailto:" + to.getText());
            mailConn = (SmtpURLConnection)url.openConnection();
            mailConn.setFrom(from.getText());
            mailConn.setSmtpServer(smtpServer.getText());

            PrintStream os = new PrintStream(mailConn.getOutputStream());
            os.print(note.getText());
            mailConn.sendIt();

            status.setText("Note successfully sent to " + to.getText());
        }
        catch (MalformedURLException e)
            status.setText("URL Error: " + e);
        catch (UnknownHostException e)
            status.setText("Host could not be found.  Try again.");
        catch (IOException e)
```

continues

Listing 17.4. continued

```
            status.setText("Stream Error: " + e);
        finally
        {
            if (mailConn != null)
            {
                try
                    mailConn.closeServer();
                catch (IOException e) {}
            }
        }
    }

    public static void main(String args[])
    {
        new EX17A("Java SMTP Client");
    }
}
```

Figure 17.2.

SMTP client application in action.

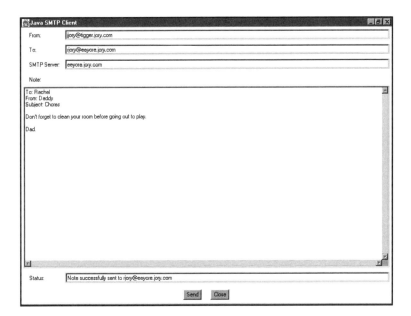

Interfacing with CGI Scripts and ISAPI Extensions

The Common Gateway Interface (CGI) and Internet Server Application Programming Interface (ISAPI) are commonly used on Web sites to get information from visitors. An HTML page can be created with input controls such as edit fields, list boxes, and check boxes, using the HTML FORM, INPUT, TEXTAREA, and SELECT tags. When the form is submitted back to the server by the user, the browser simply packages the responses in a URL-encoded sequence of characters and either sends the output on the end of the URL (GET method) or in a separate transaction (POST method). The method used to send the responses back to the server is specified in the Web page.

Using the classes already covered in this chapter plus the URLEncoder class discussed below, you will see how Java applets can extend the limited use of CGI scripts and ISAPI extensions by providing a more robust and sophisticated interface.

URLEncoder Class

URLEncoder is a utility class that cannot be instantiated (the default constructor is declared private) but provides a static method called encode() that returns an x-www-form-urlencoded version of the string passed as an argument. The x-www-form-urlencoded format has all unsafe, reserved, and non-printable characters encoded, or escaped, within the string. See the section titled "What Is a URL?" at the beginning of this chapter for a more detailed description of URL encoding.

The applet shown in Figure 17.3 allows the user to search for detailed information about a product by entering the name of the product and pressing the Search button. The encode() method is used to format the product name before it is sent back to the Web server using an HTTP POST transaction. Since the applet is using the HTTP protocol to communicate with the server, it does not matter if the server processes the request using a CGI script or ISAPI extension. Listing 17.4 includes the source code for the applet.

Figure 17.3.
CGI or ISAPI from an applet.

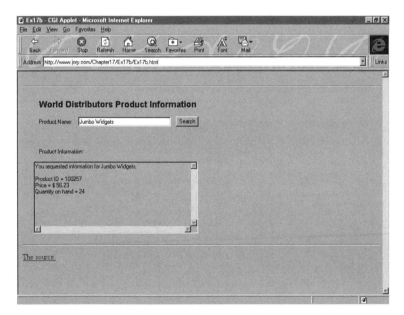

Listing 17.4. EX17B.java.

```java
import java.applet.Applet;
import java.awt.*;
import java.net.*;
import java.io.*;

public class EX17B extends Applet
{
    TextField prodName;
    TextArea prodInfo;
    Button search;
    Label status;
    URL url;

    public void init()
    {
        prodName = new TextField(30);
        prodInfo = new TextArea(10, 30);
        prodInfo.setEditable(false);
        search = new Button("Search");
        status = new Label();
        Label l;

        GridBagLayout gbag = new GridBagLayout();
        GridBagConstraints cons = new GridBagConstraints();
        cons.insets = new Insets(5, 5, 5, 5);

        setLayout(gbag);

        l = new Label("World Distributors Product Information");
        l.setFont(new Font("Helvetica", Font.BOLD, 18));
        cons.gridwidth = GridBagConstraints.REMAINDER;
        gbag.setConstraints(l, cons);
        add(l);

        cons.anchor = GridBagConstraints.NORTHWEST;
        cons.gridwidth = 1;
        l = new Label("Product Name:");
        gbag.setConstraints(l, cons);
        add(l);

        cons.fill = GridBagConstraints.HORIZONTAL;
        gbag.setConstraints(prodName, cons);
        add(prodName);

        cons.fill = GridBagConstraints.NONE;
        cons.gridwidth = GridBagConstraints.REMAINDER;
        gbag.setConstraints(search, cons);
        add(search);

        cons.fill = GridBagConstraints.HORIZONTAL;
        gbag.setConstraints(status, cons);
        add(status);

        l = new Label("Product Information:");
        gbag.setConstraints(l, cons);
        add(l);
```

```
        cons.fill = GridBagConstraints.BOTH;
        gbag.setConstraints(prodInfo, cons);
        add(prodInfo);

        resize(300, 400);
    }

    public boolean handleEvent(Event evt)
    {
        if (evt.target == search)
        {
            if (prodName.getText().length() > 0)
                search();
            else
                status.setText("Please enter a product name.");
            return true;
        }
        else
            return super.handleEvent(evt);
    }

    public void start()
    {
        try
            url = new URL("http", getCodeBase().getHost(),
                    getParameter("script"));
        catch (MalformedURLException e)
        {
            status.setText("Error initializing URL to server.");
            url = null;
        }
    }

    public void search()
    {
        if (url == null)
        {
            status.setText("Unknown URL; cannot perform query.");
            return;
        }

        try
        {
            status.setText("Querying server...");
            URLConnection conn = url.openConnection();

            PrintStream os = new PrintStream(conn.getOutputStream());
            os.println(URLEncoder.encode(prodName.getText()));
            os.close();

            status.setText("Retrieving response...");
            DataInputStream is = new DataInputStream(conn.getInputStream());

            String line = is.readLine();
            prodInfo.setText("");

            while (line != null)
            {
```

Listing 17.4. continued

```
            prodInfo.appendText(line + "\n");
            line = is.readLine();
        }
        is.close();
        status.setText("");
    }
    catch (IOException e)
    {
        status.setText("Error processing query: " + e);
    }
    }
}
```

Because the URL to the script will not change during the life of the applet, the start() method creates the URL once. To allow this applet to be reused without needing to be modified, only the name of the CGI script or ISAPI extension in the HTML page must be changed. The search() method is called each time the user presses the Search button. Within search(), a connection is made to the CGI script, an output stream is obtained from the URLConnection, and the contents of the Product Name field are encoded and sent to the script for processing. To retrieve the results from the script, an input stream is obtained from the connection and each line is read and appended to the Product Information TextField.

Although this is a simple application of using a CGI script or ISAPI extension with a Java applet, the advantages of using an applet over a traditional HTML form are apparent. Not only can client-side edits be performed with applets to eliminate unnecessary submissions of requests to the server, but the look and feel of the applet is much more interactive and sophisticated.

Content Handlers

Like URLStreamHandlers, content handlers can be used to extend Java's built-in support for Internet resources. Whereas URLStreamHandlers apply to URLs, content handlers are used to wrap the content of resources into Java-based objects. However, content handlers are much less restricted in applets than URLStreamHandlers. Indeed, you are free to create your own custom content handlers and content handler factories in applications as well as applets.

ContentHandler Class

ContentHandler is an abstract base class that declares the getContent() method called by URLConnection. To define your own content handler, you must subclass ContentHandler and provide a getContent() method to create an Object instance representing your resource. Rather than create a custom content handler or call Applet.getImage(), the applet in Listing 17.5 invokes the content handler for an image/gif resource by calling the getContent() method of URLConnection.

Listing 17.5. EX17C.java.

```java
import java.applet.*;
import java.awt.*;
import java.net.*;
import java.io.*;
import sun.awt.image.URLImageSource;

public class EX17C extends Applet
{
    Image img;
    String error = "";

    public void init()
    {
        resize(200, 100);
    }

    public void paint(Graphics g)
    {
        if (error.length() > 0)
            g.drawString(error, 10, 10);
        else
            g.drawImage(img, 10, 10, getBackground(), this);
    }

    public void start()
    {
        try
        {
            URL url = new URL("http://www.jory.com/gifs/someimage.gif");
            URLImageSource imgsrc = (URLImageSource)url.getContent();
            img = Toolkit.getDefaultToolkit().createImage(imgsrc);
        }
        catch (MalformedURLException me)
            error = me.toString();
        catch (IOException e)
            error = e.toString();
    }
}
```

Following along in the code in Listing 17.5, a URL to the image is created as normal. However, instead of calling the getImage() method of the Applet class, the URLImageSource content handler is used. Once the content handler is created, the image itself can be created by calling the toolkit's createImage() method. Now the image can be displayed in the applet's paint() method. In fact, this is the same process that getImage() goes through to create images! Of course, you would normally use getImage() to load images in your applets, but this example illustrates how content handlers are used for accessing resources. Before running the example, be sure to change the URL to point to a valid image file either on a Web server or your local hard disk.

ContentHandlerFactory Interface

The ContentHandlerFactory functions exactly like the URLStreamHandlerFactory interface, except for content handlers. To create your own content handler factory, implement the ContentHandlerFactory interface in a class and call URLConnection.setContentHandlerFactory() to install your factory. Only one content handler factory can be set for URLConnection, though. Fortunately, the content handler factory is not automatically set for applets like the URL stream handler factory in URL.

Summary

The URL classes and content handlers provide a powerful and extensible framework for implementing handlers for your own resource and MIME types. Hopefully, the security constraints that currently limit the usefulness of URLs in applets will be lifted in the future so that these classes can be used to their fullest potential.

Chapter

18

Networking with Datagrams and Sockets

In Chapter 17, "Accessing URLs," you gained access to resources on the Internet using only the URL group of classes. When a higher level of control is necessary to communicate across a network, you can use the datagram and socket classes. In this chapter, we will discuss these two primary methods of socket communication using Java, and the advantages and disadvantages of each approach.

Socket programming is usually a complex task that requires in-depth knowledge of the protocols and networking subsystems involved. Java, however, comes to the rescue again by providing intuitively designed classes that allow you to hit the ground running with low-level Internet programming. To set the stage, a brief overview of the TCP/IP protocol suite and sockets is needed.

TCP/IP Basics

The Internet, as we know it today, had its beginning in the late 1960s as a research project of the U.S. Department of Defense. The Advanced Research Projects Agency (ARPA) was commissioned to design a communications network that would allow computers on independent and dissimilar networks to share information. Although the original ARPANET has grown and changed tremendously since its inception, it laid the groundwork for what is known today as the Internet.

Over the years many contributions were made to the development of the Internet, but arguably the most valuable of these was the creation of the Transmission Control Protocol and Internet Protocol (TCP/IP) suite. TCP/IP services provide the transportation mechanisms for routing and delivering data across the network. When a stream of data is transmitted, it is divided into individual data packets called datagrams. In addition to the data itself, each datagram includes routing information that identifies the computer that is sending the data as well as the computer that should receive the data—an electronic envelope of sorts. As datagrams are relayed from network to network on the Internet, it is the job of IP to inspect the address of the destination computer and ensure that the data is traveling down the right path to reach its intended host.

To identify computers on the Internet, each is given a unique number called an IP address. IP addresses are 32-bit numbers that are commonly shown in dotted decimal notation (for example, 206.99.100.177). Because each computer is also a member of its own local network, its IP address is broken into two parts: the network and the host. The network portion identifies the network that the computer belongs to, and the host portion identifies the computer on that network. The sizes of the network and host components vary depending on the class of the address, but the overall size is always 32 bits. This scheme is similar to the street address of a business, with the street name representing a network and the number representing the building on that street.

Although dotted decimal notation is easier to remember than the numeric representation, it is still a lot to ask for humans to remember a series of numbers. To solve this problem, each IP address can also be given an alphanumeric alias. Because computers like to work with numbers, aliases must be converted to the IP address they represent before data can actually be sent. These translation services are most often provided by Domain Name System (DNS) servers located on the

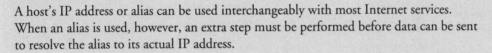

Internet. Like IP addresses, aliases also have logical components. Instead of a host being identified as part of a network, however, under DNS a host is a member of a domain. Domains form a hierarchical chain that defines each host's logical membership in the network. Consider the alias of www.jory.com, which defines a host called www, which is a member of the jory domain, which is a member of the com domain. Domain names move from general to specific as you read from right to left. The com domain is by far the largest and includes all commercial organizations. Other common base domains include edu for educational entities and gov for government institutions.

> **NOTE:**
>
> A host's IP address or alias can be used interchangeably with most Internet services. When an alias is used, however, an extra step must be performed before data can be sent to resolve the alias to its actual IP address.

As already mentioned, IP is responsible for routing individual data packets across the network. IP is not concerned with the content of each datagram or even whether the data reaches its intended destination. Higher-level protocols that work with IP assume this role. The User Datagram Protocol (UDP) is used when the amount of data being transmitted can fit within one datagram. Because UDP does not need to be concerned with segmenting and reassembling multiple datagrams on each end of a connection, it is known for being fast and efficient. UDP, however, makes no guarantee that the datagram will reach its target. Because most data transfer tasks involve more data than can fit in one datagram and function naturally with network connections as streams, TCP is the most common protocol used with IP. TCP provides a reliable connection between two nodes and ensures that the data will be reassembled in the proper sequence and be delivered error free. With a TCP connection, the sending and receiving of data is very similar to reading and writing to a file or pipe. For this reason, TCP connections are often referred to as sockets. This added abstraction, however, comes with a price. TCP adds overhead to the connection that results in slower transfer rates. Just as TCP builds on IP, the next level of protocols, including HTTP, FTP, and SMTP, build on TCP to provide familiar Internet services.

Java provides several classes that can be used to deal with IP and IP addresses, datagrams and datagram connections, and TCP connections that integrate cleanly with the stream classes covered in Chapter 13, "Using Java Streams."

The InetAddress Class

The InetAddress utility class provides a handy interface for dealing with Internet addresses and their peculiar nomenclature. Because InetAddress does not have a public constructor, it cannot be created directly. It does, however, provide three static methods that return instances of InetAddress. The three public static methods of InetAddress as well as some of its other public methods are listed in Table 18.1.

Table 18.1. The `InetAddress` methods of interest.

Method	Description
`InetAddress getByName(String)`	Static method used to retrieve the address for the host name passed as the parameter.
`InetAddress[] getAllByName(String)`	Static method used to retrieve all the addresses for the host name passed as a parameter.
`InetAddress getLocalHost()`	Static method used to retrieve the address for the current, or local, host.
`String getHostName()`	Returns the host name.
`byte[] getAddress()`	Returns the IP address.
`String getHostAddress()`	Returns the IP address as a string.

The host name passed to `getByName()` and `getAllByName()` can be the host's full name, alias, or IP address. Consider the following examples, which return equal `InetAddress` objects:

```
try
{
    InetAddress fullname = InetAddress.getByName("tigger.jory.com");
    InetAddress alias = InetAddress.getByName("tigger");
    InetAddress octets = InetAddress.getByName("199.42.65.1");

    if (fullname.equals(alias) && fullname.equals(octets))
        // All is right with the world!
}
catch (UnknownHostException e)
{
    // Exception handling here.
}
```

NOTE:

Normally, each call to get an address for a host involves a DNS lookup across the network, which can degrade performance when done repetitively. `InetAddress`, however, mitigates the delays caused by DNS lookups by keeping an internal cache of addresses as they are looked up. The cache is always checked first to see whether the address can be returned immediately.

The `DatagramPacket` Class

As already mentioned, communicating over a network using datagrams is an unreliable method of sending self-contained pieces of information. It is unreliable because the protocol does not guarantee that datagram packets will reach their intended destination. Furthermore, even if they do reach their destination, there is no guarantee that they will arrive in the same order in which they were sent. Datagrams are still valuable, however, for certain types of communication, especially those dealing with small amounts of data that are sent using a broadcast scheme. In addition, because datagrams don't include the overhead of guaranteed packet delivery and sequencing, they are typically much faster than data sent using TCP (that is, streaming sockets).

Java provides two classes to perform datagram communication. The `DatagramPacket` class encapsulates the information, or data, for each packet of information sent across the network, and `DatagramSocket` is responsible for actually sending the data. After `DatagramSocket` is discussed, an example that illustrates the use of both classes will be covered. Table 18.2 lists the methods of the `DatagramPacket` class.

Table 18.2. The `DatagramPacket` methods.

Method	Description
`DatagramPacket(byte[], int)`	Creates a `DatagramPacket` that can be used to receive packets from a network connection. The byte array passed as a parameter is used to hold the incoming packet.
`DatagramPacket(byte[], int, InetAddress, int)`	Creates a `DatagramPacket` that is suitable for sending packets across a network connection. The byte array passed as a parameter should contain the data to be sent, and the `InetAddress` and port specifying the destination address and port.
`InetAddress getAddress()`	Returns the `InetAddress` of the host that sent or received the data packet.
`int getPort()`	Returns the port number used to send or receive the data packet.
`byte[] getData()`	Returns the packet data.
`int getLength()`	Returns the length of the packet data.

Datagrams can be created in two forms: those used for sending packets and those used for receiving packets. The only difference between the two is the constructor used to create them. Consider the following code fragment, in which both types of `DatagramPacket` are created:

```
Byte buffer[] = new byte[128];
```

```
DatagramPacket recvPacket = new DatagramPacket(buffer, buffer.length);
// ... Receive some data from a network connection into recvPacket.
// Load buffer with data and create packet to send on port 9000.
DatagramPacket sendPacket = new DatagramPacket(buffer, buffer.length,
        InetAddress.getByName("somehost.somewhere.com"), 9000);
// ... send data in buffer across network connection.
```

The work of receiving and sending DatagramPackets is performed by the DatagramSocket class.

The DatagramSocket Class

A DatagramSocket object can be created to send or receive data encapsulated in DatagramPackets. Because the routing information is included in the DatagramPacket being sent or received, the DatagramSocket is simple to use. Table 18.3 lists the methods of DatagramSocket.

Table 18.3. The public DatagramSocket methods.

Method	Description
DatagramSocket()	Creates a DatagramSocket connected to the first available port. Used for sending packets.
DatagramSocket(int)	Creates a DatagramSocket connected to the specified port. Generally used for receiving data packets.
send(DatagramPacket)	Sends the DatagramPacket passed as a parameter.
receive(DatagramPacket)	Receives a packet into the DatagramPacket passed as a parameter. This method blocks until a packet is received.
int getLocalPort()	Returns the port number being used on the local host for this socket.
close()	Closes the socket.

The reason the first constructor is used to send datagrams is that a port is not specified. In these cases, the first available port is used. Rest assured that the datagram socket will attempt to deliver the datagram to the proper port on the other end of the connection based on the host and port embedded in the DatagramPacket being sent. The following example ties together the use of the InetAddress, DatagramPacket, and DatagramSocket classes.

A Datagram Example: A Live U.S. National Debt Applet

Because datagram network connections deal with small pieces of data, let's consider a datagram client applet and datagram server application that exchange datagrams. The server application accepts subscriptions from one or more applets that are interested in receiving a live feed of the current national debt for the United States. Every three seconds the application broadcasts datagrams containing the current national debt to all subscribed applets. The user can subscribe and unsubscribe from the server at any time. Figures 18.1 and 18.2 show the applet and server application in action.

Figure 18.1.
The National Debt Applet.

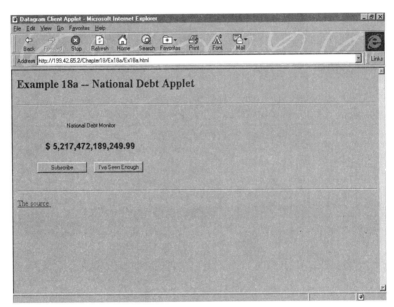

Figure 18.2.
The National Debt Server.

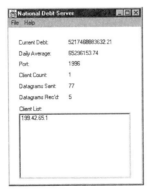

The applet uses two buttons to allow the user to subscribe and unsubscribe from the live feed from the server. When the Subscribe button is pressed, the applet opens a DatagramSocket connection to the server, sends one DatagramPacket containing the SUBSCRIBE command, starts a thread to wait for a confirmation from the server, and also starts a timer in case the server never responds. If the server is accepting subscriptions, it responds by echoing the datagram back to the applet. The timer class is discussed a bit later.

When subscribed, the applet begins to receive datagrams from the server every three seconds that contain the current national debt. The debt display is updated with the contents of each debt datagram. To stop the feed of datagrams from the server, the applet must unsubscribe from the server. This is achieved when the user either presses the I've Seen Enough button or changes to another Web page, causing the applet to stop. In both situations, a datagram is sent to the server with the UNSUBSCRIBE command. The server also echoes the unsubscribe datagram back to the applet. After the confirmation is received, the applet's thread ends. It is started back up, however, if the user subscribes again. Listing 18.1 includes some of the source code for the applet. The classes used to create and lay out the controls of the applet are not listed here but are included on the accompanying CD-ROM.

Listing 18.1. EX18A.java.

```
import java.applet.*;
import java.awt.*;
import java.net.*;
import java.io.*;
import NationalDebtRes;     // Applet controls created by Resource Wizard.
import SimpleTimer;
import SimpleTimerClient;

public class EX18A extends Applet implements Runnable, SimpleTimerClient
{
    static final int DEBT_PORT = 1996;
    static final String SUB_CMD = "SUBSCRIBE";
    static final String UNSUB_CMD = "UNSUBSCRIBE";
    InetAddress host;
    Thread thread = null;
    boolean subscribed;
    NationalDebtRes resource;
    SimpleTimer timer = null;

    public void init()
    {   // Create the resource from the Resource Wizard and
        // initialize the controls.
        resource = new NationalDebtRes(this);
        resource.CreateControls();
        resource.IDC_DEBT.setFont(new Font("Helvetica", Font.BOLD, 18));
        resource.IDC_DEBT.setText("$ 0.00");

        subscribed = false;
    }

    public void start()
    {   // Due to security, server must be running on the same
        // system as the document.
```

```
        try
            host = InetAddress.getByName(getDocumentBase().getHost());
        catch (UnknownHostException e)
            getAppletContext().showStatus("Unable to find host.");
    }

    public boolean handleEvent(Event evt)
    {
        boolean retval = false;

        if (evt.target == resource.ID_SUBSCRIBE && !subscribed)
        {   // Attempt to subscribe to server.
            getAppletContext().showStatus("Subscribing to host...");
            if (sendCommand(SUB_CMD))
                subscribed = true;
            retval = true;
        }
        else if (evt.target == resource.ID_UNSUBSCRIBE && subscribed)
        {   // Attempt to unsubscribe from server.
            getAppletContext().showStatus("Unsubscribing from host...");
            if (sendCommand(UNSUB_CMD))
                subscribed = false;
            retval = true;
        }

        return retval;
    }

    // Sends a command to the server using a datagram.
    protected boolean sendCommand(String cmd)
    {
        boolean retval = false;
        byte buf[] = new byte[cmd.length()];
        cmd.getBytes(0, cmd.length(), buf, 0);
        DatagramSocket socket = null;

        try
        {   // Kill any running timer.
            if (timer != null)
                timer.stop();
            if (thread == null)
            {   // Start up listening thread.
                thread = new Thread(this);
                thread.start();
            }
            // Create a datagram destined for the server containing the command.
            DatagramPacket packet = new DatagramPacket(buf, buf.length,
                    host, DEBT_PORT);
            socket = new DatagramSocket();
            socket.send(packet);    // Send it.
            // Wait 5 seconds for a response.
            timer = new SimpleTimer(this, 5000);

            retval = true;
        }
        catch (SocketException se)
            getAppletContext().showStatus("Unable to communicate with host.");
        catch (IOException e)
            getAppletContext().showStatus("Error communicating with host.");
```

395

continues

Listing 18.1. continued

```
        if (socket != null)
            socket.close();
        return retval;
    }

    public void run()
    {   // Listen on DEBT_PORT for debt updates.
        DatagramSocket listen;
        try
            listen = new DatagramSocket(DEBT_PORT);
        catch (SocketException se)
        {
            getAppletContext().showStatus("Unable to open socket to host.");
            return;
        }

        String msg;

        while (true)
        {
            try
            {
                DatagramPacket recv = new DatagramPacket(new byte[128], 128);
                listen.receive(recv);
                msg = new String(recv.getData(), 0, 0, recv.getLength());
            }
            catch (IOException e)
            {
                getAppletContext().showStatus("Error communicating with host.");
                break;
            }
            if (msg.equals(UNSUB_CMD))
            {   // Received unsubscribe confirmation, drop out.
                getAppletContext().showStatus("Unsubscribe confirmation " +
                        "received.");
                break;
            }
            else if (msg.equals(SUB_CMD))
            {   // Received subscription confirmation, stop timer
                // and keep listening.
                if (timer != null)
                {
                    timer.stop();
                    timer = null;
                }
                getAppletContext().showStatus("Subscription confirmation " +
                        "received.");
            }
            else if (msg.charAt(0) == '$')
                resource.IDC_DEBT.setText(msg);
        }
        // Kill any running timer.
        if (timer != null)
        {
            timer.stop();
```

```
            timer = null;
        }

        listen.close();
        thread = null;
    }

    // Called by SimpleTimer when a timer expires.
    public synchronized void timeOut()
    {
        if (subscribed)
        {   // Trying to subscribe so reset flag.
            getAppletContext().showStatus("Subscription confirmation not " +
                    "received; server may not be active.");
            subscribed = false;
        }
        else
        {   // Trying to unsubscribe so reset flag.
            getAppletContext().showStatus("Unsubscription confirmation " +
                    "not received.  Try again.");
            subscribed = true;
        }
        timer = null;
    }

    public void stop()
    {   // Make sure we unsubscribe before leaving
        // (don't bother waiting for response).
        if (subscribed)
        {
            sendCommand(UNSUB_CMD);
            subscribed = false;
        }
        if (thread != null)
        {
            thread.stop();
            thread = null;
        }
    }
}
}
```

The timer used by the national debt applet is provided by a simple utility class called SimpleTimer. SimpleTimer, shown in Listing 18.2, runs in its own thread and sleeps for a specified number of milliseconds. If the timer thread is not stopped before the call to sleep() returns, SimpleTimer calls the timeOut() method implemented by the user of the timer.

Listing 18.2. SimpleTimer.java.

```
// Implements a basic timer that runs in its own
// thread and calls an interface method when it expires.
public class SimpleTimer extends Thread
{
    long duration = 0;
    SimpleTimerClient client = null;
```

continues

Listing 18.2. continued

```
    public SimpleTimer(SimpleTimerClient client, long duration)
    {
        this.client = client;
        this.duration = duration;
        start();
    }

    public void run()
    {
        try
            sleep(duration);
        catch (InterruptedException e) {}

        if (client != null)
            client.timeOut();
    }
}
```

As already mentioned, if the timer expires, it calls the `timeOut()` method of the object that started the timer. The `timeOut()` method is defined in the `SimpleTimerClient` interface shown in Listing 18.3.

Listing 18.3. `SimpleTimerClient.java`.

```
// Client interface for SimpleTimer.
// The timeOut() method is called when a timer expires.
public interface SimpleTimerClient
{
    public void timeOut();
}
```

The national debt server is implemented as a multithreaded Java application. It uses two numbers provided by the user to calculate the current debt: the previous day's balance and the average daily increase of the debt. Every three seconds the debt is recalculated and broadcast in datagrams to all subscribed applets. To keep things simple, the server assumes that the debt balance provided by the user is current as of the previous day. The daily average is used to calculate the increase per second. The current debt is then calculated as the sum of the previous day's balance plus the number of seconds elapsed today multiplied by the increase in the debt every second. Unfortunately, it is also assumed that the debt will always be increasing.

To manage the subscription requests of multiple applets, the server uses the `SubscriptionManager` utility class. The `SubscriptionManager` runs in its own thread and listens on the predefined national debt port (1996) for new subscriptions and cancellations. It maintains a list of `InetAddress` objects in a `Vector` object to represent the currently subscribed applets. The `SubscriptionManager` informs the server when the subscription count changes and when datagrams are sent and received through the methods defined in the `SubscriptionManagerClient` interface. The server uses this information to update the statistics shown in the main window in Figure 18.2.

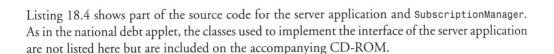

Listing 18.4 shows part of the source code for the server application and SubscriptionManager. As in the national debt applet, the classes used to implement the interface of the server application are not listed here but are included on the accompanying CD-ROM.

Listing 18.4. EX18B.java.

```java
import java.awt.*;
import java.io.*;
import java.net.*;
import java.util.*;
import DialogLayout;
import MainMenuRes;
import MainWinRes;
import OptionsRes;
import HelpAboutRes;
import MessageBoxRes;
import MessageBox;

public class EX18B extends Frame implements Runnable, SubscriptionClient
{
    static final int DEBT_PORT = 1996;
    MainMenuRes menu;
    MainWinRes mainWin;
    SubscriptionManager manager = null;
    int packetsSent = 0, packetsRecd = 0;
    Thread running = null;

    public static void main(String args[])
    {
        new EX18B("National Debt Server");
    }

    public EX18B(String caption)
    {
        super(caption);

        // Create main menu built using Resource Wizard.
        menu = new MainMenuRes(this);
        menu.CreateMenu();

        // Set up font to use.
        setFont(new Font("Dialog", Font.PLAIN, 8));
        mainWin = new MainWinRes(this);
        mainWin.CreateControls();

        // Initialize main window fields.
        mainWin.IDC_CURRENTDEBT.setText("0.00");
        mainWin.IDC_DAILYAVERAGE.setText("0.00");
        mainWin.IDC_PORTNUMBER.setText(String.valueOf(DEBT_PORT));
        mainWin.IDC_CLIENTCOUNT.setText("0");
        mainWin.IDC_DATAGRAMSENT.setText(String.valueOf(packetsSent));
        mainWin.IDC_DATAGRAMRECD.setText(String.valueOf(packetsRecd));

        // Start up the subscription manager to listen for applets.
        manager = new SubscriptionManager(this, DEBT_PORT);
```

continues

Listing 18.4. continued

```
        show();

        // Start up application thread to broadcast debt updates.
        running = new Thread(this);
        running.start();
    }

    public boolean handleEvent(Event event)
    {
        boolean retval = true;

        if (event.target == menu.ID_FILE_OPTIONS)
        {   // Show options dialog.
            new OptionsDlg(this,
                    new OptionsData(mainWin.IDC_CURRENTDEBT.getText(),
                    mainWin.IDC_DAILYAVERAGE.getText())));
        }
        else if (event.target == menu.ID_FILE_EXIT ¦¦
                event.id == Event.WINDOW_DESTROY)
        {   // Kill manager and broadcast threads.
            if (manager != null)
                manager.stop();
            if (running != null)
                running.stop();
            dispose();
            System.exit(0);
        }
        else if (event.target == menu.ID_HELP_ABOUT)
        {   // Display help¦about.
            new HelpAboutDlg(this);
        }
        else if (event.arg instanceof OptionsData)
        {   // Update options data based on values from options dialog.
            OptionsData data = (OptionsData)event.arg;
            mainWin.IDC_CURRENTDEBT.setText(data.currentDebt);
            mainWin.IDC_DAILYAVERAGE.setText(data.dailyAvg);
        }
        else
            retval = false;

        return retval;
    }

    public void run()
    {   // Thread responsible for broadcasting debt updates to
        // subscribing applets.
        DatagramSocket socket = null;
        while (true)
        {
            try
            {   // Broadcast every 3 seconds.
                Thread.sleep(3000);
                if (manager.getSubscriberCount() > 0)
                {   // Have subscribers so get debt, set up socket
                    // and send datagrams.
                    String debt = getCurrentDebt();
```

```
                byte buf[] = new byte[debt.length()];
                debt.getBytes(0, debt.length(), buf, 0);
                socket = new DatagramSocket(DEBT_PORT);
                for (Enumeration e = manager.subscribers();
                        e.hasMoreElements();)
                {   // Send datagram to each applet.
                    InetAddress addr = (InetAddress)e.nextElement();
                    DatagramPacket packet = new DatagramPacket(buf,
                            buf.length, addr, DEBT_PORT);
                    socket.send(packet);
                    datagramSent();
                }
            }
        }
        catch (InterruptedException e)
            break;
        catch (Exception e)
        {
            new MessageBox(this, "Communications error.  Server stopping.",
                    "Error");
            break;
        }
    }
    if (socket != null)
        socket.close();
}

public synchronized void subscriberCountChange(int count)
{   // Called by SubscriptionManager when count changes.
    mainWin.IDC_CLIENTCOUNT.setText(String.valueOf(count));
    mainWin.IDC_CLIENTLIST.clear();
    for (Enumeration e = manager.subscribers(); e.hasMoreElements();)
        mainWin.IDC_CLIENTLIST.addItem(e.nextElement().toString());
}

public synchronized  void datagramSent()
{   // Called by SubscriptionManager when a datagram is sent.
    mainWin.IDC_DATAGRAMSENT.setText(String.valueOf(++packetsSent));
}

public synchronized void datagramRecd()
{   // Called by SubscriptionManager when a datagram is received.
    mainWin.IDC_DATAGRAMRECD.setText(String.valueOf(++packetsRecd));
}

protected String getCurrentDebt()
{   // Calculate current debt based on previous day's balance plus
    // amount of increase up to current time.  Note: assumes that
    // debt will always increase (pretty reliable).
    String retval;
    try
    {
        Date now = new Date();
        double debt = Double.valueOf(mainWin.IDC_CURRENTDEBT.
                getText()).doubleValue();
        double avg = Double.valueOf(mainWin.IDC_DAILYAVERAGE.
                getText()).doubleValue();
        double perSecond = avg / 86400;
        int seconds = (now.getHours() * 3600) + (now.getMinutes() * 60) +
```

401

continues

Listing 18.4. continued

```
                    now.getSeconds();
        double currDebt = (perSecond * seconds) + debt;
        retval = formatBigCurrency(currDebt);
    }
    catch (NumberFormatException e)
        retval = "$ 0.00";

    return retval;
}

protected String formatBigCurrency(double value)
{   // Formats a big double as a currency string since
    // toString() returns exponential notation.
    double power = 1000000000000.00d;
    String s = "$ ";

    while ((long)value > 0)
    {
        double work = value / power;
        if ((long)work > 0)
        {
            if (work < 100 && s.length() > 2)
                s += "0";
            if (work < 10 && s.length() > 2)
                s += "0";
            int piece = (int)work;
            s += piece;
            value -= (piece * power);
            if ((long)value > 0)
                s += ",";
        }
        else if (s.length() > 2)
            s += "000,";
        power /= 1000f;
    }
    s += ".";
    int cents = (int)(value * 100);
    if (cents < 10)
        s += "0";
    s += cents;

    return s;
}
}

// Interface used by SubscriptionManager to communicate with client object.
interface SubscriptionClient
{
    public void subscriberCountChange(int count);
    public void datagramSent();
    public void datagramRecd();
}

// Monitors given port for subscription requests and cancellations.
class SubscriptionManager extends Thread
{
```

```
SubscriptionClient client;   // Client object for subscription services.
Vector subscribers;          // List of subscribers.
DatagramSocket socket;
int port = 0;
static final String SUB_CMD = "SUBSCRIBE";
static final String UNSUB_CMD = "UNSUBSCRIBE";

public SubscriptionManager(SubscriptionClient client, int port)
{
    this.client = client;
    this.port = port;
    subscribers = new Vector();
    start();
}

public int getSubscriberCount()
{
    return subscribers.size();
}

public Enumeration subscribers()
{
    return subscribers.elements();
}

protected void addSubscriber(InetAddress newAddr)
{   // Add a subscriber if not already in list.
    if (!subscribers.contains(newAddr))
    {
        subscribers.addElement(newAddr);
        // Notify client object.
        client.subscriberCountChange(subscribers.size());
    }
}

protected void removeSubscriber(InetAddress existAddr)
{   // Remove a subscriber if in list.
    int idx = subscribers.indexOf(existAddr);
    if (idx != -1)
    {
        subscribers.removeElementAt(idx);
        // Notify client object.
        client.subscriberCountChange(subscribers.size());
    }
}

public void run()
{   // Process subscription requests and cancellations.
    try
    {
        DatagramPacket recv, send;
        socket = new DatagramSocket(port);
        String cmd;

        while (true)
        {
            recv = new DatagramPacket(new byte[128], 128);
            socket.receive(recv);
```

continues

Listing 18.4. continued

```
                client.datagramRecd();
                cmd = new String(recv.getData(), 0, 0, recv.getLength());
                if (cmd.equals(SUB_CMD))
                    addSubscriber(recv.getAddress());
                else if (cmd.equals(UNSUB_CMD))
                    removeSubscriber(recv.getAddress());
                // Return command received as a form of confirmation so
                // applet knows we're here.
                send = new DatagramPacket(recv.getData(), recv.getLength(),
                        recv.getAddress(), port);
                socket.send(send);
                client.datagramSent();
            }
        }
        catch (SocketException se)
            System.err.println("Socket error: " + se);
        catch (IOException e)
            System.err.println("IO Error: " + e);
    }
}
```

The Socket Class

Communicating using datagrams severely limits the type of network services that can be written. Datagrams are used to carry small amounts of information and cannot be used as a reliable form of exchanging data. For the previously shown national debt example, it did not matter much if a datagram never reached an applet because another would be sent three seconds later. The Socket class offers a better alternative for applications that need to communicate using a more reliable connection. Socket takes care of sending data across the network to give the illusion that the data is sent and received using a stream or socket. Socket also performs any error correction needed for data packets that are corrupted or never received.

Table 18.4 lists the methods of interest from the Socket class.

Table 18.4. The Socket methods of interest.

Method	Description
Socket(String, int)	Creates a streaming socket and binds it to the host and port specified as parameters.
Socket(String, int, boolean)	Creates a socket and binds it to the host and port specified as parameters. The last parameter is used to indicate whether the socket should be a stream or datagram socket.
Socket(InetAddress, int)	Creates a streaming socket connected to the specified host and port.

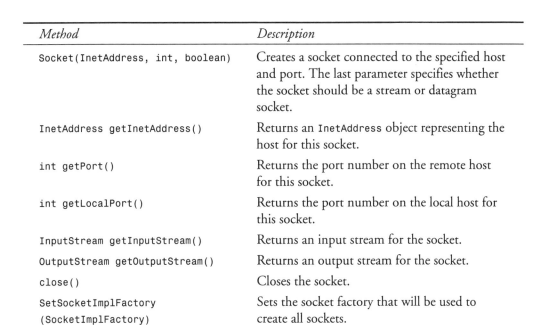

Method	Description
`Socket(InetAddress, int, boolean)`	Creates a socket connected to the specified host and port. The last parameter specifies whether the socket should be a stream or datagram socket.
`InetAddress getInetAddress()`	Returns an `InetAddress` object representing the host for this socket.
`int getPort()`	Returns the port number on the remote host for this socket.
`int getLocalPort()`	Returns the port number on the local host for this socket.
`InputStream getInputStream()`	Returns an input stream for the socket.
`OutputStream getOutputStream()`	Returns an output stream for the socket.
`close()`	Closes the socket.
`SetSocketImplFactory (SocketImplFactory)`	Sets the socket factory that will be used to create all sockets.

`Socket` objects are created slightly different from `DatagramSocket` objects because the host and port are not encapsulated in a `DatagramPacket`. A socket can be created using either a host name or an `InetAddress` object. As with `DatagramSocket`, the port can also be specified, and it defaults to the first available port if initialized to -1. Create sockets with a port number when originating a connection with a host rather than waiting for a host to initiate a connection. Input and output streams can also be retrieved from a socket to create a flexible mechanism for reading and writing data across the connection. Consider the following code fragment, which illustrates how easy it is to create, open, and perform I/O using a socket.

```
try
{
    Socket socket = new Socket("somehost.somewhere.com", -1);
    // Always a good idea to buffer the stream to mitigate blocking.
    PrintStream out = new PrintStream(
            new BufferedOutputStream(socket.getOutputStream()));
    out.println("Are you listening?");
    DataInputStream in = new DataInputStream(
            new BufferedInputStream(socket.getInputStream()));
    in.readLine();
    // ...
    // Don't forget to close the socket!
    socket.close()
}
catch (Exception e)
    // Exception handling logic.
```

A Socket Example: A POP Client Application

To illustrate how the socket class can be used, consider the following example, which implements an electronic mail program that uses the post office protocol (POP) to retrieve mail from a POP server. As the protocol name implies, POP servers are used as electronic post offices to hold mail for users who might not have permanent connections to the network. The program can be run as a Java applet or application but can be used only as an applet if the POP server is running on the same server that served the Web page containing the applet. Remember that Web browser security prohibits applets from communicating with hosts other than the originating host. The POP client running as an application is shown in Figure 18.3.

<u>Figure 18.3.</u>
The POP client.

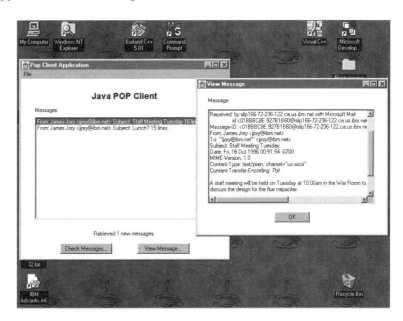

POP is a very simple protocol. After a connection has been established, the client issues a series of commands to log on, check for new mail, request each new message, and optionally have each message removed from the server. The POP server replies in the affirmative by returning +OK. A typical conversation between a POP client and server might look like this:

```
Server: +OK pop.server.com ready
Client: USER jjory
Server: +OK
Client: PASS lemmein
Server: +OK
Client: STAT
Server: +OK 1 847
Client: RETR 1
```

```
Server: +OK 847 bytes
Server: [...message is sent...]
Client: DELE 1
Server: +OK
Client: QUIT
Server: +OK
```

To retrieve new messages from a POP server using the program, the user clicks the Check Messages... button. This action causes an object of type MailRetriever to start running. MailRetriever is a subclass of Thread and is used to manage the connection and conversation with the POP server. It uses the MailRetrieverClient interface to retrieve information from the program and update the program with status information and new messages. Listing 18.5 includes the source code for the applet and mail retriever classes. The classes used for the interface, however, are not listed here but are included on the accompanying CD-ROM.

Listing 18.5. EX18C.java.

```java
import java.applet.*;
import java.awt.*;
import java.net.*;
import java.io.*;
import java.util.*;
// Classes created by Resource Wizard for interface.
import DialogLayout;
import ConnectDlgRes;
import MainMenu;
import MainWinRes;
import NoteRes;
import ViewMessageRes;
import MessageBox;

public class EX18C extends Applet implements MailRetrieverClient
{
    MainWinRes mainWin = null;      // Main window resource.
    ConnectData connectData = null; // Used to exchange data with dialog.
    MailRetriever retriever = null; // Responsible for retrieving messages.
    Vector messages = new Vector(); // Holds retrieved messages.

    public EX18C()
    {
        connectData = new ConnectData();
    }

    public static void main(String args[])
    {   // Called when run as an application.
        EX18C applet = new EX18C();
        // Set up frame and main window.
        EX18CApplicationFrame frame = new EX18CApplicationFrame(applet);
        applet.mainWin = frame.resource;
        applet.mainWin.IDC_STATUS.setText("");
        applet.mainWin.IDC_VIEWMESSAGE.disable();
        applet.start();
    }

    public void init()
```

continues

Listing 18.5. continued

```java
{   // Running as an applet.
    mainWin = new MainWinRes(this);
    mainWin.CreateControls();
    mainWin.IDC_TITLE.setFont(new Font("Helvetica", Font.BOLD, 18));
    mainWin.IDC_STATUS.setText("");
    mainWin.IDC_VIEWMESSAGE.disable();
}

public void stop()
{
    if (retriever != null)
    {
        retriever.stop();
        retriever = null;
    }
}

public boolean handleEvent(Event event)
{
    boolean retval = false;
    if (event.target == mainWin.IDC_CHECKMSGS)
    {   // Only allow connect dialog to come up if not already retrieving.
        if (retriever == null || !retriever.isAlive())
            new ConnectDialog(this, connectData);
        retval = true;
    }
    else if (event.target == mainWin.IDC_VIEWMESSAGE &&
            mainWin.IDC_MESSAGES.countItems() > 0)
    {   // Bring up message viewer for current message.
        int sel = mainWin.IDC_MESSAGES.getSelectedIndex();
        if (sel >= 0)
            new ViewMessageDialog((String)(messages.elementAt(sel)));
        else
            mainWin.IDC_STATUS.setText("Please select a " +
                    "message to display.");
    }
    else if (event.arg instanceof ConnectData)
    {   // User selected OK from connect dialog, start retriever.
        mainWin.IDC_STATUS.setText("Retrieving new messages...");
        retriever = new MailRetriever(this);
        retval = true;
    }
    return retval;
}

public String getPopAccount()
{   // Called by retriever to get POP account name.
    return connectData.acctName;
}

public String getPopPassword()
{   // Called by retriever to get password for POP account.
    return connectData.acctPassword;
}

public String getPopServer()
{   // Called by retriever to get the name of POP server.
```

```
            return connectData.popServer;
        }

    public synchronized void popStatus(String status)
    {   // Called by retriever to update app or applet on progress.
        mainWin.IDC_STATUS.setText(status);
    }

    public void popMessage(String message)
    {   // Called by retiever for each message retrieved.
        boolean fromFound = false, subjectFound = false;
        mainWin.IDC_VIEWMESSAGE.enable();

        // Parse message looking for whom the message is from and
        // the subject so we can format line in message listbox.
        StringTokenizer parse = new StringTokenizer(message, "\n");
        int lines = parse.countTokens();
        String from = "<Unknown From> ", subject = "<Unknown Subject> ";

        while (parse.hasMoreTokens())
        {
            String line = parse.nextToken();
            if (line.regionMatches(true, 0, "From", 0, 4) && !fromFound)
            {
                from = line + " ";
                fromFound = true;
            }
            else if (line.regionMatches(true, 0, "Subject", 0, 4) &&
                    !subjectFound)
            {
                subject = line + " ";
                subjectFound = true;
            }
        }
        // Add this message to list of messages.
        messages.addElement(message);

        mainWin.IDC_MESSAGES.addItem(from + subject + lines + " lines.");
    }
}

// Interface used between retriever and client applicaton/applet.
interface MailRetrieverClient
{
    public String getPopAccount();
    public String getPopPassword();
    public String getPopServer();
    public void popStatus(String status);
    public void popMessage(String message);
}

// Threaded POP mail retriever.
class MailRetriever extends Thread
{
    static final int POP_PORT = 110;
    Socket socket;
    PrintStream out;
    DataInputStream in;
```

continues

Listing 18.5. continued

```java
MailRetrieverClient client;
String popResponse; // Holds last command/response from server.

public MailRetriever(MailRetrieverClient client)
{
    this.client = client;
    start();
}

public void run()
{
    if (popConnect())
    {   // Connection established.
        client.popStatus("Logging on to POP server...");
        int messages = 0;
        if (popLogon())
        {   // Successfully logged on to server.
            client.popStatus("Checking for new messages...");
            messages = getWaitingMessageCount();
            for (int i = 1; i <= messages; i++)
            {
                client.popStatus("Retrieving message " + i + " of " +
                        messages + ".");
                getMessage(i);
            }

            client.popStatus("Disconnecting from POP server...");
            popQuit();

            if (messages > 0)
                client.popStatus("Retrieved " + messages +
                        " new messages.");
            else
                client.popStatus("No new messages retrieved.");
        }
        else
        {
            client.popStatus("Error logging on to POP server.");
            popQuit();
        }
    }
}

protected boolean popConnect()
{
    boolean retval = true;
    String server = client.getPopServer();

    client.popStatus("Opening connection to " + server + "...");
    try
    {   // Make connection and set up buffered i/o streams.
        socket = new Socket(server, POP_PORT);
        in = new DataInputStream(
                new BufferedInputStream(socket.getInputStream()));
        out = new PrintStream(
                new BufferedOutputStream(socket.getOutputStream()), true);
        client.popStatus("Connection successfully established with " +
```

```
                        server + ".");
        }
        catch (UnknownHostException e)
        {
            client.popStatus("Unable to resolve POP server's name.");
            retval = false;
        }
        catch (IOException e1)
        {
            client.popStatus("Error opening connection to POP server.");
            if (socket != null)
            {   // Close down socket.
                try
                    socket.close();
                catch (IOException e2) {}
            }
            retval = false;
        }
        return retval;
    }

    protected boolean waitForOk()
    {   // Waits for an OK response from server.
        boolean retval = true;
        try
        {
            do
            {
                popResponse = in.readLine();
            } while (!popResponse.startsWith("+OK"));
        }
        catch (Exception e)
            retval = false;
        return retval;
    }

    protected boolean popLogon()
    {   // Logs user on to server.
        boolean retval = false;
        if (waitForOk())
        {
            out.println("USER " + client.getPopAccount());

            if (waitForOk())
            {
                out.println("PASS " + client.getPopPassword());
                retval = waitForOk();
            }
        }
        return retval;
    }

    protected void popQuit()
    {   // Send QUIT command and close socket.
        out.println("QUIT");
        try
            socket.close();
        catch (IOException e) {}
    }
```

411

continues

Listing 18.5. continued

```java
protected int getWaitingMessageCount()
{   // Get the number of messages waiting at server.
    int retval = 0;
    out.println("STAT");

    if (waitForOk())
    {
        StringTokenizer stats = new StringTokenizer(popResponse);
        stats.nextToken();
        retval = Integer.parseInt(stats.nextToken());
    }
    return retval;
}

protected boolean getMessage(int number)
{   // Set the specified message number from server.
    boolean retval = false;
    out.println("RETR " + number);
    if (waitForOk())
    {
        String line, message = "";
        try
        {
            while ((line = in.readLine()) != null)
            {
                if (line.equals("."))
                    break;
                message += line;
                message += "\n";    // Put newline back on.
            }
            // Pass message along to client.
            client.popMessage(message);
            // Delete message from server.
            out.println("DELE " + number);
            retval = waitForOk();
        }
        catch (IOException e)
            client.popStatus("Error retrieving message " + number +
                    " from POP server.");
    }
    return retval;
}
}
```

Although this simple example does not compare to today's powerful mail applications, it does illustrate the ease with which Java can be used to communicate using sockets. Possible enhancements include support for MIME attachments (discussed in Chapter 17) and saving messages to disk for later viewing.

Summary

One of Java's strong points is the ease with which network-capable programs can be written. Indeed, most programmers typically don't need to get down to the level of datagrams and sockets, but it is nice to know that Java provides an intuitive set of classes that integrates well with Java's other classes and is extensible. In the next chapter, "Client/Server Programming," we will take a closer look at socket programming from the server side, as well as other alternatives for developing client/server solutions.

Chapter

19

Client/Server Programming

So far in Part IV, "Networking with Java," we have discovered how Java's URL, datagram, and socket classes can be used to perform some simple networking tasks. This chapter discusses the larger world of client/server computing, how Java fits into this world, and the future of Java related to the client/server model. We will also cover one last Java networking class, ServerSocket, that can be used to create sophisticated and robust server processes.

The Client/Server Model

During the last few years, the term client/server has taken the computing industry by storm. In companies around the world, technical management has latched onto client/server as a revolutionary concept that will propel their businesses into the next century. The truth is, however, that the client/server model has existed in one form or another in computer science for several decades. It exists in the monolithic mainframe systems that have been criticized for not delivering functionality that they were never designed to provide—as well as in the applications and operating systems running on your desktop. Boiled down to its most basic definition, the term client/server refers to one process (a client) requesting a service from another process (a server). The client and server processes could be running within the same address space on the same system or on separate systems separated by thousands of miles.

The recent trend has been to distribute computing resources and responsibility across several platforms, each specializing in providing a certain service. Although computing systems are better leveraged and can take advantage of parallel processing in this model, it does not come without a price. Specifically, the expense and administrative effort involved in supporting these systems is immense. System architects and administrators are faced with several daunting challenges including interoperability, compatibility, and configuration management.

Java's Contribution

Java brings a refreshing option to the table. Because Java is platform-independent, many of the compatibility issues that have plagued traditional client applications are solved. Developers no longer have to maintain and compile separate versions of the client application, and users are not forced to use a standardized client configuration. In addition, all or part of Java's executable components can be distributed. Because Java bytecodes can be centrally located but still executed in the client's address space, administrators only have to update the bytecodes in one location instead of deploying a newly compiled client application to every workstation. Of course, traditionally compiled client applications can also be loaded from a server but at the cost of slower load-time and increased network traffic due to the size of their executable files. Java's bytecode files (.class files) are designed to be safely transported across a network, especially a wide area network where bandwidth may be limited. Chapter 20, "Keeping Out the Riff-Raff: JavaSecurity," discusses the security features of Java in detail.

Another advantage of using Java for client/server development is its capability to be seamlessly integrated with the World Wide Web. This opens up the opportunity to quickly leverage the multimedia features of the Web with the dynamic and active nature of Java.

Finally, there have been some recent initiatives that will allow Java to become a serious player in significant client/server development in the future. These developments, as well as plans for the future, are discussed at the end of this chapter.

ServerSocket Class

In Chapter 18, "Networking with Datagrams and Sockets," you learned how to use the DatagramSocket class to originate and accept datagram-based network connections. You also saw how the Socket class can be used to initiate a socket or streaming connection. However, the Socket class cannot be used to listen for or accept connections originating from another host. That is the job of the ServerSocket class.

The role of ServerSocket is to listen for connection requests on a specific port from other hosts on the network. Once a connection is established, the accept() method of ServerSocket will create or spin off a Socket object to interact with the remote host. So, ServerSocket is a doorman of sorts. It waits for people to knock on a particular door, opens the door, and lets them in. As shown in the Internet dictionary example to follow, this design is the key to developing a robust socket server. Table 19.1 lists several of the public methods of the ServerSocket class.

Table 19.1. Public methods of interest from the ServerSocket class.

Method	Description
ServerSocket(int)	Creates a server socket on the specified port. A default backlog of 50 is used.
ServerSocket(int, int)	Creates a server socket on the specified port with the specified backlog limit.
InetAddress getInetAddress()	Returns an InetAddress object representing the host to which this server socket is connected.
int getLocalPort()	Returns the port number on the local host for this server socket.
Socket accept()	Accepts a connection on the local port and returns a Socket object that can be used to communicate over that connection.
close()	Closes the server socket.
setSocketFactory(SocketImplFactory)	Sets the system's socket factory that will be used to create all sockets.

In order for a `ServerSocket` object to be created, it must be told what port to monitor. You can bind the server socket to an anonymous port by specifying a port of `0`. Both public constructors require the port number as a parameter but the second constructor will also accept an integer representing the number of queued connection requests that the server socket will maintain before denying access. To extend the doorman analogy used above, this parameter is functionally equivalent to limiting the number of people that are allowed to stand in line waiting for the doorman to let them in. Once this backlog limit is reached, the server socket will cause the client socket to throw an `IOException` indicating that the connection request was rejected. The default connection backlog size is 50 requests.

When designing server programs, one of the primary goals is to process incoming requests as quickly and efficiently as possible. The last thing you want to do is force clients to wait in line or deny their requests because your server is not robust enough. At the same time, you do not want to limit the functionality of your server just because you cannot turn requests around fast enough. The following code fragment illustrates the challenges just described:

```
try
{
        ServerSocket listen = new ServerSocket(1234);    // Create server socket on
        ➥port 1234.
        while (true)
    {
        Socket socket = listen.accept();    // Wait here for the next connect
        ➥request.
        // Client has connected so get stream objects to communicate with.
        DataInputStream in = new DataInputStream(socket.getInputStream());
        DataOutputStream out = new DataOutputStream(socket.getOutputStream());
        // Do some useful processing... meanwhile other clients are being queued.
    }
}
catch (IOException e)
{
    // Exception handling logic.
}
```

Once the server socket has been created, the logic enters a loop where it waits for a client to connect so it can service its request. The `accept()` method will not return until a client connects. When the server is done working with the client, the loop wraps around and waits for the next connection. If one or more clients are waiting in the queue, `accept()` will grab the next one in line and return a socket to it immediately. So it is clear that if the tasks that the server must perform for each client are significant and the server is repeatedly used by several clients, each client will spend a lot of time waiting for the server to accept each connection. In addition, if the nature of the connection to the client is interactive or the duration is controlled by the client, the server is essentially reduced to serving one client at a time. By making the server multithreaded, the following example shows how to design a robust server that solves these problems and is capable of handling multiple connections quickly and efficiently.

Client/Server Example: Internet Dictionary

To illustrate a multithreaded Java server program, we will develop a simple client/server example that implements an Internet dictionary. The client can be run as an applet or application, as shown in Figures 19.1 and 19.2.

Figure 19.1.
Internet Dictionary client as an applet.

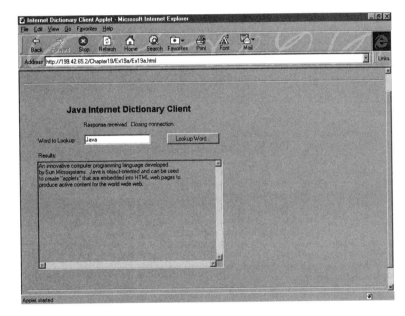

Figure 19.2.
Internet Dictionary client as an application.

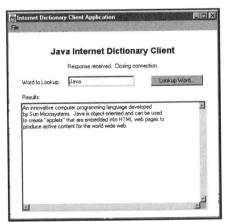

The server program is a Java application that must be run on the same host as the client class files (as specified by the CODEBASE HTML tag) if the client is run as an applet. Because applications are not bound by the security constraints imposed on applets, the server can be run on any host if the client is run as an application.

A portion of the source code for the client is shown in Listing 19.1. The user interface classes created by the Java Resource Wizard are not shown here, but are included on the accompanying CD-ROM.

Listing 19.1. EX19A.java.

```
import java.applet.*;
import java.awt.*;
import java.net.*;
import java.io.*;
public class EX19A extends Applet
{
    MainWinRes mainWin = null;
    Socket socket = null;
    static final int DICTIONARY_PORT = 2000;
    String host;
    public static void main(String args[])
    {   // Program being run as an application.
        EX19A applet = new EX19A();
        // Setup application frame for main window and start applet.
        Ex19aApplicationFrame frame = new Ex19aApplicationFrame(applet);
        applet.mainWin = frame.resource;
        applet.host = "199.42.65.2";
        applet.start();
    }
    public void init()
    {   // Program being run as applet.
        mainWin = new MainWinRes(this);
        mainWin.CreateControls();
        mainWin.IDC_TITLE.setFont(new Font("Helvetica", Font.BOLD, 18));
        // Use host that applet was served from.
        host = getCodeBase().getHost();
    }
    public void start()
    {   // Initialize screen controls.
        mainWin.IDC_STATUS.setText("");
        mainWin.IDC_RESULTS.setEditable(false);
    }
    public void stop()
    {   // Close down socket if it's active.
        if (socket != null)
        {
            try
                socket.close();
            catch (IOException e) {}
        }
    }
    public boolean handleEvent(Event event)
    {
        boolean retval = false;
```

```
        if (event.target == mainWin.IDC_LOOKUP)
        {   // Make sure the user has entered something.
            String word = mainWin.IDC_WORD.getText();
            if (word.length() == 0)
                mainWin.IDC_STATUS.setText("Please enter a word to lookup.");
            else
                lookupWord(word);
            retval = true;
        }
        return retval;
    }
    // This method does the actual lookup of the word by sending a request
    // across the network to the dictionary server.
    protected void lookupWord(String word)
    {
        mainWin.IDC_RESULTS.setText("");
        mainWin.IDC_STATUS.setText("Performing lookup...");
        try
        {   // Create socket and setup buffered input/output streams to communicate.
            socket = new Socket(host, DICTIONARY_PORT);
            DataInputStream in = new DataInputStream(new
            ➥BufferedInputStream(socket.getInputStream()));
            PrintStream out = new PrintStream(new
            ➥BufferedOutputStream(socket.getOutputStream()), true);
            mainWin.IDC_STATUS.setText("Sending word...");
            out.println("LOOKUP=" + word);    // Send lookup command to server.
            String line;
            mainWin.IDC_STATUS.setText("Waiting for response...");
            line = in.readLine();
            if (line.startsWith("DEFINITION="))
            {   // A definition was returned.
                // Strip off "DEFINITION=" response from first line of definition.
                line = line.substring(line.indexOf('=') + 1);
                // Read each line of definition from server.
                do
                    mainWin.IDC_RESULTS.appendText(line + "\n");
                while ((line = in.readLine()) != null);
                mainWin.IDC_STATUS.setText("Response received.  Closing
                ➥connection.");
            }
            else if (line.startsWith("ERROR="))
            {   // An error occurred at the server.
                // Strip off "ERROR=" response from first line of response.
                String error = line.substring(line.indexOf('=') + 1);
                if (error.equalsIgnoreCase("WordNotFound"))
                    mainWin.IDC_STATUS.setText("The word '" + word + "' not found.
                    ➥Try again.");
                else if (error.equalsIgnoreCase("DictionaryFileError"))
                    mainWin.IDC_STATUS.setText("Dictionary not available.  Try again
                    ➥later.");
                else
                    mainWin.IDC_STATUS.setText("Error looking up word.");
            }
            in.close();
            out.close();
            socket.close();
        }
        catch (UnknownHostException e1)
```

continues

421

Listing 19.1. continued

```
            mainWin.IDC_STATUS.setText("Unable to resolve dictionary server's
name.");
        catch (IOException e2)
        {
            mainWin.IDC_STATUS.setText("Error opening connection to dictionary
server.  Server may not be running.");
            if (socket != null)
            {   // Close down socket.
                try
                    socket.close();
                catch (IOException e) {}
            }
        }
        socket = null;
    }
}
// Frame used to wrap up main window when program is run as an application.
class Ex19aApplicationFrame extends Frame
{
    MainWinRes resource;
    MainMenuRes menu;
    Applet owner;
    public Ex19aApplicationFrame(Applet owner)
    {
        super("Internet Dictionary Client Application");
        this.owner = owner;
        // Since it's an application, give it a menu to allow user to exit.
        menu = new MainMenuRes(this);
        menu.CreateMenu();
        setFont(new Font("Dialog", Font.PLAIN, 8));
        resource = new MainWinRes(this);
        resource.CreateControls();
        resource.IDC_TITLE.setFont(new Font("Helvetica", Font.BOLD, 18));
        setResizable(false);    // Do not allow frame to be resized.
        show();
    }
    public boolean handleEvent(Event event)
    {   // Intercept frame messages and pass the others along to the applet.
        if (event.target == menu.ID_FILEEXIT ¦¦ event.id == Event.WINDOW_DESTROY)
        {
            dispose();
            System.exit(0);
            return true;
        }
        else
            return owner.handleEvent(event);
    }
}
```

When the user enters a word to look up and presses the Lookup Word... button, the handleEvent()
method receives the event notification and calls the lookupWord() method. This is where all of the
interaction with the server occurs.

Once the socket to the server has been opened, buffered input and output streams are created and the lookup request is sent to the server. The format of the lookup request is LOOKUP=word to lookup. Then the client waits for a response from the server. The response can take on two forms: DEFINITION=definition of word or ERROR=type of error. Because the definition can be made up of multiple lines, the program keeps reading lines from the input stream until the entire definition has been received. Each line is added to the results text area control as it is received.

On the other side of the connection, the server application shown in Figure 19.3 is responsible for looking up and returning definitions to all of the clients.

Figure 19.3.

Internet Dictionary server application.

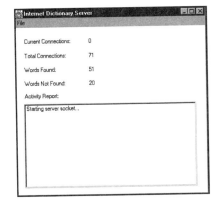

The server is composed of two parts. The application itself contains the main loop that implements a server socket. As connections are accepted in the run() method, a Lookup object is created and is handed the socket that was returned by ServerSocket.accept(). Because the Lookup class runs in its own thread, the server thread is allowed to immediately return to accepting the next connection. With this design, clients are serviced as fast as possible regardless of the complexity of the service being provided by the server.

The source code for the server is shown in Listing 19.2. Once again, the user interface classes created by the Java Resource Wizard are not shown here but are included on the accompanying CD-ROM.

Listing 19.2. EX19B.java.

```java
import java.awt.*;
import java.io.*;
import java.net.*;
public class EX19B extends Frame implements Runnable, LookupInterface
{
    static final int DICTIONARY_PORT = 2000;
    // Counts used to track server statistics.
    int currentConnections = 0;
    int totalConnections = 0;
    int wordsFound = 0;
    int wordsNotFound = 0;
    // Interface objects.
```

continues

Listing 19.2. continued

```
MainMenuRes menu;
MainWindowRes mainWin;
// Server's primary thread and socket.
Thread running = null;
ServerSocket listen = null;
public static void main(String args[])
{
    new EX19B("Internet Dictionary Server");
}
public EX19B(String caption)
{
    super(caption);
    // Create main menu built using Resource Wizard.
    menu = new MainMenuRes(this);
    menu.CreateMenu();
    // Setup font to use.
    setFont(new Font("Dialog", Font.PLAIN, 8));
    mainWin = new MainWindowRes(this);
    mainWin.CreateControls();
    // Initialize main window fields.
    mainWin.IDC_CURRENTCONNECTIONS.setText("0");
    mainWin.IDC_TOTALCONNECTIONS.setText("0");
    mainWin.IDC_WORDSFOUND.setText("0");
    mainWin.IDC_WORDSNOTFOUND.setText("0");
    setResizable(false);    // Do not allow frame to be resized.
    show();
    // Start up thread to listen for clients.
    running = new Thread(this);
    running.start();
}
public boolean handleEvent(Event event)
{
    boolean retval = false;
    if (event.target == menu.ID_FILE_EXIT ¦¦ event.id == Event.WINDOW_DESTROY)
    {   // Kill server thread if running.
        if (running != null)
            running.stop();
        dispose();
        System.exit(0);
        retval = true;
    }
    return retval;
}
public void run()
{
    mainWin.IDC_ACTIVITY.addItem("Starting server socket...");
    try
    {   // Create primary thread.
        listen = new ServerSocket(DICTIONARY_PORT);
        while (true)
        {   // Wait for connection requests and spin off Lookup threads
            // to service each request.
            Socket socket = listen.accept();
            new Lookup(this, socket);
        }
    }
```

```
            catch (IOException e)
                mainWin.IDC_ACTIVITY.addItem("Server socket error: " + e);
            // Close down the socket.
            try
                listen.close();
            catch (IOException e) {}
            listen = null;
    }
    // Called by each lookup thread to update server.
    public synchronized void connectionUpdate(String event)
    {
        mainWin.IDC_ACTIVITY.addItem(event);
    }
    // Called by each lookup thread to indicate it has started.
    public synchronized void connectionStart()
    {
        mainWin.IDC_CURRENTCONNECTIONS.setText(String.valueOf(++currentConnections));
        mainWin.IDC_TOTALCONNECTIONS.setText(String.valueOf(++totalConnections));
    }
    // Called by each lookup thread to indicate it has stopped.
    public synchronized void connectionStop()
    {
        mainWin.IDC_CURRENTCONNECTIONS.setText(String.valueOf(--currentConnections));
    }
    // Called by each lookup thread to indicate that the requested word has been
    found.
    public synchronized void wordFound()
    {
        mainWin.IDC_WORDSFOUND.setText(String.valueOf(++wordsFound));
    }
    // Called by each lookup thread to indicate that the requested word has not been
    found.
    public synchronized void wordNotFound()
    {
        mainWin.IDC_WORDSNOTFOUND.setText(String.valueOf(++wordsNotFound));
    }
}
```

As shown in Listing 19.3, the Lookup class extends the Thread class to gain the capability to run in
its own thread. The constructor simply saves references to the interface of the object that wants to
be notified of lookup activity and the socket accepted by the server, and then starts the thread.

Listing 19.3. Lookup.java.

```
import java.io.*;
import java.net.*;
public class Lookup extends Thread
{
    static final String DICTIONARY_FILE = "dictionary.dat";
    // Interface used to udpate server with lookup events.
    LookupInterface lookupUser;
    // Socket accepted from server to communicate with client.
    Socket socket;
    // Input/output streams connected to socket.
    DataInputStream in;
```

continues

Listing 19.3. continued

```
PrintStream out;
public Lookup(LookupInterface lookupUser, Socket socket)
{
    this.lookupUser = lookupUser;
    this.socket = socket;
    start();    // Kick-off thread.
}
public void run()
{
    lookupUser.connectionStart();
    try
    {   // Setup buffered streams to read/write over socket.
        in = new DataInputStream(new
        ➥BufferedInputStream(socket.getInputStream()));
        out = new PrintStream(new BufferedOutputStream(socket.getOutputStream()),
        ➥true);
        String request;
        while ((request = in.readLine()) != null)
        {   // Read until a LOOKUP command is received.
            if (request.startsWith("LOOKUP="))
            {   // Lookup word and then drop out of thread.
                wordSearch(request.substring(7));
                break;
            }
        }
    }
    catch (IOException e)
        lookupUser.connectionUpdate("I/O Error on socket: " + e);
    // Close down the socket.
    try
        socket.close();
    catch (IOException e) {}
    lookupUser.connectionStop();
}
protected void wordSearch(String word)
{
    try
    {   // Create a buffered input stream to search dictionary file for word.
        DataInputStream dis = new DataInputStream(new BufferedInputStream(new
        ➥FileInputStream(DICTIONARY_FILE)));
        String line;
        boolean found = false;
        while (!found && (line = dis.readLine()) != null)
        {   // Keep reading until word is found or end of file is reached.
            int idx;
            if (line.startsWith("^") &&  (idx = line.indexOf('^', 1)) > 0)
            {   // Format is "^Word^Definition...".  Since definitions can occupy
                // multiple lines in file, "^" indicator is used to start each
                ➥word
                // and definition sequence.
                String toMatch = line.substring(1, idx);
                if (word.equalsIgnoreCase(toMatch) && word.length() ==
                ➥toMatch.length())
                {   // Build "DEFINITION" response to be sent back to client.
                    line = "DEFINITION=" + line.substring(idx + 1);
                    // Keep reading and sending lines until the end of file is
                    ➥reached
```

```
                        // or the next word in the file is reached.
                        do
                            out.println(line);
                        while ((line = dis.readLine()) != null &&
                        ➥!line.startsWith("^"));
                        found = true;
                        lookupUser.wordFound();
                    }
                }
            }
            if (!found)
            {   // Send "ERROR" response back to client indicating word was not
            ➥found.
                out.println("ERROR=WordNotFound");
                lookupUser.wordNotFound();
            }
        }
        catch (FileNotFoundException fe)
        {   // Update client and server.
            out.println("ERROR=DictionaryFileError");
            lookupUser.connectionUpdate("Dictionary file not found.");
        }
        catch (IOException e)
        {   // Update client and server.
            out.println("ERROR=DictionaryFileError");
            lookupUser.connectionUpdate("I/O Error reading dictionary file.");
        }
    }
}
```

The run() method creates buffered input and output streams from the socket and waits for the
LOOKUP command to arrive. This method could easily be enhanced to process lookup requests for
multiple words and probably should employ a timer to drop the connection after some period of
inactivity.

Once the lookup command is received, the wordSearch() method is called to actually look up the
definition for the word. To keep the example simple, the dictionary is stored in a text file with just
a few words that are sequentially searched by each Lookup object. Of course, if we were searching
a real dictionary, this method would benefit from searching against some sort of indexed database
of words and definitions.

As shown in Figure 19.3, the server displays statistics covering server activity. Because the bulk of
the activity occurs in the Lookup class, the LookupInterface interface is used to communicate between each of the Lookup objects and the server. Using an interface as opposed to direct calls to the
server de-couples the Lookup class from the object that wants to know about lookup activity. For
example, the LookupInterface could have been implemented by a different class that wrote all
activity to a logfile, without modifying the Lookup class. The LookupInterface interface is shown
in Listing 19.4.

Listing 19.4. LookupInterface.java.

```java
// Interface used allow lookup threads to update server of events.
public interface LookupInterface
{
    public void connectionUpdate(String event);
    public void connectionStart();
    public void connectionStop();
    public void wordFound();
    public void wordNotFound();
}
```

Although the Internet dictionary example is simple in function, it illustrates how to design and develop robust server processes in Java. By taking advantage of Java's multithreading capability, the server is very fast, flexible, and efficient. However, programming client/server solutions at the socket level still requires a great deal of effort. Application-level protocols and states must be maintained and synchronized between processes, which defeats many of the advantages of the object-oriented aspects of Java. Fortunately, recent initiatives in the world of Java will allow Java programmers to take the next step in client/server development.

The Future of Java Client/Server Development

Since its initial release, Java has certainly had a significant impact on the Internet. Java applets are being deployed on more and more Web sites every day. The Internet phenomenon has also reached into private corporate intranets where Web servers and Java applets are being used not only for disseminating company information but also to assist in tasks such as administering and supporting networks and corporate applications. However, in order for Java to move from being used as a utility to supplement Web pages to the primary language used to create mission critical applications, it must garner the support of client/server platform vendors as well as be supplemented by class libraries and bridging technologies that have catapulted languages like C++ to the forefront of client/server development. Although there has never been a shortage of vendors jumping on the Java bandwagon, the tools and add-ons to Java are beginning to reach the market and make Java a player in significant client/server development. In addition, Sun has created a business unit called JavaSoft that is dedicated to developing applications, tools, and platforms to enhance Java as a programming language. A few of these enhancements are discussed below.

○ Remote Method Invocation (RMI). Through Java RMI, developers are able to truly distribute Java objects across a network. Method calls to objects located on separate systems are handled automatically and transparently. RMI is similar in concept to remote procedure calls except in the context of Java objects.

- Java Interface Definition Language (IDL). The Java IDL provides a bridge between Java objects and the industry standard Object Management Group's (OMG) Common Object Request Broker Architecture (CORBA). The CORBA IDL provides a vendor- and language-independent, distributed computing environment. Java objects are then able to talk to other Java IDL servers as well as non-Java IDL servers.

- Object Serialization. Through Java's object serialization API, objects are serialized and can thus be read from or written to a persistent source. Consider the possibilities of being able to read and write Java objects across a stream.

- Java Database Connectivity (JDBC). The JDBC API allows Java objects to access relational databases located on the same system or a remote server through structure query language (SQL) calls.

- Java Beans. The purpose of the Java Beans initiative is to develop a component architecture that is compatible with and portable to other component models. Interoperability with component models such as OpenDoc, ActiveX, and LiveConnect will be achieved by implementing bridging technology. As you will see in Chapter 21, "Using ActiveX Controls with Java," Microsoft has provided a bridge of its own to interact with ActiveX controls.

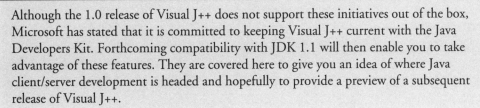

NOTE:

Although the 1.0 release of Visual J++ does not support these initiatives out of the box, Microsoft has stated that it is committed to keeping Visual J++ current with the Java Developers Kit. Forthcoming compatibility with JDK 1.1 will then enable you to take advantage of these features. They are covered here to give you an idea of where Java client/server development is headed and hopefully to provide a preview of a subsequent release of Visual J++.

Summary

One of Java's strengths is its capability to network. Combined with the fact that Java programs can be run on several platforms without source code modifications, it is no wonder that Java is rapidly becoming a popular choice for client/server development. The flexibility of Java is continuing to be enhanced. Whether you need to delve into socket-based programming or step up to interacting with distributed objects, Java provides the necessary solutions.

Chapter

20

Keeping Out the Riff-Raff: Java Security

Before Java applets arrived on the scene, the Web was primarily composed of static content and was relatively safe. Of course, CGI scripts and server-side includes opened up security concerns on the server side of the equation—but with applets, the security of the client is in question for the first time. Web developers are now able to create active content that could be executed in the client's address space. Needless to say, it is not acceptable to give wholesale access to the client's system resources. As illustrated in Figure 20.1, not only can applets originate from unknown or untrusted hosts on the Internet, the applet's class files must travel across an untrusted network before being executed on the user's system. A bulletproof security scheme is needed to allow users of the Web to run any applet without having to worry about their local files being deleted or their system being raided for sensitive information. This chapter discusses the security measures of the Java language and runtime environment.

Figure 20.1.

The origins and paths of Java applets.

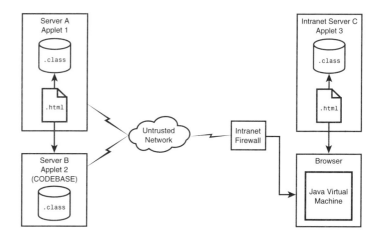

The Security Policy—Setting Limits

All Web browsers offer some level of control when it comes to executing applets. Of course, browsers that cannot execute applets offer the most security, but the others still allow users to customize the level of security to suit their needs. Most of the time this means simply enabling or disabling the execution of applets. However, Sun's HotJava browser offers a finer level of control where access to local files and network ports is fully configurable. Figure 20.2 displays the security configuration dialog for the Microsoft Internet Explorer 3.0.

The challenge is to allow an applet to perform its intended tasks, and at the same time isolate the applet from vital resources and the other processes on the host system. This concept is often referred to as the *sandbox approach*. In general, applets must operate under the constraints listed in Table 20.1.

Figure 20.2.

The security dialog for
Internet Explorer.

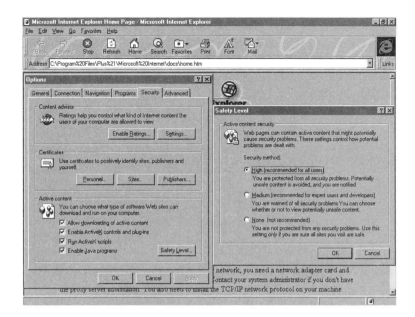

Table 20.1. Security constraints imposed on applets.

Resource	Constraint
File system	Unless otherwise configured through the browser, applets are not allowed to read, write, or manipulate files on the host machine in any way.
Network connections	Connections can be made only back to the server from which the applet came (as specified by the CODEBASE parameter of the APPLET HTML tag) or the server hosting the Web page referencing the applet.
Environment variables	Unless otherwise configured through the browser, access to environment variables via System.getProperty() is prohibited.
System calls	Starting processes, executing programs, or loading libraries on the local machine is prohibited. Furthermore, applets cannot exit or terminate the browser through calls to System.exit().
Thread control	Unauthorized manipulation of threads within the Java Virtual Machine is prohibited.
Pop-up windows	Although pop-up windows can be created with applets, they are tagged in some manner to indicate that they originated from an applet.

To enforce the constraints listed in Table 20.1, the development and runtime environments must work together. On the development side, the language itself has many attributes that make it "safe" and difficult to corrupt the runtime environment. Because the browser actually runs applets, it has the most security measures. Not only are the bytecodes of each class file verified, the loading of each class is scrutinized as well as access attempts to critical resources. The following sections discuss each of these areas in detail.

The Java Language

The creators of Java knew that if the language was going to succeed as a tool for developing active content for the Internet, the language itself would have to be safe. In fact, many of the attributes of Java that make it safe also protect programmers from the pitfalls of other languages. Perhaps one of the most obvious of these is the absence of pointers in Java. C and C++ programmers have had a love/hate relationship with pointers for many years. On one hand, pointers add flexibility and efficiency to a language. However, it is the flexibility of pointers that can add hours of debugging to a project when they are left uninitialized, pointing at deleted objects, or used to reference objects of incompatible types. As far as security is concerned, the elimination of pointers immediately protects Java programs from using them to imitate objects, violate encapsulation, and access protected areas of memory. In addition, all array access is validated to prevent out-of-bounds conditions that can lead to unauthorized access to memory.

As an alternative to pointers, Java uses strongly typed object references that are policed by the compiler and runtime environment. The compiler will flag casts between incompatible types, and all seemingly legitimate casts undergo runtime checks for casting violations. Illegal runtime casts generate ClassCastExceptions.

Memory management is also a vital ingredient to the security of Java. The garbage collector ensures that objects are disposed of only when they are no longer referenced. This prevents a program from accidentally exhausting the resources of the host system, thereby crashing or severely affecting the stability of the system. Of course, this does not prevent an evil applet from purpose-fully over-allocating resources to achieve the same end.

In addition, the Java compiler ensures that all class method and variable controls are enforced. That is, protected methods and variables are accessed internally only by a class or subclass and private methods and variables are accessed internally by the class. The final modifier also con-tributes to the security of programs by preventing critical classes from being subclassed to over-ride or circumvent access controls.

So the language specification and compiler work together to produce secure bytecodes in the form of .class files that can then be interpreted by the Java runtime environment. Unfortunately, a lot can happen to the bytecodes from the time they are constructed to the time they are interpreted. They could be modified on the file system where they reside or by a node on the Internet as the bytecode passes by. Of course, with the proliferation of Java compilers available today, the compiler itself could also produce bytecodes with security flaws. What is needed is another measure of security that ensures the bytecodes meet the same constraints imposed by the development environment.

The Code Verifier

The purpose of the code verifier is to validate the bytecodes of any class files loaded from outside the trusted domain of the runtime environment. Typically this involves any classes loaded from a network connection. Classes on the host's local disk are considered trusted and thus are not subjected to the verifier. Figure 20.3 shows the code verifier's position in the security chain.

Figure 20.3.
Java's security scheme.

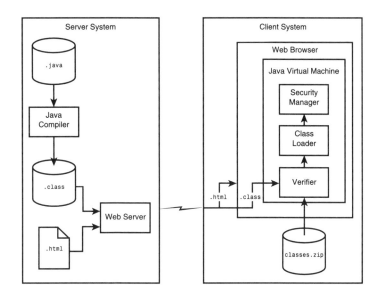

The verifier makes four passes over each class file. The first pass involves validating the format of the class file. Each class file includes the following components:

- ○ A magic constant
- ○ Major and minor version information
- ○ The constant pool, including strings, class or interface names, variable or method references, and numeric values
- ○ Class information including the name of the class and its superclass
- ○ Variable and method information for the class
- ○ Debugging information for the class

The first pass will calculate the magic number for the class file and compare it against the magic number embedded in the file. It will also do some basic validation to verify that all recognized attributes have the correct length and the constant pool contains the proper information.

The second pass looks a little closer at the class file and ensures that final classes are not subclassed; final methods are not overridden, every class has a superclass; and the names, classes, and type signatures referenced in the constant pool are legal.

The third and most complex pass actually verifies the bytecodes of each method. The stack, registers, method arguments, and opcodes are all validated in this step.

Finally, the fourth pass completes the verification process by completing tests that were deferred by the third pass as well as performing some opcode optimization.

If the verifier approves a class file to be executed, the interpreter can assume that the bytecodes possess the following qualities:

○ All register access and stores are valid.

○ No stack overflows or underflows will occur.

○ All parameter and return types match and are valid.

○ There are no illegal casting or type conversions.

Because the verifier ensures several runtime boundaries are maintained, the interpreter is free to run verified code much faster. Runtime checks that would ordinarily have to be done with the execution of each instruction are now eliminated. However, this also illustrates how vital the verifier is to the runtime environment. Just as the security of bytecodes is the responsibility of the compiler, the security and stability of the runtime environment is only as good as the verifier of the browser used to run applets. Indeed, browser vendors have had to enhance the effectiveness of their Java runtime environments to close potential security holes opened by the verifier.

The `ClassLoader`

Now that the bytecodes have been authorized to be safely interpreted, the `ClassLoader` takes over to ensure that class boundaries and namespaces are maintained. A hierarchical chain of namespaces begins with the classes loaded in the local namespace and ends with classes loaded from network connections. The local namespace is composed of the core Java classes as referenced by the `CLASSPATH` environment variable. Because these classes are trusted and implement vital objects such as `System`, they cannot be replaced by classes from any of the other namespaces. The class loader also ensures that namespaces are maintained between classes loaded from different applets from separate network sources.

This is where the package names and access modifiers come into play. The class loader keeps the classes of each package isolated and prioritized so applets cannot create their own versions of classes by the same name in different packages. In addition, access to classes that are not indicated as public by objects outside of the package is prohibited.

The SecurityManager

Now that all of the classes necessary to run an applet have been verified by the verifier and separated into executable compartments by the class loader, the security manager implements the security policy of the runtime environment. This is where perfectly legitimate requests under normal circumstances are denied by the browser. Resources such as the file system and network are protected by the security manager. Table 20.2 lists some of the methods of the abstract SecurityManager class.

Table 20.2. Public methods of the SecurityManager class.

Method	Description
checkAccept(String, int)	Called prior to accepting a socket connection from the specified host on the specified port.
checkAccess(Thread)	Called prior to performing any thread manipulation requests on the specified thread.
checkAccess(ThreadGroup)	Called prior to performing any thread group manipulation requests on the specified thread group.
checkConnect(String, int)	Called prior to opening a socket connection to the specified host and port.
checkConnect(String, int, Object)	Called prior to opening a socket to the specified host and port for the given security context.
checkCreateClassLoader()	Called to check whether a new ClassLoader object can be set.
checkDelete(String)	Called to determine whether the specified file is permitted to be deleted.
checkExec(String)	Called to determine whether a subprocess can be created for the specified command.
checkExit(int)	Called to determine whether the current process can halt the Java Virtual Machine with the specified exit code.
checkLink(String)	Called to determine whether the specified library is permitted to be dynamically loaded.
checkListen(int)	Called to determine whether the current process is permitted to listen for connections on the specified port.

continues

Table 20.2. continued

Method	Description
checkPackageAccess(String)	This method works with the class loader to determine whether the current process is permitted to access the specified package.
checkPackageDefinition(String)	Determines whether the current process is permitted to define classes within the specified package.
checkPropertiesAccess()	Called to determine whether system properties can be accessed.
checkPropertyAccess(String)	Called to determine whether the current process is permitted to access the specified environment variable.
checkRead(FileDescriptor)	Called to determine whether the current process is permitted to read the file indicated by the FileDescriptor.
checkRead(String)	Called to determine whether the current process is permitted to read the file by the specified name.
checkRead(String, Object)	Called to determine whether the specified file can be read within the given security context.
checkSetFactory()	Called to determine whether the current process is permitted to set the socket or URL stream handler factory.
boolean checkTopLevelWindow(Object)	Called to determine whether a top-level window can be displayed without display restrictions (like a warning indicator).
checkWrite(FileDescriptor)	Called to determine whether the current process can write to the file indicated by the FileDescriptor.
checkWrite(String)	Called to determine whether the current process can write to the file by the specified name.
boolean getInCheck()	Indicates whether a security check is currently in progress.
Object getSecurityContext()	Returns an object that contains information about the current execution environment to be used in subsequent security checks.

The implementation of the SecurityManager class is really quite simple. In fact, most of the methods in Table 20.2 throw only SecurityExceptions. The idea is that if you subclass SecurityManager and install your own version using System.setSecurityManager(), access to all of the resources under the security manager's control are immediately denied. In fact, this is exactly what the Web browser does (with some overridden behavior, of course). To prevent applets from installing their own more lenient security managers, the runtime system allows the security manager to be set only once.

The security manager is prewired into many of Java's classes in such a way that it cannot be bypassed. For example, before a Socket object can be successfully created, the Socket class checks to see whether a security manager has been set and if so whether a socket to the specified host and port is allowed.

```
SecurityManager security = System.getSecurityManager();
if (security != null) {
    security.checkConnect(address.getHostAddress(), port);
}
```

In addition, calls to the security manager are embedded in classes or methods that are declared final so they cannot be overridden by subclasses.

Applets Versus Applications

Up to this point, we have focused on the security constraints used to control the execution of applets. However, Java applets and applications are handled quite differently in regard to security. Because applications are explicitly executed and are from a (hopefully) trusted source, the security constraints imposed on applets are relaxed for applications. However, applications can still benefit from the built-in security features of the Java language itself as already mentioned. Furthermore, because portions of the security scheme used to monitor applets are controlled by Java classes, applications can implement their own brand of security, if necessary. The ClassLoader and SecurityManager classes already covered can be subclassed and installed by applications just as they are by the browser's Java Virtual Machine. A customized ClassLoader could provide a class cache for a networked application to cut down on the number of calls across a slow network connection for classes it has already retrieved. Likewise, a subclass of SecurityManager could be used to control what directories or files they are allowed to work with.

Summary

The security barriers imposed by Java are really quite formidable. However, Java security is not infallible. In fact, there have been some well-documented holes and back doors to the system. But Sun has been quick to answer such claims and has refined the language, compiler, bytecode verifier, class loader, and security manager over the last several releases. Likewise, Sun, Netscape, and

Microsoft have also closed security holes in their browsers related to Java applets over the last several months. In fact, most of the security concerns that have been uncovered have dealt with the implementation of the runtime environment in browsers and not the language itself. By releasing Java and the source code for its tools to the public domain, Sun has not only allowed the world to peek into every crack and crevice of Java but has also been able to rapidly solidify the language.

The future of security and active content on the Internet will continue to evolve. With the increase in use of digital signatures to authenticate the content of data, the security and confidence of dealing with information will continue to improve. Java can supplement its security model by also incorporating digital signatures. Just as the structural integrity of class files are inspected by the code verifier, it will not be long before a digital signature may also be embedded within each class file. The end result is that Web developers and users will be offered yet another level of control to safely build, retrieve, and run active content on their systems.

Part

V

Advanced Programming Concepts

Chapter 21

Using ActiveX Controls with Java

What is ActiveX? The best definition is pretty vague at best: an interface that is used to provide access to controls and code from various sources. It is mainly targeted at providing access to Internet applications. ActiveX was previously known as OLE. Then again, it is also based on the COM and DCOM models. These terms are often all used interchangeably.

There are several Visual J++ utilities that support creating the interface used to call ActiveX controls and creating an ActiveX control with Java. This chapter explores how ActiveX controls can be integrated with Java.

Creating the Java Interface Class

There are only a couple of steps required to create an interface to a COM object: registering the component and creating the Java interface class.

Registering an ActiveX Type Library

Registering a component involves putting some key information into the Windows Registry. This information must be present in the Registry to create a component.

Most installation programs automatically register a component during the install process. If, however, you have an unregistered component, you can use REGSVR32. This program must be run from a command prompt and has the following options:

```
regsvr32 [/u] [/s] dllname
```

The /u option provides the capability to unregister a DLL, and /s is used to run the program in silent mode.

To register components found in the file MYCONTROL.DLL, for example, the following line would be entered at a command prompt:

```
regsvr32 mycontrol.dll
```

Once a component is registered, a Java class can be generated to interface with the component.

Creating the Java Interface Classes

To use a COM component, a Java class and interface for use with the component must be generated. This can be accomplished by using either the Java Type Library Wizard or the command-line equivalent.

Java Type Library Wizard

The Java Type Library Wizard is used to determine the interface structure available to Java code that is used to interface to COM components. To access the Java Type Library Wizard, use the Tools | Java Type Library Wizard command. The dialog is displayed in Figure 21.1.

Figure 21.1.
Java Type Library Wizard.

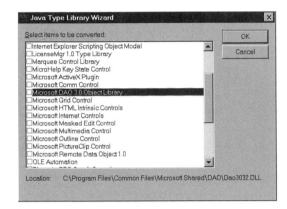

This dialog displays all of the type libraries that have been registered. The dialog shows the name of the component. If a component is highlighted, the name of the source file is displayed at the bottom of the dialog. From the figure, you can see that the type library with the name Microsoft DAO 3.0 Object Library is located in the file `C:\Program Files\Common Files\Microsoft Shared\DAO\Dao3032.DLL`.

To create a class file and summary file for the COM object, click in the box next to the object. Figure 21.2 shows the selection of the Marquee object that is automatically installed with Internet Explorer 3.0.

Figure 21.2.
Marquee object selection.

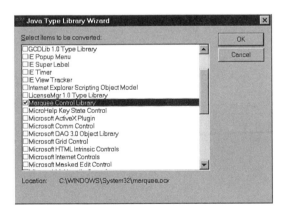

After the OK button is pressed and the wizard has completed its tasks, you can see some very important information about the generated class in the Java Type Library Wizard tab of the Output window, as shown in Figure 21.3.

Figure 21.3.
Java Type Library Wizard tab of the Output window.

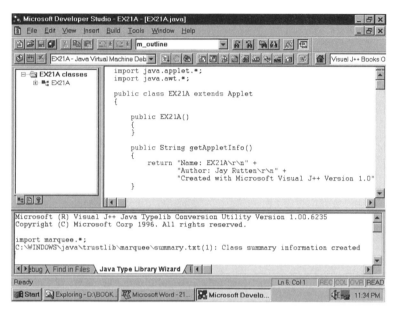

The first two lines contain the version of the wizard and let you know where the conversion utility came from. Unless you are a number cruncher, they will probably look fine. The next two lines are the most important for the developer. The import line is what needs to be added to the Java file where the COM object is to be used:

```
import marquee.*
```

The next line shows the filename of a file that was produced to show a summary of the objects created. Listing 21.1 shows the summary file that was generated for the Marquee object.

TIP:

If you double-click the SUMMARY.TXT filename in the output window, Visual J++ will automatically display the contents of the summary file.

Listing 21.1. Listing of SUMMARY.TXT for the Marquee object.

```
public class marquee/Marquee extends java.lang.Object
{
}
public interface marquee/DMarqueeEvents extends com.ms.com.IUnknown
{
    public abstract void OnStartOfImage();
    public abstract void OnEndOfImage(int);
    public abstract void OnBounce(int);
    public abstract void OnLMouseClick();
    public abstract void OnScroll(int);
}
public interface marquee/IMarquee extends com.ms.com.IUnknown
{
    public abstract java.lang.String getScrollStyleY();
    public abstract void putScrollPixelsY(short);
    public abstract short getLoopsX();
    public abstract void putLoopsX(short);
    public abstract int getOffsetFromWndX();
    public abstract void putOffsetFromWndY(int);
    public abstract int getCurrentURL();
    public abstract void Resume();
    public abstract void putWidthOfPage(int);
    public abstract void Pause();
    public abstract java.lang.String getScrollStyleX();
    public abstract short getScrollPixelsY();
    public abstract void putScrollPixelsX(short);
    public abstract int getPageHeight();
    public abstract int getWidthOfPage();
    public abstract void putOffsetFromWndX(int);
    public abstract int getPageWidth();
    public abstract short getScrollPixelsX();
    public abstract int getWhiteSpace();
    public abstract void queryURLCount(int[]);
    public abstract void putScrollStyleY(java.lang.String);
    public abstract void putScrollDelay(short);
    public abstract void putDrawImmediately(short);
    public abstract short getPageFlippingOn();
    public abstract void insertURL(int, java.lang.String);
    public abstract void AboutBox();
    public abstract short getScrollDelay();
    public abstract void putCurrentURL(int);
    public abstract void deleteURL(int);
    public abstract void queryURL(int, java.lang.String[]);
    public abstract short getZoom();
    public abstract void putZoom(short);
    public abstract void putScrollStyleX(java.lang.String);
    public abstract void putBackgroundColor(int);
    public abstract short getDrawImmediately();
    public abstract void putPageFlippingOn(short);
    public abstract int getBackgroundColor();
    public abstract short getLoopsY();
    public abstract void putLoopsY(short);
    public abstract void putWhiteSpace(int);
    public abstract int getOffsetFromWndY();
}
```

This file contains what appears to be a Java class and two Java interfaces. The `marquee/` prefixes to the class and interface names are not quite correct Java syntax, but are added for clarity. The class definition represents the COM object. Unfortunately, there are not too many methods that can be called in this class. However, the type wizard did provide two interface classes that can be called to access the COM object. A restriction of COM is that you cannot access the COM object directly for an instance of the COM class. Instead, you must always use the interface class.

The content of the interface classes represents the methods available in the COM object. Therefore, the documentation for the object would need to be consulted for the functionality of each method. For the `Marquee` example, visit the Microsoft Web page at `www.microsoft.com/activex/` for more information. The complete page is included on the accompanying CD for your convenience, in example `EX21A`.

The Java Type Library Wizard generates the class information for each type library in the same location. This location is determined by the registry key `HKEY_LOCAL_MACHINE\Software\Microsoft\Java VM\TrustedLibsDirectory`. Each library is stored in a subdirectory off of this directory with the name of the type library.

JAVATLB

Another way to generate the class information for a COM object is to use the command line equivalent of the Java Type Library Wizard, JAVATLB. The command-line syntax is

```
JAVATLB filename
```

where `filename` is the name of the type library. Again, the class information is stored off of the `HKEY_LOCAL_MACHINE\Software\Microsoft\Java VM\TrustedLibsDirectory` directory with the class files, and `SUMMARY.TXT` generated as if the Java Type Library Wizard were used.

Once the interface for the object has been created, it can be used by a Java applet.

Using a COM Object

Once an interface for a COM object has been generated, the object becomes as simple to use as any other Java class. The one exception is that when generating a COM interface, both a Java class and a Java interface are created. A COM class instance must always be allocated, but it must be accessed through the interface. This, however, will not be hard to remember, since the methods for a COM object are generated in the interface and the COM object class is rather dull.

Java applets and COM objects can communicate through two avenues: by passing a reference to a COM object directly to a Java applet so that the applet can call object methods and by passing events from a COM object to methods of a Java applet.

Passing COM Object References

The method that gives the Java applet the most control of the COM object is passing a reference to a COM object. This involves using a scripting language on an HTML page to reference both the COM object and the applet and then using the COM interface inside the applet to control the object.

Scripting Access to the COM Object

One limitation when working with COM objects is that if a COM object has a component that displays information, such as edit boxes for collecting user input information or radio buttons that allow the user to configure the use of an object, that COM object can not be instantiated in a program. However, if there are no interface components, an instance of a COM object can be instantiated directly in a program, as will be seen later.

To be able to access a visual COM object, a reference must be passed the program using a scripting language, such as VBScript or JScript. Consider the HTML of example EX21A, as shown in Listing 21.2.

Listing 21.2. HTML source for example EX21A.

```
<html>
<head>
<title>EX21A</title>
</head>
<script language=VBScript>
<!--
'Give the COM object to the applet
Sub window_onLoad
    document.EX21A.Load marquee
end sub
!-->
</script>
<body>
<OBJECT
    align=CENTER
    classid="clsid:1a4da620-6217-11cf-be62-0080c72edd2d"
    width=650 height=200 BORDER=1 HSPACE=5
    id=marquee
    >
    <PARAM NAME="ScrollStyleX" VALUE="Circular">
    <PARAM NAME="ScrollStyleY" VALUE="Circular">
    <PARAM NAME="szURL" VALUE="marquee.html">
    <PARAM NAME="ScrollDelay" VALUE=100>
    <PARAM NAME="LoopsX" VALUE=-1>
    <PARAM NAME="LoopsY" VALUE=-1>
    <PARAM NAME="ScrollPixelsX" VALUE=0>
    <PARAM NAME="ScrollPixelsY" VALUE=30>
    <PARAM NAME="DrawImmediately" VALUE=1>
```

continues

Listing 21.2. continued

```
    <PARAM NAME="Whitespace" VALUE=0>
    <PARAM NAME="PageFlippingOn" VALUE=1>
    <PARAM NAME="Zoom" VALUE=100>
    <PARAM NAME="WidthOfPage" VALUE=640>
</OBJECT>
<hr>
<applet
    code=EX21A.class
    id=EX21A
    width=650
    height=50 >
</applet>
<hr>
<a href="EX21A.java">The source.</a>
</body>
</html>
```

There are three important components of this source to examine. By examining the object from bottom to top, you see that the most obvious and familiar is the applet definition:

```
<applet
    code=EX21A.class
    id=EX21A
    width=650
    height=50 >
</applet>
```

These lines declare an applet on the page with the code contained in EX21A.class. An id of EX21A is associated with the applet so that the entity can be referred to elsewhere from the page. Sizing of the applet is the last element of the definition.

The next item is the OBJECT declaration. This object is an instance of the Marquee object discussed earlier in the chapter.

```
<OBJECT
align=CENTER
    classid="clsid:1a4da620-6217-11cf-be62-0080c72edd2d"
    width=650 height=200 BORDER=1 HSPACE=5
    id=marquee
    >
```

Notice that there is something distinctly missing from this OBJECT definition, namely, what it is. However, the classid does define the CLSID, which is a component-specific Universally Unique Global Identification (UUID) number. The Registry (using REGEDT32.EXE) can be consulted to determine what this component is. The following is some of a branch of the Registry key that gives information about this component:

```
HKEY_CLASSES_ROOT
    CLSID
        {1a4da620-6217-11cf-be62-0080c72edd2d}
            InprocSever32 = C:\WINDOWS\Sytem32\marquee.ocx
            Version = 1.0
```

This is the Marquee object. Additional information can be found in the HTML source that defines sizing of the object and an identification of marquee. Finally, before the OBJECT definition ends, there is a series of PARAM_NAME and VALUE pairs. These define values for the initial properties of the Marquee. Note that these parameters do not need to be specified as shown in this example. There are several options possible, including specifying the options in the HTML (as shown), using the default values of object (as documented in the Marquee documentation), or initializing the object via the Java interface once the object has been loaded.

The final component is the scripting portion of the HTML. This piece ties the applet and the COM object together.

```
<script language=VBScript>
<!--
'Give the COM object to the applet
Sub window_onLoad
    document.EX21A.Load marquee
end sub
!-->
</script>
```

The script language tag indicates that this code is VBScript. The only task completed in this script occurs in the window_onLoad event, which is generated when the page has been loaded. The function that is executed is the Load method of the EX21A object. The parameter passed to this method is marquee. Notice the reference to the two objects by their respective ids. As you will see in the next section, the Load method of the applet stores the reference to the object.

NOTE:

To get more information on scripting VBScript or JScript, visit the Microsoft Web pages at http://www.microsoft.com/vbscript or http://www.microsoft.com/jscript, respectively.

Using the COM Object Interface

The previous section showed how the Marquee object was passed to the applet using VBScript in the HTML page. Once the object reference is loaded in the applet, example EX21A shows what can be done.

The Load method couldn't be simpler:

```
public void Load(Object marqueeObject)
{
    // save the reference to the object in the class
    MarqueeAccess = (IMarquee)marqueeObject;
}
```

The marqueeObject passed into the method is assumed to be the Marquee object. The reference to the object is saved in the member variable MarqueeAccess. Because the marquee is passed in as an object, a cast is done to the marquee interface class, Imarquee.

Once the object reference has been saved in the class, the rest of the program follows, as shown in Listing 21.3.

Listing 21.3. Control methods and class definition of EX21A.

```
public class EX21A extends Applet
{
    protected Button StateButton = new Button("Pause");
    protected IMarquee MarqueeAccess;
    public void init()
    {
        add(StateButton);                    // provide control of marquee
        add(new Button("About"));
    }
    public boolean action(Event evt, Object obj)
    {
        boolean retval = false;
        if ("Pause".equals(obj)) {
            MarqueeAccess.Pause();           // stop the marquee
            StateButton.setLabel("Resume");
            retval = true;
        }
        else if ("Resume".equals(obj)) {
            MarqueeAccess.Resume();          // crank it back up
            StateButton.setLabel("Pause");
            retval = true;
        }
        else if ("About".equals(obj)) {
            MarqueeAccess.AboutBox();
            retval = true;
        }
        return retval;
    }
}
```

The class contains two variables, StateButton and MarqueeAccess, which are used to toggle the activity in the marquee and to hold a reference to the marquee, respectively.

The init method adds the State button to the Java portion of the page, which allows the user to control the starting and stopping of the movement in the marquee, and an About button, which is used to display a dialog containing version information about the Marquee control. The action method is similar to other examples throughout the book. If the Action button is pressed when the text on the button reads Pause, the Pause method of the marquee interface is called to stop the marquee from rotating. If the Action button is pressed when the text on the button reads Resume, the Resume method is called to continue the marquee. Lastly, if the About button is pressed, the AboutBox method is called to display some version information. Figure 21.4 shows the applet at work.

Figure 21.4.

Example EX21A.

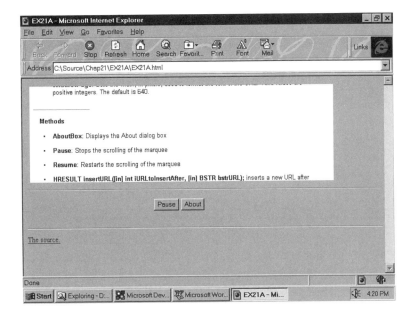

As shown in the example, once the script has passed the COM object to the applet, the interface allows access to the COM object just as if it were a normal Java class.

Event Processing

The second method that can be used to communicate between the COM object and the Java applet implements event handlers in the applet. Again, scripting needs to be used as the interface between the two components.

COM objects can generate events when the control is in predefined states. The events can be caught by a HTML script and passed on. Revisiting the script code of the HTML file for example EX21A:

```
<script language=VBScript>
<!--
'Give the COM object to the applet
Sub window_onLoad
    document.EX21A.Load marquee
end sub
!-->
</script>
```

The subprogram is actually executed on an event when the window is loaded. This is how the script language can be used to respond to events. For this example, a predefined object was used to determine where the event originated from, window. To use this event processing for COM objects, simply reference the COM object by ID and add the event. To clarify, the OnLMouseClick event is generated by the marquee when the left mouse button is clicked on the object. The sub-program used to process the event would then be

```
Sub marquee_OnLMouseClick
    document.EX21B.Play
end sub
```

When the left mouse button is clicked on the marquee of EX21B, the Play method of the applet is called:

```
public void Play()
{
    // play the sound bite
    play(getCodeBase(), "bounce.au");
}
```

This method calls Applet.play to play a short sound bite.

Example EX21B illustrates how a two-way communication channel can be established between a COM object and a Java applet. First the object can be passed to the applet, which enables the applet to call the object methods directly. Secondly, the Java applet can respond to events generated by the COM object, with the help of a scripting language.

Nonvisual COM Objects

Visual objects require that a COM object be declared in HTML on the page. There are certain COM objects that do not require this. If a COM object does not have a corresponding visual component, an object does not have to be declared. Instead, an instance of the class can be instanciated in a Java applet directly.

Example EX21C illustrates this type of COM interface and shows how to implement a self-paging system. Figure 21.5 shows the paging system interface.

To create the COM interface, use the Tools | Java Type Library Wizard in the MS Developer Studio. Select the Beeper 1.0 Type Library, as shown in Figure 21.6.

This dynamic link library contains a control that generates a beep, using the local machine's speaker. This is similar to generating an interrupt 0x07 in the olden days. The Java Type Library Wizard produces the summary file shown in Listing 21.4.

Listing 21.4. SUMMARY.TXT for the Beeper object.

```
public interface beeper/IBeeper extends com.ms.com.IUnknown
{
    public abstract int getCount();
    public abstract void Beep();
    public abstract com.ms.com.IUnknown get_NewEnum();
    public abstract java.lang.String getItem(int);
}
public class beeper/Beeper extends java.lang.Object
{
}
```

Figure 21.5.

Example EX21C.

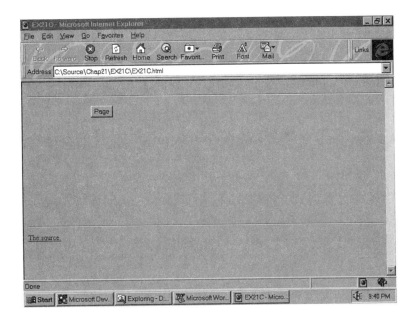

Figure 21.6.

Type Library used for
example EX21C.

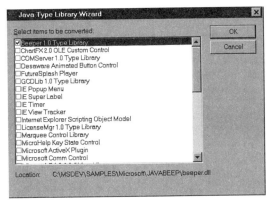

Of course, this control does not have a lot of options. Listing 21.5 shows the source for example
EX21C.

Listing 21.5. Example EX21C.

```
import java.applet.*;
import java.awt.*;
import beeper.*;
public class EX21C extends Applet
{
```

continues

Listing 21.5. continued

```
    protected IBeeper Motorola;
    public void init()
    {
        // add a button so that an action can be performed
        add(new Button("Page"));
        // allocate a new COM object
        Motorola = (IBeeper)new Beeper();
    }
    public boolean action(Event evt, Object obj)
    {
        boolean retval = false;          // assume no action
        if ("Page".equals(obj)) {
            Motorola.Beep();
            retval = true;
        }
        return retval;
    }
}
```

The beeper interface is imported as usual. The `init` method adds the single button to the applet. Additionally, the `init` method allocates the COM object with the following line of code:

```
Motorola = (IBeeper)new Beeper();
```

Note that a class is allocated, since an interface instance cannot be allocated. Then, the returned object is cast to the interface object.

NOTE:

A runtime error will occur if you attempt to use a COM object directly in a Java application, such as with the following code:

```
Beeper Motoroler = new Beeper();
Motoroler.Beep();
```

The `action` method in example EX21C responds the push of the button by calling the `Beep` method of the COM object to perform the page. I think I will recommend this pager to my boss.

Creating a COM Object with Java

So far, the discussion has been targeted to how most ActiveX objects will be used from Java applets and their interaction with Web pages. An additional feature of Visual J++ is that ActiveX objects can be generated. Follow these steps:

1. Generate a UUID for the library and components of the library using GUIDGEN.EXE.

2. Define the type library interface using the Object Definition Language (ODL).

3. Create the type library from the ODL.

4. Register the new COM component.

5. Generate the Java Interface to the COM component.

6. Implement the Java class for the COM component.

The following sections go over each step, developing a factorial example.

Generating a Universally Unique Global Identification (UUID)

The first step in creating a COM object is to establish a UUID number for the type of control. GUIDGEN.EXE can be used to create this number. Figure 21.7 shows this program in action.

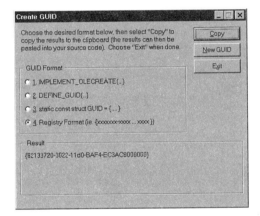

This program guarantees that every number generated, no matter when or on what computer it is run, will be unique. In this way, every ActiveX object can be identified and verified with its UUID. Additional UUIDs will be needed for each element in the type library, as you will see in the next section.

Figure 21.7 shows that the number generated for the Factorial object is

{62133720-3022-11d0-BAF4-EC3AC9000000}

Defining an Object

The next step in defining the COM object is to determine the interface to the object. This is done using the Object Definition Language (ODL). ODL takes a general form of

```
[attributes] library libraryname {
    definitions
}
```

457

The brackets ([]) and braces ({}) are part of the syntax and are required. `attributes` is a comma-delimited list of ODL attributes. Typical contents of the list that applies to libraries include the UUID for the library, help information, and version number. `libraryname` is the name of the type library. `definitions` is the heart of the library and contains the datatype, interfaces, and class contained in the type library.

Using the UUID from the previous step, the `Factorial` object library for EX21D would then be

```
[
    uuid (62133720-3022-11d0-BAF4-EC3AC9000000),
    helpstring("Factorial 1.0 Type Library"),
    version(1.0)
]
library LFactorial
{
}
```

The contents of the library can include preprocessor directives, imported libraries, interfaces, and classes. The majority of these have the same general form.

```
[attributes] elementtype elementname {
    members
};
```

Again, `attributes` is a comma-delimited list of ODL attributes. This list contains UUIDs, help information, and a potentially large list of other information for complex elements. `elementtype` is one of the following keywords:

```
module
dispinterface
interface
coclass
```

`elementname` is the user-defined name given to the element. The members of the element are dependent on the type of the element.

ODL is an extensive language used to define types for OLE automation. What has been covered here is only enough to get your feet kind of damp, so that a basic understanding of the ODL file can be obtained.

NOTE:

Microsoft's Interface Definition Language (MIDL) compiler can be used to compile ODL files, since the MIDL syntax contains complete support for ODL syntax. For a complete reference on MIDL, refer to the MIDL Programmer's Guide and Reference in the WIN32 SDK.

The `Factorial` object ODL is shown in Listing 21.6.

Listing 21.6. FACTORIAL.ODL.

```
[
    uuid (62133720-3022-11d0-BAF4-EC3AC9000000),
    helpstring("Factorial 1.0 Type Library"),
    version(1.0)
]
library LFactorial
{
    // get the standard stuff
    importlib("stdole32.tlb");
    [
        uuid (62133721-3022-11d0-BAF4-EC3AC9000000),
        helpstring("Factorial Interface")
    ]
    dispinterface IFactorial
    {
        properties:
        methods:
            [id(1)]long GetFactorial([in]long base);
    };
    [
        uuid (62133722-3022-11d0-BAF4-EC3AC9000000),
        helpstring("Factorial Class")
    ]
    coclass Factorial
    {
        dispinterface IFactorial;
    };
}
```

The Factorial object first imports the standard OLE objects using importlib. The dispinterface is used to define the properties and methods of the interface of the object. Notice that a UUID is given to the interface. The interface contains a single method, GetFactorial, that takes a number and returns the factorial of the number. Finally, the top-level Factorial class is defined with the coclass keyword. Again, a UUID is assigned to the top-level class. The class is made up of the single interface, IFactorial.

Creating a Type Library

Once an ODL file has been created, that file needs to be compiled into a type library. MKTYPLIB.EXE can be used. The syntax for this command line program is

MKTYPLIB [options] [inputfile]

The options for the program are shown in Table 21.1.

Table 21.1. MKTYPLIB options.

Option	Description
/help or /?	Display the options.
/tlb filename	Names the output filename to filename. The default is to use the input filename with the extension .tlb.
/h filename	Specifies the filename of the optionally generated .H file.
/system	Type of library that is to be made. system can be win16, win32, mac, mips, alpha, ppc, or ppc32.
/align #	Sets alignment to #.
/o filename	Causes program output to go to filename instead of screen.
/nologo	Disable display of copyright.
/w0	Disable warnings.
/nocpp	Disable the C preprocessor. Java library creators should always use this option if the C compiler is not installed.
/cpp_cmd path	Causes the C preprocessor to use path.
/cpp_opt opt	Specifies options to be sent to the C preprocessor.
/Ddefine[=value]	Defines define for the preprocesser to an optional value of value.
/I includepath	Specifies an include file path.

The majority of the options are offered when libraries are being made for use when being called from C/C++ programs. This makes the version used for Java options quite simple:

```
mktyplib factorial.odl /nocpp
```

Registering the Component

Registering the component places important information about the object in the Registry. The JAVAREG.EXE command-line tool aides in registering Java COM objects. Figure 21.8 shows the command-line options available.

The command issued to register the Factorial class specifies the class name and the UUID, which will be used for the CLSID:

```
javareg /register /class:Factorial /clsid:{62133722-3022-11d0-BAF4-EC3AC9000000}
```

Figure 21.8.

JAVAREG.EXE options.

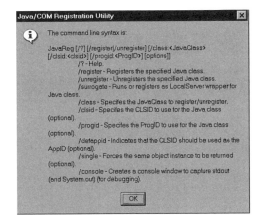

Creating the Java Interface

Once the COM object is registered, the COM interface class is generated. Once again, go to the Tools | Java Type Library Wizard, as shown in Figure 21.9, to generate the class.

Figure 21.9.

Factorial Type Library selection.

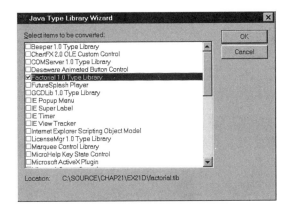

The SUMMARY.TXT file is shown in Listing 21.7, with the expected single GetFactorial method in the interface.

Listing 21.7. SUMMARY.TXT for the Factorial COM object.

```
public class factorial/Factorial extends java.lang.Object
{
}
public interface factorial/IFactorial extends com.ms.com.IUnknown
{
    public abstract int GetFactorial(int);
}
```

461

Implementing the Java Class

The final step in creating the Java Component is to implement the Java class defined in the ODL file. To do this, simply implement the interface class. Listing 21.8 contains the Factorial class.

Listing 21.8. Factorial class implementation.

```
import com.ms.com.*;
import factorial.*;
class Factorial implements IFactorial
{
    public int GetFactorial(int base)
    {
        int retval = 0;
        if (base >= 1 && base <= 20)
        {
            retval = 1;
            while (base > 1)
            {
                retval = retval * base;
                base—;
            }
        }
        return retval;
    }
}
```

The class that implements the IFactorial interface could have been named anything. There is not a direct correlation between the Factorial coclass in the ODL file with this Factorial class. It simply makes it easier for the programmer. Notice that the Factorial interface of the COM component is imported. The GetFactorial method calculates the factorial for a number between 1 and 20, returning the factorial of the number.

From this point, the Java class can be used from any application that can activate an ActiveX component. As an example, the next section will cover example EX21D, which is an applet that will use this object.

Using the Java Component

Using a COM object implemented with Java is just like using any other COM object. Figure 21.10 shows example EX21D and the COM object in use.

Figure 21.10.

Example EX21D using the Factorial COM object.

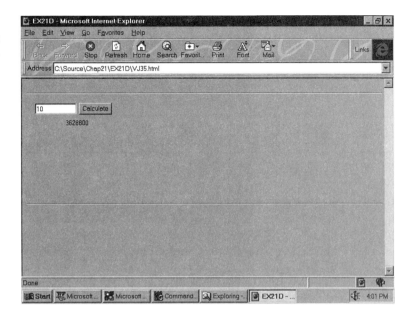

Listing 21.9 shows the action method from example EX21D, which illustrates the use of the COM object, iFac.

Listing 21.9. action method of example EX21D.

```
public boolean action(Event evt, Object obj)
{
    boolean retval = false;
    if ("Calculate".equals(obj))
    {
        try {
            int base = Integer.parseInt(BaseField.getText());
            int result = iFac.GetFactorial(base);
            if (result > 0)
                ResultLabel.setText(Integer.toString(result));
            else
                ResultLabel.setText("Error!");
        }
        catch (NumberFormatException e)
        {
            ResultLabel.setText("Bad #!");
        }
        // make sure the label is dipslaying all of its text
        ResultLabel.resize(ResultLabel.preferredSize());
        // tell the layout manager to do it's job again
        validate();
        retval = true;
    }

    return retval;
}
```

As you can see, there are just a few steps to creating an ActiveX object that can now be used in a number of situations. In addition, there are several command-line utilities in the Visual J++ suite that aide in completing these steps effortlessly. Once you have a component that is to be distributed, you must enclose the component in a signed CAB file so that a user can safely use the component without the fear of a security risk.

Creating a Signed CAB File

When distributing applets over the Internet, make sure that the users that visit your site feel safe about using any COM objects that have to be downloaded to their machine. After all, if the user does not feel safe, he or she won't use the component or visit the site. To accomplish a certain level confidence, and, in the process, gain speed of download via compressing the classes being used on your site, utilize signed cabinet files. Creating a signed CAB file is a two-step process: creating a CAB file with the classes needed for your applet and signing the file using Microsoft's Authenticode technology.

CAB Files

Cabinet file support is included on the Visual J++ disks in the \Cab&Sign directory. They are not automatically installed when installing Visual J++. To install the CAB file creation utility, copy CABDEVKIT.EXE to a directory on your local drive. Then execute the self-extracting file and follow the installation steps.

There are two steps in using a CAB file: creating the file and making use of the CAB file for your applet.

Creating a CAB File

Once the CAB Development kit has been installed, it is quite easy to create a CAB file. In fact, there are two ways to create a file: using the CABARC command or editing the sample .DDF files and running DIAMOND directly.

The CABARC utility has the following syntax:

```
CABARC [options] command cabfilename [filelist] [destdirectory]
```

command is a single letter indicating the type of function to perform: L (list), N (new CAB file), or X (extract). cabfilename is the name of the CAB file; remember to add the .CAB extension because it isn't automatically added. filelist is the list of files to add to the archive.

There are several options that can confirm files, set the compression type, and cause recursive inclusion of files in subdirectories (as well as other options) that can be seen by typing only the

name of the command. One of the most important options is the -s option, which allows the user to reserve space in the archive for signing the CAB file.

As an example on the accompanying CD, the EX21E subdirectory contains the CAB files for distributing the EX15A example. The following command was used to create the CAB file:

```
CABARC -s 6144 -r -p N ..\..\Chap21\EX21E\EX15AArc *.class *.jpg
```

Unfortunately, this does expose an error that currently exists with this version of the CAB file concept. This technology is designed to have images and audio files included in the CAB files. The CAB should be checked when loading an image using a URL that is relative to the code base, as in the following snippet of code:

```
getImage(getCodeBase(), "images\\Christopher1.jpg");
```

If the image file is not found in the CAB file, normal processing should then dictate that the codebase is referenced for the file, as usual. Currently, the images and audio clips are not loaded from the CAB file at all. Therefore, for example EX21E, there is an image subdirectory that contains the images for EX15A.

The alternative method to using CABARC is to run the cabinet generating program, DIAMOND.EXE, explicitly. To do this, however, the default DDF files need to be modified to handle the applet classes explicitly. The default DDF files are heavily commented, so the modifications are straightforward.

First, copy the files CLASSPCK.DDF, MASTER.DDF, and MASTER.INF to the release directory so that these files can be modified. Then, edit CLASSPCK.DDF to create a CAB file that will contain the class files. Following the comment in this file, modify the CAB filename that will be generated and the class files that go into this CAB file. This is not the final CAB file but only a CAB file that will contain the class files. Create the CAB file with the command

```
DIAMOND /f ClassPck.ddf
```

Next, change the MASTER.INF file. Again following the comments in the file, add the control's CLSID and some identification information for the installed library. It might be a good idea to change the name of this file to reflect the product being distributed. Example EX21F, which contains all of these files and represents a distribution of example EX21D, changed the name of the master files to EX21DDiamond.

Finally, set the name of the final CAB file, name of the class CAB file and the name of the .INF file in MASTER.DDF, and create the CAB file with the final DDF file. For our example:

```
DIAMOND /f EX21DDiamond.ddf
```

As you can see, the first method is simpler while the second method allows much more flexibility. Once the CAB files have been created, they need to be used in the APPLET tags of the HTML.

Modifying the Applet Tag for CAB File Use

Using CAB files requires a simple modification to the HTML. A single additional parameter can be specified in the APPLET tag:

```
<APPLET
    code=EX15A.class
    id=EX15A
    width=500
    height=300 >
<PARAM NAME="cabbase" VALUE="EX15AArc.CAB">
</APPLET>
```

The cabbase parameter instructs CAB-enabled browsers, such as Internet Explorer 3.0, to use the specified CAB file for class information.

Signing a CAB File

Signing a CAB file is a process that attempts to secure some reliability of code integrity through the use of public and private keys and certification authorities for code that is distributed over a virtually uncontrolled Internet. The process involves applying for a public key through a certification process by which a business shows the validity and stability of their company. Once that has been established, a key is assigned to that company that allows anyone to trace a file digitally signed with that key back to the company.

Digital signing of files support is included on the Visual J++ disks in the \Cab&Sign directory. It is not automatically installed when installing Visual J++. To install the code signing utility, copy CODESIGN.EXE to a directory on your local drive. Then execute the self-extracting file and follow the installation steps.

This section covers how to digitally sign a CAB file with the test certificate supplied with the kit. You must contact a Certification Authority to obtain an authentic certification before distributing your CAB files. Visit http://www.microsoft.com/intdev/signcode for more information on Authenticode.

To generate a test certificate, use the MAKECERT.EXE utility. A possible invocation of this program to generate MATHWORKS.CER is

```
MAKECERT -k:MathWorks.pvk -n:CN=MathWorksInc -d:MathWorksInc MathWorks.cer
```

Once a test certification file has been created, CERT2SPC.EXE can be used to generate a SPC file:

```
CERT2SPC root.cer MathWorks.cer MathWorks.spc
```

The SPC file is the file that would normally be provided by the Certification Authority. These utilities are simply provided to test the process.

The SPC file is used to actually sign the CAB files. SIGNCODE.EXE is used to add a digital signature to a file. The easiest way to use this program is to simply enter name of the program without parameters:

```
SIGNCODE
```

The Code Signing Wizard of Figure 21.11 will simplify the process.

Figure 21.11.
Code Signing Wizard.

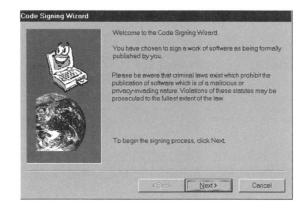

Once a CAB file has been digitally signed with a valid SPC file, it is ready to be distributed. There are two additional utilities that can be used to test the signing of files: PESIGMGR.EXE and CHKTRUST.EXE. These utilities can manipulate the certificates used in signing a file and checking the validity of a signed file, respectively. Remember that these will not work with the test certification generated with MAKECERT and CERT2SPC.

Summary

This chapter touched on several points involving the quickly changing ActiveX world. It covered how to create a Java interface of an ActiveX object using the Java Type Library Wizard for registered components. After establishing the interface, the Java applet can then be used to control the objects by calling the interface methods made available for the component. In addition, the Java applet could be used as an event handler. Combining these methods, two-way communications can be established between the object and the applet. Java can also be used to create an ActiveX object that can be packaged in a signed CAB file for trusted use on your favorite Web site.

Chapter

22

Using the Data Access Objects

In this chapter you will learn how to use the Microsoft Data Access Objects (DAO) in your Visual J++ programs. The DAO is an entire database engine that includes a set of objects and methods capable of performing just about any database operation you're likely to need. While the native database to DAO is the Jet engine used in Microsoft Access, DAO can also be used to access ODBC data sources. DAO programming could be the topic of an entire book, so this chapter will only scratch the surface. It will, however, provide you with sufficient information to get you started, and it includes examples of reading, updating, deleting, adding, and searching.

Overview of the Data Access Objects

Microsoft's Data Access Objects and Jet Database engine get around more than the Beach Boys do in that song of theirs. Jet was first introduced in November, 1992 in Access 1.0. Since then, the Jet engine and DAO have been used in Access, Visual Basic, Visual Basic for Applications (including Word and Excel), and Visual C++. Since DAO is used in so many other Microsoft products, it should not be surprising that DAO can be useful in your Visual J++ efforts.

The relationships among the Data Access Objects are shown in Figure 22.1. This figure does not show inheritance relationships. Instead it shows container relationships. In other words, from this figure you can tell that a Database contains recordsets and recordsets contain Fields.

As you can see from Figure 22.1, the DAO is made up of a large number of objects. Because these are ActiveX objects, you will access them from Visual J++ through Java interfaces. These interfaces are created with the Java Type Library Wizard.

Generating the Class Files

Before you can use DAO in your Java programs you must first create the class files that will be linked into your programs. To do this, select Java Type Library Wizard from the Tools menu in the Developer Studio. You will be presented with a list of ActiveX items installed on your system, similar to Figure 22.2. Select Microsoft DAO 3.0 Object Library and press the OK button. This will generate Java class files for your use. It will also create a file named SUMMARY.TXT. This file contains a brief list of each object and method that was generated. The file will normally be placed in C:\WINDOWS\JAVA\TRUSTLIB\SUMMARY.TXT.

Figure 22.1.
The relationships among Data Access Objects.

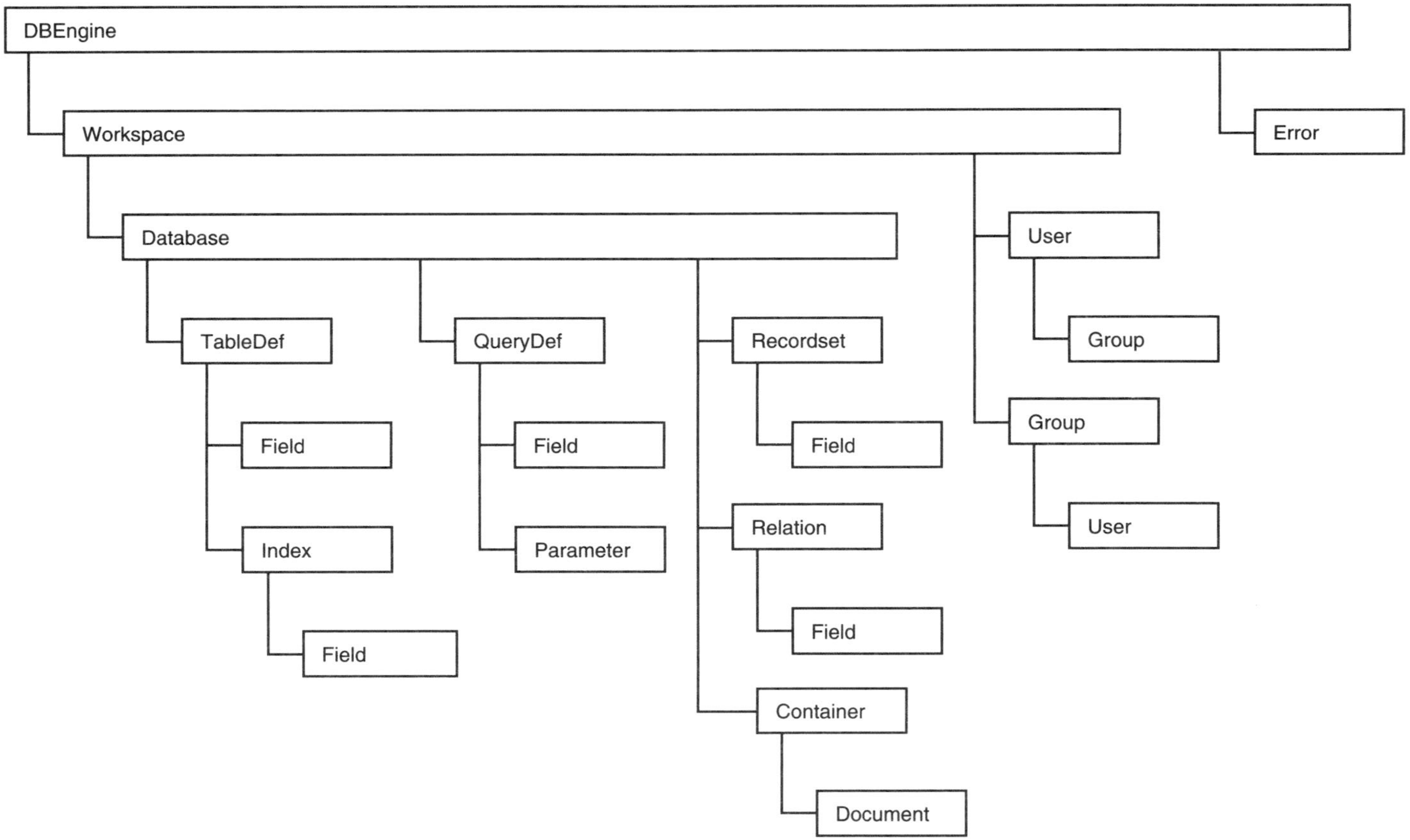

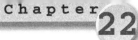
Figure 22.2.

You must run the Java Type
Library Wizard to generate
class files for DAO.

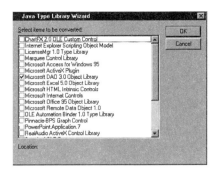

Using _DBEngine Objects

Although there are more than 30 DAO interfaces available to you, you do not need to know or use all of them. In fact, in this chapter you will focus on only a handful of them. Even so, you will be able to add powerful database access to your Java programs.

The first object you need to know about is the _DBEngine interface. This object is at the top of the DAO hierarchy and is the first object you will construct when writing a program that uses DAO. To construct a _DBEngine object you should use the method DBEngine_create in the class dao_dbengine. This class is shown in Listing 22.1 and is also provided with Visual J++.

NOTE:

Although dao_dbengine.java is included with Visual J++, it is installed only when you install the DAOSample applet. To install DAOSample, open the InfoView. First select Samples, then Microsoft Samples, and finally DAOSample. Follow the instructions that appear in the right pane of the InfoView.

Listing 22.1. dao_dbengine.java.

```
// Create a DAO DBEngine object with the license

import dao3032._DBEngine;
import com.ms.com.*;

public class dao_dbengine
{
    // The static public method creates the DBEngine object
    static public _DBEngine create()
    {
        // The return value
        _DBEngine result;
```

```
        // Create the License Manager object
        ILicenseMgr mgr = new LicenseMgr();

        // Use the License Manager to create the DBEngine
        result = (_DBEngine) mgr.createWithLic(

            // The license key for the DAO DBEngine
            "mjgcqcejfchcijecpdhckcdjqigdejfccjri",

            // The CLSID for the DAO DBEngine
            "{00025E15-0000-0000-C000-000000000046}",

            // The aggregation IUnknown* punkOuter
            null,

            // The ctxFlag to create in inproc server
            ComContext.INPROC_SERVER
            );

        return result;
    }
}
```

The `DBEngine_create` method uses the `Java LicenseMgr` class to construct the new COM (Component Object Model) component. To construct a `_DBEngine` object in your code, do the following:

```
_DBEngine dbengine = dao_dbengine.create();
```

Useful Methods

There are many methods available for use with `_DBEngine` objects; the following sections describe the most useful.

OpenDatabase

This method is used to open a new database. Its signature is as follows:

```
Database OpenDatabase(String dbname, Variant exclusive,
    Variant readonly, Variant source);
```

The `dbname` parameter is the filename of the database being opened. The remaining three parameters are each variants. The `Variant` class is used to pass data to COM objects and each `Variant` object can be used to hold any type of data—string, numeric, or Boolean. The exclusive parameter needs to hold a Boolean value indicating whether this program requires exclusive access to the database. The read-only parameter is a Boolean indicating whether the database is to be opened in read-only or read-write mode. The source parameter holds string data such as PWD=ROSEBUD that can be used when opening an ODBC data source. As an example of using OpenDatabase, consider the following:

```
// create Variants that will hold parameters that will be
// passed to OpenDatabase
Variant var1 = new Variant();
Variant var2 = new Variant();
Variant var3 = new Variant();

// set parameters for call to OpenDatabase
var1.putBoolean(false);
var2.putBoolean(false);
var3.putString("");

// Open the database for non-exclusive, read-write access
Database db = dbengine.OpenDatabase(filename, var1, var2, var3);
```

In this case, three new variants are constructed. The first two are set to false. The third is set to hold an empty string. OpenDatabase is then called with this parameter and the database is opened in non-exclusive, read-write mode.

getVersion

The getVersion method does not require any parameters and will return a string representing the version of the Jet engine in use. Table 22.1 shows the various Jet engine versions and the versions of other Microsoft products with which they were released.

Table 22.1. The versions of the Jet engine and the products they were released with.

Engine Version	Access	Visual Basic	Excel	Visual C++	Visual J++
(1992)	1.0				
(1993)	1.1	3.0			
(1994)	2.0				
2.5 (1995)		4.0 (16-bit)			
3.0 (1995)	7.0	4.0 (32-bit)	7.0	4.0	1.0

Using Database Objects

You have already seen how a Database object can be created with the OpenDatabase method of _DBEngine. In the following sections you learn about the most useful methods for using database objects.

Controlling Transactions

The three methods `BeginTrans`, `CommitTrans`, and `Rollback` are used to manage transactions. Transactions are useful because they assist in managing the integrity of a database. Use `BeginTrans` to indicate the start of a transaction block. Then use `CommitTrans` to commit the database activity since the transaction began, or use `Rollback` to undo the activity. These methods have the following signatures:

```
void BeginTrans();
void CommitTrans();
void Rollback();
```

Why would you want to do this? By thinking of your database activity in terms of transactions instead of automatic events (inserts, updates, and deletes) you can prevent some classes of data problems. For example, suppose you are writing an order entry system that will be used to take online orders. When a customer accesses your Web page he fills in a spreadsheet with a column for the product code and the quantity needed. He can order as many items as he desires but must press a Submit button before the order is sent to the shipping department.

If a customer indicates he wants 100 units of product ABC the program should check the database for stock on hand and reduce the available quantity by 100. When the customer presses the Submit button, the transaction is committed to the database. However, if the customer selects the Cancel button instead of Submit, the transaction can be rolled back.

OpenRecordset

The `OpenRecordset` method creates a recordset. A *recordset* is a collection of records. Recordset objects are among the most important in DAO and will be discussed in detail in the section "Using Recordset Objects" later in this chapter. The signature for `OpenRecordset` is as follows:

```
Recordset OpenRecordset(String source, Variant type,
    Variant options);
```

The source parameter can hold either the name of the table in the database or an SQL statement that returns a set of rows. The type parameter must hold one of the following values:

- ○ dbOpenTable
- ○ dbOpenDynaset
- ○ dbOpenSnapshot

Each of these parameters indicates a different type of recordset. A table recordset corresponds to a single table in the underlying database. Records may be added, updated, or deleted in a table recordset. A dynaset recordset is the result of a query and may include columns from more than one table. Records may be added, updated, or deleted in a dynaset. Finally, a snapshot recordset is a static copy of the records at the moment the recordset was created. A snapshot may contain fields from more than one table but additions, updates, and deletions are not allowed.

The options parameter can hold any of the values shown in Table 22.2.

Table 22.2. Valid values for the options parameter to `OpenRecordset`.

Value	Description
dbAppendOnly	Records may be added but not updated or deleted. Applies only to dbOpenDynaset.
dbConsistent	When using a recordset created from joined tables only those fields not involved in the join can be updated. Applies only to dbOpenDynaset.
dbDenyRead	Prevents other users from reading any records in the recordset. Applies only to dbOpenTable.
dbDenyWrite	Prevents other users from writing to any records in the recordset.
dbForwardOnly	The recordset only supports the MoveNext movement method.
dbInconsistent	When using a recordset created from joined tables all fields, including those involved in the join, can be updated. Applies only to dbOpenDynaset.
dbReadOnly	No changes can be made to the recordset.
dbSeeChanges	Generates an error if another program attempts to make a change to the record that is being edited.
dbSQLPassThrough	When using an ODBC data source, passes SQL code directly to the server for execution.

As an example of creating a table recordset consider Listing 22.2. First a database is opened. Then, two variants, var4 and var5, are constructed. The values dbOpenTable and dbReadOnly are placed into the variants and are passed to OpenRecordset. The name Programmer is also passed to OpenRecordset. This will cause the Programmer table to be opened in read-only mode.

Listing 22.2. Opening a table recordset.

```
// create Variants that will hold parameters that will be
// passed to OpenDatabase
Variant var1 = new Variant();
Variant var2 = new Variant();
Variant var3 = new Variant();

// set parameters for call to OpenDatabase
var1.putBoolean(false);
var2.putBoolean(false);
var3.putString("");

// Open the database for non-exclusive access
Database db = dbengine.OpenDatabase(filename, var1, var2, var3);
```

```
// create Variants that will hold parameters that will be
// passed to OpenDatabase
Variant var4 = new Variant();
Variant var5 = new Variant();

var4.putShort(Constants.dbOpenTable);
var5.putShort(Constants.dbReadOnly);

// create the recordset
recordset = db.OpenRecordset("Programmer", var4, var5);
```

Close

This method is used to close a database object. It requires no parameters and has no return value.

Using Field Objects

The Field object is used to represent the individual columns in a database table. Although there are many methods available for use with Field objects, the two you will use most frequently are putValue and getValue. These methods are used to move data into and out of Field objects, respectively. The signatures of these methods are as follows:

```
Variant getValue();
void putValue(Variant);
```

As an example of how to retrieve a value from a Field object, consider the following:

```
Variant value = new Variant();
value = salaryField.getValue();
int salary = value.toInt();
```

First, a new Variant object is constructed. The getValue method is then used to retrieve the value of salaryField. Because value is a variant, it is converted to a more useful data type. In this case, value.toInt is used to load the integer variable, salary.

Moving data in the opposite direction—into a Field object—can be done in a similar manner using putValue. For example, the following code will double the value stored in the salary field:

```
Variant value = new Variant();
value.putInt(oldSalary * 2);
salaryField.putValue(value);
```

Using Recordset Objects

In the discussion of the Database object, you were introduced to recordsets. In this section you learn how to use a recordset to view, add, update, delete, and find records. The following sections describe how to perform some of the most common operations on recordsets.

Reading Records Sequentially

To move through a recordset you can use the MoveFirst, MoveNext, MovePrevious, and MoveLast methods whose signatures are as follows:

```
void MoveFirst();
void MoveNext();
void MovePrevious();
void MoveLast();
```

Each of these methods will reposition the current record of the recordset. As an example of how these methods are used, consider Listing 22.3. This example iterates through all of the rows in the Programmer table of the supplied Access database. Information about each programmer is displayed in a TextArea, as shown in Figure 22.3.

Listing 22.3. The class EX22A demonstrates moving through a recordset sequentially.

```
import java.applet.*;
import java.awt.*;
import java.net.*;
import dao_dbengine;
import dao3032.*;
import com.ms.com.Variant;

public class EX22A extends Applet
{
    Recordset recordset;
    TextArea output;
    Database db;

    public void init()
    {
        resize(500, 400);
        output = new TextArea(20, 50);
        add(output);
    }

    public void start()
    {
        OpenDatabase();
    }

    public void stop()
    {
        // Close the recordset and database
        recordset.Close();
        db.Close();
    }

    private boolean OpenDatabase()
    {
        URL dbURL;
        try {
```

```
        // otherwise generate it relative to the applet
        dbURL = new java.net.URL(getDocumentBase(), "sample.mdb");
    }
    catch(Exception e) {
        showStatus("Error: " + e.getMessage());
        return false;
    }

    // strip "file:/" from dbURL
    String filename = dbURL.getFile().substring(1);

    // create the database engine
    _DBEngine dbengine = dao_dbengine.create();

    // create Variants that will hold parameters that will be
    // passed to OpenDatabase
    Variant var1 = new Variant();
    Variant var2 = new Variant();
    Variant var3 = new Variant();

    // set parameters for call to OpenDatabase
    var1.putBoolean(false);
    var2.putBoolean(false);
    var3.putString("");

    // Open the database for non-exclusive access
    db = dbengine.OpenDatabase(filename, var1, var2, var3);

    // create Variants that will hold parameters that will be
    // passed to OpenDatabase
    Variant var4 = new Variant();
    Variant var5 = new Variant();

    var4.putShort(Constants.dbOpenTable);
    var5.putShort(Constants.dbReadOnly);

    // create the recordset
    recordset = db.OpenRecordset("Programmer", var4, var5);

    // display all the records in this dynaset
    DisplayAllRecords();

    return true;
}

private void DisplayAllRecords()
{
    // create variants and assign the names of each column
    Variant varFirstName = new Variant();
    varFirstName.putString("FirstName");

    Variant varLastName = new Variant();
    varLastName.putString("LastName");

    Variant varSalary = new Variant();
    varSalary.putString("Salary");
```

continues

Listing 22.3. continued

```
    Variant varKnowsJava = new Variant();
    varKnowsJava.putString("KnowsJava");

    Variant varJobTitle = new Variant();
    varJobTitle.putString("JobTitle");

    // determine how many records in the recordset
    int count = recordset.getRecordCount();

    // position recordset at the first record
    recordset.MoveFirst();

    // loop through the recordset, displaying each record
    for(int recNum = 0; recNum < count; recNum++)
    {
        // get the fields in this recordset
        Fields fields = recordset.getFields();
        _Field fld;

        // create a Variant that will hold each the value
        // read from each column
        Variant value;

        // get the LastName field
        fld = fields.getItem(varLastName);
        // get its value
        value = fld.getValue();
        // display the value
        output.appendText(value.toString() + ", ");

        // get the FirstName field
        fld = fields.getItem(varFirstName);
        // get its value
        value = fld.getValue();
        // display the value
        output.appendText(value.toString() + "\r\n");

        // get the JobTitle field
        fld = fields.getItem(varJobTitle);
        // get its value
        value = fld.getValue();
        // display the value
        output.appendText("\t" + value.toString() + "\r\n");

        // get the Salary field
        fld = fields.getItem(varSalary);
        // get its value
        value = fld.getValue();
        // display the value
        output.appendText("\t" + value.toString() + "\r\n");

        // get the KnowsJava field
        fld = fields.getItem(varKnowsJava);
        // get its value
        value = fld.getValue();
```

```
        // display the value
        Boolean knowsJava = new Boolean (value.toBoolean());
        output.appendText("\tKnows Java: " + knowsJava.toString() + "\r\n");

        recordset.MoveNext();
      }
    }
}
```

Figure 22.3.

The EX22A example displays information about each programmer in the database.

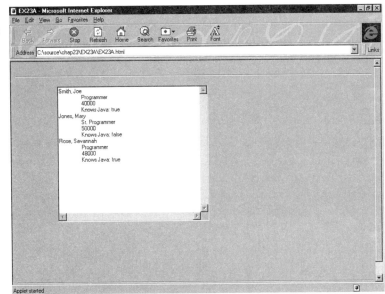

The init method of class EX22A simply resizes the screen and then places a TextArea component on the screen. The start method invokes the OpenDatabase method. OpenDatabase constructs a URL from the document base and name of the Access database file to be opened. Next, dao_dbengine.create is used to create the database engine. The database is opened using OpenDatabase and three variants. Finally, the Programmer table is opened as a table recordset in read-only mode. The DisplayAllRecords method is then called to display the record contents.

DisplayAllRecords begins with a series of lines such as the following:

```
Variant varFirstName = new Variant();
varFirstName.putString("FirstName");
```

These lines create a variant variable for each column in the Programmer table and then store the name of the column in the variant. After each of the variants is created, the number of records in the recordset is retrieved with getRecordCount. The getRecordCount method will always return the correct number of records in a table-type recordset. For a dynaset or snapshot, getRecordCount will return the correct value only after all records in the set have been retrieved.

The recordset is initially positioned on the first record with `MoveFirst`. At this point a loop begins that will iterate through each of the records in the recordset based on the quantity returned by `getRecordCount`. Each time through the loop the contents of the row will be displayed. In order to get at the fields stored in a recordset it is necessary to use the `getFields` method. In Listing 22.3 this is done as follows:

```
Fields fields = recordset.getFields();
```

This will create a collection of fields. To get at an individual item within the collection, use the `getItem` method. In Listing 22.3 the contents of the `LastName` field are retrieved with the following code:

```
// get the LastName field
fld = fields.getItem(varLastName);
// get its value
value = fld.getValue();
// display the value
output.appendText(value.toString() + ", ");
```

The method `fields.getItem` is passed the variant that contains the string `LastName`. This will cause `fld` to contain a reference to the specific field that contains data from the LastName column of the database. Next, `fld.getValue` is used to retrieve the value of this field and place it in the variant `value`. Finally, `value.toString` is used to convert the variant into a string that is passed to `appendText`. This causes the contents of the LastName column to be added to the TextArea on the applet.

After similar code is repeated for each of the columns in the database—FirstName, LastName, JobTitle, Salary, and KnowsJava—the `MoveNext` method is used to select a new current record. After the user closes the applet, the `stop` method is invoked and the recordset and database are closed.

The `MoveLast` and `MovePrevious` methods work in an analogous manner. If you need to move backward through a recordset, you can use these methods instead of `MoveFirst` and `MoveNext`.

NOTE:

You should notice from this example that it is necessary to use the following three import statements:

```
import dao_dbengine;
import dao3032.*;
import com.ms.com.Variant;
```

These lines import the `dao_dbengine` class described earlier in the chapter, the DAO objects generated by the Java Type Library Wizard, and the `Variant` class that is used with all COM objects.

Updating Records

Before the contents of a record can be updated with new values, the record must be placed in edit mode. This is done with the Edit method. Once in edit mode you can use the Resultset.getFields and the _Field.putValue methods to alter the values in a record. When the desired changes have been made, the record can be updated with the Update method. After a record is updated it is automatically taken out of edit mode. If instead of updating a record you need to take a record out of edit mode without committing any changes to the record, you can use CancelUpdate. The signatures of these new methods are as follows:

```
void Edit();
void Update();
void CancelUpdate();
```

As an example of how to update the values in a record, consider the GiveBonuses method shown in Listing 22.4. This method is from the example EX22B, which is provided on the CD-ROM that accompanies this book. The GiveBonuses method is similar to DisplayAllRecords from the previous listing in that it uses getRecordCount, MoveFirst, and MoveNext to loop through the records in a resultset. However, in this example, each programmer who knows Java will have his or her salary doubled.

Listing 22.4. Updating the salary of all Java programmers in the database.

```
private void GiveBonuses()
{
    // determine how many records in the recordset
    int count = recordset.getRecordCount();

    // create a variant for each column
    Variant varSalary = new Variant();
    Variant varKnowsJava = new Variant();

    // set the name of each column
    varSalary.putString("Salary");
    varKnowsJava.putString("KnowsJava");

    // position recordset at the first record
    recordset.MoveFirst();

    // loop through the recordset, displaying each record
    for(int recNum = 0; recNum < count; recNum++)
    {
        // get the fields in this recordset
        Fields fields = recordset.getFields();
        _Field fld;

        // create a Variant that will hold each the value
        // read from each column
        Variant value;
```

continues

Listing 22.4. continued

```
        // get the KnowsJava field
        fld = fields.getItem(varKnowsJava);
        // get its value
        value = fld.getValue();

        // if the programmer knows Java, give a good raise
        if (value.toBoolean() == true)
        {
            // get the Salary field
            fld = fields.getItem(varSalary);
            // get its value
            value = fld.getValue();
            // store the salary
            int salary = value.toInt();

            // double the programmer's salary
            int newSalary = salary * 2;

            // put the recordset into edit mode
            recordset.Edit();

            // assign the new salary to the current record
            value.putInt(newSalary);
            fld.putValue(value);

            // update the recordset
            recordset.Update();

            // display the salary change
            DisplayRaise(fields, salary, newSalary);
        }
        else
            DisplayNoRaise(fields);

        recordset.MoveNext();
    }
}
```

Inside the for loop of GiveBonuses the value of the KnowsJava field is retrieved and converted to a Boolean value. If this value is true, the salary field is retrieved from the database and stored in the integer variable salary. This value is doubled and then stored in newSalary. The actual updating of the record in the database takes place with the following lines:

```
recordset.Edit();
value.putInt(newSalary);
fld.putValue(value);
recordset.Update();
```

Depending on whether or not the programmer received a raise, either the method DisplayRaise or DisplayNoRaise will be called. These methods are as follows:

```
private void DisplayRaise(Fields fields, int oldSalary, int newSalary)
{
    String firstName = GetField(fields, "FirstName");
    String lastName  = GetField(fields, "LastName");

    output.appendText(firstName + " " + lastName +
            " got a raise from " +
            String.valueOf(oldSalary) +
            " to " + String.valueOf(newSalary) + "\r\n");
}

private void DisplayNoRaise(Fields fields)
{
    String firstName = GetField(fields, "FirstName");
    String lastName  = GetField(fields, "LastName");

    output.appendText(firstName + " " + lastName +
            " didn't get a raise.\r\n");
}
```

Rather than construct and manipulate their own variant variables, each of these methods calls the GetField method. GetField was written as follows:

```
private String GetField(Fields fields, String fldName)
{
    // create a new Variant using fldName
    Variant var = new Variant();
    var.putString(fldName);

    // get the field
    _Field fld = fields.getItem(var);
    // get its value
    Variant value = fld.getValue();

    return value.toString();
}
```

GetField works on a generic Fields container and field name. A variant is constructed and set to hold the field name. The corresponding field is then retrieved from the Fields container and its value is then returned as a string.

The result of running EX22B is shown in Figure 22.4.

Deleting Records

Deleting a record is as simple as calling the Delete method when the record to be deleted is the current record in the recordset. For example, Listing 22.5 shows the FireProgrammers method from the example EX22C, which is included on the CD-ROM. This method loops through all of the programmers in the Programmer table examining the value of the KnowsJava column. When a programmer is found who does not know Java, he is deleted from the database.

Figure 22.4.

Example EX22B doubles
the salary of all Java
programmers.

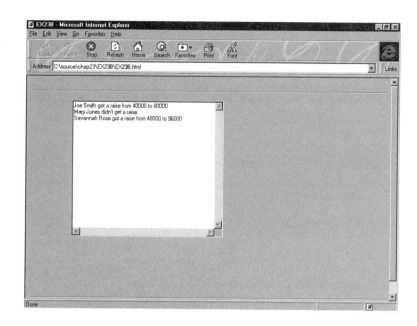

```
Joe Smith got a raise from 40000 to 80000
Mary Jones didn't get a raise.
Savannah Rose got a raise from 48000 to 96000
```

Listing 22.5. EX22C illustrates how to fire anyone who doesn't know
Java.

```
private void FireProgrammers()
{
    // determine how many records in the recordset
    int count = recordset.getRecordCount();

    // create a variant for the KnowsJava column
    Variant varKnowsJava = new Variant();
    varKnowsJava.putString("KnowsJava");

    // position recordset at the first record
    recordset.MoveFirst();

    // loop through the recordset, displaying each record
    for(int recNum = 0; recNum < count; recNum++)
    {
        // get the fields in this recordset
        Fields fields = recordset.getFields();
        _Field fld;

        // create a Variant that will hold the values
        // read from the columns
        Variant value;

        // get the KnowsJava field
        fld = fields.getItem(varKnowsJava);
        // get its value
        value = fld.getValue();

        // fire the programmer if he doesn't know Java
        if (value.toBoolean() == false)
```

```
        {
            // display a message about the fired programmer
            DisplayFiring(fields);

            // delete the current record
            recordset.Delete();
        }

        recordset.MoveNext();
    }
}
```

The Delete method does not automatically advance the recordset to the next record. It is still necessary to use MoveNext to advance to the next record in the set. The results of running EX22C are shown in Figure 22.5.

Figure 22.5.

Example EX22C fires any programmers who do not know Java.

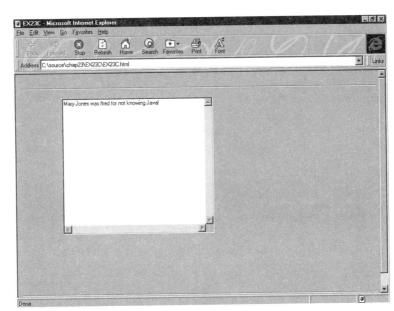

Adding New Records

Adding a record is similar to editing a record. However, instead of placing the database into edit mode with the Edit method, the database is placed into add mode with the AddNew method. The example EX22D, provided on the CD-ROM, shows how to add a new programmer to the database. Listing 22.6 shows the AddNewHire method from the EX22D class.

Listing 22.6. EX22D shows how to add a new programmer to the database.

```
private void AddNewHire()
{
    // create a variant for each column
    Variant varFirstName = new Variant();
    Variant varLastName = new Variant();
    Variant varSalary = new Variant();
    Variant varKnowsJava = new Variant();
    Variant varJobTitle = new Variant();

    // set the name of each column
    varFirstName.putString("FirstName");
    varLastName.putString("LastName");
    varSalary.putString("Salary");
    varKnowsJava.putString("KnowsJava");
    varJobTitle.putString("JobTitle");

    // tell the recordset its about to get a new record
    recordset.AddNew();

    // retrieve the fields for this recordset
    Fields fields = recordset.getFields();
    _Field fld;

    // create a Variant to hold temporary values
    Variant value = new Variant();

    // set the FirstName field
    fld = fields.getItem(varFirstName);
    value.putString("Napoleon");
    fld.putValue(value);

    // set the LastName field
    fld = fields.getItem(varLastName);
    value.putString("Solo");
    fld.putValue(value);

    // set the Salary field
    fld = fields.getItem(varSalary);
    value.putInt(63000);
    fld.putValue(value);

    // set the KnowsJava field
    fld = fields.getItem(varKnowsJava);
    value.putBoolean(true);
    fld.putValue(value);

    // set the JobTitle field
    fld = fields.getItem(varJobTitle);
    value.putString("Lead Programmer");
    fld.putValue(value);

    // commit the new record to the recordset
    recordset.Update();
}
```

In order to add a new programmer, a variant is created for each column in the database and AddNew is used to put the database into add mode. The fields in the recordset are retrieved with getFields. Then, for each column in the database the following actions are taken:

○ The field is retrieved by using the variant containing the field name.

○ The value variant is loaded with the desired value.

○ putValue is used to put the value into the field.

Finally, Update is used is to commit the new record. If an error had occurred or this was an interactive method and the user changed his mind, CancelUpdate could be used to cancel the new record. The results of running EX22D are shown in Figure 22.6.

Figure 22.6.

Example EX22D shows how to add a new programmer to the database.

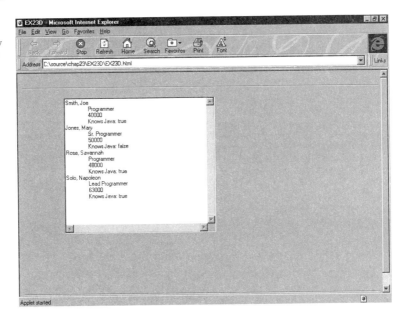

Finding Records

Sometimes you've created a Resultset and need to scan through it looking for one or more records that match certain criteria. The DAO engine provides a set of methods for doing exactly this. To find the first record that meets your criteria, you can use the FindFirst method. Additionally, there are also FindNext, FindPrevious, and FindLast methods. These methods have the following signatures:

```
void FindFirst(String);
void FindNext(String);
void FindPrevious(String);
void FindLast(String);
```

The string parameter passed to these methods is the search criteria. For example, the following two examples show valid search criteria:

```
FindFirst("Salary < 50000");
FindLast("FirstName = 'Savannah'");
```

In order to determine whether a record was found that matched the search criteria, use the method getNoMatch whose signature is as follows:

```
boolean getNoMatch();
```

This method will return true if no match was found, or false otherwise. By combining these methods, it is possible to write code that will loop through a resultset finding all records that match the desired criteria. For example, consider the following FindProgrammers method:

```
private void FindProgrammers()
{
    // setup the search criteria
    String criteria = "Salary < 50000";

    // find the first matching record
    recordset.FindFirst(criteria);

    // while there are matching records keep going
    while (recordset.getNoMatch() == false)
    {
        // display the programmer's name
        DisplayProgrammer();

        // and search for another one
        recordset.FindNext(criteria);
    }
}
```

This method is from the sample class EX22E, which is included on the accompanying CD-ROM. FindProgrammers searches for all programmers who make less than the specified salary. For each record that matches, the DisplayProgrammer method will be called. This method displays information about the underpaid programmers, as shown in Figure 22.7.

The FindFirst and other Find methods work only when the database is opened as a dynaset. This means the OpenDatabase method needs to specify dbOpenDynaset instead of dbOpenTable. This is done with the following code fragment:

```
Variant var4 = new Variant();
Variant var5 = new Variant();

var4.putShort(Constants.dbOpenDynaset);
var5.putShort(Constants.dbEditAdd);

// create the recordset
recordset = db.OpenRecordset("Programmer", var4, var5);
```

Figure 22.7.

Example EX22E identifies underpaid programmers.

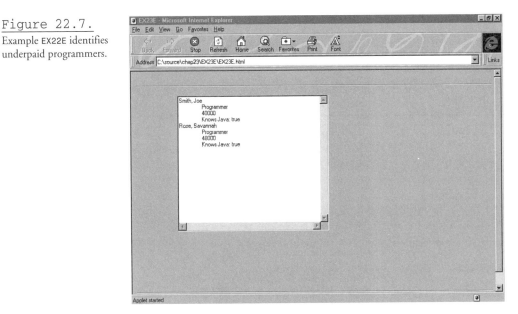

Using SQL

One of the simplest ways to manipulate your database is with SQL. SQL is a language that was designed specifically for querying and modifying relational databases. Fortunately, DAO supports the use of SQL. You can use SQL statements with DAO in the following two ways:

○ As a parameter to OpenRecordset.

○ As a parameter to the Execute method in the Database class.

In earlier examples in this chapter you passed the name of the table to be opened to OpenRecordset. For example, the following was used to open the Programmer table:

```
recordset = db.OpenRecordset("Programmer", var4, var5);
```

Instead of passing the name of a table, you can pass an SQL statement. This means you can do the following:

```
recordset=db.OpenRecordset("select * from Programmer",var4,var5);
```

Because this SQL statement selects all rows, the result set it creates will contain the same rows as the result set created by using the table name. However, you could include any valid SQL where clause to qualify the select statement. Because an SQL statement creates a dynaset, you need to pass dbOpenDynaset in the first variant passed to OpenRecordset. This can be done as follows:

```
Variant var1 = new Variant();
Variant var2 = new Variant();
var1.putShort(Constants.dbOpenDynaset);
```

```
var2.putShort(Constants.dbEditAdd);

// create the recordset
recordset=db.OpenRecordset("select * from Programmer",var1,var2);
```

> ## NOTE:
>
> The SQL language is a complex subject on its own. Therefore, this chapter doesn't
> attempt to teach SQL. For a thorough introduction to SQL, your best bet is *Understanding the New SQL: A Complete Guide* (1993) by Jim Melton and Alan Simon.

SQL has other uses beyond just creating a record set. Sometimes you just want to update rows in the database, delete a row, or add a row. To do this you can use the Execute method of the Database class. The signature of the Execute method is as follows:

```
void Execute(String sqlStr, Variant options);
```

The sqlStr parameter holds a valid SQL statement; the options parameter is used to specify one of the values in Table 22.3.

Table 22.3. Valid values for the options parameter to Execute.

Value	Description
dbConsistent	When using a recordset created from joined tables, only those fields not involved in the join can be updated.
dbDenyWrite	Prevents other users from writing to any records in the recordset.
dbFailOnError	Rolls back any updates if an error occurs.
dbInconsistent	When using a recordset created from joined tables, all fields, including those involved in the join, can be updated.
dbSeeChanges	Generates an error if another program attempts to make a change to a record that is being edited.
dbSQLPassThrough	When using an ODBC data source, it passes SQL code directly to the server for execution.

As an example of using Execute, consider the following, which sets every programmer's salary to $100,000:

```
Variant var = new Variant();
var.putShort(Constants.dbFailOnError);
db.Execute("update Programmer set Salary = 100000", var);
```

As a more complete example of using SQL with DAO, the example EX22F is provided on the accompanying CD-ROM. This example is similar to some of the non-SQL examples developed earlier in this chapter. However, because EX22F uses SQL to manipulate the database, you'll see how much easier it is. Listing 22.7 shows the OpenDatabase method of EX22F.

Listing 22.7. The OpenDatabase method of EX22F.

```
private boolean OpenDatabase()
{
    URL dbURL;
    try {
        // otherwise generate it relative to the applet
        dbURL = new java.net.URL(getDocumentBase(),
                "sample.mdb");
    }
    catch(Exception e) {
        showStatus("Error: " + e.getMessage());
        return false;
    }

    // strip "file:/" from dbURL
    String filename = dbURL.getFile().substring(1);

    // create the database engine
    _DBEngine dbengine = dao_dbengine.create();

    // create Variants that will hold parameters that
    // will be passed to OpenDatabase
    Variant var1 = new Variant();
    Variant var2 = new Variant();
    Variant var3 = new Variant();

    // set parameters for call to OpenDatabase
    var1.putBoolean(false);
    var2.putBoolean(false);
    var3.putString("");

    // Open the database for non-exclusive access
    db = dbengine.OpenDatabase(filename,var1,var2,var3);

    // create Variants that will hold parameters that
    // will be passed to OpenDatabase
    Variant var4 = new Variant();
    Variant var5 = new Variant();

    var4.putShort(Constants.dbOpenDynaset);
    var5.putShort(Constants.dbEditAdd);

    // create the recordset
    recordset=db.OpenRecordset("select * from Programmer",
            var4, var5);

    // display all the records in this dynaset
    DisplayAllRecords();
```

continues

Listing 22.7. continued

```
    // give raises to the Java programmers
    GiveRaises();
    HireNewProgrammer();

    // re-display all the records in this dynaset
    DisplayAllRecords();

    // requery the database
    Variant var6 = new Variant();
    var6.putNull();
    recordset.Requery(var6);

    // re-display all the records in this dynaset
    DisplayAllRecords();

    return true;
}
```

As you can see, this version of OpenDatabase is similar to the one used in EX22A that was shown in Listing 22.3. The first difference occurs with the call to OpenRecordset, which uses an SQL statement instead of a table name and specifies dbOpenDynaset instead of dbOpenTable. After the recordset is created the method DisplayAllRecords is called. This method is the same as was shown in Listing 22.3, so it is not repeated here. Next, the methods GiveRaises and HireNewProgrammer are called. These methods are shown in Listing 22.8.

Listing 22.8. The GiveRaises and HireNewProgrammers methods of EX22F.

```
private void GiveRaises()
{
  Variant var = new Variant();
  var.putShort(Constants.dbFailOnError);

  db.Execute("update Programmer set Salary = " +
          "Salary * 2 where KnowsJava <> 0", var);

  output.appendText("\r\nRaises given: " +
          String.valueOf(db.getRecordsAffected()) +
          "\r\n\r\n");
}

private void HireNewProgrammer()
{
  Variant var = new Variant();
  var.putShort(Constants.dbFailOnError);

  String sqlStr = "insert into Programmer (FirstName, " +
  "LastName, Salary, KnowsJava, JobTitle) " +
  "values (\"Napoleon\", \"Solo\", 63000, 0, \"Lead\")";

  db.Execute(sqlStr, var);
}
```

Both `GiveRaises` and `HireNewProgrammer` create a variant and load it with `dbFailOnError`. `GiveRaises` uses an SQL `update` statement to double the salary of every Java programmer in the database while `HireNewProgrammer` uses `insert` to add a programmer to the database. In the case of `GiveRaises`, the method `getRecordsAffected`, a member of `Database`, is used to determine how many raises were given. This method always returns the number of rows affected by the last SQL statement.

After the `OpenDatabase` method has called `GiveRaises` and `HireNewProgrammer`, `DisplayAllRecords` is again used to show the effect of these methods. As you can see in Figure 22.8, the raises are shown but Napoleon Solo does not appear. Because you're using a dynaset the raises are automatically reflected in the set; however, the new record for Napoleon Solo is not added to the dynaset until the database is requeried. This can be done by using the `Requery` method. `Requery` takes a single null variant parameter and is executed as follows:

```
// requery the database
Variant var6 = new Variant();
var6.putNull();
recordset.Requery(var6);
```

Figure 22.8.

The output of EX22F before the database is requeried.

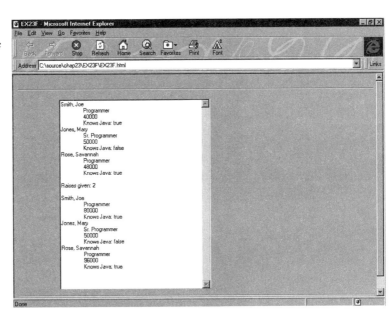

This causes all record sets to be re-created and the final call to `DisplayAllRecords` in `OpenDatabase` will now display Napoleon's name as shown in Figure 22.9.

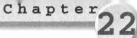
Figure 22.9.

The final output of EX22F.

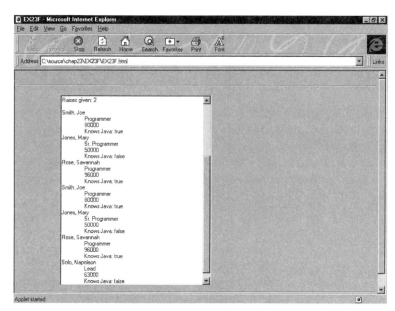

Summary

This chapter introduced you to the Data Access Objects (DAO) and showed you how to use them in your Java programs. You learned about Database, Recordset, and Field objects and how to combine these objects to perform useful tasks. You saw examples of using DAO to browse a database, add new records, update existing records, delete records, search for records, and execute SQL. Armed with the information you learned in this chapter, you are now prepared to write your own programs using the Data Access Objects.

Part VI

Sample Visual J++ Applets

Chapter 23

Software Cost Estimator

This chapter describes how to build an applet that enables you to forecast the amount of time needed to develop software. This chapter puts to use much of what you've learned throughout this book, especially on the subject of user interface programming. Additionally, you will learn some new tricks, such as how to create and use an imagemap.

The Project Overview

In this chapter you will build the CostEstimator applet. This applet is essentially a COCOMO calculator. COCOMO, which stands for Constructive Cost Model, is a method for estimating the amount of time completing a software development project will take. In COCOMO you assess a project based on 15 attributes, such as programmer capability, required reliability, and product complexity. Each of these attributes is rated on a scale from Very Low to Extra High.

The effort of a project, as measured in person months, is calculated in COCOMO with the following equation:

$$\text{Effort} = 3.0 * (\text{KLOC})^{(1.12\,*\,\text{EAF})}$$

KLOC represents a measure of the number of thousands of lines of code. For example, if you anticipate writing 10,500 lines of code, KLOC is 10.5. EAF, which stands for Effort Adjustment Factor, is calculated, as you'll see in a moment, based on the attributes of the project being estimated. The magic numbers 3.0 and 1.12 were calculated by Boehm using a form of regression analysis. These values are for what Boehm refers to as "semi-detached" projects.

As mentioned earlier, in COCOMO a project is rated from Very Low to Extra High, on 15 attributes. Because how a project is rated on these attributes influences the cost of the project, the attributes are known as cost drivers. The cost drivers and their associated values for each rating are shown in Table 23.1.

Table 23.1. COCOMO cost drivers.

Cost Drivers	Very Low	Low	Nominal	High	Very High	Extra High
Analyst capability	1.46	1.19	1.00	0.86	0.71	
Applications experience	1.29	1.13	1.00	0.91	0.82	
Complexity	0.70	0.85	1.00	1.15	1.30	1.65
Database size		0.94	1.00	1.08	1.16	
Execution time			1.00	1.11	1.30	1.66
Language experience	1.14	1.07	1.00	0.95		
Modern practices	1.24	1.10	1.00	0.91	0.82	
Programmer capability	1.42	1.17	1.00	0.86	0.70	

Cost Drivers	Very Low	Low	Nominal	High	Very High	Extra High
Reliability	0.75	0.88	1.00	1.15	1.40	
Schedule constraint	1.23	1.08	1.00	1.04	1.10	
Software tools	1.24	1.10	1.00	0.91	0.83	
Storage constraint			1.00	1.06	1.21	1.56
Turnaround time		0.87	1.00	1.07	1.15	
Virtual Machine experience	1.21	1.10	1.00	0.90		
Virtual Machine volatility		0.87	1.00	1.15	1.30	

The Effort Adjustment Factor used in the Effort equation is calculated by taking the product of all 15 cost drivers. You should notice from Table 23.1 that the Nominal value for each cost driver is 1.00. This means you can think of Nominal as the default value for each cost driver. As an example of calculating the Effort Adjustment Factor, assume that a project is rated Nominal for everything except Programmer Capability (which is High) and Complexity (which is Very High). This means that the Effort Adjustment Factor for this project is as follows:

$$\text{EAF} = 1.00^{13} * 0.86 * 1.30$$

Multiplying this out, you get EAF = 1.118. Assume that you are developing an estimate for a project you expect will include 10,000 lines of code. These values can then be plugged into the Effort equation as shown here:

$$\text{Effort} = 3.0 * (10)^{(1.12 * 1.118)}$$

As you'll be able to verify with the applet at the end of the chapter, this results in Effort equaling 53 person months.

In addition to the Effort equation, COCOMO provides an equation for calculating the duration in calendar months of a project. The equation for duration is this:

$$\text{Duration} = 2.5 * (\text{Effort}^{0.35})$$

The CostEstimator applet developed in this chapter calculates both Effort and Duration.

NOTE:

For a full description of COCOMO, see the book *Software Engineering Economics*, by Barry Boehm. This book, first published in 1981, remains valuable to this day and is one of the classics in our industry. If you have ever missed a deadline, been asked to give a deadline, met a deadline, or bet on a horse named Deadline, you should own a copy of Boehm's book.

The CostEstimator Applet

The rest of this chapter describes how to program the CostEstimator applet. The initial screen of this applet is shown in Figure 23.1. At the top left of the applet is an imagemap that includes the abbreviations PRD, CMP, PER, and PRJ. These stand for Product, Computer, Personnel, and Project. When you click the mouse over these areas on the imagemap, the applet displays a different set of cost drivers to the right of the imagemap. In Figure 23.1, the Product cost drivers are displayed because PRD has been selected in the imagemap, as shown by the highlighting around it.

Figure 23.1.

The initial screen of
CostEstimator while
Product cost drivers
are being selected.

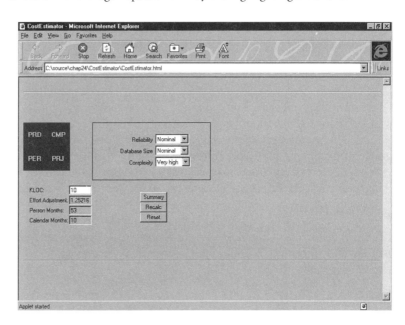

Selecting a different portion of the imagemap displays a different set of fields related to different cost drivers. For example, Figure 23.2 shows the Project attributes. In this case, two choice fields and a checkbox group are used. The four categories of cost drivers are shown in Table 23.2.

Table 23.2. Cost drivers by category.

Category	Cost Driver
Product	Reliability
	Database size
	Complexity
Computer	Execution time
	Storage constraints
	VM volatility
	Turnaround time

Category	Cost Driver
Personnel	Analyst capability
	Applications experience
	Programmer capability
	VM experience
	Language experience
Project	Modern practices
	Software tools
	Schedule constraints

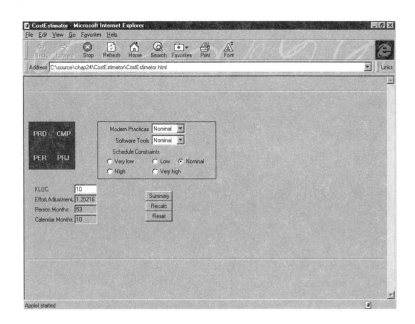

Figure 23.2.

Selecting Project cost drivers in the CostEstimator.

Figures 23.1 and 23.2 also show an area for entry of KLOC. As you recall, KLOC is shorthand for Thousand lines of code. Non-editable text fields are also provided. They will display the Effort Adjustment Factor and the COCOMO-estimated number of person months and calendar months. In these figures, numbers are shown for the example described earlier in this chapter. This is a 10,000-line program that will take 53 person months to complete.

Three buttons are also provided. The Summary button displays a frame detailing the cost-driver selections that have been made. The Recalc button performs the COCOMO calculations and updates the non-editable fields. The Reset button restores all the cost-driver selections to Nominal. This is useful for analyzing different scenarios.

The Class Overview

The classes are used to write the CostEstimator applet. Classes whose names are italicized are specific to this applet. Classes without italicized names are standard Java classes that are used as base classes for CostEstimator classes.

The CostEstimator class is, of course, the main class and extends Applet. The CostDriverPanel class is an abstract class that is implemented by ChoicePanel and ProjectPanel. These classes control the area at the top right of the applet where values for the cost drivers are entered. The fields for each of the cost-driver categories are collected into one of the subclasses of CostDriverPanel.

The Rating class is a low-level class that associates a rating (for example, "Low") with a value (1.19) within a cost driver ("Analyst capability"). The CostDriver class stores all information about the cost driver, including its name and possible ratings.

The ImagemapRect and ImageCanvas classes are used to create the imagemap. An imagemap is painted on the ImageCanvas. An ImagemapRect indicates an area on the ImageCanvas that causes the displayed CostDriverPanel to change.

Finally, the SummaryFrame class is used to provide a frame that will appear in response to pressing the Summary button. The SummaryFrame displays details on the values selected for each cost driver.

Storing Cost Drivers and Ratings

An instance of the CostDriver class, shown in Listing 23.1, is used to represent one of the 15 COCOMO cost drivers. The constructor for CostDriver is passed the name of the driver and a vector of ratings. This vector contains instances of the Rating class, which is shown in Listing 23.2.

Listing 23.1. CostDriver.java.

```java
import java.util.*;
import Rating;
// This class stores the name of a cost driver (e.g.,
// "Reliability") and the ratings (e.g., "Low", "Nominal",
// "High") that can be selected for it.
class CostDriver extends Object
{
  public String name;     // the name of the driver, for
              // example, "Reliability"
  public Vector ratings;
  public CostDriver(String name, Vector ratings)
  {
    this.name = name;
    this.ratings = (Vector)ratings.clone();
  }
}
```

Listing 23.2. Rating.java.

```java
// This class represents a rating that can be selected for a
// cost driver. It stores both the name of the rating (Low, High,
// etc.) and the multiplier to use if this rating is selected.
// For example, the High rating for Complexity implies a
// multiplier of 1.15.
public class Rating extends Object
{
  public String name;
  public float multiplier;
  Rating(String str, float value)
  {
    name = str;
    multiplier = value;
  }
}
```

The Rating class represents a paired name and multiplier. For example, the Very Low rating for Reliability implies a multiplier of 0.75. A new Rating object could be created with these values as shown here:

```java
new Rating("Very low", 0.75F);
```

To create a new instance of the CostDriver class, you create a vector of Rating objects and pass this to the CostDriver constructor. This could be carried out in the following way:

```java
// create a vector of Reliability ratings
Vector relyRatings = new Vector(5);
relyRatings.addElement(new Rating("Very low",  0.75F));
relyRatings.addElement(new Rating("Low",       0.88F));
relyRatings.addElement(new Rating("Nominal",   1.00F));
relyRatings.addElement(new Rating("High",      1.15F));
relyRatings.addElement(new Rating("Very high", 1.40F));
// create the new cost driver
CostDriver cd = new CostDriver("Reliability", relyRatings);
```

Programming the User Interface

To create the user interface for the CostEstimator, you need to use the GridBagLayout layout manager. The other layout managers do not offer the flexibility necessary to create this user interface. When you consider the main screen of the CostEstimator, you realize that it is readily partitioned into four main areas: an area for the imagemap, an area for entering values for the cost drivers, an area for entering KLOC and viewing the results, and an area containing the buttons. Figure 23.3 shows the main screen of the CostEstimator but has been annotated with lines that indicate the boundaries of these areas.

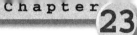
Figure 23.3.

The four main areas of
the CostEstimator
user interface.

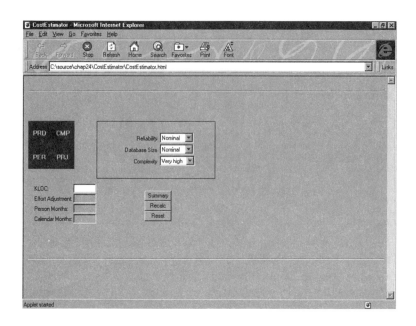

To create this interface, the init method of CostEstimator creates a new GridBagLayout layout manager and assigns it to the applet. The init method then calls four worker methods, each of which creates one of the areas shown in Figure 23.4. This can be seen in the init method, as shown here:

```
public void init()
{
  // Create a GridBagLayout and use it as the applet's
  // layout manager
  GridBagLayout layout = new GridBagLayout();
  setLayout(layout);
  // create each of the main areas of the user interface
  CreateImagemap(layout);
  CreateCardPanel(layout);
  CreateResultsPanel(layout);
  CreateButtonPanel(layout);
  resize(400, 320);
}
```

Creating the Imagemap

The first of the four areas on the applet user interface is an imagemap. An imagemap is a bitmap that includes selectable areas within it. In this case the imagemap is a bitmap showing abbreviations for each of four groupings of COCOMO cost drivers. When the user clicks the mouse over the PRD area of the imagemap, the product-related cost drivers are displayed to the right of the imagemap. Similarly, clicking the mouse over CMP displays the computer-related cost drivers, PER displays personnel-related cost drivers, and PRJ displays project-related cost drivers.

The method CreateImagemap is called from within init and is as shown here:

```
private void CreateImagemap(GridBagLayout parentLayout)
{
  // create the image
  Image image = getImage(getDocumentBase(), "map.gif");
  // create a canvas on which the image will be displayed
  imageCanvas = new ImageCanvas(image);
  // place the canvas on the applet using the applet's
  // layout manager
  GridBagConstraints gbc = new GridBagConstraints();
  gbc.gridwidth = GridBagConstraints.RELATIVE;
  gbc.fill = GridBagConstraints.BOTH;
  parentLayout.setConstraints(imageCanvas, gbc);
  add(imageCanvas);
}
```

This method loads the image map.gif from the applet's base directory. It then creates an image canvas based on the retrieved image. The image canvas is then placed on the applet using the parentLayout parameter. The ImageCanvas class encapsulates the details of the imagemap. ImageCanvas is shown in Listing 23.3.

Listing 23.3. The ImageCanvas class.

```
public class ImageCanvas extends Canvas
{
  private Image image;
  private Vector rects;
  private ImagemapRect lastrect;
  // construct an image canvas based on the specified image
  // and the currently selected portion of the imagemap
  ImageCanvas(Image image)
  {
    resize(50,50);
    this.image=image;
    // allocate a vector to hold the ImagemapRects
    rects = new Vector();
    // all the ImagemapRects that describe the hotspots
    // on the imagemap
    rects.addElement(new ImagemapRect(0,  0, 50, 50,
        "Product"));
    rects.addElement(new ImagemapRect(49, 0, 50, 50,
        "Computer"));
    rects.addElement(new ImagemapRect(0, 49, 50, 50,
        "Personnel"));
    rects.addElement(new ImagemapRect(49, 49, 50, 50,
        "Project"));
    // store the last selected ImagemapRect
    lastrect = (ImagemapRect)rects.elementAt(0);
  }
  public void paint(Graphics g)
  {
    // paint the image
    g.drawImage(image, 0, 0, this);
    // highlight the selected location
    g.setXORMode(Color.red);
```

Listing 23.3. continued

```
      g.drawRect(lastrect.x, lastrect.y, lastrect.width,
        lastrect.height);
      g.drawRect(lastrect.x+1, lastrect.y+1, lastrect.width-2,
        lastrect.height-2);
      g.drawRect(lastrect.x+2, lastrect.y+2, lastrect.width-4,
        lastrect.height-4);
  }
  // Determine if the mouse pointer was clicked over an area in
  // the imagemap that isn't already the current selection
  public boolean NewImageSelected(int x, int y,
      StringBuffer cardName)
  {
    boolean result = false;    // assume failure
    // normalize the coordinates relative to the ImageCanvas
    int xPos = x - bounds().x;
    int yPos = y - bounds().y;
    // determine which rectangle (if any) was selected
    ImagemapRect r = InWhichRect(xPos, yPos);
    // if a rectangle was selected and it isn't the same
    // one that is already selected, a new area has been
    // selected
    if (r != null && r != lastrect)
    {
      lastrect = r;
      cardName.append(r.cardName);
      result = true;
    }
    return result;
  }
  // determine which ImageMapRect (if any) the mouse pointer
  // is in
  private ImagemapRect InWhichRect(int x, int y)
  {
    // use an enumeration to move through each ImagemapRect
    // until finding one which encloses the point (x, y)
    for (Enumeration enum = rects.elements();
        enum.hasMoreElements(); )
    {
      ImagemapRect r = (ImagemapRect)enum.nextElement();
      if (r.inside(x, y))
        return r;
    }
    return null;
  }
}
```

ImageCanvas extends Canvas by drawing an image on the canvas and by storing a vector of areas that represent the selectable areas of the imagemap. The ImageCanvas constructor is passed the image that will be displayed and stores a reference to it. It then allocates a vector named rects and uses addElement to add four new instances of the ImageRect class to the vector.

The ImageRect class stores the location and dimensions of a rectangle and a name representing that area. For example, ImagemapRect(0, 49, 50, 50, "Personnel") creates an ImageRect named Personnel that begins at 0, 49 with both width and height of 50. The ImageRect class is written as follows:

```
class ImagemapRect extends Rectangle {
  String cardName;
  public ImagemapRect(int x, int y,int w,int h, String cardName)
  {
    super(x,y,w,h);
    this.cardName = cardName;
  }
}
```

The paint method for ImageCanvas uses drawImage to display the image. To indicate which area in the imagemap is currently selected, a red border is drawn around the most recently selected ImageRect. The member variable lastrect always holds the most recently selected ImageRect, so setXORMode and three calls to drawRect are used to draw the red border.

The methods NewImageSelected and InWhichRect are used to determine whether the user has clicked the mouse over an ImageRect within the imagemap. NewImageSelected is passed the x and y coordinates of the mouse click. It then normalizes these relative to the coordinates of the canvas using bounds. NewImageSelected then calls InWhichRect to determine in which ImagemapRect, if any, the mouse click occurred. If the mouse was clicked inside an ImagemapRect that is not the same as lastrect, the new value is stored in lastrect and the name of the selection is stored.

In the CostEstimator applet class it is necessary to override the mouseDown method to look for mouse button presses that occur when the mouse pointer is over the imagemap. This is done as shown here:

```
public boolean mouseDown(Event e, int x, int y)
{
  StringBuffer cardName = new StringBuffer();
  // if the button was pressed when the mouse pointer was
  // over the imagemap, get the name of the card to display
  // in the cardPanel.
  if (imageCanvas.NewImageSelected(x,y,cardName) == true) {
    cardLayout.show(cardPanel, cardName.toString());
    imageCanvas.repaint();
  }
  return true;
}
```

Selecting Project Attributes

The second area on the applet user interface is for entering values for the various cost drivers. The group of fields displayed in this area is controlled by the user's selection in the imagemap. Because this area is used to display different fields at different times, a panel is placed over this entire area, and a `CardLayout` is assigned as the panel's layout manager. Depending on the imagemap selection, the appropriate card is displayed on the panel. This can be seen in the following code:

```
private void CreateCardPanel(GridBagLayout parentLayout)
{
  // create the panel
  cardPanel = new Panel();
  // place the panel on the applet using the applet's
  // layout manager
  GridBagConstraints gbc = new GridBagConstraints();
  gbc.gridwidth = GridBagConstraints.REMAINDER;
  gbc.fill = GridBagConstraints.BOTH;
  gbc.weightx=1;
  parentLayout.setConstraints(cardPanel, gbc);
  add(cardPanel);
  // create a CardLayout and assign it to the panel
  cardLayout = new CardLayout();
  cardPanel.setLayout(cardLayout);
  // create a vector to hold the CostDriverPanels that
  // will be placed on cardPanel
  CostDriverPanelVector = new Vector(4);
  // create each of the panels that can be displayed
  // on this card
  CreateProductPanel();
  CreateComputerPanel();
  CreatePersonnelPanel();
  CreateProjectPanel();
}
```

The `CreateCardPanel` method allocates a new `Panel` instance named `cardPanel`. It then creates an instance of `GridBagConstraints` and establishes constraints that the panel is the last item on the line and that it should grow in both directions. The panel is added to the applet using `parentLayout`, the `GridBagLayout` layout manager that was allocated in `init` to handle the applet's overall layout.

Next, a new `CardLayout` is constructed and assigned to the panel. A four-element vector is then allocated. This vector will be used to store each of the four panels that will be placed on the `CardPanel` and that will be toggled using the imagemap. Finally, each of the four methods at the end of `CreateCardPanel` creates one of the panels displayed on `CardPanel`.

The `CostDriverPanel` Class

Each of the panels that will be placed on `CardPanel` will be of type `CostDriverPanel`. `CostDriverPanel`, however, is an abstract class. Two subclasses of `CostDriverPanel`, `ChoicePanel` and `ProjectPanel`, are provided and are concrete classes that can be constructed.

The `CostDriverPanel` class, as shown in Listing 23.4, provides an overridden `paint` method that draws a border around the panel. Additionally, three abstract methods (`getMultiplier`, `SetDefaults`, and `GetSummary`) are declared. The `getMultiplier` method is used to get the partial Effort Adjustment Factor for the cost drivers on the panel. The `SetDefaults` method is used to restore each of the cost drivers on the panel to its default value. `GetSummary` is used to generate a string summarizing the selections for the cost drivers on the panel.

Listing 23.4. CostDriverPanel.java.

```java
import java.applet.*;
import java.awt.*;
import java.util.*;
// This is an abstract base class that can be extended
// for displaying cost drivers
public abstract class CostDriverPanel extends Panel
{
  public CostDriverPanel()
  {
    super();
  }
  public void paint(Graphics g)
  {
    // draw a rectangle around the panel
    Rectangle rect = bounds();
    g.drawRect(rect.x, rect.y, rect.x+rect.width-1,
        rect.y + rect.height-1);
  }
  // calculate the effort adjustment multiplier for
  // the cost drivers on this panel
  public abstract float getMultiplier();
  // set the default values for all cost drivers on this panel
  public abstract void SetDefaults();
  // return a String summarizing selections on this panel
  public abstract String GetSummary();
}
```

The ChoicePanel Class

The ChoicePanel class is a non-abstract subclass of CostDriverPanel. A ChoicePanel can be used to automatically position and display cost drivers. Each cost driver will be displayed as a choice field. Figure 23.4 shows the ChoicePanel created using the personnel cost drivers.

Each ChoicePanel object contains the following member variables:

```java
Choice choiceArray[];
Vector costDrivers;
```

The choiceArray is an array of choice variables. One item is allocated in the array for each of the cost drivers displayed on the ChoicePanel. The costDrivers vector holds instances of the CostDriver class that was described earlier in this chapter. These variables are both used extensively in the ChoicePanel constructor, which is shown in Listing 23.5.

The constructor is passed a vector of CostDriver objects, and these are cloned into the costDrivers member variable. The choiceArray is allocated based on the size of this vector. Next, the layout manager for the ChoicePanel is constructed and assigned to the object. Because we want to place a Label and Choice objects on the same lines, a GridBagLayout is used.

Figure 23.4.

A ChoicePanel displaying personnel-related cost drivers.

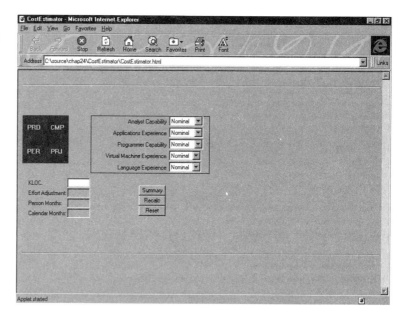

Listing 23.5. The `ChoicePanel` constructor.

```
public ChoicePanel(Vector drivers)
{
  super();    // construct the parent class
  // clone the drivers
  costDrivers = (Vector) drivers.clone();
  // allocate an array of Choice fields, each cost driver
  // will be entered in a Choice field
  choiceArray = new Choice[costDrivers.size()];
  // create and use a GridBagLayout layout manager
  GridBagLayout layout = new GridBagLayout();
  GridBagConstraints gbc = new GridBagConstraints();
  setLayout(layout);
  // use an enumeration to move through the cost drivers to
  // be displayed on this panel
  int i = 0;
  for (Enumeration e=costDrivers.elements();
      e.hasMoreElements(); i++)
  {
    CostDriver cd = (CostDriver)e.nextElement();
    // allocate a Choice for each cost driver
    choiceArray[i] = new Choice();
    // use an enumeration to move through the ratings
    // within each cost driver (e.g., Low, Nominal, High)
    for (Enumeration enum = cd.ratings.elements();
        enum.hasMoreElements() ;)
    {
      Rating r = (Rating)enum.nextElement();
      // add the name of the rating to the Choice
      choiceArray[i].addItem(r.name);
    }
```

```
      // select this item by default
      choiceArray[i].select("Nominal");
      // add the label to the panel
      gbc.gridwidth = 1;
      Label label = new Label(cd.name);
      gbc.anchor = GridBagConstraints.EAST;
      layout.setConstraints(label, gbc);
      add(label);
      // add the Choice field to the panel
      gbc.gridwidth = GridBagConstraints.REMAINDER;
      gbc.anchor = GridBagConstraints.WEST;
      gbc.insets.left=5;
      layout.setConstraints(choiceArray[i], gbc);
      add(choiceArray[i]);
   }
}
```

Next, an enumeration is used to move through the elements in the costDrivers vector. For each element, the CostDriver is cast into a local variable, cd, and an item in the choiceArray is allocated to hold the choice object that will contain the selections for this cost driver. After the elements are added to the choice, select("Nominal") is used to set the default item. Finally, a label and the choice are added to the panel.

Within the CostEstimator class, ChoicePanel objects are constructed for the product, computer, and personnel cost-estimator categories. The project category uses a different subclass of CostDriverPanel to display its cost drivers. These choice panels are created by the methods CreateProductPanel, CreateComputerPanel, and CreatePersonnelPanel. These methods are very similar. The CreatePersonnelPanel method is shown in Listing 23.6.

Listing 23.6. CreatePersonnelPanel in the CostEstimator class.

```
private void CreatePersonnelPanel()
{
   // allocate a vector that will hold the cost drivers
   // that are displayed on this panel
   Vector costDrivers = new Vector(5);
   // create a vector of Analyst Capability ratings
   Vector acapRatings = new Vector(5);
   acapRatings.addElement(new Rating("Very low",  1.46F));
   acapRatings.addElement(new Rating("Low",     1.19F));
   acapRatings.addElement(new Rating("Nominal",  1.00F));
   acapRatings.addElement(new Rating("High",      0.86F));
   acapRatings.addElement(new Rating("Very high", 0.71F));
   // create the Analyst Capability CostDriver and add it to
   // the vector
   costDrivers.addElement(new CostDriver("Analyst Capability",
      acapRatings));
   // create a vector of Applications Experience ratings
   Vector aexpRatings = new Vector(5);
   aexpRatings.addElement(new Rating("Very low",  1.29F));
   aexpRatings.addElement(new Rating("Low",      1.13F));
   aexpRatings.addElement(new Rating("Nominal",  1.00F));
```

continues

Listing 23.6. continued

```
    aexpRatings.addElement(new Rating("High",      0.91F));
    aexpRatings.addElement(new Rating("Very high", 0.82F));
    // create the Applications Experience CostDriver and add
    // it to the vector
    costDrivers.addElement(new CostDriver(
        "Applications Experience", aexpRatings));
    // create a vector of Programmer Capability ratings
    Vector pcapRatings = new Vector(5);
    pcapRatings.addElement(new Rating("Very low",  1.42F));
    pcapRatings.addElement(new Rating("Low",       1.17F));
    pcapRatings.addElement(new Rating("Nominal",   1.00F));
    pcapRatings.addElement(new Rating("High",      0.86F));
    pcapRatings.addElement(new Rating("Very high", 0.70F));
    // create the Programmer Capability CostDriver and add
    // it to the vector
    costDrivers.addElement(new CostDriver(
        "Programmer Capability", pcapRatings));
    // create a vector of Virtual Machine Experience ratings
    Vector vexpRatings = new Vector(4);
    vexpRatings.addElement(new Rating("Very low",  1.21F));
    vexpRatings.addElement(new Rating("Low",       1.10F));
    vexpRatings.addElement(new Rating("Nominal",   1.00F));
    vexpRatings.addElement(new Rating("High",      0.90F));
    // create the Virtual Machine Experience CostDriver and
    // add it to the vector
    costDrivers.addElement(new CostDriver(
        "Virtual Machine Experience", vexpRatings));
    // create a vector of Language Experience ratings
    Vector lexpRatings = new Vector(4);
    lexpRatings.addElement(new Rating("Very low",  1.14F));
    lexpRatings.addElement(new Rating("Low",       1.07F));
    lexpRatings.addElement(new Rating("Nominal",   1.00F));
    lexpRatings.addElement(new Rating("High",      0.95F));
    // create the Language Experience CostDriver and add
    // it to the vector
    costDrivers.addElement(new CostDriver(
        "Language Experience", lexpRatings));
    // create the new panel and add it to the card
    ChoicePanel personnelPanel = new ChoicePanel(costDrivers);
    cardPanel.add("Personnel", personnelPanel);

    // add this panel to the vector of all CostDriverPanels
    CostDriverPanelVector.addElement(personnelPanel);
}
```

CreatePersonnelPanel allocates a vector, costDrivers, that is used to hold the cost drivers that will be displayed when the personnel area of the imagemap has been selected. For each individual cost driver, a vector is allocated and addElement is used to add new Rating objects. As you saw earlier in this chapter, a Rating object is constructed with the name and value for the rating. For example, a Very Low rating for Language Experience is associated with an Effort Adjustment Factor of 1.14. After each of the vectors is created and added to costDrivers, a new choice panel is created and the new choice panel is added to the vector of all ChoicePanels.

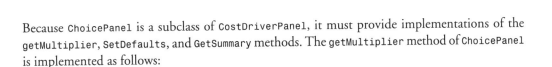

Because ChoicePanel is a subclass of CostDriverPanel, it must provide implementations of the getMultiplier, SetDefaults, and GetSummary methods. The getMultiplier method of ChoicePanel is implemented as follows:

```
public float getMultiplier()
{
  float value = 1.0f;
  int i = 0;
  // Use an enumeration to move through each of the cost
  // drivers on this panel.
  for (Enumeration e=costDrivers.elements();
      e.hasMoreElements(); i++)
  {
    // For each cost driver, get the rating associated
    // with the current selection in the Choice field.
    CostDriver cd = (CostDriver)e.nextElement();
    int index = choiceArray[i].getSelectedIndex();
    Rating r = (Rating)cd.ratings.elementAt(index);
    // multiply each of the multipliers together to
    // get the final result.
    value *= r.multiplier;
  }
  return value;
}
```

To calculate the multiplier, a local variable, value, is declared and set to 1.0 initially. An enumeration then steps through each of the cost drivers on the choice panel. For each cost driver, getSelectedIndex selects the item number of the selection for each cost driver. The rating associated with each item is then retrieved from cd.ratings.elementAt(index). As the enumeration proceeds through the cost drivers, the value is updated by multiplying it with the multiplier member in the Rating object, r.

The SetDefaults method is much simpler. All that is necessary is to loop through the items in the array of Choice objects using select to ensure that the item labeled Nominal is selected for each choice. This is done as shown here:

```
public void SetDefaults()
{
  int qty = costDrivers.size();
  for (int i=0; i < qty; i++)
    choiceArray[i].select("Nominal");
}
```

The GetSummary method is used to generate a string that summarizes the selections made on a choice panel. For example, a string summarizing the personnel category of cost drivers could appear as shown here:

```
Analyst Capability
  Nominal
  1
Applications Experience
  Nominal
  1
```

```
Programmer Capability
  Nominal
  1
Virtual Machine Experience
  Nominal
  1
Language Experience
  High
  0.95
```

The GetSummary method of ChoicePanel is written like this:

```java
public String GetSummary()
{
  StringBuffer buf = new StringBuffer();
  // use an enumeration to move through each of the drivers
  int i=0;
  for (Enumeration e=costDrivers.elements();
      e.hasMoreElements(); i++)
  {
    // append the name of the driver
    CostDriver cd = (CostDriver)e.nextElement();
    buf.append(cd.name+"\r\n");
    // append the name of the selected value
    buf.append("\t" + choiceArray[i].getSelectedItem() +
        "\r\n");
    // retrieve and then append the multiplier for the
    // selected value for this cost driver
    int index = choiceArray[i].getSelectedIndex();
    Rating r = (Rating)cd.ratings.elementAt(index);

    buf.append("\t" + r.multiplier + "\r\n");
  }
  return buf.toString();
}
```

As with many other ChoicePanel methods, an enumeration is used to move through the costDrivers vector. Because this method will be dynamically building a string of unknown length, a StringBuffer, rather than a String, is used to hold the text under construction. First, the name of the cost driver is added to the string buffer. Next, getSelectedItem is used to get the name of the selection for the Choice object. Finally, getSelectedIndex is used to get the index number of the selected item, and this value is passed to cd.ratings.elementAt to retrieve a Rating object. From this object, the Effort Adjustment Factor is read from r.multiplier and appended to the buffer.

The ProjectPanel Class

The ProjectPanel class, like ChoicePanel, is a subclass of CostDriverPanel. The ProjectPanel class is used only for displaying the project-related cost drivers. It is similar to ChoicePanel in that it also uses Choice objects to solicit user input. Choice objects, however, are used only for the Modern Practices and Software Tools cost drivers. Options for the Schedule Constraints cost driver are shown as a checkbox group, as shown in Figure 23.5.

Figure 23.5.

The ProjectPanel display-
ing the project-related
cost drivers.

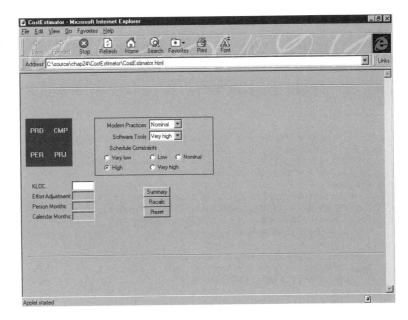

Because the ProjectPanel uses both Choice and Checkbox objects, the following member variables are defined in ProjectPanel:

```
Choice choiceArray[];
Vector costDrivers;
Vector cbVector;
CheckboxGroup cbGroup;
```

The choiceArray and costDrivers members are used in the same way each was used in ChoicePanel. The cbVector member holds the individual checkbox objects that are placed on the panel. The variable cbGroup is a CheckboxGroup that consists of all the checkboxes on the panel.

The ProjectPanel constructor is shown in Listing 23.7. After calling super to create the panel, the constructor calls the method LoadCostDrivers. This method, shown in Listing 23.8, is similar to the method CreatePersonnelPanel that was shown in Listing 23.6. All that LoadCostDrivers does is create the costDrivers vector that will be used throughout ProjectPanel's other methods.

Listing 23.7. The ProjectPanel constructor.

```
public ProjectPanel()
{
  super();
  LoadCostDrivers();      // load values into costDrivers
  // allocate an array of Choice fields that will hold
  // all but one cost driver
  int qty = costDrivers.size();
  choiceArray = new Choice[qty - 1];
  // create and use a GridBagLayout layout manager
```

continues

Listing 23.7. continued

```
GridBagLayout layout = new GridBagLayout();
GridBagConstraints gbc = new GridBagConstraints();
setLayout(layout);
// Loop through the cost drivers, creating a Choice field
// for each. Process all but the last one. The last one
// will be displayed using Checkboxes instead of a Choice
// field.
int i = 0;
for (i=0; i<qty-1; i++)
{
  CostDriver cd = (CostDriver)costDrivers.elementAt(i);
  // allocate a Choice for each cost driver
  choiceArray[i] = new Choice();
  // use an enumeration to move through the ratings
  // within each cost driver (e.g., Low, Nominal, High)
  for (Enumeration enum = cd.ratings.elements();
      enum.hasMoreElements() ;)
  {
    Rating r = (Rating)enum.nextElement();
    // add the name of the rating to the Choice
    choiceArray[i].addItem(r.name);
  }
  // select this item by default
  choiceArray[i].select("Nominal");
  // add the label to the panel
  gbc.gridwidth = 1;
  Label label = new Label(cd.name);
  gbc.anchor = GridBagConstraints.EAST;
  layout.setConstraints(label, gbc);
  add(label);
  // add the Choice field to the panel
  gbc.gridwidth = GridBagConstraints.REMAINDER;
  gbc.anchor = GridBagConstraints.WEST;
  gbc.insets.left=5;
  layout.setConstraints(choiceArray[i], gbc);
  add(choiceArray[i]);
}
// use the last cost driver to make a CheckboxGroup
CostDriver cd = (CostDriver)costDrivers.elementAt(qty-1);
// create a vector to hold the Checkboxes
cbVector = new Vector(6);
// add the label for the Checkbox group
gbc.gridwidth = 1;
Label label = new Label(cd.name);
gbc.gridwidth = GridBagConstraints.REMAINDER;
gbc.anchor = GridBagConstraints.WEST;
layout.setConstraints(label, gbc);
add(label);
// keep track of how many items are on each line, so that
// items can be properly positioned.
int itemsOnLine=0;
// create a new CheckboxGroup
cbGroup = new CheckboxGroup();
// all the checkbox items will be anchored on the west
// side, so set this value before the loop
gbc.anchor = GridBagConstraints.WEST;
```

```
  // use an enumeration to move through the ratings for the
  // cost driver
  for (Enumeration enum = cd.ratings.elements();
      enum.hasMoreElements(); itemsOnLine++)
  {
    Rating r = (Rating)enum.nextElement();
    // the "Nominal" item should be checked by default
    boolean checked = r.name.equals("Nominal");
    // if line is almost full of items, tell this item to
    // use the remainder of the space
    if (itemsOnLine == 2)
    {
      gbc.gridwidth = GridBagConstraints.REMAINDER;
      itemsOnLine = 0;
    }
    else
      gbc.gridwidth = 1;
    // create the new checkbox and add it to the screen
    Checkbox cb = new Checkbox(r.name, cbGroup, checked);
    layout.setConstraints(cb, gbc);
    add(cb);
    // then add it to the vector of checkboxes
    cbVector.addElement(cb);
  }
}
```

Listing 23.8. The `ProjectPanel.LoadCostDrivers` method.

```
private void LoadCostDrivers()
{
  // allocate a vector that will hold the cost drivers
  // that are displayed on this panel
  costDrivers = new Vector(3);
  // create a vector of Modern Practices ratings
  Vector modpRatings = new Vector(5);
  modpRatings.addElement(new Rating("Very low",  1.24F));
  modpRatings.addElement(new Rating("Low",       1.10F));
  modpRatings.addElement(new Rating("Nominal",   1.00F));
  modpRatings.addElement(new Rating("High",      0.91F));
  modpRatings.addElement(new Rating("Very high", 0.82F));
  // create the Modern Practices CostDriver and add it to
  // the vector
  costDrivers.addElement(new CostDriver("Modern Practices",
      modpRatings));
  // create a vector of Software Tools ratings
  Vector toolRatings = new Vector(5);
  toolRatings.addElement(new Rating("Very low",  1.24F));
  toolRatings.addElement(new Rating("Low",       1.10F));
  toolRatings.addElement(new Rating("Nominal",   1.00F));
  toolRatings.addElement(new Rating("High",      0.91F));
  toolRatings.addElement(new Rating("Very high", 0.83F));
  // create the Software Tools CostDriver and add it to
  // the vector
  costDrivers.addElement(new CostDriver("Software Tools",
      toolRatings));
```

continues

Listing 23.8. continued

```
    // create a vector of Schedule Constraints ratings
    Vector scedRatings = new Vector(5);
    scedRatings.addElement(new Rating("Very low",  1.23F));
    scedRatings.addElement(new Rating("Low",       1.08F));
    scedRatings.addElement(new Rating("Nominal",   1.00F));
    scedRatings.addElement(new Rating("High",      1.04F));
    scedRatings.addElement(new Rating("Very high", 1.10F));
    // create the Schedule Constraints CostDriver and add
    // it to the vector
    costDrivers.addElement(new CostDriver(
        "Schedule Constraints",  scedRatings));
}
```

After the costDrivers vector has been loaded, a for loop is used to iterate through all but the last cost driver on this panel. The last driver is skipped because it will be displayed using checkboxes. To do this, the last element in the costDrivers vector is cast into the variable cd as shown here:

```
CostDriver cd = (CostDriver)costDrivers.elementAt(qty-1);
```

Next, cbVector is allocated to hold up to six elements, the most required by any COCOMO cost driver. After adding a label to the display, the variable itemsOnLine is set to 0. This variable will be used to count how many checkbox objects have been placed on the current line so that the layout manager can be correctly told when to move to the next line in the layout.

After a new CheckboxGroup object is constructed and placed in cbGroup, the GridBagConstraints are set to WEST. This means that items will be aligned along their left edges. Because this constraint holds true for all the checkbox items, the constraint is set outside the loop. The loop uses an enumeration to move through the ratings associated with this cost driver. Before each new checkbox is added, checks are made to determine whether the current item is the default item (in which case its name is Nominal) and to ensure that no more than three checkboxes are on any line.

ProjectPanel is a subclass of CostDriverPanel, and therefore it provides implementations of getMultiplier, SetDefaults, and GetSummary. Each of these methods is similar to the equivalent method in ChoicePanel, with the addition of retrieving or setting a value in a checkbox. Because these methods are so similar, they are not described here but are included on the CD that accompanies this book.

The Results Panel

The third area of the CostEstimator user interface is the results panel. As you saw in Figure 23.4, the results panel is displayed at the lower left of the applet's main screen. Creating the results panel is a relatively straightforward process. To maintain precise control over the placement of objects on the screen, however, a GridBagLayout layout manager is used. This makes the CreateResultsPanel method, shown in Listing 23.9, fairly long.

Listing 23.9. The `CreateResultsPanel` method in `CostEstimator`.

```
private void CreateResultsPanel(GridBagLayout parentLayout)
{
  // create a panel and add it to the applet using the
  // applet's layout manager
  Panel p = new Panel();
  GridBagConstraints gbc = new GridBagConstraints();
  gbc.gridwidth = GridBagConstraints.RELATIVE;
  gbc.fill = GridBagConstraints.BOTH;
  parentLayout.setConstraints(p, gbc);
  add(p);
  // create and assign a GridBagLayout as the layout manager
  // for this panel
  GridBagLayout layout = new GridBagLayout();
  p.setLayout(layout);
  // place some space at the top of the panel
  Panel space = new Panel();
  gbc.gridheight =3;
  gbc.weighty =1;
  gbc.gridwidth = GridBagConstraints.REMAINDER;
  gbc.fill = GridBagConstraints.BOTH;
  layout.setConstraints(space, gbc);
  p.add(space);
  gbc.weighty = 0;
  // create a Label and TextField for KLOC
  Label klocLabel = new Label("KLOC:");
  gbc.gridheight = 1;
  gbc.gridwidth = GridBagConstraints.RELATIVE;
  layout.setConstraints(klocLabel, gbc);
  p.add(klocLabel);
  gbc.gridwidth = GridBagConstraints.REMAINDER;
  klocField = new TextField(5);
  layout.setConstraints(klocField, gbc);
  p.add(klocField);
  // create a Label and TextField for Effort Adjustment
  Label effortAdjustLabel = new Label("Effort Adjustment:");
  gbc.gridwidth = GridBagConstraints.RELATIVE;
  layout.setConstraints(effortAdjustLabel, gbc);
  p.add(effortAdjustLabel);
  gbc.gridwidth = GridBagConstraints.REMAINDER;
  effortAdjustmentField = new TextField(5);
  // make the field read-only
  effortAdjustmentField.setEditable(false);
  layout.setConstraints(effortAdjustmentField, gbc);
  p.add(effortAdjustmentField);
  // create a Label and TextField for Person Months
  Label personMonthsLabel = new Label("Person Months:");
  gbc.gridwidth = GridBagConstraints.RELATIVE;
  layout.setConstraints(personMonthsLabel, gbc);
  p.add(personMonthsLabel);
  gbc.gridwidth = GridBagConstraints.REMAINDER;
  personMonthsField = new TextField(5);
  // make the field read-only
  personMonthsField.setEditable(false);
  layout.setConstraints(personMonthsField, gbc);
  p.add(personMonthsField);
  // create a Label and TextField for Calendar Months
```

continues

Listing 23.9. continued

```
Label calendarMonthsLabel = new Label("Calendar Months:");
gbc.gridwidth = GridBagConstraints.RELATIVE;
layout.setConstraints(calendarMonthsLabel, gbc);
p.add(calendarMonthsLabel);
gbc.gridwidth = GridBagConstraints.REMAINDER;
calendarMonthsField = new TextField(5);
// make the field read-only
calendarMonthsField.setEditable(false);
layout.setConstraints(calendarMonthsField, gbc);
p.add(calendarMonthsField);
// create some space at the bottom of the panel
// so the fields above are properly located
space = new Panel();
gbc.gridheight =3;
gbc.weighty =1;
gbc.gridwidth = GridBagConstraints.REMAINDER;
gbc.fill = GridBagConstraints.BOTH;
layout.setConstraints(space, gbc);
p.add(space);
}
```

The key to understanding CreateResultsPanel is understanding the various panels that are used. Overall, a panel is created and added to the applet. This panel is the full size of the results area of the user interface. Both this panel and the applet it is placed on use GridBagLayout as their layout manager. On this large panel, the following smaller panels are placed:

- ○ An empty panel
- ○ A panel containing the labels and text fields
- ○ Another empty panel

The empty panels are both created with the following GridBagConstraints:

```
gbc.gridheight =3;
gbc.weighty =1;
gbc.gridwidth = GridBagConstraints.REMAINDER;
gbc.fill = GridBagConstraints.BOTH;
```

These constraints allow the empty panels to fill up the vertical space evenly, thereby centering the panel that contains the labels and text fields.

Creating the Button Panel

The final part of the CostEstimator applet's user interface is the set of three buttons at the bottom right of the applet's main screen. As shown in Figure 23.4, the buttons are labeled Summary, Recalc, and Reset. These buttons are created by the CreateButtonPanel method shown in Listing 23.10.

Listing 23.10. The CreateButtonPanel method in CostEstimator.

```
private void CreateButtonPanel(GridBagLayout parentLayout)
{
  // create a panel and add it to the applet using the
  // applet's layout manager
  Panel p = new Panel();
  GridBagConstraints gbc = new GridBagConstraints();
  gbc.gridwidth = GridBagConstraints.REMAINDER;
  parentLayout.setConstraints(p, gbc);
  add(p);
  // create and assign a GridBagLayout as the layout manager
  // for this panel
  GridBagLayout layout = new GridBagLayout();
  p.setLayout(layout);
  // place some space above the buttons
  Panel space = new Panel();
  gbc.gridheight =3;
  gbc.weighty =1;
  gbc.gridwidth = GridBagConstraints.REMAINDER;
  gbc.fill = GridBagConstraints.BOTH;
  layout.setConstraints(space, gbc);
  p.add(space);
  // place some space to the left of the buttons
  space = new Panel();
  gbc.gridheight = 4;
  gbc.weighty = 1;
  gbc.gridwidth = GridBagConstraints.RELATIVE;
  gbc.weightx=1;
  layout.setConstraints(space, gbc);
  p.add(space);
  gbc.gridheight = 1;
  gbc.gridwidth = GridBagConstraints.REMAINDER;
  // add the Summary button
  gbc.fill = GridBagConstraints.HORIZONTAL;
  gbc.weightx =1;
  gbc.anchor = GridBagConstraints.EAST;
  Button b = new Button("Summary");
  layout.setConstraints(b, gbc);
  p.add(b);
  // add the Recalc button
  b = new Button("Recalc");
  layout.setConstraints(b, gbc);
  p.add(b);
  // add the Reset button
  b = new Button("Reset");
  layout.setConstraints(b, gbc);
  p.add(b);
}
```

CreateButtonPanel works much like CreateResultsPanel. First, a panel is constructed and placed onto the applet. Then a panel named space is constructed and placed across the top of the large panel. Next, another panel is constructed and also stored in the space variable. This panel is then assigned the following GridBagConstraints:

```
gbc.gridheight = 4;
gbc.weighty = 1;
gbc.gridwidth = GridBagConstraints.RELATIVE;
gbc.weightx=1;
```

These constraints will cause the panel to be aligned vertically along the left edge of the panel, beginning just below the previously placed panel. This is shown in Figure 23.6. After the empty panels have been placed, the three buttons are constructed and added.

Figure 23.6.

Two empty panels are placed on a larger panel to create the Button panel.

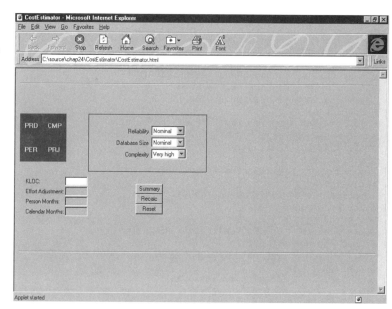

The CostEstimator Buttons

To respond to button presses, it is necessary to include an action method in the CostEstimator class. In this case the action method checks the label of the button and then simply calls an appropriate method based on which button was pressed. This is carried out in the following way:

```
public boolean action(Event evt, Object obj)
{
  boolean result=false;
  if("Reset".equals(obj))
  {
    DoReset();
    result = true;
  }
  else if("Recalc".equals(obj))
  {
    DoRecalc();
```

```
      result = true;
   }
   else if("Summary".equals(obj))
   {
      ShowSummary();
      result = true;
   }
   return result;
}
```

Resetting Default Values

If the Reset button has been pressed, the `DoReset` method is called. This method is written as follows:

```
private void DoReset()
{
   // use an enumeration to move through the CostDriverPanels
   for (Enumeration enum = CostDriverPanelVector.elements();
         enum.hasMoreElements(); )
   {
      // for each panel, call SetDefaults
      CostDriverPanel p = (CostDriverPanel)enum.nextElement();
      p.SetDefaults();
   }
}
```

`DoReset` uses the `CostDriverPanelVector` that contains a reference to each of the `CostDriverPanels`. This vector includes three `ChoicePanel` objects (for the product, computer, and personnel cost driver categories) and one `ProjectPanel` object. An enumeration is used to move through the vector, and for each item the `SetDefaults` method is called. Because `SetDefaults` was declared as abstract in `CostDriverPanel` and was overridden in `ChoicePanel` and `ProjectPanel`, the implementations of `SetDefaults` in these subclasses will be called.

Estimating the Project Schedule

Selecting the Recalc button causes the `DoRecalc` method to be executed. This method is shown in Listing 23.11. `DoRecalc` reads the user's entry from the `klocField` text field. This field should contain the number of lines of code in thousands. Because `klocField` might be blank or contain non-numeric entries, however, the call to `Float.valueOf(klocField.getText())` is enclosed in a `try...catch` block that will catch the exception `NumberFormatException` that could be thrown.

Listing 23.11. The `DoRecalc` method in the `CostEstimator` class.

```
private void DoRecalc()
{
   try
   {
      // make sure a number was entered in klocField
```

Listing 23.11. continued

```
    Float kloc = Float.valueOf(klocField.getText());
    // for this level of semidetached COCOMO, start with
    // 1.12 as the base effort adjustment factor
    float effortAdjustment = 1.12F;
    // calculate the Effort Adjustment Factor by calling
    // getMultiplier for each CostDriverPanel
    for (Enumeration e=CostDriverPanelVector.elements();
        e.hasMoreElements(); )
    {
      CostDriverPanel p = (CostDriverPanel)e.nextElement();
      effortAdjustment *= p.getMultiplier();
    }
    // display the Effort Adjustment Factor
    effortAdjustmentField.setText(String.valueOf(
        effortAdjustment));
    // calculate and display the number of person months
    // on the project
    int personMonths=(int)(3.0D*(Math.pow(kloc.floatValue(),
        effortAdjustment)));
    personMonthsField.setText(String.valueOf(personMonths));
    // calculate and display the number of calendar months
    // on the project
    double calendarMonths=2.5*(Math.pow(personMonths, 0.35F));
    calendarMonthsField.setText(String.valueOf(Math.round(
        calendarMonths)));
  }
  catch (NumberFormatException e)
  {
    // if klocField doesn't contain a number, set all
    // the fields to blank
    effortAdjustmentField.setText("");
    personMonthsField.setText("");
    calendarMonthsField.setText("");
  }
}
```

Next, the Effort Adjustment Factor is calculated by setting the variable effortAdjustment to 1.12 initially and then multiplying effortAdjustment by the multiplier calculated for each cost driver category. After the Effort Adjustment Factor is calculated, it is displayed in the effortAdjustmentField with the following code:

```
effortAdjustmentField.setText(String.valueOf(effortAdjustment));
```

After the Effort Adjustment Factor has been calculated, the estimated person months and calendar months are calculated. These calculations are performed according to the intermediate COCOMO equations described earlier in this chapter. When calculated, each of these fields is displayed using setText.

Summarizing Project Attributes

The CostEstimator applet's final button is the Summary button. Pressing this button causes a new instance of the SummaryFrame class to be constructed and shown. This is achieved by the method ShowSummary, which appears as shown here:

```
private void ShowSummary()
{
  SummaryFrame frame=new SummaryFrame(CostDriverPanelVector);
  frame.show();
}
```

The SummaryFrame Class

The SummaryFrame class is used to display text summarizing the selections the user has made describing the project being estimated. Figure 23.7 shows a sample SummaryFrame and examples of the text that could appear within it. As you can see in this figure, for each cost driver the name of the cost driver is given, along with the user's selection and the multiplier associated with that selection.

Figure 23.7.

A SummaryFrame summarizes the cost driver selections.

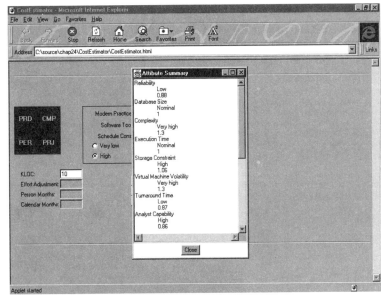

The SummaryFrame class, shown in Listing 23.12, is a subclass of Frame. The SummaryFrame constructor is passed a vector named CostDriverPanelVector. This is the vector that contains an element for each category panel. An enumeration is used to move through each entry in this vector. For each item the GetSummary method is invoked. The string returned by GetSummary is appended to the text area that is displayed on the SummaryFrame.

Listing 23.12. The `SummaryFrame` class.

```
class SummaryFrame extends Frame {
  private TextArea Summary; // text area for displaying results
  public SummaryFrame(Vector CostDriverPanelVector)
  {
    super("Attibute Summary");
    // create the TextArea for displaying the results
    Summary = new TextArea(10, 25);
    add("Center", Summary);
    // use an enumeration to move through each
    // CostDriverPanel
    for (Enumeration enum = CostDriverPanelVector.elements();
        enum.hasMoreElements(); )
    {
      // for each CostDriverPanel, use the GetSummary method
      // to retrieve a String summarizing the values on
// that panel
      CostDriverPanel p = (CostDriverPanel)enum.nextElement();
      Summary.appendText(p.GetSummary());
    }
    // create a panel and put a Close button on it at the
    // bottom of the frame
    Panel p = new Panel();
    p.add(new Button("Close"));
    add("South", p);
    resize(250, 400);
  }
  public boolean action(Event evt, Object arg)
  {
    boolean result = false;
    // if the Close button is pressed, dispose of the frame
    if("Close".equals(evt.arg)) {
      dispose();
      result = true;
    }
    return result;
  }
}
```

A Close button is added to the frame. The `action` method of the `SummaryFrame` class watches for a press of this button. When the Close button is detected, the SummaryFrame is disposed of.

Summary

In this chapter you combined much of what you learned in previous chapters to create a useful real-world applet. The CostEstimator involved some in-depth user interface programming and provided opportunities to work with vectors and arrays. You also learned about imagemaps and how to use an imagemap to control the appearance of an applet.

You should not stop here, however. You could extend this applet in many ways. For example, you could create a new subclass of `CostDriverPanel` that allows data entry with scrollbars. Or you could draw a pie graph showing the relative impact of each cost driver. You could use the Data Access Objects to store projects in a database and then support comparisons between different projects.

24

Development Request Online

This chapter develops a sample applet that can be used to submit Development Request forms to a database server and to track their progress. It covers many of the aspects that have been covered throughout this book, with an added emphasis on storing the collected information in an Access database.

Project Overview

This chapter features the creation of an applet that replaces a typical office form with a Web site. Any form from any office can be put on a Web site, allowing universal access. This enables a variety of users, from marketing geeks to programmers to managers, to quickly get an idea of the state of certain requests. Figure 24.1 shows an example of a Development Request form.

For the sake of brevity, only a few of the possible fields were added to this example. However, I encourage developers to enhance this applet so that it contains all of the fields required to take that next step toward a paperless office.

DevRequest Applet

The DevRequest applet has three basic screens, as described in Table 24.1.

Table 24.1. DevRequest screens.

Screen	Purpose
Login	Enables the user to log into the system with a username and password.
Control	The main screen of the applet, used to enter and review requests in the system.
Administration	Enables an administrator of the system to enter and modify both users and departments tracked by the system.

The login screen simply enables the user to access the system by entering a username and the associated password. It is assumed that the first administrator entry is entered by another means (for example, using Microsoft Access). However, a "back door" could have easily been incorporated into DevRequest. Figure 24.2 shows the login screen.

The main screen of the applet is displayed immediately after the user has logged in. Figure 24.3 shows the control screen.

Figure 24.1.

Example of a request form to be put online.

ITG Tracking Number_____

ITG Development Request

Please use this form if you have a ITG request to investigate a new system capability or development initiative

Your Name: **Date Requested**

Product (s) Involved:

Description of desired enhancement or capability:

Impact on business and functional groups (sales, marketing, clinical, etc.) affected if enhancement is developed?

Does exisiting budget in your area include this development? (y/n)
Department?
If not, are you aware of other departments with budget earmarked for this developed or a client commitment to pay for development?

Priority Assigned by Executive Committee:

☐ **Immediate** (*push other projects and release immediately*)
☐ **High** (*dedicate resources and include in next release*)
☐ **Medium** (*include in next release if resources permit*)
☐ **Low** (*include in future releases as appropriate*)
☐ **Do Not Develop at This Time**

Projected Completion Date:_____

Date Started:_____ ITG Project Lead:_____

Date completed:_____ Customer Champion:_____

Figure 24.2.
The DevRequest login
screen.

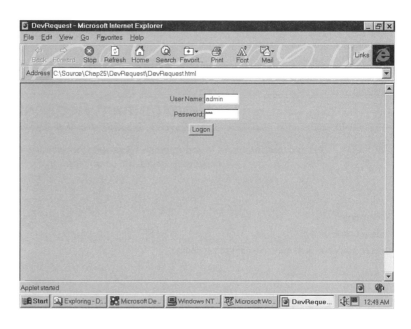

Figure 24.3.
The DevRequest control
screen.

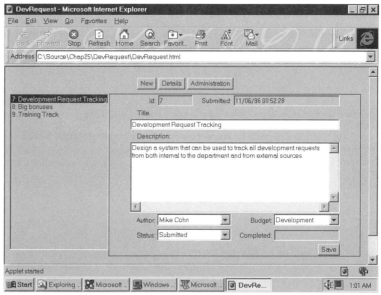

Using this screen, the user can see a list of all requests in the system by tracking ID and title in the list at the left of the screen. In addition, if a request is highlighted in the list, the user can select the Details button, displaying all of the information about the request on the right side of the screen.

This information includes the title and complete description of the request, when and by whom the request was submitted, the budget in which the resources to complete the request are allocated, and the current status of the request. If the New button is pressed, the currently displayed details will be cleared and the controls will be readied for a new request to be entered. Any modifications that are made to either an existing or new request can be saved to the database by using the Save button located at the bottom of the details form.

When the user is an administrator, the Administration button will bring up the screen in Figure 24.4.

Figure 24.4.
The DevRequest administration screen.

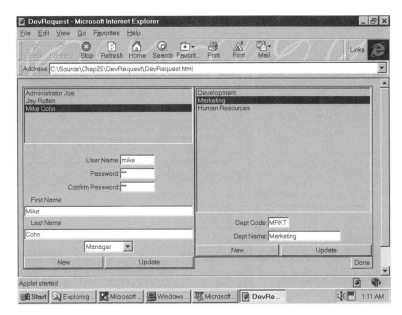

This screen is used to update both the operator and department tables. An operator is simply a user of the system. The department indicates through which budget requests are funded. All of the pertinent information about each of these entities can be updated, or new entities can be added, using this screen.

Class Overview

The classes used in the DevRequest applet are diagrammed in Figure 24.5. Classes whose names are italicized are specific to this applet. Classes without italicized names are standard Java classes used as base classes for DevRequest classes. A short summary for each class can be found in Table 24.2.

Figure 24.5.

DevRequest class overview.

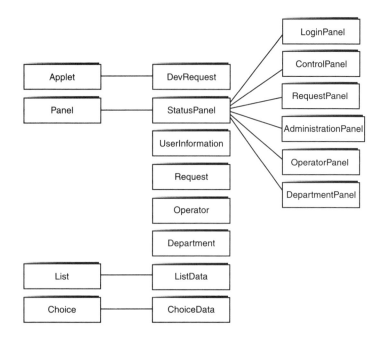

Table 24.2. DevRequest class summary.

Class	*Extends*	*Description*
DevRequest	Applet	Main class of the applet that contains the login, control, and administration screens.
UserInformation		Utility class that holds information about the current user. Provides a mechanism to control the flow of the screens.
StatusPanel	Panel	Base class for panels in the system providing basic messaging capabilities.
LoginPanel	StatusPanel	Contains the controls used to log into the system.
ControlPanel	StatusPanel	Contains the controls used to display and modify requests in the system.
RequestPanel	StatusPanel	Contains the controls used to display the detail information of a request.
Request		Holds information about a single request. Also used to read and write request information from and to the database.
AdministrationPanel	StatusPanel	Contains the controls used to perform administration duties on the database.

Class	Extends	Description
OperatorPanel	StatusPanel	Contains the controls used to display a list and details of the operators of the system.
Operator		Holds information about a single operator. Also used to read and write operator information from and to the database.
DepartmentPanel	StatusPanel	Contains the controls used to display a list and details of the departments of the system.
Department		Holds information about a single department. Also used to read and write department information from and to the database.
ListData	List	Associates a data item with each item in the list.
ChoiceData	Choice	Associates a data item with each item in the drop-down list.

The DevRequest applet uses a CardLayout to display each of the three main screens of the system. The information in UserInformation is used to track who is logged onto the system. It controls which of the cards is currently being displayed and what is to be displayed next. Each panel of the CardLayout contains either just controls, or displays its information in additional panels so as to help divide the display functionality into logical groupings. All database access is contained within the low-level entity classes: Request, Operator, and Department. Additional utility classes are provided to aid in displaying messages to the user and associate database information with list items.

Database Schema

The storage of all of the collected information is in a Microsoft Access database. There are three tables involved, as can been seen in Table 24.3.

Table 24.3. Types of storage tables.

Table	Description
REQUEST	Contains all of the information stored for each request, such as title, submission date, and so on.
OPERATOR	Contains all of the information stored for each operator (user) of the system, such as username, password, access level, and so on.
DEPARTMENT	Contains all of the information stored for each department, such as department code and name.

Figure 24.6 contains that physical database model. The arrows on the drawing represent referential integrity constraints. This means that the column from which the arrow originates must exist as a primary key of the table to which it points. For the DevRequest model, the relationship exists that each requester must be an operator in the system. Additionally, the approved budget must come from a department registered in the system.

That covers the basics of the applet. The remaining sections of this chapter cover the implementation details.

Figure 24.6.

DevRequest physical database model.

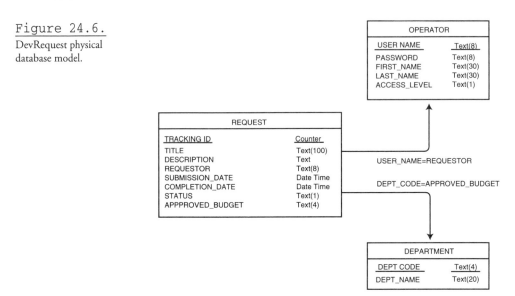

Access to the Data

All of the data for this applet is stored in a Microsoft Access database consisting of three tables: REQUEST, OPERATOR, and DEPARTMENT. The information will be retrieved using the Microsoft Data Access Objects (DAO). For more information on the nuts and bolts of DAO, see Chapter 22, "Using the Data Access Object." In this applet, the information retrieved can be logically grouped based on the tables from which it is being retrieved. Therefore, there are three corresponding Java classes that handle access to these tables: Request, Operators, and Departments.

Request

`Request` is used to hold and access database information about a single request. This is one of the key classes in the database. There are several members of the class that hold the request information:

```
public int TrackingId;
public Operator Requestor;
public String Title;
public String Description;
public Date SubmissionDate;
public Date CompletionDate;
public String Status;
public Department ApprovedBudget;
```

Each of the fields corresponds directly to a column in the REQUEST table.

Additionally, two sets of constant values are defined. The first set is for general use and contains values that indicate the state of the object:

```
public final static Date DATE_NOT_SET = new Date(0);
public final static int NEW_REQUEST_ID = -1;
```

`DATE_NOT_SET` is used to indicate that a date has not been assigned a value. Because this is a `Date` instance, it is pretty hard to store a flag in the class to show a special kind of date. However, it is pretty safe to assume that there never will be a submission date or completion date before January 1, 1970, which is the value to which this constant is set. `NEW_REQUEST_ID` is used to flag that a request is a new request; all existing requests will have an ID greater than 0.

The status of a request can be one of four predefined values. The values that are stored in the database are given by the following constants strings:

```
public final static String SUBMITTED = "S";
public final static String APPROVED  = "A";
public final static String COMPLETED = "C";
public final static String POSTPONED = "P";
```

There are three key methods in the class: `read`, `write`, and `readAll`. `read` is used to read the details of a request. It assumes that the tracking ID of the desired request is set when this method is called. Listing 24.1 contains this method.

Listing 24.1. The read method of class `Request`.

```
public boolean read(Database db)
{
    boolean retval = false;       // assume database error
    String command = "select * from REQUEST where TRACKING_ID = " +
            Integer.toString(TrackingId);
    Variant type = new Variant();
    Variant options = new Variant();
```

continues

Listing 24.1. continued

```
Variant fieldName = new Variant();
Variant fieldValue = new Variant();
type.putShort(Constants.dbOpenDynaset);
options.putShort(Constants.dbReadOnly);
// create the recordset and get the number of records returned
Recordset recordset = db.OpenRecordset(command, type, options);
int recordCount = recordset.getRecordCount();
// retrieve the first row
if (recordCount > 0) {
    recordset.MoveFirst();
    // get the fields of the row
    Fields fields = recordset.getFields();
    _Field field;
    // retrieve all of the information and store it
    fieldName.putString("TITLE");
    field = fields.getItem(fieldName);
    fieldValue = field.getValue();
    Title = fieldValue.toString();
    fieldName.putString("DESCRIPTION");
    field = fields.getItem(fieldName);
    fieldValue = field.getValue();
    Description = fieldValue.toString();
    fieldName.putString("REQUESTOR");
    field = fields.getItem(fieldName);
    fieldValue = field.getValue();
    Requestor.setUserName(fieldValue.toString());
    fieldName.putString("SUBMISSION_DATE");
    field = fields.getItem(fieldName);
    fieldValue = field.getValue();
    SubmissionDate = new Date(fieldValue.toString());
    fieldName.putString("COMPLETION_DATE");
    field = fields.getItem(fieldName);
    fieldValue = field.getValue();
    if (fieldValue.getvt() != Variant.VariantNull)
        CompletionDate = new Date(fieldValue.toString());
    fieldName.putString("STATUS");
    field = fields.getItem(fieldName);
    fieldValue = field.getValue();
    Status = fieldValue.toString();
    fieldName.putString("APPROVED_BUDGET");
    field = fields.getItem(fieldName);
    fieldValue = field.getValue();
    ApprovedBudget.setCode(fieldValue.toString());
    retval = true;
}
if (retval)
{
    retval = Requestor.read(db);
    if (retval)
        retval = ApprovedBudget.read(db);
}
return retval;
}
```

The first task is to determine the defining mechanism for the recordset to be returned. This is accomplished with the following SQL statement, which returns all REQUEST columns for the request with the given ID:

```
String command = "select * from REQUEST where TRACKING_ID = " +
        Integer.toString(TrackingId);
```

Next, a recordset that contains the information selected by the SQL statement is opened. Since the ID is the primary key of the table, only a single row is returned. Therefore, the record count returned is used to flag the success of the record set retrieval. The next rather large section of code is used to retrieve the individual fields of the row. The process is common throughout the applet and consists of the following steps:

1. Load the name of the field in the field name Variant.

2. Get the field from the fields of the record.

3. Get the value of the field returned.

4. Convert the value of the Variant value returned to a usable type and store that information.

The final task to be completed in the read method is to read in the requester information and the approved budget-department information.

The write method is used to insert a new request into the database or update an existing request. This method assumes that the fields of the current instance of the Request class have been updated with the latest information. Notice that this class has very little, if any, coupling with any interface components being used to gather this information. This allows this class to have the potential of being reused in a number of situations. Listing 24.2 contains the write method.

Listing 24.2. The write method of class Request.

```
public void write(Database db)
{
    StringBuffer command = new StringBuffer();
    // set completion date if needed
    if (Status.equals(COMPLETED) && CompletionDate.equals(DATE_NOT_SET))
        CompletionDate = new Date();
    if (TrackingId == NEW_REQUEST_ID)
    {
        command.append("insert into REQUEST(TITLE,DESCRIPTION,");
        command.append("REQUESTOR,SUBMISSION_DATE,COMPLETION_DATE,");
        command.append("STATUS,APPROVED_BUDGET) values(");
        command.append("'" + Title + "',");
        command.append("'" + Description + "',");
        command.append("'" + Requestor.UserName + "',");
        command.append("'" + SubmissionDate.toLocaleString() + "',");
        command.append((CompletionDate != DATE_NOT_SET) ?
                "'" + CompletionDate.toLocaleString() + "'," : "NULL,");
```

continues

539

Listing 24.2. continued

```
            command.append((Status != null) ? "'" + Status + "'," : "NULL,");
            command.append("'" + ApprovedBudget.Code + "')");
    }
    else
    {
            command.append("update REQUEST set ");
            command.append("TITLE = '" + Title + "',");
            command.append("DESCRIPTION = '" + Description + "',");
            command.append("REQUESTOR = '" + Requestor.UserName + "',");
            command.append("SUBMISSION_DATE = '" +
                    SubmissionDate.toLocaleString() + "',");
            command.append("COMPLETION_DATE = ");
            command.append((CompletionDate != DATE_NOT_SET) ?
                    "'" + CompletionDate.toLocaleString() + "'," : "NULL,");
            command.append("STATUS = ");
            command.append((Status != null) ? "'" + Status + "'," : "NULL,");
            command.append("APPROVED_BUDGET = '" + ApprovedBudget.Code + "' ");
            command.append("where TRACKING_ID = " +
                    Integer.toString(TrackingId));
    }
    Variant options = new Variant();
    options.putShort(Constants.dbFailOnError);
    db.Execute(command.toString(), options);
}
```

Because this is the last call before being written out to the database, the completion date of the request is set, if necessary, to the current time. Next, the ID is checked to see if this will be an insert action or an update action. Probably the most straightforward way to perform either of these actions is to write a SQL statement to perform the action, embedding any values necessary directly into the statement. In this way, Variant instances for each field are avoided. The write method creates either an insert statement or update statement based on the value of the ID. Next, the Database.Execute method is used to carry out the action.

Finally, the readAll method is used to return a stripped-down version of each request. This is done to minimize the amount of data returned so as not to jeopardize performance. Listing 24.3 contains this method.

Listing 24.3. The readAll method of class Request.

```
public static boolean readAll(Database db, Vector requestList)
{
    boolean retval = false;          // assume database error
    String command = "select TRACKING_ID, TITLE from REQUEST " + "
            order by TRACKING_ID";
    Variant type = new Variant();
    Variant options = new Variant();
    Variant fieldName = new Variant();
    Variant fieldValue = new Variant();
```

```
    type.putShort(Constants.dbOpenDynaset);
    options.putShort(Constants.dbReadOnly);
    // create the recordset and get the number of records returned
    Recordset recordset = db.OpenRecordset(command, type, options);
    int retrievedRecordCount = 0;
    // retrieve the first row
    if (recordset.getRecordCount() > 0)
        recordset.MoveFirst();
    // read all of the records
    while (retrievedRecordCount < recordset.getRecordCount())
    {
        int trackingId;
        String title;
        // get the fields of the row
        Fields fields = recordset.getFields();
        _Field field;
        // retrieve all of the information and store it
        fieldName.putString("TRACKING_ID");
        field = fields.getItem(fieldName);
        fieldValue = field.getValue();
        trackingId = fieldValue.toInt();
        fieldName.putString("TITLE");
        field = fields.getItem(fieldName);
        fieldValue = field.getValue();
        title = fieldValue.toString();
        // save the request
        requestList.addElement(new Request(trackingId, title));
        // move the element indexing
        recordset.MoveNext();
        retrievedRecordCount++;
    }
    return retval;
}
```

Notice that this method is static. This is done so that the method can be called before a Request instance has been allocated. The SQL statement used shows only a limited number of columns being returned:

```
String command = "select TRACKING_ID, TITLE from REQUEST order by TRACKING_ID";
```

TIP:

The order by clause in the Request.readAll method tells Access to return the requests in the order in which the IDs were assigned. This most likely will be the same order in which they were submitted. However, it is much more efficient on larger databases to use the primary key as an ordering column.

The readAll method is very similar to the read method with respect to the order in which things are accomplished. The difference is in the while statement and the fact that multiple rows are returned, thus cycling through all of the rows.

CAUTION:

When retrieving the record count from a recordset, the value returned will always be accurate when dealing with a table-type recordset, and it will be accurate for a dynaset or snapshot only after all records have been returned. Even when moving sequentially through a dynaset, the count returned will not always be a sequentially incrementing count, as would be expected. To handle this, the following code from Request.readAll could be used:

```
Recordset recordset = db.OpenRecordset(command, type, options);
int retrievedRecordCount = 0;
// retrieve the first row
if (recordset.getRecordCount() > 0)
    recordset.MoveFirst();
// read all of the records
while (retrievedRecordCount < recordset.getRecordCount())
{
    // process the record...
    // move the element indexing
    recordset.MoveNext();
    retrievedRecordCount++;
}
```

If the value returned after opening the recordset is greater than 0, at least one record was returned. Then, as long as the number of records that have been read is less than the record count being returned, continue reading records.

The public methods of the Request are summarized in Table 24.4.

Table 24.4. Public methods of class Request.

Method	Purpose
Request()	Constructs a new request.
Request(int, String)	Constructs a request representing an existing request with the given ID and title.
getTrackingIdStr()	Returns the ID in a displayable string.
getCompletionDate()	Returns the completion date in a displayable string.
toString()	Returns a string representing this class, containing the ID and title of the request.

Method	Purpose
clear()	Clears the current request. Upon return, the request looks like a "new" request.
set(Request)	Sets the values to the same as the passed in request.
read(Database)	Reads the details of an existing request from the database.
write(Database)	Writes the current request to the database.
readAll(Database)	Static method used to read the basics of all requests in the system.

Operator

`Operator` is used to hold information about a single user or operator of the system. The stored information about the operator corresponds to the columns in the `OPERATOR` table:

```
public String UserName;
public String Password;
public String FirstName;
public String LastName;
public String AccessLevel;
```

The access level can be used to control the types of services or fields accessible by each operator. The values stored in the database are represented by the following constants in the `Operator` class:

```
public final static String ADMINISTRATOR = "A";
public final static String EXECUTIVE = "E";
public final static String MANAGER = "M";
public final static String PROGRAMMER = "P";
public final static String GUEST = "G";
```

Database access in the `Operator` class is found through the `read`, `insert`, `update`, and `readAll` methods.

The `read` method reads in the operator details for the operator represented by the string found in the `UserName` member. Listing 24.4 contains the `read` method.

Listing 24.4. The read method of Operator.

```
public boolean read(Database db)
{
    boolean retval = false;           // assume database error
    String command = "select * from OPERATOR where USER_NAME = '" +
            UserName + "'";
    Variant type = new Variant();
    Variant options = new Variant();
    type.putShort(Constants.dbOpenDynaset);
    options.putShort(Constants.dbReadOnly);
```

continues

Listing 24.4. continued

```
    // create the recordset and get the number of records returned
    Recordset recordset = db.OpenRecordset(command, type, options);
    int recordCount = recordset.getRecordCount();
    // retrieve the first row
    if (recordCount > 0) {
        recordset.MoveFirst();
        // get the fields of the row
        getFields(recordset.getFields());
        retval = true;
    }
    return retval;
}
```

Because the user name is the primary key of the OPERATOR table, only a single row is returned from the SQL statement:

```
String command = "select * from OPERATOR where USER_NAME = '" +
        UserName + "'";
```

Once again, even though a dynaset is being returned, because only a single row is expected in the recordset, the record count can be used as a flag to determine if a row was found in the table. To read the values of the row returned, the private method getFields is called. The code for getFields can be found in Listing 24.5.

Listing 24.5. The getFields method of Operator.

```
private void getFields(Fields fields)
{
    Variant fieldName = new Variant();
    Variant fieldValue = new Variant();
    _Field field;
    // retrieve all of the information and store it
    fieldName.putString("USER_NAME");
    field = fields.getItem(fieldName);
    fieldValue = field.getValue();
    UserName = fieldValue.toString();
    fieldName.putString("PASSWORD");
    field = fields.getItem(fieldName);
    fieldValue = field.getValue();
    Password = fieldValue.toString();
    fieldName.putString("FIRST_NAME");
    field = fields.getItem(fieldName);
    fieldValue = field.getValue();
    FirstName = fieldValue.toString();
    fieldName.putString("LAST_NAME");
    field = fields.getItem(fieldName);
    fieldValue = field.getValue();
    LastName = fieldValue.toString();
    fieldName.putString("ACCESS_LEVEL");
    field = fields.getItem(fieldName);
    fieldValue = field.getValue();
    AccessLevel = fieldValue.toString();
}
```

This method takes the `Fields` instance returned for the current record of the recordset. The same field retrieval steps discussed in the previous section are used to retrieve the value for each column and place it in the appropriate class member.

The `insert` and `update` methods, shown in Listing 24.6, embed the values being written to the database directly in the SQL statement used to perform the action.

Listing 24.6. The insert and update methods of `Operator`.

```
public void insert(Database db)
{
    write(db, "insert into OPERATOR values('" + UserName +
            "','" + Password + "','" + FirstName + "','" +
            LastName + "','" + AccessLevel + "')");
}
public void update(Database db)
{
    write(db, "update OPERATOR set PASSWORD = '" + Password +
            "', FIRST_NAME = '" + FirstName +
            "', LAST_NAME = '" + LastName +
            "', ACCESS_LEVEL = '" + AccessLevel +
            "' where USER_NAME = '" + UserName + "'");
}
```

Both of the functions use the private `write` method to execute the SQL statement. This method simply passes the SQL statement to the appropriate `Database` method.

```
private void write(Database db, String command)
{
    Variant options = new Variant();
    options.putShort(Constants.dbFailOnError);
    db.Execute(command, options);
}
```

Listing 24.7 shows that the `readAll` method is very similar to `Request.readAll`. One of the differences is that all of the rows of the table are being returned, so that an open table is used instead of a dynaset. Additionally, `getFields` is used to retrieve the contents of the fields of each record.

Listing 24.7. The readAll method of `Operator`.

```
public static boolean readAll(Database db, Vector operatorList)
{
    boolean retval = false;              // assume database error
    Variant type = new Variant();
    Variant options = new Variant();
    type.putShort(Constants.dbOpenTable);
    options.putShort(Constants.dbReadOnly);
    // create the recordset and get the number of records returned
    Recordset recordset = db.OpenRecordset("OPERATOR", type, options);
    int recordCount = recordset.getRecordCount();
```

continues

Listing 24.7. continued

```
    // retrieve the first row
    if (recordCount > 0)
        recordset.MoveFirst();
    // read all of the records
    while (recordCount > 0)
    {
        Operator op = new Operator();
        // get the fields of the row
        op.getFields(recordset.getFields());
        // save the operator
        operatorList.addElement(op);
        // move the element indexing
        recordset.MoveNext();
        recordCount—;
    }
    return retval;
}
```

The public methods of Operator are summarized in Table 24.5.

Table 24.5. Public methods of class Operator.

Method	Purpose
Operator()	Constructs a new operator.
toString()	Returns a string representing this class, containing the name of the operator.
clear()	Clears the current operator. Upon return, the operator looks like a "new" operator.
set(String, String, String, String, String)	Sets the values of the member variables to the parameters passed in.
set(Operator)	Sets this operator to an operator with the given operator information.
setUserName(String)	Sets the username of the current operator to the parameter passed in.
insert(Database)	Inserts a new row into the database table with the current information.
update(Database)	Updates the row with the operator's information with the given username.
read(Database)	Reads the details of an existing operator from the database.
readAll(Database)	Static method used to read all operators in the system.

Department

The final database-access class is used for the DEPARTMENT table. This class is a simpler version of the Operator class. The only information is stored in the two members:

```
public String Code;
public String Name;
```

The remainder of the class is very similar to the Operator class, and the public methods are summarized in Table 24.6.

Table 24.6. Public methods of class Department.

Method	Purpose
Department()	Constructs a new department.
toString()	Returns a string representing this class, containing the name of the department.
clear()	Clears the current department. Upon return, the department looks like a "new" department.
set(String, String)	Sets the values of the member variables to the parameters passed in.
set(Department)	Sets this department to a department with the given information.
setCode(String)	Sets the code of the current department to the parameter passed in.
insert(Database)	Inserts a new row into the database table with the current information.
update(Database)	Updates the row with the department's information using the given department code.
read(Database)	Reads the details of an existing department from the database.
readAll(Database)	Static method used to read all departments in the system.

User Interface

The user interface is created with CardLayout to control the displaying of the three screens in the DevRequest applet. Each contains a single panel, which includes the more sophisticated GribBagLayout to place various controls on the dialog.

Common Classes

During the course of developing the DevRequest applet, it was apparent that there was a need for several common classes. This need included controls to associate a data element with each item in both a Choice and List control, and a common Panel class that provides messaging methods.

Data Aware Choice and List Controls

To display a list of options on a Panel, a Choice or a List control might be used. When developing more involved applets, there will often be times when the choice made in a Choice or List will imply the use of not only the selected string, but also the entity that that selected string represents. For example, the DevRequest has the potential of displaying a list of all operators in the system in a Choice control for selecting by whom the request was generated. Additional fields could also be added to the DevRequest applet to collect data on who reviewed the request, who approved the request at every management level needed, among other locations throughout the applet. For each of these situations, the logical item to place in the Choice control is the name of the person. However, the name is not what is used to uniquely identify operators. Therefore, you would like to be able to associate the username with each name in the list. Even more appropriate would be to associate an Operator instance with each name in the list.

A simple extension to the Choice class would be to add a Vector that holds an object reference for each item added to the list. Listing 24.8 contains the complete class implementation for the ChoiceData class that associates a data element with each item in the list.

Listing 24.8. The ChoiceData class.

```
/*
 *
 * ChoiceData
 *
 * This class extends the choice control and adds the ability
 *    to associate a data element with each item in the choice
 *    list.
 */
public class ChoiceData extends Choice
{
    protected Vector Data = new Vector();
    public void addItemData(String item, Object obj)
    {
        addItem(item);                  // add item to choices
        Data.addElement(obj);           // add date to the data list
    }
    public void selectByData(Object obj)
    {
```

```
            // find the data in the data list
            int index = Data.indexOf(obj);
            // select the corresponding element
            select(index);
    }
    public Object getSelectedData()
    {
        return getSelectedIndex() >= 0 ?
                Data.elementAt(getSelectedIndex()) : null;
    }
    public void load(Vector data)
    {
        // add each element to the choice list and the data list
        for (Enumeration enum = data.elements();
                enum.hasMoreElements();)
        {
            Object ob = enum.nextElement();
            addItemData(ob.toString(), ob);
        }
    }
}
```

ChoiceData now allocates a Vector instance, Data, that will be a list of data items associated with each item in the control. Because all of the items are added to the end of the list in the control, the same can be done for the respective data elements. Additionally, the control and the Vector index their respective items with a zero relative offset. Both of these facts enable an easy one-to-one correspondence between the elements in the Choice control and the elements in the Vector.

A new set of data methods are added to the ChoiceData class that operate on both items and data elements. addItemData is used to add a string item to the control and an object to the data list. Both entities are added to the end of their respective lists so that index relationships are maintained. selectByData uses this index relationship to find a data element in the data list and select its corresponding item in the control. Similarly, getSelectedData is used to return the data element associated with the currently selected item in the control.

load is used to fill the control with a list of items in a single method call. This method uses an Enumeration to add each item of the Vector to the control. The toString method of the list elements is used to determine the string displayed in the control.

The corresponding ListData class contains all of the methods described in the ChoiceData class. One additional functionality that the list provides is the ability to clear the list. The ListData equivalent simply has to clear both the control and the data elements:

```
public void clear()
{
    super.clear();                  // clear the list
    Data.removeAllElements();       // clear the data
}
```

StatusPanel

The DevRequest applet contains a number of Panel-derived classes that are used to logically group controls. There are a couple of concepts used with the DevRequest panels that are not possible with the standard Java classes. These include drawing a border around the perimeter of the panel and displaying a message to the applet status bar. Listing 24.9 contains the listing of the StatusPanel class that provides these capabilities.

Listing 24.9. The StatusPanel class.

```
/*
 *
 * StatusPanel
 *
 * This class provides a simple means to display a status message to
 *    the applet's status bar.
 */
public class StatusPanel extends Panel
{
    protected boolean hasBorder = false;
    public StatusPanel()
    {
        hasBorder = false;
    }
    public StatusPanel(boolean hasBorder)
    {
        this.hasBorder = hasBorder;
    }
    public void paint(Graphics g)
    {
        if (hasBorder)
        {
            // draw a rectangle around the panel
            Rectangle rect = bounds();
            g.drawRect(0, 0, rect.width - 1, rect.height - 1);
        }
    }
    protected void setStatus(String msg)
    {
        Applet applet = getAppletParent();
        applet.showStatus(msg);
    }
    protected void setStatus(ComException comE)
    {
        Applet applet = getAppletParent();
        if (applet instanceof DevRequest)
        {
            Variant comError = new Variant();
            comError.putShort((short)(comE.getHResult()));
            Errors errs = ((DevRequest)applet).dbEngine.getErrors();
            dao3032.Error err = errs.getItem(comError);
            applet.showStatus("DB Error: " + err.getDescription());
        }
        else
            applet.showStatus(comE.getMessage());
```

```
    }
    private Applet getAppletParent()
    {
        java.awt.Container parent = getParent();
        while (!(parent instanceof Applet))
            parent = parent.getParent();
        return (Applet)parent;
    }
}
```

The hasBorder member is a flag used in the paint method to draw a simple border around the perimeter of the panel. It is defaulted to not have a border, but it can be modified by passing a parameter to the constructor. The setStatus method is used to place a message on the status bar of the browser the applet is being run from. It uses the private getAppletParent method to retrieve the applet from the parent container of the panel control. getAppletParent assumes that every control eventually has an ancestor that is Applet derived. It uses a while loop to traverse the parent chain and the instanceof operator to find the applet where the panel resides. The second version of the setStatus method takes a COM exception raised by a DAO object and displays the error message associated with the exception.

DevRequest

DevRequest is derived from the Applet class and implements the Observer interface to monitor when the user information has changed so that the appropriate screen can be displayed. The init method first allocates the database connection that will be used throughout the applet. This is done with the following OpenDatabase method:

```
protected boolean OpenDatabase()
{
    URL dbURL;
    try {
        // otherwise generate it relative to the applet
        dbURL = new java.net.URL(getDocumentBase(),
                "DevDb.mdb");
    }
    catch(Exception e) {
        showStatus("Error: " + e.getMessage());
        return false;
    }
    // strip "file:/" from dbURL
    String filename = dbURL.getFile().substring(1);
    // create the database engine
    dbEngine = dao_dbengine.create();
    // create Variants that will hold parameters that
    // will be passed to OpenDatabase
    Variant exclusive = new Variant();
    Variant readOnly = new Variant();
    Variant source = new Variant();
    // set parameters for call to OpenDatabase
    exclusive.putBoolean(false);
```

```
        readOnly.putBoolean(false);
        source.putString("");
        // open the database for non-exclusive access
        db = dbEngine.OpenDatabase(filename, exclusive, readOnly, source);
        return true;
}
```

Next, `init` adds the applet to the observer list of the `UserInformation` instance. This causes the `update` method of the applet to be called every time the `UserInformation` is updated. Finally, the `CardLayout` is allocated and the panels are added to the applet with the `AllocatePanels` method:

```
protected void AllocatePanels()
    {
        // the main layout manager will be a card layout
        layout = new CardLayout();
        setLayout(layout);
        add(UserInformation.LOGIN, new LoginPanel(db, UserInfo));
        add(UserInformation.CONTROL, new ControlPanel(db, UserInfo));
        add(UserInformation.ADMINISTRATION, new AdministrationPanel(db, UserInfo));
    }
```

Notice that the name used when adding the panel components is defined as a constant in the `UserInformation` class. The `update` method of `DevRequest` looks at the currently logged-on user information for the next screen to be displayed:

```
public void update(Observable o, Object arg)
{
    // if the user information has changed, assume login
    //    has been successful and go to control
    if (o instanceof UserInformation)
        layout.show(this, UserInfo.NextScreen);
}
```

The `UserInformation` class is used in conjunction with the `DevRequest` class to control displaying of the screens at various points in the application. There are two sets of constants defined in the `UserInformation` class. The first set are the names used for the screens of the dialog:

```
public final static String LOGIN = "Login";
public final static String CONTROL = "Control";
public final static String ADMINISTRATION = "Administration";
```

These define the names of the dialogs and are used when signaling the next screen to be displayed. The second set of constants is used when associating the access level of the currently logged-on user with a numerical value. This value can then be queried to determine if certain elements are available to the user. The following is the list of possible values:

```
public final static int ADMINISTRATOR = 0;     // database level
public final static int EXECUTIVE = 1;
public final static int MANAGER = 2;
public final static int PROGRAMMER = 3;
public final static int GUEST = 4;
```

The `setAccessLevel` method takes an access-level string, presumably read from the database, and associates one of the preceding constants to the current user.

`signalNextScreen` and `done` are methods used to notify the observers of this class that the next screen has been changed and needs to be displayed. `signalNextScreen` is used to control the order in which screens are displayed:

```
// This method controls the order that the screens are displayed.
public void signalNextScreen()
{
    // if at the login or administration screens, then go back
    //    to the control; otherwise, go to the administration
    if ((NextScreen == LOGIN) || (NextScreen == ADMINISTRATION))
        NextScreen = CONTROL;
    else
        NextScreen = ADMINISTRATION;
    // notify on lookers for actual changing of the panels
    done();
}
```

In the DevRequest applet, the order of the display of the screens is straightforward and boils down to a simple `if` statement. If the current screen is not the control screen, then the next screen will be. Otherwise, go to the administration screen. The private `done` method is used to call the `Observable` class methods that notify the observers that a change has occurred.

```
// This method is used to signal all observers that
//    this class is done changing.
private void done()
{
    setChanged();
    notifyObservers();
}
```

The panels that are added to the applet correspond to the three screens of the applet: Login, Control, and Administration.

LoginPanel

`LoginPanel` is a simple panel that displays text fields to collect the username and password (see Figure 24.2). The layout is performed with a `GridBagLayout` manager in the constructor:

```
public LoginPanel(Database db, UserInformation UserInfo)
{
    super();
    // save the passed in information
    this.db = db;
    this.UserInfo = UserInfo;
    // make a grid bag layout for the panel
    GridBagLayout layout = new GridBagLayout();
    GridBagConstraints gbc = new GridBagConstraints();
    setLayout(layout);
    // put a little space above and below the controls
    gbc.insets.top = gbc.insets.bottom = 4;
    // create the controls for this panel
    gbc.weightx = 1.0;                    // center 2 controls side-by-side
    gbc.anchor = GridBagConstraints.EAST;
    Label lbl = new Label("User Name:", Label.RIGHT);
```

```
        layout.setConstraints(lbl, gbc);
        add(lbl);
        // make the text field the last on the line
        gbc.anchor = GridBagConstraints.WEST;
        gbc.gridwidth = GridBagConstraints.REMAINDER;
        layout.setConstraints(UserNameField, gbc);
        add(UserNameField);
        gbc.anchor = GridBagConstraints.EAST;
        gbc.gridwidth = 1;
        lbl = new Label("Password:", Label.RIGHT);
        layout.setConstraints(lbl, gbc);
        add(lbl);
        // make the text field the last on the line
        gbc.anchor = GridBagConstraints.WEST;
        gbc.gridwidth = GridBagConstraints.REMAINDER;
        layout.setConstraints(PasswordField, gbc);
        PasswordField.setEchoCharacter('*');
        add(PasswordField);
        // add the button on its own line
        gbc.anchor = GridBagConstraints.CENTER;
        Button btn = new Button("Logon");
        layout.setConstraints(btn, gbc);
        add(btn);
        // put all of the space at the bottom
        gbc.fill = GridBagConstraints.BOTH;
        gbc.weighty = 1.0;
        Panel space = new Panel();
        layout.setConstraints(space, gbc);
        add(space);
}
```

First, the passed-in information is stored in member variables for use later on in the class. Next, a GridBagLayout is allocated and set as the layout manager for the panel. To add some format to this form, the sets of two controls are added so that the inner sides are centered horizontally on the form. The button is next placed on a line of its own and centered. So that the buttons are not vertically centered, but rather at the top of the form, an empty panel is added on the line following the button. It was given the capability to grow in the vertical direction, yet leave the vertical height of the rest of the controls the same. Therefore, the space panel fills the area below the button and above the bottom of the form.

The action method of the LoginPanel class processes the pushing of the Logon button. It first assumes that both a username and a password are required, so appropriate checks are made. If either field is empty, a message is written to the status bar. Next, the username and password are validated using the following validation routine:

```
protected boolean ValidateUser()
{
    boolean retval = false;                    // assume no logon
    String command = "select * from OPERATOR where USER_NAME = '" +
            UserNameField.getText().toLowerCase() +
            "' and PASSWORD = '" +
            PasswordField.getText().toLowerCase() + "'";
    Variant type = new Variant();
    Variant options = new Variant();
    type.putShort(Constants.dbOpenDynaset);
```

```
options.putShort(Constants.dbEditAdd);
// create the recordset
Recordset recordset = db.OpenRecordset(command, type, options);
// if there was a record returned, then get the user's info
if (recordset.getRecordCount() > 0)
{
    Variant fieldName = new Variant();
    Variant fieldValue = new Variant();
    // retrieve the first (and only) row
    recordset.MoveFirst();
    // get the fields of the row
    Fields fields = recordset.getFields();
    _Field field;
    // retrieve all of the information and store it
    fieldName.putString("USER_NAME");
    field = fields.getItem(fieldName);
    fieldValue = field.getValue();
    UserInfo.UserName = fieldValue.toString();
    fieldName.putString("FIRST_NAME");
    field = fields.getItem(fieldName);
    fieldValue = field.getValue();
    UserInfo.FirstName = fieldValue.toString();
    fieldName.putString("LAST_NAME");
    field = fields.getItem(fieldName);
    fieldValue = field.getValue();
    UserInfo.LastName = fieldValue.toString();
    fieldName.putString("ACCESS_LEVEL");
    field = fields.getItem(fieldName);
    fieldValue = field.getValue();
    UserInfo.setAccessLevel(fieldValue.toString());
    retval = true;                      // found an entry
}
    return retval;
}
```

This method is similar to the read method of the Operator class. The distinguishing factor is that the row selected must match both the username and the password, as evident in the SQL statement:

```
String command = "select * from OPERATOR where USER_NAME = '" +
        UserNameField.getText().toLowerCase() +
        "' and PASSWORD = '" +
        PasswordField.getText().toLowerCase() + "'";
```

The last task performed by the action processing of the Logon button is to change to the next screen via the UserInformation class.

ControlPanel

The ControlPanel is separated into three sections of the screen: the button panel across the top enabling the user to enter a new request, get detailed information about an existing request, or go to the administration screen; a list of all of the currently active requests; and a panel containing the detailed information about the request. Once again, these controls are placed on the dialog using a GridBagLayout manager allocated in the constructor:

```
public ControlPanel(Database db, UserInformation UserInfo)
{
    super();
    // save the passed in information
    this.db = db;
    this.UserInfo = UserInfo;
    // make a grid bag layout for the panel
    GridBagLayout layout = new GridBagLayout();
    GridBagConstraints gbc = new GridBagConstraints();
    setLayout(layout);
    // put a little space above and below the controls
    gbc.insets.top = gbc.insets.bottom = 2;
    // create the controls for this panel
    gbc.gridwidth = GridBagConstraints.REMAINDER;
    AdministrationButton.hide();
    Panel p = new Panel();
    p.add(new Button("New"));
    p.add(new Button("Details"));
    p.add(AdministrationButton);
    layout.setConstraints(p, gbc);
    add(p);
    gbc.weightx = 1.0;                  // equally space remaining
    gbc.weighty = 1.0;                  // let list fill remaining space
    gbc.gridwidth = GridBagConstraints.RELATIVE;
    gbc.fill = GridBagConstraints.BOTH;
    layout.setConstraints(RequestList, gbc);
    add(RequestList);

    gbc.gridwidth = GridBagConstraints.REMAINDER;
    ReqPanel = new RequestPanel(this, db);
    layout.setConstraints(ReqPanel, gbc);
    add(ReqPanel);
    readRequests();
}
```

The last task performed in the ControlPanel constructor is the reading of the requests from the database using the readRequest method:

```
public void readRequests()
{
    // kill existing list
    RequestList.clear();
    Vector requests = new Vector();
    // query the database for all of the requests
    Request.readAll(db, requests);
    // load the list
    RequestList.load(requests);
    // clear the current panel
    ReqPanel.setRequest(new Request());
}
```

Because this method can be called multiple times throughout the life of the panel, the current contents of the list are cleared before adding the new contents. Request.readAll is used to read in all of the requests from the database. The ListData.load method is used to bulk load the list. The last task performed is to clear the contents of the Details panel.

The action method handles the button-press event by sending a newly allocated request to the details panel, sending the data item associated with the selected list item to the details panel, or using the UserInformation class to go to the administration screen.

The show method of the ControlPanel class selectively shows the administration button if the user has the appropriate access level. Notice that this check must be performed in the show method, as opposed to the constructor, because the UserInformation has not been filled in when the constructor gets called.

```
public void show()
{
    if (UserInfo.AccessLevel <= UserInformation.ADMINISTRATOR)
        AdministrationButton.show();
    super.show();
}
```

The RequestPanel class represents the detailed information about a request. Figure 24.7 shows the bounds of the RequestPanel class on the control screen.

Figure 24.7.

RequestPanel display on the control screen.

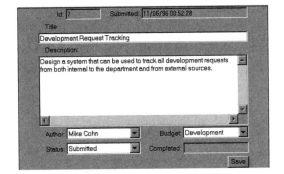

Once again, the placement of the controls on the panel becomes an exercise on the use of a GridBagLayout manager in the constructor of the RequestPanel. Additionally, in the constructor, the following two methods are called to populate the Choice controls with the operators and departments:

```
private void loadOperators()
{
    Vector operators = new Vector();
    Operator.readAll(db, operators);
    RequestorChoice.load(operators);
}
private void loadDepartments()
{
    Vector depts = new Vector();
    Department.readAll(db, depts);
    ApprovedBudgetChoice.load(depts);
}
```

Both of these methods use the bulk-loading capabilities of the `ChoiceData` control.

To display a new request, the `setRequest` method is called. This method simply saves the request class instance and populates the controls:

```
public void setRequest(Request req)
{
    // save the request as the current request
    CurrentRequest = req;
    TrackingIdField.setText(CurrentRequest.getTrackingIdStr());
    SubmissionDateField.setText(
            CurrentRequest.SubmissionDate.toLocaleString());
    CompletionDateField.setText(CurrentRequest.getCompletionDate());
    TitleField.setText(CurrentRequest.Title);
    DescriptionArea.setText(CurrentRequest.Description);
    RequestorChoice.select(CurrentRequest.Requestor.toString());
    StatusChoice.selectByData(CurrentRequest.Status);
    ApprovedBudgetChoice.select(CurrentRequest.ApprovedBudget.toString());
}
```

To save any details that were modified, the `action` method responds to the Save button:

```
public boolean action(Event evt, Object obj)
{
    boolean retval = false;              // assume no action
    if ("Save".equals(obj))
    {
        if (validateFields())
        {
            try
            {
                CurrentRequest.write(db);
                conPanel.readRequests();
            }
            catch(ComException e)
            {
                setStatus(e);
            }
        }
        retval = true;
    }
    return retval;
}
```

Before the details are written to the database, the fields are validated with a call to the `validateFields` method:

```
private boolean validateFields()
{
    boolean retval = false;              // assume not enough info
    if (TitleField.getText().length() > 0)
    {
        CurrentRequest.Title = TitleField.getText();
        CurrentRequest.Description = DescriptionArea.getText();
        CurrentRequest.Requestor =
                (Operator)RequestorChoice.getSelectedData();
        CurrentRequest.Status = (String)StatusChoice.getSelectedData();
```

```
        CurrentRequest.ApprovedBudget =
                (Department)ApprovedBudgetChoice.getSelectedData();
        retval = true;
    }
    return retval;
}
```

DevRequest requires that a title be specified for every request entered in the system. Therefore, the length of the title is checked to make sure one has been entered. If so, then the control information is saved, gathered, and placed in the current request structure before returning to the action method.

After the fields have been validated, the action method writes the information to the database. If no exceptions were raised, the list of the ControlPanel is updated to reflect any changes that may have occurred as a result of saving the request.

AdministrationPanel

The final screen in the system is the Administration screen (see Figure 24.8), which is composed of two panels displaying the operator and department information, and a button used to return to the ControlPanel. Once again, the GridBagLayout manager is used in the constructor:

```
    public AdministrationPanel(Database db, UserInformation UserInfo)
    {
        super();
// save the passed in information
        this.db = db;
        this.UserInfo = UserInfo;
        // make a grid bag layout for the panel
        GridBagLayout layout = new GridBagLayout();
        GridBagConstraints gbc = new GridBagConstraints();
        setLayout(layout);
        gbc.weightx = 1.0;                    // let list fill remaining space
        gbc.weighty = 1.0;                    // let list fill remaining space
        gbc.gridwidth = 1;
        gbc.gridheight = 2;
        gbc.fill = GridBagConstraints.BOTH;
        OperatorPanel opPanel = new OperatorPanel(db);
        layout.setConstraints(opPanel, gbc);
        add(opPanel);
        gbc.gridheight = 1;
        gbc.gridwidth = GridBagConstraints.REMAINDER;
        DepartmentPanel deptPanel = new DepartmentPanel(db);
        layout.setConstraints(deptPanel, gbc);
        add(deptPanel);
        gbc.weightx = 0.0;
        gbc.weighty = 0.0;
        gbc.anchor = GridBagConstraints.EAST;
        gbc.fill = GridBagConstraints.NONE;
        Button btn = new Button("Done");
        layout.setConstraints(btn, gbc);
        add(btn);
    }
```

You might be wondering why the GridBagLayout manager is used so extensively. The reason is that this layout manager is great at laying out controls relative to other controls. Because the majority of controls have some type of relationship to other controls being added to the container, this layout manager is an excellent choice. Also, if additional controls are added later, a lot of the positioning manipulation of existing controls is eliminated—the layout manager takes care of it.

The only other method in AdministrationPanel is the action method that handles the processing of the Done button click and uses the UserInformation class to return to the control screen.

```
public boolean action(Event evt, Object obj)
{
    boolean retval = false;              // assume not processed
    if ("Done".equals(obj))
    {
        UserInfo.signalNextScreen();
        retval = true;
    }
    return retval;
}
```

There are two panels added to the AdministrationPanel: OperatorPanel and DepartmentPanel. As you might have guessed, these panels display operator (Figure 24.8) and department (Figure 24.9) information.

Figure 24.8.

OperatorPanel display on the Administration screen.

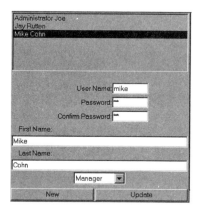

Figure 24.9.

DepartmentPanel display on the Administration screen.

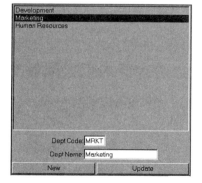

The `OperatorPanel` uses a, you guessed it, `GridBagLayout` manager to place an adjustable-height
List control above a detail panel and two side-by-side buttons on the panel:

```
public OperatorPanel(Database db)
{
    super(true);
    // save the passed in information
    this.db = db;
    // make a grid bag layout for the panel
    GridBagLayout layout = new GridBagLayout();
    GridBagConstraints gbc = new GridBagConstraints();
    setLayout(layout);
    // put a little space above around the controls
    gbc.insets.left = gbc.insets.top =
            gbc.insets.right = gbc.insets.bottom = 2;
    gbc.weighty = 1.0;                 // let list fill remaining space
    gbc.gridwidth = GridBagConstraints.REMAINDER;
    gbc.fill = GridBagConstraints.BOTH;
    layout.setConstraints(OperatorList, gbc);
    add(OperatorList);
    gbc.weighty = 0.0;                 // don't resize remaining controls
    StatusPanel opInfo = getOperatorInfoPanel();
    layout.setConstraints(opInfo, gbc);
    add(opInfo);
    // add two side-by-side buttons
    gbc.weightx = 1.0;                 // equally space horizontally
    gbc.gridwidth = 1;
    gbc.fill = GridBagConstraints.HORIZONTAL;
    Button btn = new Button("New");
    layout.setConstraints(btn, gbc);
    add(btn);
    gbc.gridwidth = GridBagConstraints.REMAINDER;
    btn = new Button("Update");
    layout.setConstraints(btn, gbc);
    add(btn);
    // read in the operators from the database
    readOperators();
}
```

Additionally, the `readOperators` method is called to populate the list:

```
private void readOperators()
{
    // kill existing list
    OperatorList.clear();
    Vector operators = new Vector();
    Operator.readAll(db, operators);
    OperatorList.load(operators);
}
```

The `action` method handles the processing of the buttons:

```
public boolean action(Event evt, Object obj)
{
    boolean retval = false;              // assume not processed
    if ("New".equals(obj))
    {
```

```
        if (validateFields())
        {
            try
            {
                CurrentOperator.insert(db);
                readOperators();
            }
            catch(ComException e)
            {
                setStatus(e);
            }
        }
        retval = true;
    }
    else if ("Update".equals(obj))
    {
        if (validateFields())
        {
            try
            {
                CurrentOperator.update(db);
                readOperators();
            }
            catch(Exception e)
            {
                setStatus("DB Error: " + e.getMessage());
            }
        }
        retval = true;
    }
    return retval;
}
```

If the New button is pressed, the fields are validated and moved into the CurrentOperator instance using the validateFields method. The operator is then written to the database as a new row. If an operator is duplicated in the database, then an exception will be raised and the error message will be displayed on the status line of the browser. If the Update button is pressed, the fields are again validated and placed in the CurrentOperator class. The row in the database is then updated with the new information.

The fields are validated by making sure the username has been entered and the two password entries are identical:

```
private boolean validateFields()
{
    boolean retval = false;                 // assume not enough info
    if ((UserNameField.getText().length() > 0) &&
            (PasswordField.getText().equals(ConfirmPasswordField.getText())))
    {
        // move information to the current operator
        CurrentOperator.set(UserNameField.getText(),
                PasswordField.getText(),
                FirstNameField.getText(),
                LastNameField.getText(),
                (String)AccessLevelChoice.getSelectedData());
```

```
        retval = true;
    }
    return retval;
}
```

The final functionality provided in this class is to automatically populate the details when an operator is selected from the list. This is handled by overriding the `handleEvent` method.

```
public boolean handleEvent(Event evt)
{
    boolean retval;
    switch(evt.id) {
    case Event.LIST_SELECT:
    case Event.LIST_DESELECT:
        fillCurrentOperator();
        retval = true;
        break;
    default:
        retval = super.handleEvent(evt);
        break;
    }
    return retval;
}
```

When an item in a list is selected, an event is generated with an ID of `Event.LIST_SELECT`. Similarly, when the item is deselected, an `Event.LIST_DESELECT` event is generated. By trapping both of these events and calling the `fillCurrentOperator` method every time the selection changes, the details can be modified to show the currently selected operator.

`fillCurrentOperator` simply queries the list for the selected item and uses the data associated with that item to populate the detail information controls. If there is no item selected, then the List will generate an `ArrayIndexOutOfBoundsException` exception. This method traps that exception and simply clears the current operator so that the detail fields will be cleared.

```
private void fillCurrentOperator()
{
    try
    {
        Operator op = (Operator)OperatorList.getSelectedData();
        CurrentOperator.set(op);
    }
    catch (ArrayIndexOutOfBoundsException e)
    {
        CurrentOperator.clear();
    }
    UserNameField.setText(CurrentOperator.UserName);
    PasswordField.setText(CurrentOperator.Password);
    ConfirmPasswordField.setText(CurrentOperator.Password);
    FirstNameField.setText(CurrentOperator.FirstName);
    LastNameField.setText(CurrentOperator.LastName);
    AccessLevelChoice.selectByData(CurrentOperator.AccessLevel);
}
```

`DepartmentPanel` is very similar to the `OperatorPanel`.

Summary

This chapter took a first step toward developing an online request system. It involved a multiscreen applet that displayed a number of controls. In addition, the data collected was stored in a database using Microsoft's DAO so that information could be stored for later retrieval. As in any trip, there are many steps to follow, which take you down a number of paths. This applet could be easily modified to include additional controls specific to your needs. Additional types of forms could be included along with the appropriate routing mechanisms, and the database could be expanded or the DAO modified to access existing databases.

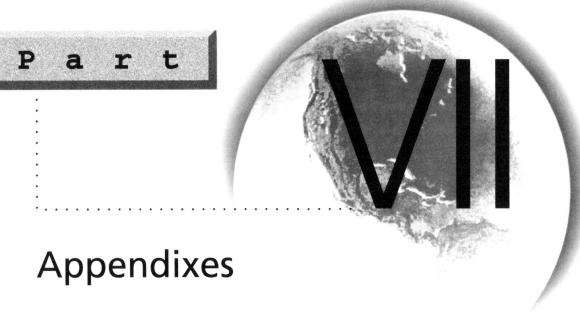

Part

VII

Appendixes

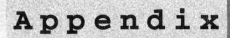

Appendix A

A Whirlwind Tour of the Java Language

If you are an experienced programmer already comfortable with an object-oriented language but don't know Java, or if you have already started learning Java but need a quick refresher, this appendix is for you. This appendix outlines the core syntax and constructs of the Java language. You learn how to declare Java variables and write Java functions. You will see how Java's minimal set of primitive types can be combined with its rich object model to fulfill the goals of object-oriented programming. You will also learn how to make use of exception handling to trap errors.

The Structure of a Java File

This appendix presents the Java language by starting with its smallest pieces—reserved words, operators, and primitive types. Building on this foundation you'll learn how to control the flow of a Java program and then how to create new Java classes. However, to augment this bottom-up approach, it is useful to start by examining an example of a Java class in its entirety. This overview will help place the rest of this appendix in context.

The following code is the complete definition of a Java class named `MyClass`:

```java
import java.applet.*;
import java.awt.Graphics;

public class MyClass extends Applet
{
    private String aString;
    private int xPosition;

    public void init()
    {
        xPosition = 32;
        aString = "This is a string";
    }

    public void paint(Graphics g)
    {
        g.drawString(aString, xPosition, 10);
    }
}
```

The statement `public class MyClass extends Applet` creates a new class named `MyClass`. This class `extends Applet`, meaning that `MyClass` inherits the properties of the class named `Applet` but that `MyClass` extends `Applet` by adding additional functionality or modifying the functionality of `Applet`. If a class did not extend the functionality of the class on which it is based, there would be little reason for defining the new class.

Within the class, its member variables and methods are defined. In the case of `MyClass`, it includes a variable named `aString` of type `String` and a variable named `xPosition` that is of type `int`. Each of these variables is defined as `private`, indicating that the variable cannot be accessed from outside the class.

Next within the class is the definition of a method called `init`. This method is defined as `public` and `void`. The `public` keyword indicates that the method can be accessed outside the current class while `void` indicates that the method has no return value. The `init` method sets the initial values of the `aString` and `xPosition` variables.

Finally, the `paint` function, also declared as `public` and `void`, is presented. Unlike `init`, `paint` is passed a parameter. The parameter is named `g` and is of type `Graphics`. The code within `paint` invokes the `drawString` method of the `Graphics` class to draw the string stored in `aString` on the screen.

At the top of this sample class were the following lines:

```
import java.applet.*;
import java.awt.Graphics;
```

In Java, classes are collected into packages. Classes and packages may then be reused in other programs by using the `import` statement. The first import line in this example is used to instruct Java to import all the classes stored in the package identified by the name `java.applet`. The `.*` at the end of the import statement indicates that all classes in this package are to be imported. Instead, a specific class name could have been listed, as with the second line of this example.

Comments

Missing in the example class you just saw were comments. I'd like to correct that right now so that code samples throughout the rest of this appendix can include comments. Java supports three types of comment delimiters—the traditional `/*` and `*/` of C, the `//` of C++, and a new variant that starts with `/**` and ends with `*/`.

The `/*` and `*/` delimiters are used to enclose text that is to be treated as a comment by the compiler. These delimiters are useful when you want to designate a lengthy piece of code as a comment, as shown in the following:

```
/* This is a comment that will span multiple
source code lines. */
```

The `//` comment delimiter is borrowed from C++ and is used to indicate that the rest of the line is to be treated as a comment by the Java compiler. This type of comment delimiter is particularly useful for adding comments adjacent to lines of code, as shown in the following:

```
Date today = new Date();      // create an object with today's date
System.out.println(today);    // display the date
```

Finally, the `/**` and `*/` delimiters are new to Java and are used to indicate that the enclosed text is to be treated as a comment by the compiler, but that the text is also part of the automatic class documentation that can be generated using JavaDoc. JavaDoc is fully described in Chapter 9, "Documenting Your Visual J++ Code." These delimiters can be used to enclose multiple lines of text, identically to how `/*` and `*/` behave, as follows:

```
/** The NeuralNetwork class implements a back-propagation
network and ... */
```

The Java comment delimiters are summarized in Table A.1.

Table A.1. Java comment delimiters.

Start	End	Purpose
/*	*/	The enclosed text is treated as a comment.
//	(none)	The rest of the line is treated as a comment.
/**	*/	The enclosed text is treated as a comment by the compiler but is used by JavaDoc to automatically generate documentation.

CAUTION:

You cannot nest comments in Java source code. Therefore, /* and */ appearing within a // comment are ignored as is the pattern // appearing within /* or /** comments. Comments cannot be placed within quoted strings, and if comment delimiters occur within a quoted string, they will be considered part of the quoted string.

Java Keywords

The following is a list of Java keywords:

Java Keywords

abstact	float	public
boolean	for	return
break	if	short
byte	implements	static
case	import	super
catch	instanceof	switch
char	int	synchronized
class	interface	this
continue	long	throw
default	native	throws
do	new	transient
double	null	try

Java Keywords

else	operator	void
extends	package	volatile
final	private	while
finally	protected	

The Java specification reserves additional keywords that will be used in the future but are not part of the current language specification. The following is a list of reserved Java keywords that are not currently used:

Reserved Java Keywords

byvalue	generic	outer
cast	goto	rest
const	inner	var
future	operator	

CAUTION:

You may have noticed that `true` and `false` are missing from the list of Java keywords. These are actually Boolean literals, but can be thought of as keywords.

Primitive Types

A language's primitive types are the building blocks from which more complicated types, such as classes, are built. Java supports a set of eight primitive types, which are shown in Table A.2.

Table A.2. Java primitive types.

Type	Description
byte	8-bit signed integer
short	16-bit signed integer
int	32-bit signed integer
long	64-bit signed integer
float	32-bit floating-point number
double	64-bit floating-point number
char	16-bit Unicode characters
boolean	Can hold `true` or `false`

Because most of the machines that will run Java programs will do so in a 32-bit environment, the sizes of the primitive types have been defined with 32-bit optimization in mind. This means that some Java primitives may use more storage space than you are accustomed to if you come to Java from a 16-bit programming background.

In Java you declare a variable by giving its type followed by its name, as in the following examples:

```
int x;
float LifeRaft;
short people;
long TimeNoSee;
double amountDue, amountPaid;
```

In the preceding code, x is declared as an int (integer), LifeRaft is declared as a floating-point variable, people is declared as a short integer, TimeNoSee is declared as a long integer, and amountDue and amountPaid are declared as double-precision floating-point values.

C++ NOTE:

From this list, you can tell that Java adds both the byte and boolean types. Some recent C++ compilers have added support for the new C++ boolean type, so you may already be using it in your code. Because Java provides Unicode support, you should notice that its char type is 16 bits wide. This is also why the 8-bit byte type is included as a primitive type. In C++, you have probably been emulating a byte type with something similar to the following:

```
type unsigned char byte;
```

There are a couple of other extremely important differences between the Java and C++ primitive types. The Java primitives are each of a known and guaranteed size. This is critical to Java because of its goal of portability across hardware and operating systems. If an int is 16 bits on one platform and 32 bits on another platform, a program is asking for trouble if it expects to be run on both platforms. C++ guarantees certain relationships among its primitive types. For example, a C++ long is guaranteed to be at least as big as a C++ int. Java takes this further and prescribes an exact size for each primitive. You should take care to notice the sizes of the Java primitives. In particular, you should notice that a Java int is 32 bits and a Java long is 64 bits.

Also worth pointing out is that all Java primitive types are signed. This means that C++ declarations like the following are not allowed in Java:

```
unsigned long bigLong;     // not legal in Java
unsigned double salary;    // not legal in Java
```

Finally, the Java boolean primitive can be set to a value of true or false. In traditional C and C++ programming, true and false were defined by using the preprocessor to be equal to 1 and 0, respectively.

Integer Types

Java consists of four integer types: byte, short, int, and long, which are defined as 8-, 16-, 32- and 64-bit signed values as summarized in Table A.3.

Table A.3. The Java integer primitive types.

Type	Bit Size	Minimum Value	Maximum Value
byte	8	-256	255
short	16	-32,768	32,767
int	32	-2,147,483,648	2,147,483,647
long	64	-9,223,372,036,854,775,808	9,223,372,036,854,775,807

The operations that may be performed on integer primitives are shown in Table A.4. A more detailed discussion of the Java operators is deferred until later in this appendix.

Table A.4. Operators on integer primitives.

Operator	Operation
=	Equality
!=	Inequality
>	Greater than
<	Less than
>=	Greater than or equal to
<=	Less than or equal to
+	Addition
-	Subtraction
*	Multiplication
/	Division
%	Modulus
++	Increment
--	Decrement
~	Bitwise logical negation
&	Bitwise AND
¦	Bitwise OR

continues

Table A.4. continued

Operator	Operation
^	Bitwise XOR
<<	Left shift
>>	Right shift
>>>	Right shift with zero fill

If either or both of the operands is of type long, the result of the operation will be a 64-bit long. If either operand is not a long, it will be cast to a long prior to the operation. If neither operand is a long, the operation will be performed with the 32-bit precision of an int. Any byte or short operands will be cast to int prior to the operation.

CAUTION:

In Java, you cannot cast between an integer type and a Boolean type.

Floating-Point Types

Support for floating-point numbers in Java is provided through two primitive types—float and double, which are 32- and 64-bit values, respectively. The operators available for use on these primitives types are shown in Table A.5.

Table A.5. Operators on floating-point primitives.

Operator	Operation
=	Equality
!=	Inequality
>	Greater than
<	Less than
>=	Greater than or equal to
<=	Less than or equal to
+	Addition
-	Subtraction
*	Multiplication
/	Division

Operator	Operation
%	Modulus
++	Increment
- -	Decrement

Java floating-point numbers will behave as specified in IEEE Standard 754. Java variables of type `float` and `double` can be cast to other numeric types but cannot be cast to be of the `boolean` type.

If either or both of the operands is a floating-point type, the operation is considered to be a floating-point operation. If either of the operands is a `double`, each will be treated as a `double` with the necessary casts being performed. If neither operand is a `double`, each operand will be treated as a `float` and cast as necessary.

Floating-point numbers can take on any of the following values:

○ Negative infinity
○ Negative, finite values
○ Negative zero
○ Positive zero
○ Positive, finite values
○ Positive infinity
○ NaN, or "not a number"

This last value, NaN, is used to indicate values that do not fit within the scale of negative infinity to positive infinity. For example, the following will produce a value of NaN:

```
0.0f / 0.0f
```

The inclusion of NaN as a floating-point value can cause some unusual effects when floating-point values are compared with the relational operators. Because NaN does not fit within the scale of negative infinity through positive infinity, comparing against it will always result in `false`. For example, both `5.3f > NaN` and `5.3f < NaN` are `false`. In fact, when NaN is compared to itself with `==`, the result is `false`.

On the other hand, although negative and positive zero may sound like different values, comparing them with `==` will result in `true`.

Other Primitive Types

In addition to the integer and floating-point primitive types, Java includes two additional primitive types—Boolean and character. Variables of type `boolean` can hold either `true` or `false`, while variables of type `char` can hold a single Unicode character.

A

Default Values

One common source of programming errors is the use of an uninitialized variable. Frequently, this type of bug shows itself in a program that behaves erratically. Sometimes the program does what it's supposed to; other times it reformats your hard drive, overwrites your CMOS, declares war on a foreign country, or manifests some other undesirable side effect. It does this because an uninitialized variable may take on the value of whatever random garbage is in its memory location when the program runs. Java circumvents this problem, and possibly prevents World War III, by assigning a default value to any uninitialized variables. Default values are assigned based on the type of the variable, as shown in Table A.6.

Table A.6. Standard default values for Java primitive types.

Primitive	Default
byte	0
short	0
int	0
long	0L
float	0.0f
double	0.0d
char	null
boolean	false
all references	null

TIP:

It's certainly convenient and beneficial that Java will take care of assigning default values to uninitialized variables, but it is not wise to rely on this. Good programming practice suggests that you should initialize every variable you declare, without relying on default values. Although it is very unlikely that the default values would change (for example, the Boolean default of false is unlikely to change to true), other side effects are possible.

In a C program, I once spent hours tracking down a bug that was caused by my reliance on the compiler defaulting a global integer to 0. The compiler did its job correctly; unfortunately, another programmer saw my bad practice of using an uninitialized global and corrected it by initializing it for me—to 1. When I was reassigned to the maintenance of the program, I had no idea the change had been made.

Casting Between Primitive Types

Sometimes you have a variable that is of one type and you want to use it as another. For example, one of the first programs I wrote was used to predict the final scores in baseball games based on a huge number of input statistics. It would come up with results like the Chicago Cubs beating the San Diego Padres with scores like 3.2 to 2.7. Because it was clearly impossible in real life to score a partial run, the results needed to be converted from floating-point to integer values. This is known as *casting* a variable. In Java, you can cast a variable of one type to another as follows:

```
float fRunsScored = 3.2f;
int iRunsScored = (int)fRunsScored;
```

In this case, the floating-point value 3.2 that is stored in fRunsScored will be cast into an integer and placed in iRunsScored. When cast into an integer, the nonwhole portion of the fRunsScored will be truncated so that iRunsScored will equal 3.

This is an example of what is known as a *narrowing conversion*. A narrowing conversion may lose information about the overall magnitude or precision of a numeric value, as you saw in this case. You should always be careful when writing a narrowing conversion because of this potential for data loss.

The other type of conversion is called a *widening conversion*. A widening conversion may lose information about precision in the least significant bits of the value, but it will not lose information about the magnitude of the value. In general, widening conversions are much safer. Table A.7 shows the widening conversions that are possible between Java primitive types.

Table A.7. Available widening conversions among Java primitive types.

From	*To*
byte	short, int, long, float, or double
short	int, long, float, or double
char	int, long, float, or double
int	long, float, or double
long	float or double
float	double

C++ NOTE:

Related to casting is the concept of *automatic coercion*. Automatic coercion occurs when a compiler *coerces*, or casts, a variable of one type into another automatically. For example, consider the following C++ code:

```
long aLong = 65536L;
unsigned int justAnInt;
justAnInt = aLong;
printf("%d", justAnInt);
```

In this example, the 65,536 stored in aLong is also placed into justAnInt. Because no explicit cast is performed, an automatic coercion from a long to an unsigned int is performed. Unfortunately, on a 16-bit platform, this will result in an error because the value in aLong is too large to fit in justAnInt. The automatic coercion will place 0 into justAnInt instead of the desired 65,536.

Because Java does not perform automatic coercions, you may need to slightly alter your thinking about some of your C++ programming habits. For example, in C++ you could write the following loop:

```
int count=10;
while (count) {
    // use count to do something
    count--;
}
```

In C++, the while loop will execute as long as count is nonzero. However, a Java while loop must be formed according to the following syntax:

```
while (booleanExpression)
    statement
```

What this means is that statements like while(count) do not work in Java because there is no automatic coercion of an integer (such as count) to the boolean that a Java while loop expects. You need to rewrite the C++ code fragment to work in Java as follows:

```
int count=10;
while (count > 0) {
    // use count to do something
    count--;
}
```

This creates a Boolean expression that is evaluated on each pass through the loop. You will need to make similar adjustments with the Java for and do...while loops, as well.

Literals

A literal is an explicit value that is used by a program. For example, your program may include a literal value of 3.1415 that is used whenever the value of *pi* is necessary, or it may include 65 as the mandatory retirement age. These values, 3.1415 and 65, are both literals.

Integer Literals

Integer literals can be specified in decimal, hexadecimal, or octal notation. To specify a decimal value, simply use the number as normal. To indicate that a literal value is a long, you can append either L or l to the end of the number. Hexadecimal values are given in base 16 and include the digits 0-9 and the letters A-F. To specify a hexadecimal value, use 0x followed the digits and letters that comprise the value. Similarly, an octal value is identified by a leading 0 symbol.

For examples of specifying integer literals, see Table A.8.

Table A.8. Examples of integer literals.

Integer	Long	Octal	Hexadecimal
0	0L	0	0x0
1	1L	01	0x1
10	10L	012	0xA
15	15L	017	0XF
16	16L	020	0x10
100	100L	0144	0x64

Floating-Point Literals

Similar to integer literals are Java's floating-point literals. Floating-point literals can be specified in either the familiar decimal notation (for example, 3.1415) or exponential notation (for example, 6.02e23). To indicate that a literal is to be treated as a single precision float, append either f or F. To indicate that it is to be treated as a double precision value, append either d or D.

Java includes predefined constants, POSITIVE_INFINITY, NEGATIVE_INFINITY, and NaN, to represent the infinity and Not-a-Number values.

The following list shows some valid floating-point literals:

```
43.3F
3.1415d
-12.123f
6.02e+23f
6.02e23d
6.02e-23f
6.02e23d
```

Boolean Literals

Java supports two Boolean literals—`true` and `false`.

Character Literals

A character literal is a single character or an escape sequence enclosed in single quotes, for example, `'b'`. Escape sequences are used to indicate special characters or actions, such as line feed, form feed, or carriage return. The available escape sequences are shown in Table A.9. For examples of character literals, consider the following:

```
'b'
'\n'
\u15e'
'\t'
```

Table A.9. Escape sequences.

Sequence	Purpose
\b	Backspace
\t	Horizontal tab
\n	Line feed
\f	Form feed
\r	Carriage return
\"	Double quote
\'	Single quote
\\	Backslash
\uxxxx	Unicode character

String Literals

Although there is no string primitive type in Java, you can include string literals in your programs. Most applications and applets will make use of some form of string literal, probably at least for error messages. A string literal consists of zero or more characters (including the escape sequences shown in Table A.9) enclosed in double quotes. As examples of string literals, consider the following:

```
"A String"
"Column 1\tColumn 2"
"First Line\r\nSecond Line"
```

```
"First Page\fSecond Page"
" "
```

Because Java does not have a string primitive type, each use of a string literal causes an object of the `String` class to be created behind the scenes. However, because of Java's automatic memory management, your program doesn't need to do anything special to free or release the memory used by the literal or string once you are finished with it.

Arrays

In Java you declare an array using enclosing square bracket symbols (`[ ]`).

For example, consider the following array declarations:

```
int intArray[];
float floatArray[];
double [] doubleArray;
char charArray[];
```

Notice that the brackets can be placed before or after the variable name. Placing the `[]` after the variable name follows the conventions of C, and if you are coming to Java from C or C++, you may want to continue that tradition. However, there is an advantage to placing the brackets before the variable name. By placing the brackets in front of the variable name, you can more easily declare multiple arrays. For example, consider the following declarations:

```
int [] firstArray, secondArray;
int thirdArray[], justAnInt;
```

On the first line both `firstArray` and `secondArray` are arrays. On the second line, `thirdArray` is an array but `justAnInt` is, as its name implies, a lone integer. The ability to declare singleton variables and arrays in the same statement, as on the second line in the preceding example, is the source of many problems in other programming languages. Java helps prevent this type of problem by providing an easy, alternative syntax for declaring arrays.

Allocation

Once an array is declared, it must be allocated. You probably noticed that the size of the arrays have not been specified in the examples so far. This is because, in Java, all arrays must be allocated with `new`. Declaring the following array would have resulted in a compile-time error:

```
int intArray[10];    // this is an error
```

To allocate an array you use `new`, as shown in the following examples:

```
int intArray[] = new int[100];
float floatArray[];
floatArray = new float[100];
long [] longArray = new long[100];
double [][] doubleArray = new double[10][10];
```

Initialization

An alternative way of allocating a Java array is to specify a list of element initializers when the array is declared. This is done as follows:

```
int intArray[] = {1,2,3,4,5};
char [] charArray = {'a', 'b', 'c'};
String [] stringArray = {"A", "Four", "Element", "Array"};
```

In this case, intArray will be a five-element array holding the values 1 through 5. The three-element array charArray will hold the characters 'a', 'b', and 'c'. Finally, stringArray will hold the strings shown.

Array Access

Items in a Java array are known as the components of the array. You can access a component at runtime by enclosing the component number you want to access with brackets as shown in the following:

```
int intArray[] = {100, 200, 300, 400, 500};

int a = intArray[0];        // a will be equal to 100
int b = intArray[1];        // b will be equal to 200
int c = intArray[2];        // c will be equal to 300
int d = intArray[3];        // d will be equal to 400
int e = intArray[4];        // e will be equal to 500
```

Java arrays are numbered from 0 to one less than the number of components in the array. Attempting to access an array beyond the bounds of the array (for example, intArray[42] in the preceding example) will result in a runtime exception, ArrayIndexOutOfBoundsException.

Operators

A language's operators can be used to combine or alter a program's values. Java contains a very rich set of operators. The complete list of Java operators is as follows:

A Complete List of Java Operators

=	>	<	!	~
?	:	==	<=	>=
!=	&&	||	++	--
+	-	*	/	&
|	^	%	<<	>>
>>>	+=	-=	*=	/=
&=	|=	^=	%=	<<=
>>=	>>>=			

Operators on Integers

The bulk of the Java operators work on integer values. The binary operators (those that require two operands) are shown in Table A.10. The unary operators (those that require a single operand) are shown in Table A.11. Each table gives an example of the use of each operator.

Table A.10. Binary operators on integers.

Operator	Operation	Example
=	Assignment	a = b
==	Equality	a == b
!=	Inequality	a != b
<	Less than	a < b
<=	Less than or equal to	a <= b
>=	Greater than or equal to	a >= b
>	Greater than	a > b
+	Addition	a + b
-	Subtraction	a - b
*	Multiplication	a * b
/	Division	a / b
%	Modulus	a % b
<<	Left shift	a << b
>>	Right shift	a >> b
>>>	Right shift with zero fill	a >>> b
&	Bitwise AND	a & b
¦	Bitwise OR	a ¦ b
^	Bitwise XOR	a ^ b

Table A.11. Unary operators on integers.

Operator	Operation	Example
-	Unary negation	-a
~	Bitwise logical negation	~a
++	Increment	a++ or ++a
--	Decrement	a-- or -a

In addition to the operators shown in Tables A.10 and A.11, Java also includes an assortment of assignment operators that are based on the other operators. These operators will operate on an operand and store the resulting value back in the same operand. For example, to increase the following of a variable x, you could do the following:

```
x += 3;
```

This is equal to the more verbose x = x + 3. Each of the specialized Java assignment operators performs its normal function on the operand and then stores the value in the operand. The following assignment operators are available:

Integer Assignment Operators

+=	-=	*=
/=	&=	!=
^=	%=	<<=
>>=	>>>=	

C++ NOTE:

You may have noticed that operator overloading is not mentioned in this discussion of operators. Initially, operator overloading was an exciting feature of C++ that promised to enable programmers to treat all data types, whether primitive or not, equivalently. The reasoning went that if there was a logically intuitive action that should be performed by an operator, the language should support overloading the operator to perform that action. Unfortunately, reality intervened, and many uses of operator overloading in C++ have led to unnecessary bugs. Because of the potential for introducing bugs through operator overloading, the developers of Java wisely chose to leave it out.

Operators on Floating-Point Values

The Java operators on floating-point values are a subset of those available to Java integer types. The operators on floats and doubles are shown in Table A.12, which also gives examples of their use.

Table A.12. Binary operators on integers.

Operator	Operation	Example
=	Assignment	a = b
==	Equality	a == b
!=	Inequality	a != b

Operator	Operation	Example
<	Less than	a < b
<=	Less than or equal to	a <= b
>=	Greater than or equal to	a >= b
>	Greater than	a > b
+	Addition	a + b
-	Subtraction	a - b
*	Multiplication	a * b
/	Division	a / b
%	Modulus	a % b
-	Unary negation	-a
++	Increment	a++ or ++a
--	Decrement	a-- or -a

Operators on Boolean Values

The Java Boolean operators are summarized in Table A.13. If you are coming to Java from a C or C++ background, you are probably already familiar with these. If not, however, the conditional operator will be a new experience.

Table A.13. Operators on Boolean values.

Operator	Operation	Example
!	Negation	!a
&&	Conditional AND	a && b
||	Conditional OR	a || b
==	Equality	a == b
!=	Inequality	a != b
?:	Conditional	a ? expr1 : expr2

The conditional operator is Java's only ternary (three-operand) operator and has the following syntactic form:

```
booleanExpr ? expr1 : expr2
```

The value of `booleanExpr` is evaluated and if `true`, the expression `expr1` is executed; if `false`, expression `expr2` is executed. This makes the conditional operator a convenient shorthand for the following:

```
if(booleanExpression)
    expr1
else
    expr2
```

C++ NOTE:

In Java, unlike C++, Boolean operators operate only on Boolean expressions. For example, consider the following C++ fragment:

```
int x = 1;
int y = 7;
if (x && y) {
    // do something
}
```

This same code is illegal in Java. Because the `&&` operator expects two `boolean` operands and there is no automatic coercion from an integer, the Java compiler does not know how to interpret this statement. In Java, it needs to be rewritten as follows:

```
int x = 1;
int y = 7;
if (x != 0 && y != 0) {
    // do something
}
```

In this case, the two integer values have been converted into explicit tests. Because these tests are Boolean expressions, the code can now be compiled.

Controlling Your Program

The Java keywords for controlling program flow are nearly identical to C and C++. This is one of the most obvious ways in which Java shows its legacy as a derivative of these two languages. In this section, you will see how to use Java's control flow commands to write methods.

Selection

The Java language provides two alternative structures—if statements and switch statements—for selecting among alternatives. Although it would be possible to spend your entire Java programming career using only one of these at the expense of the other, each has its definite advantages.

The `if` Statement

A Java `if` statement is a test of any Boolean expression. If the Boolean expression evaluates to `true`, the statement following the `if` is executed. On the other hand, if the Boolean expression evaluates to `false`, the statement following the `if` is not executed. For example, consider the following code fragment:

```
import java.util.Date;
Date today = new Date();
if (today.getDay == 0) then
    System.out.println("It is Sunday.");
```

This code uses the java.Util.Date package and creates a variable named `today` that will hold the current date. The `getDay` member method is then applied to `today` and the result compared to `0`. A return value of `0` for `getDay` indicates that the day is Sunday, so if the Boolean expression `today.getDay == 0` is true, a message is displayed. If today isn't Sunday, no action occurs.

C++ NOTE:

If you are coming to Java from a C or C++ background, you may have been tempted to rewrite the preceding example as follows:

```
import java.util.Date;
Date today = new Date();
if (!today.getDay) then
    System.out.println("It is Sunday.");
```

In C and C++, the expression `!today.getDay` would evaluate to `1` whenever `today.getDay` evaluated to `0` (indicating Sunday). In Java the expression used within an `if` statement must evaluate to a Boolean. Therefore, this code doesn't work because `!today.getDay` will evaluate to `0` or `1`, depending on which day of the week it is. And, as you learned earlier in this chapter, integer values cannot be cast to Boolean values. This is, of course, an example where Java's nuances may take a little getting used to for C and C++ programmers. Once you're accustomed to the change, however, you will find your code more readable, reliable, and maintainable.

Of course, an `if` statement without an `else` is as incomplete as a Labrador Retriever without a bandanna around his neck. Not wanting to be accused of cruelty to animals or programmers, the Java developers included an `else` statement that can be executed whenever an `if` statement evaluates to `false`. This can be seen in the following sample code:

```
import java.util.Date;
Date today = new Date();
if (today.getDay == 0) then
    System.out.println("It is Sunday.");
else
    System.out.println("It is NOT Sunday.");
```

In this case, the same message will be displayed whenever it is Sunday, but a different message will be displayed whenever it is not Sunday. Both examples so far have only shown the execution of a single statement within the `if` or the `else` cases. By enclosing the statements within curly braces, you can execute as many lines of code as you'd like. This can be seen in the following example that makes some suggestions about how to spend each day of the week:

```java
import java.util.Date;
Date today = new Date();
if (today.getDay == 0) then {
    System.out.println("It is Sunday.");
    System.out.println("And a good day for golf.");
}
else {
    System.out.println("It is NOT Sunday.");
    System.out.println("But still a good day for golf.");
}
```

Because it's possible to execute whatever code you desire in the `else` portion of an `if...else` block, you may have already reasoned that it is possible to execute another `if` statement inside the `else` statement of the first `if` statement. This is commonly known as an `if...else if...else` block, an example of which follows:

```java
import java.util.Date;
Date today = new Date();
if (today.getDay == 0) then
    System.out.println("It is Sunday.");
else if (today.getDay == 1) then
    System.out.println("It is Monday.");
else if (today.getDay == 2) then
    System.out.println("It is Tuesday.");
else if (today.getDay == 3) then
    System.out.println("It is Wednesday.");
else if (today.getDay == 4) then
    System.out.println("It is Thursday.");
else if (today.getDay == 5) then
    System.out.println("It is Friday.");
else
    System.out.println("It must be Saturday.");
```

The `switch` Statement

As you can see from the previous code sample, a lengthy series of `if...else if...else` statements can get convoluted and hard to read as the number of cases increases. Fortunately, you can avoid this problem by using Java's `switch` statement. Like its C and C++ cousins, the Java `switch` statement is ideal for testing a single expression against a series of possible values and executing the code associated with the matching `case` statement, as shown in the following example:

```java
import java.util.Date;
Date today = new Date();
switch (today.getDay) {
    case 0:     // Sunday
        System.out.println("It is Sunday.");
        break;
```

```
    case 1:    // Monday
        System.out.println("It is Monday.");
        break;
    case 2:    // Tuesday
        System.out.println("It is Tuesday.");
        break;
    case 3:    // Wednesday
        System.out.println("It is Wednesday.");
        break;
    case 4:    // Thursday
        System.out.println("It is Thursday.");
        break;
    case 5:    // Friday
        System.out.println("It is Friday.");
        System.out.println("Have a nice weekend!");
        break;
    default:   // Saturday
        System.out.println("It must be Saturday.");
}
System.out.println("All done!");
```

You should have noticed that each day has its own case within the switch. The Saturday case (where today.getDay = 6) is not explicitly given but is instead handled by the default case. Any switch block may include an optional default case that will handle any values not caught by an explicit case.

Within each case, there can be multiple lines of code. The block of code that will execute for the Friday case, for example, contains three lines. The first two lines will simply display informational messages, but the third is a break statement. The keyword break is used within a case statement to indicate that the flow of the program should move to the first line following the switch block. In this example, break appears as the last statement in each case except the default and will cause program execution to move to the line that prints "All done!". The break statement was left out of the default block because by that point in the code, the switch block was ending, and there was no point in using an explicit command to exit the switch.

If, as the previous example seems to imply, you always need to include a break statement at the end of each block, why not just leave break out and have Java assume that after a block executes, control should move outside the switch block? The answer is that there are times when you do not want to break out of the switch statement after executing the code for a specific case value. For example, consider the following code that could be used as a scheduling system for physicians:

```
import java.util.Date;
Date today = new Date();
switch (today.getDay) {
    case 0:    // Sunday
    case 3:    // Wednesday
    case 6:    // Saturday
        System.out.println("It's Golf Day!");
        break;
    case 2:    // Tuesday
        System.out.println("Tennis at 8:00 am");
```

589

```
    case 1:        // Monday
    case 4:        // Thursday
    case 5:        // Friday
        System.out.println("Office Hours: 10:00 - 5:00");
        break;
}
System.out.println("All done!");
```

This example illustrates a couple of key concepts about switch statements. First, you'll notice that it is possible to have multiple cases execute the same block of code, as follows:

```
case 0:        // Sunday
case 3:        // Wednesday
case 6:        // Saturday
    System.out.println("It's Golf Day!");
    break;
```

This code will result in the message "It's Golf Day" being displayed if the current day is Wednesday, Saturday, or Sunday. If you collect the three cases together without any intervening break statements, each will execute the same code. But consider what happens on Tuesday when the following code executes:

```
case 2:        // Tuesday
    System.out.println("Tennis at 8:00 am");
```

Certainly a reminder about the message match will be displayed, but this case doesn't end with a break statement. Because Tuesday's code doesn't end with a break statement, the program will continue executing the code in the following cases until a break is encountered. This means that Tuesday's code flows into the code used for Monday, Thursday, and Friday as shown in the following:

```
case 2:        // Tuesday
    System.out.println("Tennis at 8:00 am");
case 1:        // Monday
case 4:        // Thursday
case 5:        // Friday
    System.out.println("Office Hours: 10:00 - 5:00");
    break;
```

This will result in the following messages being displayed every Tuesday:

```
Tennis at 8:00 am
Office Hours: 10:00 - 5:00
```

On Monday, Thursday, and Friday, only the latter message will display.

In addition to writing switch statements that use integer cases, you can use character values as shown in the following example:

```
switch (aChar) {
    case 'a':
    case 'e':
    case 'i':
    case 'o':
    case 'u':
```

```
        System.out.println("It's a vowel!");
        break;
    default:
        System.out.println("It's a consonant!");
}
```

Iteration

Iteration is an important concept in any computer language. Without the capability to loop or iterate through a set of values, our ability to solve real-world problems would be severely limited. Java's iteration statements are nearly identical to those found in C and C++ and include for loops, while loops, and do...while loops.

The for Statement

The syntax of the Java for statement is very powerful and concise. The first line of a for loop enables you to specify a starting value for a loop counter, specify the test condition that will exit the loop, and indicate how the loop counter should be incremented after each pass through the loop. This is definitely a statement that offers a lot of bang for the buck. The syntax of a Java for statement is as follows:

```
for (initialization; testExpression; incremement)
    statement
```

For example, a sample for loop may appear as follows:

```
int count;
for (count=0; count<100; count++)
    System.out.println("Count = " + count);
```

In this example, the initialization statement of the for loop sets count to 0. The test expression, count < 100, indicates that the loop should continue as long as count is less than 100. Finally, the increment statement increments the value of count by one. As long as the test expression is true, the statement following the for loop setup will be executed, as follows:

```
System.out.println("Count = " + count);
```

Of course, you probably need to do more than one thing inside the loop. This is as easy to do as using curly braces to indicate the scope of the for loop, as shown in the following:

```
int count;
for (count=0; count<100; count++) {
    YourMethod(count);
    System.out.println("Count = " + count);
}
```

One nice shortcut that can be taken with a Java for loop is to declare and initialize the variable used in the loop. For example, in the following code, the variable count is declared directly within the for loop:

```
for (int count=0; count<100; count++)
    System.out.println("Count = " + count);
```

It may look like an inconsequential difference whether you declare a variable before a for loop or within the loop. However, there are advantages to declaring the variable within the loop. First, it makes your intention to use the variable within the loop clear. If the variable is declared above the for loop, how will you remember (and how will future programmers know) that the variable was intended for use only *within* the loop? Second, a variable declared within the for loop will go out of scope at the end of the loop. This means you could not write the following code:

```
for (int count=0; count<100; count++)
    System.out.println("Count = " + count);
System.out.println("Loop exited with count = " + count);
```

The last line cannot find a variable named count because count goes out of scope when the for loop terminates. This means that, in addition to making the intended purpose of the variable more clear, it is also impossible to accidentally bypass that intent and use the variable outside the loop.

You can also leave out portions of the first line of a for loop. In the following example, the increment statement has been left out:

```
for (int count=0; count<100; ) {
    count += 2;
    System.out.println("Count = " + count);
}
```

Of course, leaving the increment statement out of the for loop declaration in this example doesn't achieve any useful purpose because count is incremented inside the loop.

It is possible to get even fancier with a Java for loop by including multiple statements or conditions. For example, consider the following code:

```
for (int up=0, down = 20; up < down; up++, down -= 2 ) {
    System.out.println("Up = " + up + "\tDown = " + down);
}
```

This loop starts the variable up at 0 and increments it by 1. It also starts the variable down at 20 and decrements it by 2 for each pass through the loop. The loop continues until up has been incremented enough that it is equal to or greater than the variable down.

The test expression portion of a Java for loop can be any Boolean expression. Because of this, it does not need to be a simple test (x < 10) as shown in the preceding examples. The test expression can be a method call, a method call combined with a value test, or anything that can be phrased as a Boolean expression. For example, suppose you want to write a method that will display a message indicating the first year since World War II that the Chicago Cubs appeared in the World Series. You could do this as follows:

```
public boolean DidCubsPlayInWorldSeries(int year) {
    boolean retval;

    switch(year) {
        case 1907:                    // these are years the Cubs won
        case 1908:
```

```
            retval = true;
            break;
        case 1906:              // these are years the Cubs lost
        case 1910:
        case 1918:
        case 1929:
        case 1932:
        case 1935:
        case 1938:
        case 1945:
            retval = true;
            break;
        default:
            retval = false;
    }
    return retval;
}

public void FindFirstAfterWWII() {
    for (int year=1946; DidCubsPlayInWorldSeries(year)==false; year++) {
        System.out.println("The Cubs didn't play in " + year);
    }
}
```

The method `DidCubsPlayInWorldSeries` is passed an integer value indicating the year and returns a Boolean value that indicates whether or not the Cubs made it to the World Series in that year. This method is an example of the `switch` statement shown earlier in this chapter.

The method `FindFirstAfterWWII` uses a `for` loop to find a year in which the Cubs played in the World Series. The loop starts `year` with 1946 and increments `year` by one for each pass through the loop. The test expression for the loop will allow the loop to continue as long as the method `DidCubsPlayInWorldSeries` returns `false`. This is a useful example because it shows that a method can be called within the test expression of a `for` loop. Unfortunately, it is a bad example in that the Cubs haven't won the World Series since the goose step was popular in Berlin, and there is no sign of that changing in the near future. In other words, a loop that looks for a Cubs World Series appearance after 1945 is an infinite loop.

The `while` Statement

Related to the `for` loop is the `while` loop. The syntax for a `while` loop is as follows:

```
while (booleanExpression)
    statement
```

As you can tell from the simplicity of this, the Java `while` loop does not have the built-in support for initializing and incrementing variables that its `for` loop does. Because of this, you need to be careful to initialize loop counters prior to the loop and increment them within the body of the `while` loop. For example, the following code fragment will display a message five times:

```
int count = 0;
while (count < 5) {
    System.out.println("Count = " + count);
    count++;
}
```

The do...while Statement

The final looping construct in Java is the do...while loop. The syntax for a do...while loop is as follows:

```
do {
    statement
} while (booleanExpression);
```

This is similar to a while loop except that a do...while loop is guaranteed to execute at least once. It is possible that a while loop may not execute at all depending on the test expression used in the loop. For example, consider the following method:

```
public void ShowYears(int year) {
    while (year < 2000) {
        System.out.println("Year is " + year);
        year++;
    }
}
```

This method is passed a year value, and then loops over the year displaying a message as long as the year is less than 2000. If year starts at 1996, messages will be displayed for the years 1996, 1997, 1998, and 1999. However, what happens if year starts at 2010? Because the initial test, year < 2000, will be false, the while loop will never be entered. Fortunately, a do...while loop can solve this problem. Because a do...while loop performs its expression testing after the body of the loop has executed for each pass, it will always be executed at least once. This is a very valid distinction between the two types of loop, but it can also be a potential source of errors. Whenever you use a do...while loop, you should be careful to consider the first pass through the body of the loop.

Jumping

Of course, it is not always easy to write all your for, while, and do...while loops so that they are easy to read and yet terminate on exactly the right pass through the loop. Java makes it easier to jump out of loops and to control other areas of program flow with its break and continue statements.

The break Statement

Earlier in this chapter, you saw how the break statement is used to exit a switch statement. In a similar manner, break can be used to exit a loop. This can be seen in Figure A.1.

Figure A.1.

Flow of control with a break statement.

```
while (boolean expression){
        statement1
        statement2
        if (boolean expression)
            break;
        statement3
}
statement4
```

As Figure A.1 illustrates, if the `break` statement is encountered, execution will continue with `statement4`. As an example of this, consider the following code:

```
int year = 1909;
while (DidCubsWinTheWorldSeries(year) == false) {
    System.out.println("Didn't win in " + year);
    if (year >= 3000) {
        System.out.println("Time to give up. Go White Sox!");
        break;
    }
}
System.out.println("Loop exited on year " + year);
```

This example shows a `while` loop that will continue to execute until it finds a year that the Chicago Cubs won the World Series. Because they haven't won since 1908 and the loop counter `year` starts with 1909, it has a lot of looping to do. For each year they didn't win, a message is displayed. However, even die-hard Cubs fans will eventually give up and change allegiances to the Chicago White Sox. In this example, if the year is 3000 or later, a message is displayed and then a `break` is encountered. The `break` statement will cause program control to move to the first statement after the end of the `while` loop. In this case, that will be the following line:

```
System.out.println("Loop exited on year " + year);
```

The `continue` Statement

Just as a `break` statement can be used to move program control to immediately after the end of a loop, the `continue` statement can be used to force program control back to the top of a loop. This can be seen in Figure A.2.

Figure A.2.
Flow of control with a continue statement.

```
while (boolean expression){
        statement1
        statement2
        if (boolean expression)
            continue;
        statement3
}
statement4
```

Suppose you want to write a method that will count and display the number of times the Cubs have won the World Series this century. One way to do this would be to first see if the Cubs played in the World Series and then see if they won. This could be done as follows:

```
int timesWon = 0;
for (int year=1900; year <= 2000; year++) {
    if (DidCubsPlayInWorldSeries(year) = false)
        continue;
    if (DidCubsWinWorldSeries(year)) {
        System.out.println("Cubbies won in " + year + "!");
        timesWon++;
    }
}
System.out.println("The Cubs won " + timesWon + " times.");
```

In this case, a for loop is used to iterate through the years from 1900 to 2000. The first line within the loop tests to see if the Cubs played in the World Series. If they didn't, the continue statement is executed. This moves program control back to the for loop. At that point, year is incremented and the expression year <= 2000 is retested. If year is less than or equal to 2000, the loop continues. If, however, DidCubsPlayInWorldSeries equals true, the continue statement is skipped, and the next test is performed to see if the Cubs won that year.

Using Labels

Java does not include a goto statement. However, the fact that goto is a reserved word indicates that it may be added in a future version. Instead of goto, Java enables you to combine break and continue with a label. This has an effect similar to a goto in that it allows a program to reposition control. In order to understand the use of labels with break and continue, consider the following example:

```java
public void paint(Graphics g) {
    int line=1;

    outsideLoop:
    for(int out=0; out<3; out++) {
        g.drawString("out = " + out, 5, line * 20);
        line++;

        for(int inner=0;inner < 5; inner++) {
            double randNum = Math.random();
            g.drawString(Double.toString(randNum), 15, line * 20);
            line++;
            if (randNum < .10) {
                g.drawString("break to outsideLoop", 25, line * 20);
                line++;
                break outsideLoop;
            }
            if (randNum < .60) {
                g.drawString("continue to outsideLoop", 25, line * 20);
                line++;
                continue outsideLoop;
            }
        }
    }
    g.drawString("all done", 50, line * 20);
}
```

This example includes two loops. The first loops on the variable out, and the second loops on the variable inner. The outer loop has been labeled by the following line:

```java
outsideLoop:
```

This statement will serve as a placeholder and as a name for the outer loop. A random number between 0 and 1 is generated for each iteration through the inner loop. This number is displayed on the screen. If the random number is less than 0.10, the statement break outsideLoop is executed. A normal break statement in this position would break out of the inner loop. However, because this is a labeled break statement, it has the effect of breaking out of the loop identified by the name. In this case, program control passes to the line that displays "all done" because that is the first line after outsideLoop.

On the other hand, if the random number is not less than 0.10, the number is compared to 0.60. If it is less than this, the statement continue outsideLoop is executed. A normal, unlabeled continue statement at this point would have the effect of transferring program control back to the top of the inner loop. Because this is a labeled continue statement, program control is transferred to the start of the named loop. A sample run of this method, as captured in the Java Applet Viewer, is shown in Figure A.3.

Figure A.3.

Sample results demonstrating the use of labels.

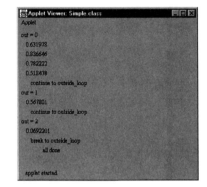

As you can see in Figure A.3, the first pass through the outer loop resulted in four passes through the inner loop. When the value 0.518478 was generated, it caused the continue outsideLoop to execute because the number is less than 0.60. The next pass through the outer loop was similar except that it did a continue of the outer loop after only one iteration through the inner loop. Finally, on the third pass through the outer loop, the program generated a value lower than 0.10, which caused the program to break to the outer loop. You can see that, at this point, the next line of code to be executed was the first line of code after the outer loop (the line that prints the message "all done").

Java Classes

Now that you've seen most of the low-level details of the Java language, it's time to turn your attention to Java classes and see how Java is able to live up to its claim of being an object-oriented language. A Java class is a compile-time concept that represents a runtime object. In other words, a class is a definition or template for an object that will exist within the program. For example, if you have a class called Car, you may have a particular instance of that class that is a 1966 Volkswagen Beetle. The instances (1966 Volkswagen Beetle) of a class (Car) are known as objects. In order to define a class in Java, you would do something similar to the following:

```
class Car {
    // member variables
    // member methods
}
```

C++ NOTE:

The design of Java's object model and its support for classes was certainly influenced by C++. However, Java classes borrow less from C++ than do many other aspects of Java and its syntax. Although classes are undeniably important in C++, classes are mandatory and central to everything you do in Java. In Java, there are no free-standing variables or functions. Everything must be encapsulated within a class. Further, every class in Java can trace back through its inheritance hierarchy and find itself a descendant of the Object class.

Field Declarations

Car is now an empty class. In order to make it usable and useful, you need to add some fields to the class. A field can be either a member variable or a member method. To declare member variables, all you need to do is identify the variable by type and name in the class definition, as shown in the following:

```
class Car {
    // these are member variables
    String manufacturer;
    String model;
    int year;
    int passengers;
}
```

In this example, Car has been extended to include string variables for manufacturer and model, and integer variables for the year it was built and the number of passengers it can hold. From this class definition, it is then possible to create instances, or objects, at runtime, as shown in Figure A.4.

Field Access

One of the principal advantages of object-oriented programming is *encapsulation*. Encapsulation is the capability to define classes that hide their implementation details from other classes, exposing only their public interfaces to those other classes. Support for encapsulation in Java comes from the three keywords public, private, and protected. When you are defining a class, these field access modifiers are used to control who has access to each field in the class. By declaring a

field as public, you are indicating that it is entirely accessible to all other classes. Continuing with the Car class example, to declare all the fields as public, do the following:

```
class Car {
    public String manufacturer;
    public String model;
    public int year;
    public int passengers;
}
```

Figure A.4.

The Car class and objects.

Class

Class Automobile

String manufacturer
String model
int year
int passengers

Objects

Manufacturer = VW	Manufacturer = Honda	Manufacturer =Ford
Model = Bus	Model = Accord	Model = Explorer
Year = 1966	Year = 1996	Year = 1994
Passengers = 8	Passengers = 4	Passengers = 5

Of course, declaring everything as public doesn't exactly achieve the goal of encapsulation because it lets other classes directly access variables in the Car class. Consider what would happen if you needed to create an instance of this class for a 1964-and-a-half Mustang. Because year only holds integer values, it would have to be changed to a float so that it could hold 1964.5. If code in other classes directly accessed year, that code could conceivably break.

To restrict access to a field, use the keyword private. A class cannot access the private fields of another class. Suppose the Car class is intended for use in a used car sales application. In this case, you may want to define Car as follows in order to hide your cost for a car from potential buyers:

```
class Car {
    public String manufacturer;
    public String model;
    public int year;
    public int passengers;
    private float cost;
}
```

Finally, the keyword protected is used to indicate that fields are accessible within the current class and all classes derived from the class but not to other classes. The capability to derive a class from another class will be discussed later in this appendix.

599

Setting Initial Values

One extremely nice aspect of Java class declarations is the capability to specify initial values for member variables in the variable declaration. For example, because most cars will hold four passengers, it may be reasonable to default the passengers member variable to 4, as shown in the following code:

```java
class Car {
    public String manufacturer;
    public String model;
    public int year;
    public int passengers = 4;
    private float cost;
}
```

Static Members

In addition to private, protected, and public members, a Java class can also have static members. A static member is one that belongs to the class itself, not to the instances of the class. Regardless of how many instances of a class have been created by a program at runtime, there will exist exactly one instance of each static member. Declaring a static member is done by adding the keyword static to any of the other field access modifiers, as shown in the following:

```java
class Car {
    public String manufacturer;
    public String model;
    public int year;
    public int passengers = 4;
    private float cost;
    public static int tireQty = 4;
}
```

In this case, the variable tireQty has been added and is set to 4. Because every car will have four tires, tireQty was declared as static. Also, because we want tireQty to be accessible to other classes, it has been declared public.

It is also possible to declare member methods as static, as will be shown later in this appendix.

Member Methods

In addition to member variables, most classes will also have member methods. Because member methods, like member variables, are fields, access to them can be controlled with the public, protected, and private modifiers. A member method is declared according to the following syntax, in which elements enclosed in square brackets "[...]" are optional:

```java
[methodModifiers] resultType methodName [throws exceptionList] {
    // method body
}
```

The methodModifiers are the familiar public, protected, and private keywords you've already seen as well as some additional modifiers. The method modifiers are described in Table A.14.

Table A.14. Method modifiers.

Modifier	Purpose
public	Accessible outside the class in which it is declared
protected	Accessible by the class in which it is declared and by subclasses of that class
private	Accessible only by the class in which it is declared
static	A method of the class rather than of a particular instance of the class
final	Cannot be overriden in subclasses
native	A platform-dependent implementation of the method in another language, typically C or assembly
Synchronized	Used to indicate a critical method that will lock the object to prevent execution of other methods while the synchronized method executes

The resultType of a method declaration can be one of the primitive types (for example, int, float, char), another class, or void. A resultType of void indicates that no result is passed back to the caller of the method. After the method name is given, a list of exceptions throwable by the method is given. If no exceptions are thrown by the method, this list is not necessary. Exception handling is discussed in full later in this appendix.

As an example of adding a method to the Car class, consider the following sample code:

```
class Car {
    public String manufacturer;
    public String model;
    public int year;
    public int passengers;
    public float CalculateSalePrice() {
        return cost * 1.5;
    }
    private float cost;
}
```

In this case, the Car class has had a public member method, CalculateSalePrice, added. The method returns a float, and the body of the method calculates this return value. To calculate the sale price of a car, the private member variable cost is multiplied by 1.5, reflecting a markup of 50 percent over the amount for which the car was purchased.

Overloaded Methods

The capability to overload methods is one of the biggest advantages to working in an object-oriented language, and Java certainly doesn't disappoint. Overloading a method means to use the same method name for more than one method. For example, the Car class can include two CalculateSalePrice methods, as follows:

```java
public float CalculateSalePrice() {
    return cost * 1.5;
}

public float CalculateSalePrice(double margin) {
    return cost * (1 + margin);
}
private float cost;
```

In this case, the first version of CalculateSalePrice is not passed any parameters and bases the sale price on the cost plus 50 percent (cost * 1.5). The second version is passed a margin by which the car should be marked up in determining the car's sale price.

At runtime, Java is able to distinguish between these methods by the parameters passed to each. Because of this you can overload a method as many times as you want as long as the parameter lists of each version are unique. In other words, you could not do the following:

```java
public float CalculateSalePrice() {
    return cost * 1.5;
}

public float CalculateSalePrice(double margin) {
    return cost * (1 + margin);
}

// this method declaration conflicts with the preceding method
public float CalculateSalePrice(double multiplier) {
    return cost * margin;
}
private float cost;
```

In this situation, the last two declarations are in conflict because each is passed a double. Different parameter names are insufficient to distinguish between two versions of the same overloaded function. They must differ by at least one parameter type.

Constructors

A special type of member method is known as a *constructor*. A constructor is used to create new instances of a class. You can identify a constructor because it will have the same name as the class. Like any other method, a constructor can be overloaded as long as the versions are distinguishable by the parameter types passed to each. Typically, a constructor will set the member variables of an object to values appropriate for that instance. As an example, consider the following variation on the Car class:

```java
public class Car {
    String manufacturer;
    String model;
    int year;
    int passengers;
    float cost;

    // calculate the sale price of a car based on its cost
    public double CalculateSalePrice() {
        return cost * 1.5;
    }

    // a public constructor
    public Car(String madeBy, String name, int yr, int pass,
            float cst) {
        manufacturer = madeBy;
        model = name;
        year = yr;
        passengers = pass;
        cost = cst;
    }

    // create and return a string with the basic details about
    // this particular car
    public String GetStats() {
        return new String(year + " " + manufacturer + " " + model);
    }
}
```

A constructor, Car, has been added to this version of the Car class. The constructor is passed five parameters that will be used as initial values for the instance variables manufacturer, model, year, passengers, and cost. The code for the constructor simply sets the five instance variables. The Car class has also received a new public member, GetStats, that creates a string that contains the basic facts about the car. By using the constructor and the new GetStats method, you can now display some information about a car. For example, the following code will display "1967 VW Bug":

```java
Car myCar = new Car("VW", "Bug", 1967, 4, 3000);
String str = myCar.GetStats();
System.out.println(str);
```

The new instance of the class Car was created with the following line:

```java
Car myCar = new Car("VW", "Bug", 1967, 4, 3000);
```

The use of the Java keyword new instructs Java to create a new object of type Car by allocating memory for it and to invoke the constructor for Car whose signature matches the parameter list. In this case, Car has only one constructor, so it is invoked and will set the instance variables to the values of the parameters. Once the variable myCar goes out of scope at the end of the function in which it is declared, the automatic memory management features of Java will detect that the memory that was allocated by new is no longer referenced, and it will be released.

> **TIP:**
>
> If a class does not specifically include a constructor, Java will provide a default constructor that takes no parameters. This constructor will enable you to create new instances of a class and will set all member variables to their Java system default values. However, it is a dangerous and unwise practice to rely on the existence of a Java default constructor. In general, you should always provide at least one constructor for each class you define.

The this Variable

All Java classes contain a hidden member variable named this. The this member can be used at runtime to reference the object itself. One excellent use of this is in constructors. It is very common to have a set of instance variables in a class that must be set to values that are passed to a constructor. When you are doing this, it would be nice to have code that was similar to the following:

```
year = year;
```

Ideally the variable on the left could be the instance variable, and the variable on the right could be the parameter passed to the constructor. Unfortunately, I don't know of any languages that would be able to make this distinction. The typical solution most programmers have settled on is similar to the following:

```java
public class Car {
    String manufacturer;
    String model;
    int year;
    int passengers;

    // a public constructor
    public Car(String madeBy, String name, int yr, int pass,
            float cst) {
        manufacturer = madeBy;
        model = name;
        year = yr;
        passengers = pass;
        cost = cst;
    }
}
```

Here, we've had to come up with two names for each concept: The best variable names (manufacturer, model, and so on) are used as the instance variables in the class declaration. The less satisfactory names are passed as parameters so as to distinguish them from the instance variables. The assignment statements are then very readable by Java but seem a little contrived to human readers. Java's this keyword provides a very effective solution to this problem in that the constructor can be written as follows:

```java
public class Car {
    String manufacturer;
    String model;
    int year;
    int passengers;
    float cost;

    // calculate the sale price of a car based on its cost
    public double CalculateSalePrice() {
        return cost * 1.5;
    }

    // a public constructor
    public Car(String manufacturer, String model, int year,
            int passengers, float cost) {
        this.manufacturer = manufacturer;
        this.model = model;
        this.year = year;
        this.passengers = passengers;
        this.cost = cost;
    }
}
```

In this case, the variables like this.year refer to the instance variables, whereas the unqualified variables like year refer to the constructor's parameters.

Of course, this is only one example of how you can use this. It is also frequently used as a parameter to other functions from within member methods.

Class Inheritance

In Java, every class you declare will be derived from another class. You can specify the class to derive from by using the extends keyword as follows:

```java
public class ClassicCar extends Car {
    // member methods and variables
}
```

As you probably noticed, extends was left out of all the prior examples in this chapter. This is because if a class is not declared as being derived from a specific class, it is assumed to be derived from the Java base class, Object. This means that the following two class declarations are equivalent:

```java
public class Car {
    // member methods and variables
}

public class Car extends Object {
    // member methods and variables
}
```

Because Object is the class from which all other Java classes are ultimately derived, this provides a common set of functionality among all Java classes. Most notably, garbage collection is possible because all classes will ultimately trace their lineage back to Object as shown in Figure A.5.

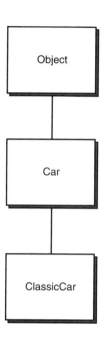

Figure A.5.

Everything is (eventually) derived from Object.

A derived class is commonly referred to as a *subclass*, while the class it is derived from is commonly referred to as a *superclass*. The term *immediate superclass* is used to describe the class from which a subclass is directly derived. In Figure A.5, for example, ClassicCar is a subclass of both Car and Object. Car and Object are both superclasses of ClassicCar, but only Car is the immediate superclass of ClassicCar.

Overriding Member Methods

When you create a subclass, you inherit all the functionality of its superclass, and then you can add or change this functionality as desired. As an example of this, consider the altered declaration of the Car class in the following code:

```
public class Car {
    private int year;
    private float originalPrice;

    // calculate the sale price of a car based on its cost
    public double CalculateSalePrice() {
        double salePrice;
        if (year > 1994)
            salePrice = originalPrice * 0.75;
        else if (year > 1990)
            salePrice = originalPrice * 0.50;
        else
            salePrice = originalPrice * 0.25;
        return salePrice;
    }
```

```
    // a public constructor
    public Car(int year, float originalPrice) {
        this.year = year;
        this.originalPrice = originalPrice;
    }
}
```

This version of the Car class holds information about the year and the original purchase price of the car. It has a member method, CalculateSalePrice, that determines the price for which to sell the car based on its age. Depending upon the age of the car, it can sell for either 75, 50, or 25 percent of its original price.

Although very simplistic, this is a good start for most cars. However, it is completely inadequate for classic, old cars. This algorithm would indicate that a 1920 Model T would be worth only 25 percent of its original 1920 price. A slight improvement on this would be to assume that every ClassicCar is worth $10,000. To do this, ClassicCar is derived from Car, as follows:

```
public class ClassicCar extends Car {
    // calculate the sale price of a car based on its cost
    public double CalculateSalePrice() {
        return 10000;
    }

    // a public constructor
    public ClassicCar(int year, float originalPrice) {
        super(year, originalPrice);
    }
}
```

Because ClassicCar is derived from Car, it inherits all the functionality of Car, including its member variables year and originalPrice. The function CalculateSalePrice appears in both class declarations. This means that the occurrence of this function in ClassicCar overrides the occurrence of it in Car for object instances of ClassicCar. As an example of how this works, consider the following:

```
ClassicCar myClassic = new ClassicCar(1920, 1400);
double classicPrice = myClassic.CalculateSalePrice();

Car myCar = new Car(1990, 12000);
double price = myCar.CalculateSalePrice();
```

The variable myClassic is of type ClassicCar and is constructed using that class's constructor, which is passed an original price for the car of $1,400. The sale price of this car is calculated and stored in classicPrice. Because myClassic is a ClassicCar, the sale price will be $10,000. Next, myCar is constructed as a new object of type Car with an original cost of $12,000. Its sale price is determined and stored in price. Because myCar is a Car, its sale price will be based on the year it was made (1990) and will be 25 percent of $12,000, or $3,000.

The **super** Variable

In the preceding declaration for `ClassicCar`, you may have noticed that the constructor made use of a variable named super. Just as each object has a this variable that references itself, each object (other than those of type `Object` itself) has a super variable that represents the parent class. In this case, `super(year, originalPrice)` invokes the constructor of the superclass `Car`.

Class Modifiers

Classes that are created in Java can be modified by class modifiers. The Java class modifiers are `public`, `final`, and `abstract`. If no class modifier is used, then the class may only be used within the package in which it is declared. A `public` class is a class that can be accessed from other packages. A class that is declared as `final` cannot be derived from, meaning it cannot have subclasses.

abstract Classes

Sometimes you may want to declare a class and yet not know how to define all the methods that belong to that class. For example, you may want to declare a class called `Mammal` and include in it a member method called `MarkTerritory`. However, you don't know how to write `MarkTerritory` because it is different for each type of `Mammal`. Of course, you plan to handle this by deriving subclasses of `Mammal`, such as `Dog` and `Human`. But what code do you put in the `MarkTerritory` function of `Mammal` itself?

In Java you can declare the `MarkTerritory` function of `Mammal` as an `abstract` method. Doing so lets you to declare the method without writing any code for it in that class. However, you can write code for the method in the subclass. If a method is declared `abstract`, then the class must also be declared as `abstract`. For `Mammal` and its subclasses, this means they would appear as follows:

```java
abstract class Mammal {
    abstract void MarkTerritory();
}

public class Human extends Mammal {
    public void MarkTerritory() {
        // mark territory by building a fence
    }
}

public class GangMember extends Mammal {
    public void MarkTerritory() {
        // mark territory with graffiti
    }
}

public class Dog extends Mammal {
    public void MarkTerritory() {
```

```
            // mark territory by doing what dogs do
    }
}
```

In the preceding declarations, the Mammal class contains no code for MarkTerritory. The Human class could contain code that would mark territory by building a fence around it, while the GangMember class could contain code that would mark territory by spray-painting graffiti. The Dog class would mark territory by raising the dog's leg and doing what dogs do to mark territory.

> **NOTE:**
>
> A method that is private or static cannot also be declared abstract. Because a private method cannot be overridden in a subclass, a private abstract method would not be usable. Similarly, because all static methods are implicitly final, static methods cannot be overridden.

Implementing Interfaces

Typically, an abstract class will have some methods that are declared as abstract and some that are not. If you find yourself declaring a class that is entirely abstract, you are probably declaring what is known in Java as an *interface*. An interface is an entirely abstract class. You can derive subclasses from an interface in a manner completely analogous to deriving a subclass from another class.

As an example, suppose you are building an application that must display the hour of the day. Users will have two options for getting this information. They can get it from either a watch or a cuckoo clock. This could be implemented as follows:

```
interface Clock {
    public String GetTime(int hour);
}

class Cuckoo implements Clock  {
    public String GetTime(int hour) {
        StringBuffer str = new StringBuffer();
        for (int i=0; i < hour; i++)
            str.append("Cuckoo ");
        return str.toString();
    }
}

class Watch implements Clock  {
    public String GetTime(int hour) {
        return new String("It is " + hour + ":00");
    }
}
```

In this example, Clock is an interface that provides a single function, GetTime. What this means is that any class that is derived from (or, in other words, *implements* the Clock interface) must provide a GetTime function. Cuckoo is an example of a class that implements Clock, and you'll notice that instead of the class Cuckoo extends Clock syntax that would have been used if Clock were an abstract class, it is instead declared with class Cuckoo implements Clock.

Because Cuckoo implements the Clock interface, it provides a GetTime function. In this case, a string is created that will hold as many Cuckoos as specified by the hour parameter. The class Watch also implements Clock and provides a GetTime function. Its version is a simple message stating the hour.

Interfaces and superclasses are not mutually exclusive. A new class can be derived from a super-class and one or more interfaces. This could be done as follows for a class that implements two interfaces and has one superclass:

```
class MySubClass extends MySuperClass implements FirstInterface,
        SecondInterface {
    // class implementation
}
```

Because it is possible for one class to implement more than one interface, interfaces are a very convenient method for implementing a form of multiple inheritance.

Exception Handling

When something goes wrong inside a Java method, the method can *throw an exception*. Throwing an exception refers to generating an instance of a class that represents an error or warning and passing the object back to the calling code. Exception handling can streamline the code you must write to handle errors or unlikely conditions.

Trying and Catching

In Java, exception handling is performed through the use of try…catch blocks. The code within a try block is executed, and if an exception occurs, execution is transferred to a catch block if one is provided that handles the type of exception that occurred. As an example, consider the following code:

```
public class MyClass extends Applet
{
    public void paint(Graphics g)
    {
        String [] stringArray = {"A", "Four", "Element", "Array"};

        try {
            for(int i=0;i<5;i++)
                g.drawString(stringArray[i], 10, 30+10*i);
        }
        catch (ArrayIndexOutOfBoundsException e) {
```

```
                g.drawString("oops: array too small", 10, 10);
        }
    }
}
```

In this example, a try block surrounds a for loop. The for loop will iterate one time too many through a four-element array. This will generate the exception ArrayIndexOutOfBoundsException, which is caught by a catch block.

Sometimes a block of code can generate more than one possible exception. In these cases you can use multiple catch blocks, one for each of the possible exceptions, as shown in the following code:

```
public class MyClass extends Applet
{

    public void paint(Graphics g)
    {
        String [] stringArray = {"A", "Four", "Element", "Array"};

        try {
            for(int i=0;i<4;i++)
                g.drawString(stringArray[i], 10, 30+10*i);

            char ch = stringArray[0].charAt(43);
        }
        catch (ArrayIndexOutOfBoundsException e) {
            g.drawString("oops: array too small", 10, 10);
        }
        catch (StringIndexOutOfBoundsException e) {
            g.drawString("oops: string index error", 10, 10);
        }
    }
}
```

In this case, the program loops through the four items in the array and then uses charAt to get the character at position 43 in a one character string. This generates the StringIndexOutOfBoundsException that is handled by the second catch block.

Using a finally Block

In addition to try and catch blocks, Java also enables you to specify a finally block that will execute, regardless of any exceptions that may have occurred. As an example of a finally block, consider the following class:

```
public class MyClass extends Applet
{

    public void paint(Graphics g)
    {
        String [] stringArray = {"A", "Four", "Element", "Array"};

        try {
            for(int i=0;i<5;i++)
                g.drawString(stringArray[i], 10, 30+10*i);
```

```
        }
        catch (ArrayIndexOutOfBoundsException e) {
            g.drawString("oops: array too small", 10, 10);
        }
        finally {
            g.drawString("in the finally", 10, 100);
        }
    }
}
```

Here, an exception will be thrown when the loop attempts to access the fifth item in the four-item array. The exception is caught and handled by displaying a message on the screen; then the `finally` block is executed, and another message is displayed. Executing this class will display the messages shown in Figure A.6.

Figure A.6.

Catching thrown exceptions and executing a `finally` block.

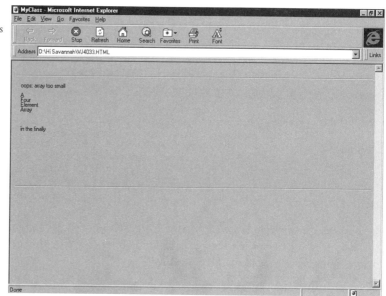

Summary

This chapter covered a great deal of information. You were introduced to Java's primitive types and the operators that are available for these types. Next, you learned how to control the flow of a Java program through its selection statements (`if`, `switch`, and `case`), its iteration statements (`for`, `while`, and `do…while`), and jumping (`break` and `continue`). You learned how to put all of this together and create new classes by deriving them from existing classes or interfaces. Finally, you learned how to effectively handle errors with exception handling.

Pointers and Memory Management

In the last few chapters you worked through some complicated subjects. In this chapter you will learn everything you need to know about pointers and memory management in Java.

Summary

This appendix reminded you how refreshing it is not to have to worry about pointers and memory management while working with complicated subjects like those covered in prior chapters.

Index

617

Web Programming with Visual Basic

—Craig Eddy & Brad Haasch

This book is a reference that quickly and efficiently shows the experienced developer how to develop Web applications using the 32-bit power of Visual Basic 4. It includes an introduction to and overview of Web programming and quickly delves into the specifics, teaching readers how to incorporate animation, sound, and more to their Web applications.

CD-ROM contains all the examples from the book, plus additional Visual Basic programs.

Includes coverage of Netscape Navigator and how to create CGI applications with Visual Basic

Discusses spiders, agents, crawlers, and other Internet aids

Covers Visual Basic

$39.99 USA/$56.95 CDN
ISBN: 1-57521-106-8

User Level: Accomplished–Expert
Internet/Programming

7 3/8× 9 1/8
08/01/96
400 pp.

Web Programming with Java

—Harris & Jones

This book gets readers on the road to developing robust, real-world Java applications. Various cutting-edge applications are presented, allowing the reader to quickly learn all aspects of programming Java for the Internet.

CD-ROM contains source code and powerful utilities.

Readers will be able to create live, interactive Web pages.

Covers Java

$39.99 USA/$56.95 CDN
1-57521-113-0

User Level: Accomplished–Expert
Internet/Programming

7 3/8× 9 1/8
09/01/96
500 pp.

Teach Yourself Visual J++ in 21 Days

—Laura Lemay, Patrick Winters, and David Blankenbeckler

Readers will learn how to use Visual J++, Microsoft's Windows version of Java, and how to design and create Java applets for the World Wide Web. Visual J++ includes many new features to Java including visual resource editing tools, source code control, syntax coloring, visual project management, and integrated bills. All of those tools are covered in detail, giving readers the information they need to write professional Java applets for the Web.

Includes information on the Java class libraries and how to use them to create specific applet effects

Provides a detailed tutorial to developing applications with the new Java

CD-ROM includes all the source code from the book and all the examples.

Covers Visual J++

$39.99 USA/$56.95 CDN
1-57521-158-0

User Level: Casual–Accomplished
Internet/Programming

7 3/8× 9 1/8
11/01/96
500 pp.

Visual J++ Unleashed

—Bryan Morgan, et al.

Java is the hottest programming language being learned today. And Microsoft's Windows version of Java, code-named Visual J++, may prove to be even hotter as Microsoft has added several new development features, such as graphic designing, to the Java language. *Visual J++ Unleashed* shows readers how to exploit the Java development potential of Visual J++.

Shows how to add interactivity and Java applets to Web pages

Details how the Windows enhancements to the Java environment can be exploited for "quick and easy" programming

CD-ROM includes source code from the book and powerful utilities.

Covers Visual J++

$49.99 USA/$70.95 CDN	*User Level: Accomplished–Expert*	*7 3/8× 9 1/8*
1-57521-161-0	*Internet/Programming*	*11/01/96*
		1,000 pp.

Web Programming Unleashed

—Breedlove, et al.

This comprehensive tome explores all aspects of the latest technology craze: Internet programming. Programmers will turn to the proven expertise of the Unleashed series for accurate day-and-date information on this hot new programming subject.

Gives timely, expert advice on ways to exploit the full potential of the Internet

CD-ROM includes complete source code for all applications in the book, additional programs with accompanying source code, and several Internet application resource tools.

Covers the Internet

$49.99 USA/$70.95 CDN	*User Level: Accomplished–Expert*	*7 3/8× 9 1/8*
1-57521-117-3	*Internet/Programming*	*11/01/96*
		1,200 pp.

VBScript Unleashed

—Brian Johnson

With VBScript Unleashed, Web programming techniques are presented in a logical and easy-to-follow sequence that helps readers understand the principles involved in developing programs. The reader begins with learning the basics to writing a first program and then builds on that to add interactivity, multimedia, and more to Web page designs.

Provides the reader with a thorough understanding of the VBScript language

Teaches communication across the Internet, safety, security, CGI, and more

CD-ROM includes valuable source code and powerful utilities.

Covers Latest Version

$39.99 USA/$56.95 CDN	*User Level: Casual–Accomplished–Expert*	*7 3/8× 9 1/8*
1-57521-124-6	*Internet/Programming*	*12/01/96*
		650 pp.

Laura Lemay's Web Workshop:
ActiveX and VBScript

—Paul Lomax & Rogers Cadenhead

ActiveX is an umbrella term for a series of Microsoft products and technologies that add activity to Web pages. Visual Basic Script is an essential element of the ActiveX family. With it, animation, multimedia, sound, graphics, and interactivity can be added to a Web site. This book is a compilation of individual workshops that show the reader how to use VBScript and other ActiveX technologies within their Web site.

CD-ROM contains the entire book in HTML format, a hand-picked selection of the best ActiveX development tools, scripts, templates, backgrounds, borders, and graphics.

Covers ActiveX and VBScript

$39.99 USA/$56.95 CDN	*User Level: Casual–Accomplished*	*7 3/8× 9 1/8*
1-57521-207-2	*Internet/Programming*	*12/01/96*
		450 pp.

ActiveX Programming Unleashed

—Weiying Chen, et al.

ActiveX is Microsoft's core Internet communication technology. This book describes and details that technology, giving programmers the knowledge they need to create powerful ActiveX programs for the Web and beyond. Covers ActiveX controls—the full-featured components of the Internet.

Teaches how to use ActiveX documents, server framework, ISAPI, security, and more

CD-ROM includes various tools, demos, and code examples.

Covers ActiveX

$39.99 USA/$56.95 CDN	*User Level: Accomplished–Expert*	*7 3/8× 9 1/8*
1-57521-154-8	*Internet/Programming*	*12/01/96*
		700 pp.

Add to Your Sams.net Library Today
with the Best Books for Internet Technologies

ISBN	Quantity	Description of Item	Unit Cost	Total Cost
1-57521-106-8		Web Programming with Visual Basic (Book/CD-ROM)	$39.99	
1-57521-113-0		Web Programming with Java (Book/CD-ROM)	$39.99	
1-57521-158-0		Teach Yourself Visual J++ in 21 Days (Book/CD-ROM)	$39.99	
1-57521-161-0		Visual J++ Unleashed (Book/CD-ROM)	$49.99	
1-57521-117-3		Web Programming Unleashed (Book/CD-ROM)	$49.99	
1-57521-124-6		VBScript Unleashed (Book/CD-ROM)	$39.99	
1-57521-207-2		Laura Lemay's Web Workshop: ActiveX and VBScript (Book/CD-ROM)	$39.99	
1-57521-154-8		ActiveX Programming Unleashed (Book/CD-ROM)	$39.99	
		Shipping and Handling: See information below.		
		TOTAL		

Shipping and Handling: $4.00 for the first book, and $1.75 for each additional book. If you need to have it NOW, we can ship product to you in 24 hours for an additional charge of approximately $18.00, and you will receive your item overnight or in two days. Overseas shipping and handling adds $2.00. Prices subject to change. Call between 9:00 a.m. and 5:00 p.m. EST for availability and pricing information on latest editions.

201 W. 103rd Street, Indianapolis, Indiana 46290

1-800-428-5331 — Orders   1-800-835-3202 — FAX   1-800-858-7674 — Customer Service

Book ISBN 1-57521-174-2

Installing the CD-ROM

The companion CD-ROM contains Visual J++ Publisher's Editon, all the source code and project files developed by the authors, plus an assortment of evaluation versions of third-party products. To install, please follow the steps listed here.

Windows 95/NT 4 Installation Instructions

1. Insert the CD-ROM into your CD-ROM drive.
2. From the Windows 95 or NT 4 desktop, double-click the My Computer icon.
3. Double-click the icon representing your CD-ROM drive.
4. Double-click the icon titled setup.exe to run the CD-ROM installation program.

This program will create a Program group with the icons to run the programs on the CD. No files will be copied to your hard drive during this installation.

NOTE:

If you have the Autoplay feature enabled, the setup.exe program is executed automatically once the CD is inserted into the drive.

Visual J++ 1.0, Publishers Edition

Microsoft® Corp Visual J++™, Publishers Edition included on the accompanying CD allows you to create your own Visual J++™ programs without purchasing the commercial version. The Publishers Edition does differ from the commercial version in some ways. These include no Database support for SQL and ODBC databases through Data Access Objects (DAO) and Remote Data Objects (RDO). No JET engine for creating programs that work with Access and other DAO databases. No Zoomin and WinDiff Tools. No third party tools and libraries that integrate with Visual J++™. No redistribution of Java Virtual Machine and Internet Explorer. No code samples. No Microsoft technical support. No free or discounted upgrades to later versions of Visual J++™, Professional Edition.

Microsoft Corp Visual J++™, Publishers Edition requires the following to operate:

- Personal computer with a 486 or higher processor running MS Windows 95 ® or Windows NT® Workstation version 4.0 or later operation systems
- 8 MB of memory (12 MB recommended) if running Windows 95; 16 MB (20 recommended) if running Windows NT Workstation
- Hard-disk space:

  Typical installation: 20 MB

  Minimum installation: 14 MB

  CD-ROM installation (tools run from the CD): 14 MB total tools and information on CD/UCT/: 50 MB
- A CD-ROM drive
- VGA or higher resolution monitor (super VGA recommended)
- Microsoft Mouse or compatible point device

END-USER LICENSE AGREEMENT FOR MICROSOFT SOFTWARE

MICROSOFT VISUAL J++ , Publisher's Edition

IMPORTANT—READ CAREFULLY: This Microsoft End-User License Agreement ("EULA") is a legal agreement between you (either an individual or a single entity) and Microsoft Corporation for the Microsoft software product identified above and Microsoft Internet Explorer, which include computer software and associated media and printed materials, and may include "online" or electronic documentation (together, the "SOFTWARE PRODUCT" or "SOFTWARE"). By installing, copying, or otherwise using the SOFTWARE PRODUCT, you agree to be bound by the terms of this EULA. If you do not agree to the terms of this EULA, promptly return the unused SOFTWARE PRODUCT to the place from which you obtained it for a full refund.

Software product LICENSE

The SOFTWARE PRODUCT is protected by copyright laws and international copyright treaties, as well as other intellectual property laws and treaties. The SOFTWARE PRODUCT is licensed, not sold.

1. GRANT OF LICENSE. This EULA grants you the following rights:

You may use one copy of the Microsoft Software Product identified above on a single computer. The SOFTWARE is in "use" on a computer when it is loaded into temporary memory (i.e., RAM) or installed into permanent memory (e.g., hard disk, CD-ROM, or other storage device) of that computer. However, installation on a network server for the sole purpose of internal distribution to one or more other computer(s) shall not constitute "use" for which a separate license is required, provided you have a separate license for each computer to which the SOFTWARE is distributed.

You may only use copies of the Microsoft Internet Explorer software only in conjunction with a validly licensed copy of Microsoft operating system products (e.g., Windows® 95 or Windows NT®). You may make copies of the SOFTWARE PRODUCT for use on all computers for which you have licensed Microsoft operating system products.

Solely with respect to electronic documents included with the SOFTWARE, you may make an unlimited number of copies (either in hardcopy or electronic form), provided that such copies shall be used only for internal purposes and are not republished or distributed to any third party.

2. UPGRADES. If the SOFTWARE is an upgrade, whether from Microsoft or another supplier, you may use or transfer the SOFTWARE only in conjunction with upgraded product. If the SOFTWARE is an upgrade from a Microsoft product, you may now use that upgraded product only in accordance with this EULA.

3. SUBSCRIPTION UPDATES. If you have acquired the SOFTWARE PRODUCT as part of a subscription package, then you must treat as an upgrade any subsequent versions of SOFTWARE PRODUCT received as an update to your subscription package.

4. COPYRIGHT. All title and copyrights in and to the SOFTWARE PRODUCT (including but not limited to any images, photographs, animations, video, audio, music, text, and "applets" incorporated into the SOFTWARE PRODUCT), the accompanying printed materials, and any copies of the SOFTWARE PRODUCT are owned by Microsoft or its suppliers. The SOFTWARE PRODUCT is protected by copyright laws and international treaty provisions. Therefore, you must treat the SOFTWARE PRODUCT like any other copyrighted material except that you may either (a) make one copy of the SOFTWARE PRODUCT solely for backup or archival purposes or (b) install the SOFTWARE PRODUCT on a single computer provided you keep the original solely for backup or archival purposes. You may not copy the printed materials accompanying the SOFTWARE PRODUCT.

5. DESCRIPTION OF OTHER RIGHTS AND LIMITATIONS.

a. Limitations on Reverse Engineering, Decompilation, and Disassembly. You may not reverse engineer, decompile, or disassemble the SOFTWARE PRODUCT, except and only to the extent that such activity is expressly permitted by applicable law notwithstanding this limitation.

b. No Separation of Components. The SOFTWARE PRODUCT is licensed as a single product and neither the software programs making up the SOFTWARE PRODUCT nor any UPDATE may be separated for use by more than one user at a time.

c. Rental. You may not rent or lease the SOFTWARE PRODUCT.

d. Software Transfer. You may permanently transfer all of your rights under this EULA, provided that you retain no copies, you transfer all of the SOFTWARE PRODUCT (including all component parts, the media and printed materials, any upgrades, this EULA, and, if applicable, the Certificate of Authenticity), and the recipient agrees to the terms of this EULA. If the SOFTWARE PRODUCT is an upgrade, any transfer must include all prior versions of the SOFTWARE PRODUCT. Notwithstanding the foregoing, you may permanently transfer all your rights under this EULA that pertain to the Microsoft Internet Explorer only in conjunction with a permanent transfer of your validly licensed copy of a Microsoft operating system product.

← Flip back to see the rest of the agreement.

e. Termination. Without prejudice to any other rights, Microsoft may terminate this EULA if you fail to comply with the terms and conditions of this EULA. In such event, you must destroy all copies of the SOFTWARE PRODUCT. In addition, your rights under this EULA that pertain to the Microsoft Internet Explorer software shall terminate upon termination of your Microsoft operating system product EULA

6. REDISTRIBUTABLE COMPONENTS.

a. Redistributable Files. In addition to the license granted in Section 1, Microsoft grants you a nonexclusive, royalty-free right to reproduce and distribute the object code version of those portions of the SOFTWARE designated in the SOFTWARE as: (i) the files identified in the REDISTRB.WRI file located in the \MSDev\Redist subdirectory on the "Microsoft Visual J++ version 1.00" CD-ROM (collectively, "REDISTRIBUTABLES"), provided you comply with Section 6.b.

b. Redistribution Requirements. If you redistribute the REDISTRIBUTABLES, you agree to: (i) distribute the REDISTRIBUTABLES in object code form only in conjunction with and as a part of your software application product which adds significant and primary functionality and which is designed, developed, and tested to operate in the Microsoft Windows and/or Windows NT environments; (ii) not use Microsoft's name, logo, or trademarks to market your software application product; (iii) include a valid copyright notice on your software product; (iv) indemnify, hold harmless, and defend Microsoft from and against any claims or lawsuits, including attorney's fees, that arise or result from the use or distribution of your software application product; and (v) not permit further distribution of the REDISTRIBUTABLES by your end user. Contact Microsoft for the applicable royalties due and other licensing terms for all other uses and/ or distribution of the REDISTRIBUTABLES.

7. U.S. GOVERNMENT RESTRICTED RIGHTS. The SOFTWARE PRODUCT and documentation are provided with RESTRICTED RIGHTS. Use, duplication, or disclosure by the Government is subject to restrictions as set forth in subparagraph (c)(1)(ii) of the Rights in Technical Data and Computer Software clause at DFARS 252.227-7013 or subparagraphs (c)(1) and (2) of the Commercial Computer Software—Restricted Rights at 48 CFR 52.227-19, as applicable. Manufacturer is Microsoft Corporation/One Microsoft Way/Redmond, WA 98052-6399.

8. EXPORT RESTRICTIONS.

You agree that you will not export or re-export the SOFTWARE PRODUCT to any country, person, entity or end user subject to U.S.A. export restrictions. Restricted countries currently include, but are not necessarily limited to Cuba, Iran, Iraq, Libya, North Korea, Syria, and the Federal Republic of Yugoslavia (Serbia and Montenegro, U.N. Protected Areas and areas of Republic of Bosnia and Herzegovina under the control of Bosnian Serb forces). You warrant and represent that neither the U.S.A. Bureau of Export Administration nor any other federal agency has suspended, revoked or denied your export privileges.

9. NOTE ON JAVA SUPPORT. THE SOFTWARE PRODUCT CONTAINS SUPPORT FOR PROGRAMS WRITTEN IN JAVA. JAVA TECHNOLOGY IS NOT FAULT TOLERANT AND IS NOT DESIGNED, MANUFACTURED OR INTENDED FOR USE OR RESALE AS ONLINE CONTROL EQUIPMENT IN HAZARDOUS ENVIRONMENTS REQUIRING FAIL-SAFE PERFORMANCE, SUCH AS IN THE OPERATION OF NUCLEAR FACILITIES, AIRCRAFT NAVIGATION OR COMMUNICATIONS SYSTEMS, AIR TRAFFIC CONTROL, DIRECT LIFE SUPPORT MACHINES, OR WEAPONS SYSTEMS, IN WHICH THE FAILURE OF JAVA TECHNOLOGY COULD LEAD DIRECTLY TO DEATH, PERSONAL INJURY, OR SEVERE PHYSICAL OR ENVIRONMENTAL DAMAGE.

miscellaneous

If you acquired this product in the United States, this EULA is governed by the laws of the State of Washington.

If you acquired this product in Canada, this EULA is governed by the laws of the Province of Ontario, Canada. Each of the parties hereto irrevocably attorns to the jurisdiction of the courts of the Province of Ontario and further agrees to commence any litigation which may arise hereunder in the courts located in the Judicial District of York, Province of Ontario.

If this product was acquired outside the United States, then local law may apply.

Should you have any questions concerning this EULA, or if you desire to contact Microsoft for any reason, please contact the Microsoft subsidiary serving your country, or write: Microsoft Sales Information Center/One Microsoft Way/Redmond, WA 98052-6399.

LIMITED WARRANTY

LIMITED WARRANTY. Except with respect to Microsoft Internet Explorer and the REDISTRIBUTABLES, which are provided "as is," without warranty of any kind, Microsoft warrants that (a) the SOFTWARE PRODUCT will perform substantially in accordance with the accompanying written materials for a period of ninety (90) days from the date of receipt, and (b) any hardware accompanying the SOFTWARE PRODUCT will be free from defects in materials and workmanship under normal use and service for a period of one (1) year from the date of receipt. Some states and jurisdictions do not allow limitations on duration of an implied warranty, so the above limitation may not apply to you. To the extent allowed by applicable law, implied warranties on the SOFTWARE PRODUCT and hardware, if any, are limited to ninety (90) days and one year, respectively.

CUSTOMER REMEDIES. Microsoft's and its suppliers' entire liability and your exclusive remedy shall be, at Microsoft's option, either (a) return of the price paid, or (b) repair or replacement of the SOFTWARE PRODUCT or hardware that does not meet Microsoft's Limited Warranty and which is returned to Microsoft with a copy of your receipt. This Limited Warranty is void if failure of the SOFTWARE PRODUCT or hardware has resulted from accident, abuse, or misapplication. Any replacement SOFTWARE PRODUCT or hardware will be warranted for the remainder of the original warranty period or thirty (30) days, whichever is longer. Outside the United States, neither these remedies nor any product support services offered by Microsoft are available without proof of purchase from an authorized international source.

NO OTHER WARRANTIES. To the maximum extent permitted by applicable law, Microsoft and its suppliers disclaim all other warranties, either express or implied, including, but not limited to, implied warranties of merchantability AND fitness for a particular purpose, with regard to the SOFTWARE PRODUCT, and any accompanying hardware. This limited warranty gives you specific legal rights. You may have others, which vary from state/jurisdiction to state/jurisdiction.

NO LIABILITY FOR CONSEQUENTIAL DAMAGES. TO THE MAXIMUM EXTENT PERMITTED BY APPLICABLE LAW, IN NO EVENT SHALL MICROSOFT OR ITS SUPPLIERS BE LIABLE

FOR ANY special, incidental, indirect, or consequential DAMAGES WHATSOEVER (INCLUDING, WITHOUT LIMITATION, DAMAGES FOR LOSS OF BUSINESS PROFITS, BUSINESS INTERRUPTION, LOSS OF BUSINESS INFORMATION, OR ANY OTHER PECUNIARY LOSS) ARISING OUT OF THE USE OF OR INABILITY TO USE THE software PRODUCT, EVEN IF MICROSOFT HAS BEEN ADVISED OF THE POSSIBILITY OF SUCH DAMAGES. BECAUSE SOME STATES and JURISDICTIONS DO NOT ALLOW THE EXCLUSION OR LIMITATION OF LIABILITY FOR CONSEQUENTIAL OR INCIDENTAL DAMAGES, THE ABOVE LIMITATION MAY NOT APPLY TO YOU.